EXPLORING INNER SPACE

AWARENESS GAMES FOR ALL AGES

by
Christopher Hills
and
Deborah Rozman

University of the Trees

A handbook for parents, teachers and everyone

University of the Trees Press
P.O. Box 644
Boulder Creek, California 95006
(408) 338-3855

UNIVERSITY OF THE TREES PRESS
P.O. Box 644
Boulder Creek, California 95006

EXPLORING INNER SPACE, Awareness Games for All
Ages: a handbook for parents, teachers and everyone
by Christopher Hills and Deborah Rozman

Printed in the United States of America, by R.R. Donnelley Co.
Cover: Original Artwork by Geoffrey Chandler
Cover design and photography: John Hills
Text photography: Michael Hammer

Library of Congress Cataloging in Publication Data

Hills, Christopher.
    Exploring inner space

    1. Consciousness-Problems, exercises, etc.
I. Rozman, Deborah, joint author
II. Title
BF311.H47   158'1   78-14948
ISBN 0-916438-05-8

DEDICATION

*This book is dedicated to the bubbling child-like
heart that lights up all of us.*

*It is for those who feel confined by the routine
of life, like the child who does not want to go to school
and only waits for playtime to spark the wild freedom within.*

*These awareness games are given to all those teachers
who tried so hard to pass on their knowledge, but utterly
failed to penetrate our stubborn resistance.*

*May the parents, teachers and children of today
discover the miracle of the cosmic child playing
inside them on the timeless shores of inner space.*

About the authors:

Christopher Hills, Ph.d., D.Sc., is founder and director of University of the Trees, Boulder Creek, California. A world renowned yogi, philosopher, and scientist, he spent many years traveling and lecturing before retiring to the giant redwoods to write. In 1970 he was elected President of the World Conference on Scientific Yoga in New Delhi, India. This conference was a breakthrough event in uniting the philosophies of East and West. In response to his writings, students gathered to study with him at the University of the Trees which has evolved as a Consciousness Research School. Dr. Hills is author of many books, including *Supersensonics, Nuclear Evolution: Discovery of the Rainbow Body, Rays from the Capstone,* a correspondence study course *Into Meditation Now*, and soon to be published (1979) *The Rise of the Phoenix*, a book on social, economic and political reform based on the new consciousness teachings.

Deborah Rozman, Ph.d. is the author of *Meditating With Children: The Art of Concentration and Centering*, and *Meditation for Children,* new consciousness books for parents and teachers. She has studied psychology and the nature of consciousness for many years, beginning her training in yoga with Paramahansa Yogananda and Self-Realization Fellowship in 1970. In 1974 she felt drawn to study with Christopher Hills because as she says, "He puts it all together—psychology, science, yoga, spiritual awareness, education." Deborah is an educational consultant for many school districts and Director of Psychology of Consciousness at the University of the Trees. She has taught transpersonal psychology, awareness games, creative conflict and meditation to children, teenagers and senior citizens in California Public Schools. Her books have been sponsored by superintendents of several school districts as effective educational tools.

TABLE OF CONTENTS

This book has been written in a conversational tone and style for your easy reading and use. We have tried to be sensitive to the modern feelings regarding sexism in literature. We have avoided using words that are strictly masculine as much as possible. In some places it was just too awkward to say he/she or him/her. In spite of our struggles to find a suitable word that included both sexes, at times we had to resort to using he or him for easy and clear reading.

A WORD OF ACKNOWLEDGEMENT

The idea of using educational games to get across difficult techniques in a simple way first came to me in 1963 when I did a six months tour of America. Visiting many groups and teaching techniques of healing visualisations, memory developments and telepathy, I found that if I gave the usual lecture the audience listened and was duly entertained but they never *used* the information, and so they never really learned.

One of the first people to encourage me to develop these games was Bob Stone who was then Public Relations Director for the Long Island Board of Education. Several years later, on another six months tour in 1969, I happened to have one of my awareness seminars for group leaders in Los Angeles. Winifred Babcock, of the Babcock Reynolds Foundation, had offered me her villa for a weekend seminar to share these techniques with twenty of the foremost leaders of spiritual movements at that time. This was long before the present interest in yoga and Eastern teachings had become the fashion, and I thought this would be an ideal opportunity for seeding these ideas surreptitiously in the awakening consciousness stream of America, which was then only a small trickle of metaphysical groups. Since those days I have seen thousands of metaphysical bookstores with Eastern teachings spring up in every city, and the small stream has become a mighty river.

I invited Bob Stone to that seminar and he approached me afterwards about writing a book of these games in simple language for the layman, a book that could be sold in mass market paperback. I was a bit dubious because he said that the high, spiritual tone and intent of these games was not for the masses and we would have to compromise. New American Library eventually brought out the book two years later as a Signet classic entitled *Conduct Your Own Awareness Sessions*. The book was poorly marketed with an atrocious cover and did not go into a second printing. But it was encouraging to see several imitative books come out in hardback a year or two later, which made me think that some interest was still there. But the interest then was not with the masses so much as with the awakening movement towards research into consciousness.

Bob Stone had always encouraged me to write these games in a simplified way for use by educators with children as well as for adults. It was not until I had left London and founded the University of the Trees that our Director of Psychology of Consciousness, Dr. Deborah Rozman, came up with the inspiration to rewrite these games to suit this need. She had tried these games with her own classes of adults and children for two years and found the ones which the students liked best and how the book could be used not only in the classroom but also with senior citizens' groups and youth groups run by the County Board of Education. After her successful book, *Meditating With Children,* became an in-service training manual for teachers who were interested in getting tranquility and peace in the classroom and in centering the children in their work, she decided to take all the games I had originated and bring them up to date with the new interest in educational games, so that the book would serve a dual purpose in bringing a feeling of community in the family as well as in the classroom. The book you have therefore in your hands in this edition has been completely rewritten and restructured in an easy format, thanks to loving helpers. I am indebted to Dr. Rozman for editing and rewriting these games and for adding to them. I also thank Pamela Osborn and Ary King for typesetting and Phil Allen, Wendy McFadzen and Myra Williams for editing the manuscript.

When I first authored these games and tried them out at Centre House in London before bringing them to America in the 60s, we would often get twenty-five percent of the people succeeding with the telepathy and group mind experiments. I am now told that today's children who use meditation or centering and try these experiments in the classrooms are getting fifty percent success rates. This means that something really fundamental is taking place in the development of our human powers of communication. Our world is suffering deeply from a great lack of understanding and communication, almost to the point of self-destruction. Judging by the fifty percent divorce rate, the home life of our children is being destroyed. Perhaps our children who cannot communicate with their parents will one day remember those moments in school when they used higher levels of consciousness to learn and to know what was in the mind and heart of another person.

I hope the book serves the same purpose first intended when I originated the games, which is to use them as a method of teaching esoteric and spiritual knowledge without setting oneself up as a teacher. They are a first-class way of getting rid of the teacher-student hang-up and are not only extremely effective ways of getting into people, underneath their egos, but they are a great deal of fun. So whether you are a little kid or a big kid at heart, you will enjoy this opportunity to laugh at yourself and discover hidden domains of the heaven which lies all about you. I believe you will find that the children or your friends whom you invite to participate in these games will develop an open, spontaneous relationship which cannot be got by ordinary methods of teaching and learning.

Please send us any new games you think of and try out. A second volume of games may be published if we get sufficient response. Meantime, have lots of fun with your groups of children or friends, and send me some of it telepathically so that I can feel your joy.

Christopher Hills

A NEW WAY FOR EDUCATION

When I first went to school I was completely turned off by the way I was taught. I lived in one world and school was another—a prison—where the multiplication tables were chanted and writing and reading were the punishments. Outside the class I found freedom, green grass, butterflies, a flowing stream with sticklebacks* in it, and a whole universe waiting to be explored. That universe was in me then. I would tune my imagination outside the classroom walls, for inside the class I felt regimentation, stress, and hatred of learning.

For many years I was shut off. I was told to stay after school to catch up, and tutored until my teachers gave up in desperation at my utter resistance to knowledge. It was not until I left school that I began to learn and teach myself what I could have learned in school if only my teachers had known how to make learning an exciting adventure—an exploration.

Things have changed since then, and we now have so many aids to make education interesting, from movies to television, from simulations to audio-visual aids, from story book physics to wholistic history, but what we do not have in the classroom yet is a feeling of community and the peaceful vibrations of the natural world I experienced outside the classroom walls. We know the human world outside those walls was not peaceful, wars were brewing, and even now the togetherness of the community becomes more fragmented day by day. But in the child's mind there is freedom out there in the vast spaces beyond the classroom. How my heart longed for those vast spaces and how my being hated the restrictive walls of the educational system.

Can we as teachers find the materials for helping students discover who they are within the traditional system? Of course we can, but the way we present them to students cannot be found in the past methods. A born teacher can take any material and with considerable skill can turn it into

*Sometimes called minnows.

exciting material. But born teachers are few and even the greatest have made little impact on our ego structures or influenced the growth of the enormous potential lying within. A child is left alone to explore the enormous potential in that vast universe in which he roams outside the classroom.

We all know the traditional truths and we all learn from our cultures those values which make our society what it is. But most teachers are made, not born, and unfortunately they are made by the status quo. Staff and parents alike may even resist a particular innovation with children in the fear that a new way may do more harm than good. New ways of teaching mathematics, new ways of learning languages, new ways abound— but do the children do better at sums? Do they speak and write any better, or do the new fangled televisions and expensive equipment, that every school must have, just make us raise lazy youngsters who are less effective, and less able to communicate?

We must look at the results in the quality of life and in the evolution of society for the answer. And if we are honest, the answer is disturbing. There is less interest in change, less interest in thinking for oneself, more and more "big government" deciding everything from cradle to grave. Yet in education we are still free to teach our materials in the most effective ways we can and thereby influence those young minds and beings who will be the citizens in a few years time from now.

Education is still the best investment of time and energy in terms of getting more out of a system than you put into it. In five years time our teenagers will vote for the kind of society they want. Will they also become a charge on the welfare state or will they be thinking for themselves? This is the challenge of any new method—to get across that knowledge which gives the certainty and confidence of relationships and makes our words integral. On the integrity of our words and actions hangs our communication with the total environment and future happiness. Our sense of conviction decides the way people will relate to us. Our first emphasis then, must not be on *learning* information and knowledge, but on learning to retrieve it and how to communicate it. A person who knows a lot but can only communicate a few stilted sentences is worse off in society than someone who knows a little but communicates all of it. We see these people rise to power. We see them govern us. We see them deciding the very important issues of the day. Because they communicate!

★ The first duty of a teacher or parent then is to teach *how to learn.*

★ The second duty is to teach *how to listen* in depth.

★ The third duty is to teach how to remember what is heard.

★ The fourth duty is to teach us how to put the truths we learn to work for ourselves and for the welfare of all.

★ The fifth duty is to teach us how to communicate on different levels of our being and to know and recognize the levels of consciousness in another.

★ The sixth duty is to teach how to love and care not only for others but the total environment around us.

★ The seventh duty is to become a model of the intelligence in the nucleus of all things so that information becomes wisdom, and much learning becomes humility.

The whole problem of an education which includes all these seven skills can be found in the question, "Who is going to teach the teachers?" The problem is a circular one like the chicken and the egg. Where are the teachers who will teach the teachers of the teachers?

Teaching these skills is the essence of the book *Exploring Inner Space*, which uses games that are chock full of information, to be learned as a by-product of having fun. If you aim to teach directly you will eventually have resistance, but if you teach the skill of acquiring knowledge by drawing it out of the student from inside, then the outside knowledge will flow in with the ease of a student's breath. By encouraging communication with others, in a group setting designed to discover who we are, we automatically create a school of natural wisdom for a new society. Writing, reading, working out results, all become necessary for us in playing the games. Because the games concentrate on what our consciousness is doing, they relate to every subject capable of being learned and they can be adapted to suit any learning environment.

These explorations or games are excellent ways to settle the atmosphere of a class so that it is quiet enough for listening. Noise and expression are part of the integrated communication and not some wild uncontrollable chaos needing release, so often found in the modern classroom. The administration of a new wholistic form of education, including the cultivation of reverie and meditation as learning methods, is now just being discovered. *Exploring Inner Space* uses many of these techniques hidden amongst the instructions for playing the games. Within the scope of this book is secreted every known type of technique for self-development from yoga to memory tests, from meditation to the deep spaces through which children so easily enter the depths within. The fruits of some of these games may not be harvested for many years to come. Profound and unquantifiable, they may nevertheless be that subtle power which transforms the individual and through him changes the nature of society.

Our children are the psychological capital which we invest in the transformation of our culture. Our psychic income and happiness will depend on their eventually fulfilling themselves as individuals. The lasting ·influence of a teacher's personality on students will always overshadow the environment of a school system, however regimented, in any society. These new methods have been written down to get beyond the personality into the real being of the teacher, parent and child, and enter beyond the walls of the prison into the universal being of everyone.

They are therefore as important for adults, families, groups, communities and companies in business as they are for the dreamers of tomorrow's world—our future heroes and saints—the children.

Christopher Hills

A group collage of some of our students practicing yoga. From 7 years old to 80 years old, the yoga postures in this book can be enjoyed by all.

THE LAUNCHING PAD

AN INTRODUCTION

FOR KIDS!

(And to be read to kids who don't know how to read yet)

Have you ever wanted to travel to another planet or to the sun or moon? Now you can, for real!

If you wanted to go to the star Sirius, that blue star you see bright in the night sky, nicknamed "the dog star," and you had a spaceship that travels as fast as light, you'd whiz by Sirius at 648 million miles per hour. Most cars go about 60 miles per hour on the freeway so the speed light moves is about 10 million times as fast as the car. It would still take you over 8 years, even travelling at that incredibly fast pace, to arrive at Sirius and another 8 years to get back. That is if you used an ordinary spaceship travelling at the speed of light.

But the spaceship of your own imagination travels faster than the speed of light. Presto and you're there in your consciousness, which means in your awareness. Can we really explore outer space in our minds? We can and do and we can even share it scientifically with each other. It's not just playing pretend. It's just beyond pretend and it's for real! We can also share feelings, thoughts, moods, happiness, sadness, joys and our secret places inside with each other in a way that makes us feel good, not afraid. This is what *Exploring Inner Space* is all about. Close your eyes. You still see space inside and feel your inner mind and inner vision at work with your eyes shut. This is a very important secret. Your inner space is really a whole lot bigger than all of outer space. That's hard to believe because your body is so small. But inside your mind is space enough for the whole universe and everything in it to live. Everything you know and everything you don't know is in your inner space waiting for you to find it. How do you know it's all in there? Because the only place you can experience *any-thing* is inside you, inside your awareness.

Adults don't know this secret very well either, so they will need to explore their inner worlds with you too. Do you know how sometimes your Mom or Dad looks like something is bothering them? Dad has a funny wrinkle or Mom's mouth sags, and you know deep inside that something is bothering them even if they say no, or don't know, or pretend it's not. By *Exploring Inner Space* we are going to have the chance to share and care and get in touch with our inner worries and wishes with each other, with our friends and parents. What would it be like if everyone could share with each other inside-out? What if everyone liked you and you liked everyone else, no matter how ugly or scared or funny you or they were? Wouldn't it feel good? On the inside we're all pretty much alike in what we need from life. We get happy, sad, angry, loving, or bored. But we're very different in what we do with our feelings. If we're scared that we'll be punished or thought less of, we hide some of our deeper feelings. If we feel we'll get praise and people will like us more, then we express and share what we think and feel.

Now we can learn that it's okay to share what we feel and think whatever is really happening inside us and be sure that others will understand. But we have to learn how to do this so we don't judge others and make them feel like running away or closing up like a clam. What we want to do with this book is to be able to share our real selves.

You know how you can turn your socks inside-out? Well, when we feel upset, our inside feelings come outside as we cry or scream or mope. And many times it seems like nobody understands. When we're happy inside that shows outside too, in a smile or laughter or the light of joy on our faces. Do you know what other people feel inside? Can you put your awareness inside them and look out through their hearts and eyes and feel how they feel? Wouldn't it be nice if other people could feel your feelings that way? Well that is what we learn by exploring inner space. We can feel what stars and trees, animals and other people feel and we can feel ourselves better too. It doesn't happen all at once, but it happens more and more as we explore. All this means we can be happier.

You can only have this happiness if you see others as *your Self.* This means you see everyone—birds, grass, animals, trees, people as part of *your Self.* You are a big umbrella of the universe with everything inside you. Close your eyes for a minute and imagine what that would feel like. Your *body* isn't a big umbrella, but *you* are, your awareness is. When we can really imagine this then we don't blame others and separate ourselves saying, "It's all her fault," or "She did it." She is part of you! We don't need to lie so that we can look good because we will know that others understand how we feel; and we also will know how they feel inside. We are One with them. We have to accept that this oneness is okay and learn to feel it. As little babies we all experienced this oneness, but as we grew older we covered it up with our sense of me, mine. We got an ego that said to itself, "I'm here, stuck in this body and you are over there in your body." What we want to become in *Exploring Inner Space* is "I'm here and you're here too. We are both more than our bodies. Sirius and the sun are here too, as part of myself. They're part of my *consciousness.*" You can travel to them anytime by tuning in to them with your consciousness, just like you tune in a radio station on the radio. Turn a dial in your "mind-radio" and you can read someone's thoughts, tell how they are feeling, or get a signal from them. Turn another dial inside your mind and you can tell what it's like to be in the center of the sun, your whole being sizzling in light. What an endless inner T.V. set we have! There's much more to you than you know. Come and find out!

THIS WHOLE BOOK IS ABOUT DISCOVERING YOU

AND EXPLORING WHAT YOUR MIND CAN DO.

EVERY GAME WILL TAKE YOU THROUGH

OUTER SPACE AND INNER SPACE TOO!

THE LAUNCHING PAD

AN INTRODUCTION

FOR BIG KIDS! (ADULTS)

Exploring Inner Space simplifies the results of Christopher Hills' research on Nuclear Evolution into fun and practical awareness games that people of all ages can do to discover their own inner worlds of consciousness. Many of these games were originated at Centre Community in London, England, by Christopher for a group of people working together on consciousness evolution as far back as 1967. You may recognize the ones that have become popularized by word of mouth or by authors who visited the community and have since written books on sensitivity training, awareness development or group therapy. The falling exercise, the love seat, full length mirror and some of the E.S.P. games for learning to read auras and experience telepathy are among the most well-known.

In 1970, Christopher and group leader Robert Stone compiled eighty of the games together which Signet Classics published and called *Conduct Your Own Awareness Sessions.* At that time the touchy-feely groups were becoming popular so the publisher decided to put a sexy, touchy-feely picture on the cover. But the book was not a touchy-feely book. It was a journey into many different parts of ourselves on many levels of awareness. So the people who wanted to do the serious work on themselves took one look at the sexy cover and never thought to open the book. The people who wanted the sensual stuff took one look inside and found that it was deeper than they wanted to go. The true audience for the book never really heard about it. Those of us who were fortunate enough to discover what it had to offer were rewarded with wonderful and stimulating exercises that brought forth previously undiscovered parts of our being that we had always wanted to develop but didn't know how.

21

As a psychology teacher, I was particularly eager to teach these simple games to groups of adults and to children, and watch them discover themselves. For three years I taught them as part of a class in transpersonal psychology, linking them with the philosophy of Nuclear Evolution. The classes always began with large numbers of people who had heard how exciting they were from friends, but usually whittled down a bit to those who were sincerely wanting to grow and look at themselves. We weren't sorry to lose the others and were even glad when some of the fence-sitters left, because we always had a very intense and close group by the end of the sixteen-week class period. Some continued on to join the even deeper Creative Conflict classes that we give at the University of the Trees. For most people, when the challenge to grow becomes a little difficult they turn away to the nearest excuse which is always readily at hand.

I had been studying with Christopher for several years before I began my classes. His discoveries on the awakening of humans to universal awareness, which he calls Nuclear Evolution, seemed to me to be the most tremendous insight into human nature I'd seen in all my psychology and spiritual studies. The wisdom in it tuned me into a dynamic intuitive plane of consciousness of an order of being I had rarely experienced, only in peak moments. I felt here was the breakthrough, the true New Age synthesis of yoga, science, religion and psychology put in a way never before given to mankind.

When Christopher asked me to prepare the old *Conduct Your Own Awareness Sessions* for reprinting, the thought struck me, why not put it into the same format of Nuclear Evolution as I did in my Monday night classes to which people had responded so well! In my classes it had seemed the natural thing to group the awareness games according to the seven levels of consciousness and the energies they developed. People attending were the general public of all ages from fifteen to sixty, and not necessarily spiritually-minded. So each week we explored together one of the energy levels from the many different perspectives that everybody experiences in their daily lives. We all wore clothes of the color related to the psychology of the level we were exploring. First we would discuss the Nuclear Evolution research of that aspect of consciousnes, then do a few yoga postures which put us in touch with the energy center governing this level inside us. (These postures were designated by one of Christopher's students, Malcolm Strutt, who is now director of the Centre School of Alternative Education in London and a hatha yoga expert. Malcolm has written a comprehensive book on yoga postures*) Then we would do a short clearing and centering meditation to tune us into a direct experience of that state of consciousness so we were all vibrating on the same frequency of awareness—in resonance. From this space we explored our own actions and reactions to this part of ourselves through one of the awareness games. Finally, we always discussed our feelings and wrote our impressions and experiences into journals. Often the rapport between the people in the class would grow so close that a large group would adjourn to the nearest coffee shop and share inner-worlds and mind spaces to the early hours of the morning. There was always a solid core of those who felt the experiences in the class were the most important thing that had happened to them in their lives.

When Christopher started a new consciousness research community and school for enhancing evolution in 1974, he made it clear that he only wanted students who were really committed to change. Willingness to change is the theme at the University of the Trees in Boulder Creek, because it is the vital force needed for evolution, for awakening hidden potential. *Exploring Inner Space* evokes that evolutionary force of change inside you. As you do the games and exercises you will go on a journey from which you will emerge a different person. You will feel new movements of energy, new thoughts, new feelings and perceptions arise as you discover that you live in a universe of seven distinct energy dimensions. You will awaken your intuitive faculties for the most important achievement of all—the ability to see in-tu-it, into the hidden nature of life with direct perception.

It's the intuition that expands the faculties of all the senses and other levels to tune them to a wider range of vibrations. Just to hear about people who can do telepathy, or divine the location of lost or hidden objects, or read auras is not the same thing as doing it yourself. When you can actually feel the telepathic transfer of thought from another person to yourself or from you to another, there is a vibration that makes you know you are a radar set and tunes you into an entirely different time-space dimension. Your inner eye becomes like a homing device, sensing with extra-sensory attunement the most profound answers to the deepest questions in yourself.

---

*See Malcolm's book, *Wholistic Health and Living Yoga,* University of the Trees Press, 1978. (See appendix.)

We all want to feel we are a cosmic being, not from hear-say or belief, but from the direct knowing of being it. This is entirely different from intellectual knowledge. How to communicate to you the "inner sense" in a way that you'll receive a direct feeling transference of what it is like is our task through these games and exercises. Kids usually pick it up just like that! That's why so many thousands of children were able to bend spoons like Uri Geller, just by watching him do it on television. They were able to get inside his mind by putting their thoughts in resonance with his. Then the door opened in their mind and they knew. Children do that with adults all the time so that they can psyche us out. We don't out-grow this ability, we just block it as we grow older. Really, it's a natural part of everyone, requiring no great talent to unfold, just an open heart and mind.

Christopher has brought us tremendous new knowledge of our hidden potential in his book *Nuclear Evolution: Discovery of the Rainbow Body**. It shows scientifically how we humans literally "eat" cosmic light. We are made of this light from the one cosmic intelligence which some call God and we unconsciously transform the light into seven distinct levels of awareness which compose our self, much like a prism transforms sunlight into color. This light in the nucleus of being is our reality. Through our consciousness we transform, filter and shade the light we absorb, and then radiate it back out into the cosmos in the form of our aura and personality expression. By understanding the functions of our seven centers of consciousness we can scientifically gain complete self-mastery. Some people get confused when they try to put the ideas of light, color and psychology together. Light is color and energy, and does affect us. So, too, our thoughts are energy and project different colors into our aura depending on what we are doing with our consciousness. You don't have to believe it by hearsay, you can soon prove it and now see it for yourself by following the instructions in this book.

Exploring Inner Space is a Nuclear Evolution handbook to bring direct experience of these seven different levels to everyone. The seven levels of awareness work through seven *chakras* or wheels of energy, located along the spinal column. Traditionally they have been known but have been veiled behind a cloak of mystery in the Eastern Hindu, Buddhist and Yoga

* University of the Trees Press, (see Appendix.)

traditions. In the West they have also been symbolically represented in the Book of Revelation in the Bible as seven golden candlesticks or seven stars, but no direct mention is made that they are vital instruments of our own consciousness. Now you can contact them and increase their capacity for radiating light and awareness by exploring them consciously.

Realization that Cosmic *light and consciousness are One and the same and are inside you* is what fuses science and religion, and *is* the revelation of the New Age. Nuclear Evolution presents this realization in such a way that it is being heralded as a bible of the coming age by people in different parts of the globe.

Is your personality shining or dull? You will be able to experience your own drives and responses to different situations and release more light. You can become the kind of person you truly want to be by getting in touch with your real nature. Nuclear Evolution is the unfolding of the seed in the heart of yourself to encompass every level and go beyond into the light of a pure consciousness. These awareness games powerfully bring you direct practice and experience right in your own living room or class room. You don't have to go to a special school, or a sensory deprivation tank, or all the places and gimmicks where things happen *to* you. You can explore new worlds with friends and family right where you are.

The outcome of doing all this evolutionary work on yourself with others is trust, something we all want but often fear. With trust we gain more acceptance and more love. Other people in a nuclear evolution group are wonderful mirrors for our own growth, via the exercises that teach us how to mirror to each other in kindness, the strengths and blind spots which we are unable to see alone. To accomplish this mirroring, the group work is to create first an atmosphere of openness where we can let our defenses down so that we are able to explore together. Mutual feedback and growth are essential to the evolution of all humanity. We call it Group Consciousness.

At the University of the Trees we have a community of individuals and families sharing and growing together in Group Consciousness.* With a

---

* In my books *Meditating With Children* and *Meditation For Children* I have given a 5-step process for evolutionary growth that includes some of these awareness games which can transform the entire family or classroom into a higher state of evolution.

strong love and the purpose of conscious growth, we learn to polish the mirrors of our own seeing in the perceptions of each other. Through the kinds of awareness activities presented here, creative communication, and an even deeper commitment to selfless service, meditation, and dedication to truth, we are evolving a wholistic way of life from the inside-out, from the inner being out to the personality. It is very important to deepen inner relationships as that is where the spring of love lies, and where the understanding that brings peace to you and the world is nourished.

Children often receive the greatest benefits from these games because the games fill that need to have the deeper parts of themselves recognized. They take into account every aspect of a person's development. Not only do kids often do the best on the E.S.P. games, but they can come up with personality feedback in the mirroring game that will floor you. One of the leaders at the University of the Trees plays the mirroring game and does the creative conflict exercises with local neighborhood kids once a week and they just love it! They frequently ask for it on their own initiative.

One important thing about these games and exercises is that they are non-competitive. Rather than gain ego satisfaction by beating someone else with a higher score, you seek out the more lasting joy of co-exploration and challenging yourself. When you see an awakening in any of the energy levels occur in yourself and in your friends or family, the joy of discovery and the deepened communication bring you a fulfillment you wouldn't trade for anything. Exploring the unsullied virgin territory in the depths of inner being is the most thrilling adventure. And the many inner worlds keep the journey endlessly stimulating. So the mission of this adventure into your real self is basically two-fold, it is to open you to new awareness of the great untapped potential lying dormant within you, and to bring you a deeper understanding of your own conditioning drives and motives and those of others. Automatically this will bring you closer to others, to nature and to your ultimate fulfillment.

INSTRUCTIONS:

Most of these games can be played by two to twenty people. There are many that you can do alone and others which require at least six or seven participants. The ideal way to use this book is to first read it yourself, then bring it into a group that you are already a part of or form your own group to embark on the exploration together. Families, groups of families, children, classmates, neighbor friends, teen groups, business groups, social groups, bridge groups, parties, religious groups—all have enjoyed breaking away from their usual superficial socializing or political discussions to entertain some of the deeper questions of life and discover answers within. If your group or family will meet regularly for an awareness session it is good to progress through the book from start to finish in order. However, if you wish to skip around the book, first familiarize yourself with the different levels of consciousness and then decide which you would like to explore at any given time. Pick one of the games in that level that feels right for you or your group. Prepare ahead of time if possible. Each game explores a different part of you. The games proceed in order, to increasingly more challenging ones. Keep a journal to write your answers to the questions in the games and to have a record of your inner development.

If you don't have a group or are unsure how to form one, you can consult with friends, put notices on bulletin boards, contact different centers, schools and social groups, or put an ad in the paper asking if anyone is interested in an awareness group. Take responsibility for initiating it and you will discover there are others interested who are just waiting for someone else to take the lead and give direction. Once the people express interest, commitment is the next thing to discuss. Commitment to regular attendance will build a close group. Whether you decide to meet weekly, twice a week, monthly or whatever, the group grows in depth based upon each person's commitment. If you have rotating leaders who prepare an exploration to do each time, then everyone becomes responsible. Decide to meet for a specific number of times to begin with so that people don't have to feel that they are eternally committed. Seven sessions will give you a chance to explore each level one time and give each person a taste. Everybody should read the Introduction and Chapters One and Two for personal study. Set a policy for latecomers and visitors. You may even want to set a limit to size. Some people find the cozier groups from seven to ten members maximum are the ideal size for depth and variety. Others prefer just two or three and still others find fulfillment in a large group of twenty functioning together. Latecomers and new people will feel left behind if they have no background. Curiosity seekers wandering in and out will break the vibration of the group. Hold your sessions in a place where you can have uninterrupted peace and invite only those new people who are sincerely interested and may want to join regularly. It's very easy for certain people who have strong egos to come in and try to disrupt or take over a group, even unconsciously, so you should be discriminating and honest with your feelings. Discuss admitting new members before-hand and make the decision be unanimous. If each person is responsible for the success of his or her group, then you will have few problems.

The first two games are prerequisites to the rest of the book and should be the ones you start with before jumping off on your own. The first *few* games in every level are "getting to know you" and "learning to recognize that level" exercises. These will help any group break the ice and guide the group into the deeper sessions to follow. With these guidelines, let the book be your leader. Whether you go through the entire book alone, with a partner or with several friends, the more consciousness you put into the games and exercises the more you will get out of them. As one who has seen myself and others grow dramatically and change their personalities through exploring inner space creatively together, there is nothing more that I'd like to give you than this joy of discovering your Self. Happy Loving!

Deborah Rozman

PART I
THE TAKE-OFF

Stage One

OUTER SPACE AND INNER SPACE

(A Nuclear Evolution View)

by Deborah Rozman

Most of us walk around on this planet believing that space is out there somewhere and we are in here, inside our body and inside our mind which is inside our brain. This is what we are taught from birth by our parents, teachers and the whole of society. A few people have broken away from this strong suggestion and experience themselves differently. They feel that they are the whole of space and that everything in space goes on inside of them, inside their awareness. Their body and senses are only one part of their awareness. "How else,"they ask,"can anything be known? If the sun is not inside your awareness then how do you experience it?" Our awareness is not confined to just the physical body, but extends wherever we let it go, to the farthest galaxy, the feelings inside another person, the mind of a Christ, the heart of a flower, the starving children in Africa, the millions of war dead. It's only we who limit our awareness by deciding not to extend it to everything, and by believing the hypnotic suggestion of those who believe they are confined to a fleshy shell.

As a child of four, I remember playing one day in the large family room in the back of my house. No adults were around. I had been looking into outer space the night before and its impression was still fresh in my mind. I wondered if one day we would be able to travel to Mars and what it would be like. As I considered the prospect, I decided that I would play I was going to Mars. I dragged out my little musical rocking chair, tied some rope to it, strapped the rope to some other objects and pretended this was my rocket ship. After strapping myself tightly in the chair for safety with the rest of the rope I closed my eyes and started the count down. 10-9-8-7-6-5-4-3-2-1-take off! And in my mind I saw myself breezing through dark space on my way to Mars, my chair rocking faster and faster as the ship picked up speed. When I landed on Mars I breathlessly opened my eyes fully expecting to see a new land and was disappointed to be faced with the same two-tone green square of the linoleum tile in my family room. I played awhile longer, but my faith had been shaken by the rude presence of the family room and my fantasy no longer seemed very real. There must be a way, I thought, of going to Mars. One night, as I went off to sleep, I dreamt that I was going into a spiralling tunnel of light and that it was taking me to Mars! I knew I was travelling through some light barrier.

When I awoke in the morning I remembered I had dreamt I had gone to Mars, but it all quickly faded away over breakfast and the day's activities. I was left wondering, did I really go there?

If you think back in your own life, you can see we all have had these tussles in our minds as to what's real and what isn't. How many children have gone running, a few blocks at least, to see if they can find the pot of gold at the rainbow's end? Fact or fantasy, we are continually bombarded with the concreteness of this physical world pulling us back from our hopes, dreams, and aspirations more and more as we grow up. Is there a way we can integrate the two without ending up in the looney bin with all those people who say they're the messiah while they can't even feed themselves?

"Somewhere over the Rainbow, dreams that we dare to dream really do come true." This song, considered the height of fantasy, is actually becoming the height of reality. The evolutionary discovery is that we can fly over the rainbow when we embark on the journey into our own consciousness. To dissolve the separation between our inner space – our minds, feelings, drives, hopes, fantasies – and our outer space – everything that we sense lies out there – we have to discover the being inside us who believes in the separation. We call it the ego. Underlying this separating being is your real Self who is like a rainbow of consciousness in you. Discovering your Rainbow Body in the nucleus of being is the real life task of Nuclear Evolution.

Not many people know that all of life is a rainbow – for real. When we shine pure, transparent sunlight through a clear raindrop or prism we see the seven rainbow colors. All colors and shades of color are derived from the basic primary light colors in various combinations. Pigment colors that we see in paints and on objects are secondary light colors (or reflected light) and require primary light like the sun in order to be seen. Have you ever noticed in early dawn, just as the sun rises, that there is no color? The objects around are discernable but they are all different shades of grey. As the sunlight gets brighter the greys become more distinctive until they absorb enough sunlight to reflect a strong enough intensity to make color. The color is in the light and not in the object. Sunlight is absorbed according to the surface's molecular structure and the object reflects its characteristic vibration of light which we see as color. It's a profound experience and available to everyone each morning, to realize that colors only exist due to sunlight, and that your favorite green chair isn't green at all but mousy grey before light shines on it. Try looking at the objects around you at dawn or dusk and notice what light does.

Primary light is also shining *in you* or you wouldn't be able to be aware in the dark, or be self-aware of your own thoughts and images and feelings. If you close your eyes right now and become aware of your thoughts, feelings, and images that are coming to you inside, you see them as reflected light bouncing off the blackboard of your mind. But the primary light of pure awareness *is* you! That is why the yogis say to watch your thoughts, so you can get behind them to the real you. This primary light in you is not coming out of your eyes strongly enough to light up the colors of objects in a dark room, just as starlight is too weak to light them. So you cannot see in the dark. But the light of awareness in you is pure and clear and powerful in the nucleus of your being, just like sunlight, once you remove the filters.

There is an etheric body that surrounds your physical body which refracts cosmic light pouring in you from space just like a prism refracts sunlight. Your human awareness is cosmic light refracted by seven whirling energy centers located along the spine in your etheric body.

Science is just beginning to be able to photograph these centers. Each of the centers absorbs and steps down the light into distinct vibratory frequencies of rainbow color.

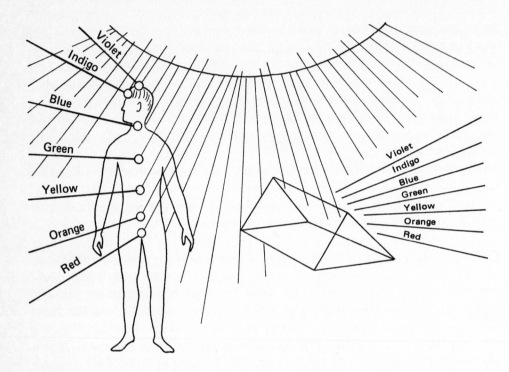

Why seven centers and why the rainbow shades, is nature's design and secret. The rainbow body is distinguishable to clairvoyants who can see the subtle aura around the physical body. They have their intuitive center open. It is also detectable by you through certain awareness games. Your aura color is the shade of the centers that are active and aware in you. Someone with all seven centers clearly open and radiating has a golden white aura like the sun, all light colors combined, and is considered a very spiritual person. Most of us are hung up in at least one of our drives in one or more of our centers so people's auras are all different colors and shades. As the light passes through these centers and is refracted into color, it is also refracted into seven distinct kinds of awareness. This light is our awareness. What we need to know is: how does light become awareness and create our experience of life?

Cosmic light energy is intelligent and aware, so we call it *consciousness.* Atoms have consciousness, rocks have consciousness, crystals have consciousness, plants and animals have it too. Anything that has a behavior pattern has consciousness. Atoms behave in certain ways. Everything behaves in certain ways. Even light behaves in certain ways. It has laws from within that direct it. We have to stop thinking that there's some old man with a long white beard somewhere up in the sky pulling the strings, and light, atoms, and people jump like puppets to the pulls. The intelligence and consciousness is within the light. It is within you. Where? Within the nuclear center which leads you into black holes and white holes everywhere in the center of being. But we have to learn how to get into the higher energy levels of awareness to be able to experience this for ourself. So our awareness comes from these seven chakras or centers of whirling light which act like step-down transformers of cosmic energy.

When we look out of our eyes right now and hear through our ears and feel through our skin, we create a picture of the world. This picture is a three dimensional experience in you. When we sit in front of a big wide Cinemascope screen at the movie theatre we know it's all just a movie, but while we are in the theatre we get caught up in the action and it feels real. Well, in the same way, science and psychology says that our real life experience is also a movie. They call it a *hologram* going on inside us.

A hologram is a 3-D picture. In science laboratories they make holograms with laser beams of light. Presto and you see a 3-D picture in front of you. It looks real. But stick your finger through to pick up the real-looking object and there's nothing there. It's like magic. You can buy hologram toys now in stores and in the movie Star Wars they have a hologram T.V. set, where a picture is projected in the middle of the floor in 3-D. Well, we make holograms, or 3-D pictures, inside our own head and project them out onto the screen of our mind and believe they are *out there,* not realizing it's all happening *in here.* We are creating a three dimensional seeming reality of life by the actions of our consciousness. But really everything is happening inside us, inside our seven whirling chakras of awareness. Nuclear Evolution teaches that sunlight, plus starlight, plus the primary light of our own consciousness, plus the mind come together inside our head to recreate the universe into the size and shape and form we perceive it. It teaches that right now there are at least two stars with light beams intersecting inside your consciousness creating the hologram of light which you think you see as the reality in front of

AURA ENERGY

Gland	Nerve Plexus	Chakra	Color	Level	Function: a Few Characteristics both Positive and Negative
Pineal	Brain Dendrites	Crown, Sahasrara	Violet	7th	*Imagination*—fantasy, spiritual perception, charm, magic, oneness, divine order, sense of eternity, chaos, hallucination, creating our reality, seeing how we create life, creativity
Pituitary	Medulla Oblongata	Brow, Ajna	Indigo	6th	*Intuition*—direct perception, sixth sense, seeing into reality, psychic, future-orientated, fear of future, spacey
Thyroid	Pharyngea, Plexus Cervicus	Throat, Vissudha	Blue	5th	*Mental ideals*—concepts, devotion to authority, conservative, memory, lives in the past, tradition, the blues
Thymus	Cardiac	Heart, Anahata	Green	4th	*Security*—insecurity, vital force, heart love, belonging, desire to acquire energy (money, love, antiques, knowledge, etc.) life force, jealousy, possessiveness
Adrenal	Coeliac, Solar Plexus Epigastricus	Intellect, Manipura	Yellow	3rd	*Intellectual*—separative and mechanical thinking, logical, analytical, linear thinking, penetrating insight
Spleen	Splenic, Hypogastricus	Spleen, Swadisthana	Orange	2nd	*Social*—political and cultural dependence, ambitious, social climber, love of fellow beings, herd instinct
Gonads	Coccygeal,	Genital, Muladhara	Red	1st	*Sensual*—the 5 senses, reactive to stimulus, physical activity, action-orientated, anger, sexual, self-preserving, sensory

you. Think about it. Let it blow your mind. Solid objects seem hard, but actually they are made of this same light or energy. Light is our reality and is us. The entire universe is in our mind. How we filter light as it pours through our seven refracting centers determines how clear our perception is, how aware we are and how much of the total universe we can experience.

I've probably lost some of you in this short explanation of how humans imagine, but the important thing to remember is that we get caught up in life not realizing how we are creating it, just like we get caught up in the big wide movie, forgetting that the projector is behind us shining it all on the screen in front of us. If you want to go into a more complete understanding you'll need to read *Nuclear Evolution* where Christopher has spent 1,000 pages explaining the direct experience as well as the scientific understanding of it all.

Now we come right back to the beginning with the question, "Well how can I know all this for myself?"Only by opening up the full functioning of your seven centers can you know it. And it is for that purpose that we have put together this Nuclear Evolution handbook. Now you can experience the fast-moving space age discoveries of science for yourself. You become them, so they are no longer theories, but living reality from within your being.

The rainbow of consciousness is experienced as the above seven chakras or faculties of awareness which contain all your unconscious and conscious impulses, motives, drives, instincts, thoughts, feelings, memories, physical organs and senses. They are all interrelated and work together. Body, mind and soul link the pure light of spirit and matter in one continuum of light.

Since each level of consciousness vibrates at a certain color frequency, your response to color in the second awareness game will hold a mirror to your inner self giving you a glimpse of your own inner psychology. Your consciousness is a kaleidoscope of colors moving and changing. Although we all have seven chakras, most people have only one or two of them functioning most of the time. The others are active only a bit. Your aura color reveals the state of your centers at any moment. Although the aura changes as you feel, think and do different things inside yourself, it has a basic color which it returns to that is the most active center in you. Only when you can get in touch with each level and find out what is happening inside your consciousness can you open your ability to give out light and unfold your hidden potential. Usually we grow unconsciously. Many techniques, both psychological and spiritual, help us dissolve blocks and radiate more joy, love and light. When you work with all the levels consciously, you are speeding up your evolution because you can say that you are truly growing wholistically, completely.

These seven levels function just like worlds within worlds inside. They interpenetrate so that your sense of insecurity will affect your physical well-being or your memory will influence your imagination. Nevertheless, they can be experienced as distinct levels and vibrations which enables you to gain mastery over each chakra. As you can see from the above chart, the activity in the different centers affects the nervous system and its responses to stimuli as well as the hormone secretions which regulate body activity. Dis-ease in the body is caused by problems in any of the levels. If you are repressing some angry feelings and thoughts, your mental constipation can give you hemorrhoids. If you are worried your boyfriend may be out with another girl, your chronic insecurity can eat away at your cells and give you ulcers. If you have a negative imagination you might avoid people for fear they will hurt you, and so you cut yourself off from the social level and love.

We are only able to absorb as much light as the opening or conditioning of our centers will allow. They become filtered or they open and close in combinations according to our life experiences. When you have negative imaginings, fearing the worst, the violet center will be cloudy. The aura will appear muddy. If you try to gain power to stop your fears, your aura will turn purple and be dark. If you are very concerned about what others think of you and about social propriety (orange) then you may never open up your intuitive center (indigo world) which sees deep into the real nature of things beyond pretense. You'll be too busy spending all your energy on what others might be thinking. If you love intellectual stimulation too much you may never have the joy of experiencing the wholistic view of life that the conceptual, blue level mind is capable of, and you could just miss the beingness of life that comes from an open heart.

Nuclear Evolution unites the philosophies of the past and present and shows that the future thrust of man's evolutionary development is to purify and expand all the seven levels so that our spirit can shine through a clear prism, realize its oneness with the creator and radiate the full enlightenment of Cosmic Consciousness. The biggest shadow that blocks the light is what we have to work on first; it is our ego sense of being a separate mind, separate from light and separate from others because we feel we're locked in here, into our physical world of awareness. I'm sure you can discover many examples within yourself of how you filter the light and close off your chakras. Through the exercises to follow you will see even more clearly what they are and what to do about them.

Now we have a basic groundwork from which we can take off with some idea of where we are headed and why. These games and experiences are all developed to awaken and activate your seven chakras and enable you to take in and radiate more light, more consciousness, and realize that you are that pure consciousness that is omnipresent, omnipotent and omniscient. If you can bear in mind the one thought that consciousness is the ground of your being in which all vibrations and patterns of experience arise, then the practice of these awareness exercises will prove to you that light and consciousness are one. Getting to know that One who is the indestructible consciousness in us is the most exciting adventure known to man.

Stage Two

THERE IS ONLY ONE

by Deborah Rozman

Most of us have heard the saying, "We are all One." What image does that Oneness conjure up in the mind? Is it that we all have similar bodies, drives and needs? Or we're all "in it" together sandwiched between sky and ground? Or does that phrase convey some actual feeling of being everyone?

Try to imagine that every person and every thing is composed of you, your consciousness, which can become hard like stone or take many forms like eyes, minds and feelings. Now imagine that you are your consciousness emanating life force that is creating everything. When your mind and body are calm, when your memory has stopped playing tapes, you become your essence being which is the original stuff. Being this substance, which is the cause of all you know, you are everything and everyone.

This state is Pure *Consciousness* before it becomes things. When we thoroughly explore and expand mind, memory and the awareness of our whole self, we come to understand how we create reality. With such understanding we have a new ability to let go of our *identification* with the effects of pure consciousness – memory and body especially – which makes us feel separate from the essence in all. Then something happens. We let go and become the original stuff, even if only for a glimpse. To know ourself as pure consciousness all the time even while we are also using our minds and bodies takes a great deal of concentration, inner patience and discovery. It's like exploring unconquered land in the new world. As we explore we release limits on our ego which only thinks it knows who it is.

One of the best ways to experience this change is with people. Often if you meditate alone you can feel at-one with life. But as soon as you see someone do something you don't like – there you are separating again. Sometimes it just seems impossible to let go of that ego sense of ME, me sitting there meditating, thinking, judging. When you explore inner space together with other people, it can be a great meditation if you apply your full awareness and forget yourself enough to put yourself inside what is happening in the other person. While someone is describing his inner world you can feel it as he feels it if you concentrate *in* him and let go into him so you merge with his imagination and it becomes one with yours. When this happens new feelings which are going on in that person arise in you too. For a moment you become that person even if that person is feeling something painful or sorrowful. You feel it, but in this state it doesn't bring you down. You're in your pure being and you know you're their pure being too, working through their images, their feelings and mind. This keeps you centered in a peaceful place even while you are experiencing their pain. Concentration plus expansion into the other gives this feeling of uplifting compassionate oneness. This takes practice, love and time to develop. But even from the beginning you can feel the change of experience working slowly inside. The first thing you must learn is to really listen without thoughts about you, or opinions coming up all the time. When you listen to another person without your own ideas inter- fering you become open so his *being* and your *being* can merge. If you don't stay attuned in this way, but wander around in your thoughts, you may pick up on his emotions and they will affect you. You'll identify with the mood just like he is doing, and you'll lose touch with the underlying purity of being. Then you can't be of any help to him or yourself. That's why some people avoid relationships. They don't want to be affected by someone else. Or else they are afraid to share what they are really feeling. So instead people play lots of social games with each other in their relationships. We talk about this, and not that. We wouldn't want to tread on that tender territory, that's not our business. These games in Exploring Inner Space are games to let more light in and to open up our tenderness, whereas society's games are to shut things out and keep ourselves hidden.

The oneness we're looking for is that pure consciousness which is free, free to feel, to love, to become, but without getting stuck as anything rigid. If you judge someone's space you can never feel what it's like for him in his own world. You cut yourself off from him by judging. So oneness means first *acceptance,* then you can feel the other as if you are him. Much understanding comes and misunderstanding goes. You don't have to agree with his trip, you may not even like it, but more important than liking or agreeing is real understanding which is loving. It's more rewarding. When you can say to someone, now I really understand how you feel from inside-out, then both of you feel like you've loved. The door to deep, real communication is open.

When it comes down to facing another person, much less a group of people in this way, most of us shrink inside at first. Kids giggle, adults get nervous. What are you fearing but your own unknown self? And what is fearing? It is the familiar ego that is going to be asked to expand. But deep in the heart, behind those fears is the awakening urge of expectation, of hope for something new and bigger. These explorations have the understanding of your fears, needs and desires written into them to take you through to the awakening you want, in spite of yourself.

Not all communication in this adventure is with other people. Much of it is first with the different parts of yourself as you open up your centers. One part of you can be as afraid of another part of you as it is of someone else. Your blue level moral self can be afraid of your red level sexual self. Your yellow level rational self can be afraid of your violet level imaginative self. So you also have to create a safe "getting to know you" space inside yourself. The meditations in this book set the environment to create a safe inner communication. Most people are schizophrenic to some degree depending on how well the different levels within work together as one harmonious being. Inner conflicts are really the divisiveness between levels.

Often we project our inner divisiveness out onto other people. So our conflicts with them are really a result of a conflict inside ourself. The meditations are one way to create an inner atmosphere of peace, tuning body, feelings, mind and spirit in one harmonious major chord. From here we can play tunes of life on the different levels of minor chords in resonance with the primary one. This helps us stay centered as we explore. In Part III we go into understanding our inner conflicts more deeply with a method called "Creative Conflict," which is part of our creative communication. Sometimes we have blind spots, and no matter how we meditate we cannot see our gaps or our egos. This is where group mirroring and creative communication are important.

As we penetrate the depth of the imagination in the seventh level we border on complete dissolution of our little self. The images no longer are drawn from stored memories, but emerge from the primal substratum of creative life. As we transmute life energy into light we travel through the light barrier into our selfless self. I remember the first time I led my class through the regression exercise, to the birth experience and the state before birth. My imagination slipped away until it became all the stars spread out in space and there was no Debbie left. Instead of Debbie there was awareness and a feeling of suffused love – union. I had died and become the stars, totally identified as them and spread out through space too. When this happened there was no time or space or me. Space doesn't exist because you become it.

The promise of these games is directly proportional to what you put into them. For those who want to go even deeper into this type of universal experience, there are several courses the University of the Trees community offers.* In these courses, as in all the games you will find in this book, the main purpose is to enable you to feel and enter into the vibration of each chakra for a total experience of many dimensions of life. When you find yourself ready for a deeper plunge into outer/inner space, the urge for a continuous experience through daily exploration on your part, then "games" cease and become reality.

---

* Christopher Hills and his students have developed a number of maps and guidelines. Having gone beyond space and time in his own consciousness and achieved Self-Realization, Christopher has written a three year daily course of study to help others arrive. It trains you to penetrate through all these levels in what he has called "A Space Odyssey" to Pure Consciousness. (See appendix.)

PART II
THE VOYAGE

THE VOYAGE

As we prepare ourselves for a new look at space and what lies within it, we need to keep in mind the idea that we are exploring different parts of ourself. All activities, all awareness or mind games, from whatever source, act upon certain levels of consciousness. In fact, whatever action we take reflects our chakra energies. This book is a *chakra handbook* into which we can fit many, many more games and exercises than are found on the pages to follow. The awareness explorations given are some of the first created in the field, and also include many designed specifically to open a certain chakra. By no means is exploring inner space limited solely to the sessions which follow. We can incorporate any group activity, or personal exercise into the *chakra* framework, to allow us an endless voyage.

Our *reactions* are just as important a part of each exploration as our *actions*. This is an important point to keep in mind. Whenever something arises that you find difficult, or when someone reacts in a different way from how you would react, look at it as a challenge for yourself. If we judge or begin to separate ourself from others, or from the games, we need to ask:
"What part of myself am I rejecting and why?"
If an uncertainty rises within you about what the group is doing, or about your own actions, again you must ask:
"From what level are my feelings and reactions coming?"
In this way we make all of our inner feelings and thoughts food for growth. No matter what blocks we may encounter, if we have this attitude of self-honesty we will grow and have the joyful discovery that we are doing our best. Our integrity will bring us fulfillment.

Attitude is the most important requirement for growing from these experiences.

a) An open mind
b) honesty with yourself
c) daring to be open and honest with your other selves

will guarantee that these explorations will work for you. If you feel at any time that the group is going too slow for you, or something is not working as it should, ask yourself which of the above attitudes (a, b or c) is weak or missing. You can provide the missing element and re-create the scene to your own image. The power and the responsibility lie within each person who goes on the voyage and nowhere else. Once you find out which attitude needs some attention on your part, you will have the tool to dissolve your block. The action is up to you. It will bring the Cosmic response. Fueled by your willingness, guided by the mirror of the group and your own honesty, you will be able to go through the door and leave the earth-bound orbit of your own ego into the ever-expanding territory of your vaster being.

MAPPING THE VOYAGE

SUMMARY OF INSTRUCTIONS:
Follow these instructions carefully and refer back to them frequently as you would a map, especially if you ever feel lost. They are meant to guide, not to limit, and in guiding provide freedom for spontaneity within the structure.

★ Leaders rotate. Choose a leader before each session. That leader may choose the exploration as a surprise or lead an exploration chosen by the group. In your first meeting, plan how you are going to approach the games. Create a map of the course you are going to follow. Are you going to proceed through each level doing one game from each level? Are you going to explore all of one world before going onto the next? Are you going to wear the color of the level in your clothes so everybody is resonating to that color frequency? Decide what is best for your group.

★ The leader should prepare all of the needed accessories ahead of time and study the game beforehand so that he knows what steps will come and be ready for them during the exploration.

★ Begin each session with the yoga postures that put you in touch with the world you are exploring. (Except for the first two games which do not have postures.)

★ After the yoga postures do the centering meditation for that level, which you can continue to practice on your own at home.

★ Sit in a circle, close together, yet with room to relax and move.

★ Proceed through the exploration, step by step, modifying only when needed to fit your particular group. The leader reads the goal to the group before going into the first step, and then reads each step as he goes. Certain points of instruction that need to be kept secret so as not to give away the purpose of that step *should not* be read by the leader. Other points of instruction that are solely to aid the leader and may be distracting if read to the group while they are in the middle of an activity, *need not* be read by the leader. Most of these points will be in italics and easy to recognize.

★   If you are working with young children in these games, let yourself spontaneously simplify the words and ideas when needed to fit the age level. Kids are more suited to some games than to others. Pick and choose ahead of time.

★   Gauge the time you have. You may want to go more deeply into certain exercises in the shorter games, or eliminate an exercise in a longer game if you are pinched for time. If you don't have time to complete all the steps go as far as you can but still leave some time for discussion and journal writing at the end. You may want to continue the session next time and then choose another game from that level to do as well.

★   Have your pen and journal ready all the time to keep a record of your voyage. Jot down in your journals the answers to all questions you are asked to answer in the games. Write your insights, impressions, feelings, questions and ideas to get a mirror of your inner self which you share with yourself and maybe with others, if you feel moved to, at the end of the game. You may use poetry and drawings as well as prose to express yourself. Journals may be shared, but they are your private space.

★   Close with a love circle, linking arms and sharing your oneness in gratitude to each other for the contribution of everyone to higher group consciousness.

★   You may get so turned on by one of the dimensions that you'll want to go straight through all the journeys in that world before going on to a new level. Some groups were so into the heart chakra that they just wanted more and more of the feeling it brought them. Other groups want to really master the E.S.P. games, so they repeat the exercises over and over in the intuitive world until they can do them at will.

Second grade public school classroom practicing concentration on the Centering symbol of Nuclear Evolution.

THE CENTERING MEDITATION

At the start of each exploration and after you do the yoga postures, it is very centering and relaxing to begin with a meditation. We can explore more deeply the consciousness in each level by awakening our finer sensitivities to it. The centering meditation here is a step by step introduction into your inner space. In a group it will be a guided meditation. The meditations on each of the levels take up where this basic centering leaves off. For those of you who are new to exploring the cosmos through meditation, you will need to go through each of these five steps to start. Soon you will be able to do them quickly and on your own without need for a guiding voice. Then you can be centered wherever you are, in whatever world you find yourself.

Real meditation is a wholistic experience that includes your entire being. The first step is to ask your body what it is trying to say to you. You get in touch with your body and relax it in this way. What is its message? In the East they use yoga postures as a means to relax the body and prepare it for meditation. The body is like a battery. It starts your consciousness going and gives it a storehouse of energy. To keep it running smoothly you have to keep the energy circuits free from tension. So before each exploration and before each meditation we do a few yoga postures to put us in touch with the part of the body related to the chakra we are going to be working with. We get in touch with the tensions and relax them, letting go of the kinks within our bodies. In "The Centering Meditation" we also go through an exercise in tensing and relaxing to quickly put ourselves in touch with our whole body and at ease.

The second step is to get in touch with your feelings. Your breath is a very powerful tool you can use to change your emotional feelings at will. Conscious breathing puts you in touch with your feelings, and charges your emotions and body with fresh life force. The third step is what we call concentration or centering. It is when you draw all your life force into the center of your being. You draw your inner energies up to the point between your eyebrows, into your intuitive center of sensitivity. This is the magnetic part of your mind, beyond thoughts. You have tuned into your body and into your feelings, and now you want to tune into your center of direct perception. To do this successfully you have to have done steps 1 and 2 first, because only with a relaxed body and calm emotions can the energies be released to rise into this spiritual eye center between the brows, just in back of the forehead. Concentration is a focussing of attention so no distracting thoughts take you back into fidgeting, or into old memories and old dreams or feelings. We need all of our energies clear to meditate properly. Then, in this concentrated state, the intuition is given the chance to open. We stay there waiting, focussed, not demanding, just open. Let go of the mind, of any thoughts that come in. Just let them pass as they come. You wait in the stillness, centered, and you may experience intuitive flashes, an insight, a core feeling or thought where you just know it's real. You don't seize it with your mind and start to work on it, or try to remember it, because then you are back into the mind. Your intuition will remember what it needs to. Just let the thoughts go and higher consciousness can come in. If you stay centered and attuned throughout the exploration, intuition will come and work through you and work through all the levels as you explore.

The fourth step is expansion. Here you expand beyond your idea of being a separate self in a little body. Here is where you are ready to do the special meditations for each of the inner worlds, to expand your consciousness of how they work, to experience them all as part of yourself. The fifth step is the most important. It is when you apply your newly expanded awareness into action. Like an electric current, you must ground this new energy into creative activity for it to become useful to your growth.

When our activity serves our evolution, serves our expanded Self, then it is the highest action we can be doing on earth. So we enter into one of the awareness explorations as our fifth step to explore our greater Self. Not only do we go on an exciting adventure, but we serve the highest purpose in life, furthering our evolution. The more you can bring these five steps into your everyday life, the more you gain the fulfillment of your own Self-mastery.

CENTERING MEDITATION

The reader does as much of the same meditation as he can while slowly reading. Whenever three dots appear (. . .) that means to pause. Whenever there is to be a long pause (over thirty seconds) it will be indicated. Anyone can read or lead a guided meditation. In the home and classroom we often have the children take turns guiding a meditation which they have made up or which they read from the book. The reader needs to be sensitive to the group as he is reading in order to gauge his pace.

The leader reads the following:

Begin the centering by sitting with your spine straight, either cross-legged in a comfortable position on a pillow on the floor, or else sit in a chair with your feet flat on the floor. It's important that you be comfortable. One way to help keep the spine straight is to place your hands at the junctures where the legs and pelvis meet. Keep the palms upturned unless you are used to meditating another way. Lean forward so that the pelvis is tilted forward, then sit up straight but keep the pelvis in the same tilted forward position. Now the pelvis will help you keep the spine in place by pushing the lower back forward while you relax. The hand position will help by keeping the shoulders back and the chest out. Keeping the back straight is important so that the energy in the seven spinal centers can flow freely up and down the spine from your brain. You can even feel the energy moving in the spine after awhile if you tune your mind into it. Once your posture feels comfortable, you can begin to relax each part of the body in turn. It's best to close your eyes from here on and let yourself be guided by the leader until you know how to do it on your own.

Tense the toes, put your mind inside them and relax them. . . Then draw your awareness out of the toes into the feet. Tense them and let them go. Relax the feet. Draw your consciousness up into the ankles and legs. Tense the ankles and calves, don't tense too hard, then let them go, relaxed, released . . . Draw your awareness and your energy up your legs some more into the thighs. Tense the thighs, charge them with energy

The Leader continues reading. . .

and then let them go, releasing all the muscle tensions, releasing all the pent-up energy. Relax. Tense the pelvis and buttocks and hip area, then let it all go relaxing it as you release the tension. As you practice this your body will feel so light that you will hardly know that it exists from the waist down. . . Now tense the stomach and let it go. Then the chest, tense and relax . . . Now the hands and lower arms. Tense and relax. Move your consciousness to the upper arms and shoulders and tense and relax them. Now put your awareness in your back and tense and relax your spine and back muscles in three parts. First the lower back, then the middle back, then the upper back and neck. . . Feel the consciousness move up the back as you withdraw your awareness up and up as you go. . . Now tense the face, squish it all up and tense all the facial muscles. Relax. Finally, tense the head and scalp, let them go and focus your awareness into the center of the brain on top of the head. Your whole body should feel loose, free, relaxed, and your consciousness awake and ready. Ask it how it feels. If any part still feels tense, or fidgety, you tense it and then let it go, letting all its pent up energy relax. . .

Now begin to watch your breathing for one or two minutes. Watch it go up and down inside your nose and in your heart or lungs. . . Feel its rhythm slow you down and calm you inside-out as you let it flow up and down like a wave on the sea. . . Ask yourself, do I have any old feelings, old pains and hurts still in my heart? Or, when was the last time I got upset at someone, or someone got angry with me? Feel your old feelings and as the breath goes out let them go. Each time you breathe in, feel you are charging up with new life force and fresh feelings. . . Now inhale slowly and gently through your nostrils to a count of five, then hold the breath for the same count, then slowly exhale through the nostrils to the same count. . . Gradually you will be able to increase the count to 20 and feel deep effects in your feelings. As you breathe, you draw in fresh life and love which rides piggy back on the breath. As you hold your breath circulate this love through your whole body, washing it with fresh life force and love, and as you breathe out you let go of any old worries, tensions, or painful feelings you may have. Get in touch with your deep

The leader continues reading. . .

feelings. Let go of your old emotions and inhale fresh, uplifting emotions. You are a child at heart. You are transforming your own inner space at will. Repeat this rhythmic breathing while imaging fresh love and life five times, the same count as you use in the breath. It's important to really put yourself into it, to bring yourself a new feeling, a new experience of energy. . . (long pause).

Now let yourself breathe naturally again. . . To relax your mind more deeply, get in touch with its thoughtmaking. Let the thoughts go, don't hold onto any of them. . . Saying a sound in the mind as you watch your breath helps calm the thoughts. As the breath flows in naturally, say the word *sa* to yourself, mentally. As the breath flows out naturally, say the word *ha* to yourself. This will quiet your thoughts. Practice it a few moments. . . (long pause) . . . Now draw the mind and all the awareness into the center behind your forehead. You can do this by pretending all the energy is flowing up from all your nerves and collecting in one point at the place behind your forehead in between your two eyebrows. It may be like light rays focussing into the sun, or like all your energy flowing into a magnet at that point. Here, you feel centered inside yourself.

If you feel you are still having trouble keeping your mind steady, you can do the same centering but this time bring the energy into your heart center which is near the center of your chest, and let your mind flow into a feeling of love. Send that love out like a sun shining from your heart into the room, and into every person present. Meditation on the heart opens up a feeling of love and sweetness. Meditation on the magnetic center between the brows opens up sensitive perception. Together they help each other to expand your whole being.

Now when you are centered, you are ready to expand into new awareness and to explore with a more refined and attuned consciousness.*

---

* The instructions for 5-step centering and beginning meditation are available on tape. (See appendix.)

Neighborhood family meditation

THE EXPLORATIONS

GETTING TO KNOW YOU

Exploration

1

Introductory

PREPARATION:
*Choose a leader for this session
who will keep it moving.*

1 blindfold per 8 people

GOAL: Our goal is to get to know each other, to break the ice and dig below the social superficiality we all unconsciously use to protect our identity. The moment we start groping for words that describe our basic beliefs about life and our innermost aspirations, the problems that have seemed so important to us fade away. Business headaches, the garbage bag we forgot to take out, school pressures, the gripe against wife, mother, husband or boss, all seem irrelevant for the moment as we probe to a deeper stratum of life.

When you are just yourself, no matter how inadequate your words feel to you inside, it brings a closeness with all people present beyond anything that just social friendship can give. You feel a broadening of horizons and a change in the vibration in the room which gets away from small talk to an instant uplifting of all present to a higher level of awareness.

No one is to be changed by others, only by his own free will and his own growth in consciousness.

If we try to prepare a speech beforehand it will come out like a press release or something canned, as we try to figure out what we're "supposed to say." It is more important that these expressions of your being be spontaneous, open and real for you. You may think you're being honest when you are really building your personal image to look good in the eyes of others. Also, it is a cop out to say "I feel like Joe does." Even if you do feel like Joe, express your own view from your own being.

EXPLORATION:

Be sure to begin with the Centering Meditation for a few minutes.

1. Everyone, in turn, expresses their personal life situation by answering the following:

   a) Your name, lifestyle, occupation, favorite activities, etc.
   b) What do you want to gain from the group?
   c) What do you hope to *give* to the group experience?
   d) Is there any problem or difficulty you would like the group to help you work on?

You may want to make notes on the answers shared for future use, to see if the group has really helped each person work on his personal problem.

2. Each person in turn expresses how he views the universe. First we will begin with a short tuning-in to get deeper in touch with feelings and to look within.

    Read slowly and repeat the questions several times.

    > Sit comfortably, close the eyes . . . watch your breathing for a few moments to center yourself . . . Feel the area within near your heart, your center of feeling. Ask yourself the following questions and let your heart give you the answer. Listen. Relax and let go . . . (long pause).

    > What is your idea of a source, creator, or God if any?
    > Does the universe have a purpose?
    > Why are you here?
    > What is your personal goal in life?

    > Now begin to share as soon as you feel ready. We will take a few minutes per person. Go around the room in order after the first person begins. If anyone needs more time we will skip that person for the moment and then return to him or her later.

    As everyone shares, you may ask each other questions for points to be clarified. Avoid argumentative questions at this time. This is a time for listening, acceptance and openness. As we listen to each other, let us watch our judgements and try to let them go for the moment.

3. After each person has shared, go around the group again and each person asks only one question of someone in the group who spoke. Choose someone whom you didn't understand or who didn't say enough. Try to draw each other out and share minds.

4. Discuss the experience. Entertain the following questions one at a time with each other, drawing out those who don't say too much. Do not let one or two people monopolize the conversation.

The Trust Exercise. The person in the middle keeps the eyes closed or is blindfolded.

How many found it hard to put their beliefs into words?
How many had to search inside to find what they really do believe?
Was anyone surprised or shocked at someone else's belief?
Do you feel you want to change anyone's beliefs?
Can we trust people who believe differently?

LEARNING TO TRUST

Do this exercise if you have time, or begin the next session with it.

Form a circle, or if there are more than eight people form several circles. Huddle close together. One person at a time goes into the center and is blindfolded. He turns around once or twice, stops, then falls gently backwards. At first falling backwards is difficult to do, as very few people trust enough to "let go" completely. You must keep the legs stiff and straight when you are in the center and the fall should be one that rocks you on your heels in a way which forces people to your aid to save you from falling down. The closer together the trustees are to each other, the safer the person in the middle will feel. Everyone must be very alert, arms ready to catch. The group prevents the person from falling by catching and support-ing him and then gently pushing him forward to fall and be caught by the other people in the circle. The person in the center doesn't move but is passed to and fro by his trustees. This "giving" the person to each other is done with love and care flowing through your arms and hands and this feeling is passed on to each person until it permeates the entire group. Spend a minute or two on each person, then go on to the next person so everyone has a turn. You can repeat this exercise before other sessions too, until everyone can do it without fear.

5. Write in your journals.

COLOR AND YOU

Exploration

2

Introductory

PREPARATION:

You will need seven pieces of colored felt or paper, as close to the seven pure colors of the rainbow as possible, and as close to the same size as possible. These colors are red, orange, yellow, green, blue, indigo and violet. Construction paper is acceptable as long as you choose the bright hues and not muddy colors. Try to pick out a true green instead of a blue-green or a dirty green, for example.

Paste or tape the colored pieces on a doorway or plain colored wall. Place them in the order given with red to the left.

GOAL: Our color choices present a mirror for our personality. Through color we can discover more about our natural drives. We go into color more deeply with the Luscher Color Test in session 25. Here we begin to explore the levels of consciousness and understand a bit why some colors attract you and others repel you, and why just the opposite colors attract and repel someone else. Don't try to "second-guess" yourself by choosing colors you think you "should" like. It's not always what we like that is our aura color. Many people discover that the very color they reject is the color they have an abundance of in their aura and a part of themselves they do not like. But there is a reason why people live by color in their choices of food, clothes and furnishings. At times we can be comfortable in surroundings dominated by one frequency of light, say blue, and repulsed in an environment of another, say pink. I know a woman who once decorated her entire house in pink, including dishwasher, refrigerator, living room carpet, drapes, etc. Then, after a few years she couldn't stand the color anymore and changed it all over to blue! She never related the change to the change that happened in her inner life at that time until she came upon *Nuclear Evolution*. She told me the interpretations fit exactly with what she went through. This beginning exercise should give you a clue about your own personality, even though we are just scratching the surface of the whole field of color psychology.

EXPLORATION:

Be sure to begin with the Centering Meditation for a few minutes.

1. Write down the answers to the following questions in your journal.

   a) What is usually your favorite color?
   b) What color do you like least?

c) What color do you usually choose to wear?
d) What color wouldn't you "be seen in"?

2. What do you spend your *inner* time doing? Check each of the following on a scale of one to five, one being not at all and five being a lot. Inner time is not the same as outer time. For example you might never think about food or sense pleasures or the joy of action, but you still outwardly eat meals and act. You then might choose one for (a) below.

a) Looking for things to keep doing, to be busy, busy in activity, thinking about sports, sex, sense pleasures—wine, eating, movies, drinks, etc. [1 2 3 4 5]

b) Wishing you had friends to socialize with frequently, looking to parties, outings, social occasions, enjoying gossip, or political ambitions, social welfare groups. Do you think a lot about serving society? [1 2 3 4 5]

c) Analyzing your life, your thoughts, people, movements, picking problems apart, wanting to figure it all out. [1 2 3 4 5]

d) Feeling insecure or secure, jealous, miserly, seeking to earn a lot of money, seeking love, worrying about a love object or possessions. [1 2 3 4 5]

e) Devotion or religious feelings. Having a lot of memories of the past, referring to the past, the family, how things were, thinking about how things should be, not liking change, craving peace. [1 2 3 4 5]

f) Always peering into the future, wondering what will happen next. What will life bring? Living so much in tomorrow that today seems almost yesterday. Intuitive flashes. [1 2 3 4 5]

g) Living in fantasies, creating worlds, people, situations in your imagination. Dreaming, wishes of what you'd like to see, erotic fantasies, images of nature or poetic images of feelings. Seeing pictures in your mind when you close your eyes. [1 2 3 4 5]

3. Walk up to the colors on the wall and after a moment of contemplation write down on another piece of paper which color you like best and which you like least and all the ones in between in your order of preference. Write the color–red, orange, yellow, green, blue, indigo or violet. Does the color you like best jump out at you, so to speak?

The leader then reads out loud the following descriptions of the psychological meaning of each color. It is very important in this exercise to put aside any pre-conceptions of what you have heard from other sources about what the colors mean and just try out these interpretations. As the leader reads, write down whether you feel the description applies to you or to others you know.

Red   Red in your aura is the level of awareness that seeks stimulation and excitement for the senses. It is the color of vitality and action. In color therapy red can increase muscular tension, or stimulate higher blood pressure and respiration. Red is the sex drive. In its negative form it can be lust, hatred and quickness to anger. In its positive form the senses are an enjoyable servant. They do not control or dominate. A person on the red level lives in the sensory now. He has little awareness of past or future and depends on externals to satisfy his sensory cravings. He is aggressive and if he cannot express his aggressiveness creatively in work and love making, he will find another way, such as eating aggressively or participating in physical sports. The positive red level person is quick on the mark and will excel in physical work and getting things done. You need a positive red level to manifest your physical goals successfully. The red level has to watch quick reactions which often come without thought. "Red with anger" is a common expression. Red for revolutionary activity is another. Red for danger means action has gone too fast or too far.

Write down your impressions of red in yourself, in others in the group, in friends and family.

Orange Orange in your aura means you crave social contact, social acceptance and security in group protection. It stands for the herd instinct, following the crowd or letting it pull you along. It is wanting to be in on what's happening, in on what everybody else is doing. The negative orange level drive is to "Keep up with the Jones'es" and worry about what everybody else is thinking about you. The positive orange wants to explore and is ambitious, not just for its own sense gratification like the red level, but for the whole community. A person operating in orange likes to feel admired by others and achieve success in their eyes. Often people who have a strong orange aura will be social butterflies, party goers, politicians, volunteer workers. On the highest level orange is the humanitarian interested in the social welfare. Orange level awareness stimulates you to be an extrovert, outgoing towards others. Orange stimulates digestion, being associated with that part of the body, and many restaurants are decorated in orange. The color orange means always going out.

Write down your impressions of orange in yourself, in others in the group, in friends and family.

Yellow   Yellow is cheerful and bright. It is an intellectually invigorating color. When it is muddy or tending towards olive it means cowardice. "He's yellow!" Yellow level likes to think and have new ideas to challenge his analytic ability. The drive is for change, and intellectual stimulation, but often the yellow-auraed person is so much in the head that he over-plans everything and gets bogged down in details or confines life to the narrow view of intellect. Some people plan all the time and never get around to doing anything besides figuring it out. The positive yellow drive is towards self-expression through creative thought or penetrating insight like the sun's rays. Yellow means always hunting for something new, looking for problems to solve, being logical and thinking things through before acting.

Write down your impressions of your own yellow level, yellow in others in the group, in friends and family.

Green   Green is the color of consciousness inside you that is concerned with security, especially of the heart. Whether you are feeling insecure, jealous, uncertain about something, or whether you are feeling secure and harmonious with life, one with nature (which is green), you are operating in that band of consciousness. "Green with envy" is a common expression. People with muddy green auras are often misers or selfish with their possessions. Green can lead to hoarding like a pack rat or accumulating knowledge to store it up. It is also the color that wants to possess the things it loves, to belong to someone and receive self-confirmation. When you feel pangs of emotional uncertainty you are in the negative green world. When your heart flows out in care and trust, you are radiating the healing positive green of life force, living love. Green means seeking to store up life force or being close to someone with a lot of it.

Write down your impressions of green in yourself, in friends, loved ones, in the group.

Blue   A person with a blue aura may be religious, seeking peace and contentment. While the red level is an activist, the blue level is a pacifist. The blue level wants peace and quiet so much it will often tolerate a bully or a dictator. Blue level people resist change and want things to be ordered, conservative, just like the good old days. If you are blue dominant, you can be uncomfortable with new ideas that are not yet accepted by existing authorities. The blue level loves ideals and often finds that his idealism is in the mind only, at the expense of what is real. If you think a lot about the past, how your mother did things, how things *should* be done, and take a while to deliberate over what people say and your own feelings, then you most likely are functioning from the blue level of consciousness. If you're "feeling blue" or are depressed about something, then you are usually in the negative past and your aura will be a murky blue. If you are devoted to high moral or spiritual concepts your aura may be a bright electric blue.

Write down your impressions of blue in yourself, in friends, loved ones, the group.

Indigo   This darker blue is the color of mystery and intuition. "It came in from out of the blue" is the intuitive awareness that knows, but doesn't know how it knows. When you receive hunches from nowhere, have E.S.P., can tune into what others are thinking, then you are in the indigo level. A person with a strong indigo drive lives in the future. What is happening now, or what's happened in the past has no interest to him, which may stun a blue level person who lives in the past. Since the indigo is always off in the future, into what will happen, he is often impatient. He is often late for appointments as he feels he's already there in his mind, and is waiting for the body to catch up. Often the indigo is spiritual, but not religious, as his experience is based on vision and direct perception rather than on what religious authorities say. But the indigo problem is that he can be on a false cloud nine and his visions unreal, or even caught in a world of superstition. The indigo believes he knows, he believes that the thoughts that come in, the symbols he perceives are true because so often in the past they have been. This is how superstition is born. While the indigo person envisions, he may not have the skill on the other levels to make it happen, test them out, or carry out his goals practically. The indigo urge is always to be somewhere where he's not, except in the peak moments when the "future" and the "now" merge. Indigo goes towards the mysterious and is usually out on a limb.

Write down your insights into indigo in yourself, in the group members, in friends and family. Do you see any of the described characteristics?

Violet   Violet is the level where past, present and future merge in the now. It is the color of imagination and charm. It is a drive toward absolute, cosmic order. The violet level person loves to use the imagination to condition himself and his environment rather than be subject to it. So the realm of magic, the occult, poetry, fantasy, music, art and inspiration turn him on. It is also the realm of people on power trips who seek to use powers to overwhelm others. It is the level where we glimpse the eternal vision and dream our dreams, real or unreal. Persons with violet auras are very descriptive or poetic. They like the bizarre and are usually original.

Write down the impressions you have of violet in yourself, in the group, in your family and in others.

4.   The next step is to discuss how your choices of color relate to how you saw yourself in the descriptions, and in the checklist of the questions on page 64. Did you choose red as your favorite and find that you are also quite a sensual person? Did you reject violet and find that you are somehow suppressing your own imaginative ability?

See if you can find any correlations. Compare notes on how you see each other. Share your insights into each other, what made you feel someone was strongly on one level or another. Note what others say about you without defending or rebutting. Just receive their feedback, right or wrong, and try to see how they are seeing you. Share and discuss the color levels in relation to people you know and explore the possibility of understanding others' motives, needs and drives better by realizing they are on a different level of consciousness from you. See how meaningful a sharing you can make this discussion by being as open as you can about your feelings, impressions and how you see these drives operating. Which do you need to work on the most for growth? Draw everyone out to express themselves. Don't bully anyone, coax them!

There are other colors of course in the aura besides the seven pure rainbow shades, but these are all combinations or derivatives of the seven rainbow colors. A few are mentioned below, as well as their meaning in the aura.

Grey   The feeling of not wanting to be left out, washed out, being deceived, or approaching death.

White   A blend of all the colors: purity, spiritual awareness of light.

Black   No color, total absorption of light without letting any radiate out. Usually deep depression or black anger—hidden resentment, suicidal. In rare cases a spiritual void of pure invisible light.

Brown   Paranoia, sexual problems possibly.

5. Journal writing.

RED WORLD
THE PHYSICAL LEVEL

Children doing yoga exercises

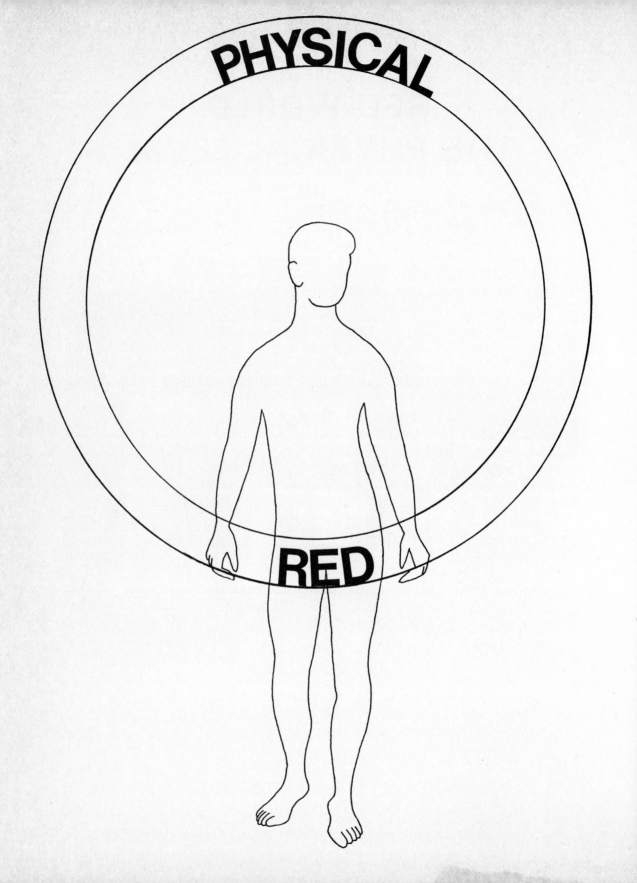

RED
I

The Red world of awareness within every person is the physical world of the five senses: *TASTE, TOUCH, SIGHT, HEARING AND SMELL.* These are five portholes through which we know about this world. They are all part of our body and its nervous system, sometimes called the Tree of Knowledge. The senses can only be experienced now! They are not like thoughts which come *after* the sense stimulation. When we see a tree it is now; afterwards we reflect or think about it. If we taste something hot we react quickly, now! Then we moan and say, "My tongue is burnt," and then we think about getting a glass of water to cool it off.

You've heard kids being told, "Touch that vase only with your eyes." When the urge is to find out about everything by touching its smooth or rough surface and experiencing the feel of the texture, it is hard to keep one's hands to oneself. The eyes are a sensitive piece of skin that can also give the *feel* of an object in a different way. You have to use the energy coming out of your eyes to put your being inside the object and feel it like it feels itself, with empathy. Actually the eye, the ear, the nose and the tongue are all pieces of skin which can feel. They are sensitized to experience special vibrations. Enjoying hugs and all skin to skin communication comes from this physical level.

Children are more frequently in this physical world, exploring their bodies and the objects around, than adults. More often than any other color, children will choose the color red when offered a choice. They move with ease in the body and know what a wonderful world the five senses bring to us to discover. The red level is also the level of action, manifestation. The person who gets things done quickly has a well-functioning red level of consciousness. The person who is slow or sluggish to complete tasks, who ponders so much he never acts, has a problem on the red level. By getting into the feel of what red level energy feels like we can learn to recognize it both when it's turned on and when it's turned off in ourselves and others. We can also learn how to activate it and calm it down. Heart failure is due to too much physical red level stress and highly strung action. Start to watch for signs of red level energy in your group. Is someone always referring to food? sex? anger? work? reacting to others?

YOGA POSTURES I

The standing postures of yoga are related to the chakra or center in the spine which governs the red, physical level of awareness. By practicing these physical exercises we learn to get in touch with that part of our nervous system and to ground our consciousness into the earth on a firm foundation. Many people who have a problem with the red level, for example those who never seem to have it together in terms of physical living on the earth—rent, food, clothes, child support—are flightly and not relaxed or well-grounded. They need to plant their feet firmly on the ground and build up from that solid foundation. These three postures help to put you in touch with the earth. Practice the postures as a way to loosen up and prepare for each session in the red world. As you do these postures keep your mind inside the base of the spine, the coccyx, and try to feel the movement of energy in that area, moving down through the legs into the earth.

TRIANGLE

Stand with arms straight out to the side, feet about three feet apart with the left foot turned inwards and the right foot turned out. Keep the palms facing down. Inhale. As you exhale stretch the torso to the right and extend the right arm out, then down as in diagram. Weight should shift to the left leg mostly. Keep the legs firm and do not bend the knees. Bring the right arm down to the calf or ankle without bending legs. Only stretch as far as you can without strain. Look up at the left hand which should be straight up in the air. Hold for a count of ten. Inhale and slowly come up. Repeat on the other side with the right foot turned inwards and the left foot out. Inhale. As you exhale stretch the torso to the left and extend left arm out,then down as in diagram. Weight should shift to the right leg. Keep the legs firm and do not bend the knees. Bring the left arm down to the calf or ankle without bending legs. Stretch as far as you can without strain. Look up at the right hand which should be straight up in the air. Hold for a count of ten. As you hold feel the current of energy going through your legs into the ground. Feel your weight balanced on both feet now and your feet firmly secured on the earth. Inhale and slowly come up.

REVERSE TRIANGLE

Begin with the feet three feet apart as you did in the triangle, standing up straight with arms out to the side. Turn the left foot in and the right foot out. Inhale and twist at the waist so the left arm moves in a circle to the right and you are looking behind yourself. Exhale so the left arm stretches down and place the left hand on the right side of the right foot, keeping your legs and knees straight and firm. Place the right hand and arm straight up in the air and look up at the right hand. Hold for a count of ten, as you feel the grounding. Inhale and come up slowly. Come back to the center, beginning position. Do the same on the opposite side. Turn the right foot in and the left foot out. Arms out at the sides. Inhale and twist to the left so the right arm comes to the left side and you are looking backwards. Exhale as you place the right hand to the left side of the left foot. Stretch left arm up in air and keep knees and legs and arms straight. Look up at the left hand, feeling the current of energy flow through your body into the ground. Hold to a count of ten. Inhale and come up.

 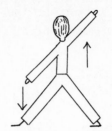 

THE WARRIOR

This time your feet are four feet apart, arms again out to the side. Put the left foot in and the right foot out. Bend the right knee. Inhale and raise the arms over the head, clasp hands and straighten the arms. Exhale and turn the torso to the right. Stretch the left leg so it is straight but the foot is flat on the ground, heel and toe. Look up at your hands and stretch up like an Indian warrior. Feel as though you are grounded in the earth and reaching toward heaven. Look up as you stretch. Hold for a count of ten. Inhale and come up and back to center. Repeat on the other side, legs four feet apart. Put the right foot in and the left foot out. Bend left knee. Inhale and raise arms over the head, clasp hands, straighten arms. Exhale and turn torso to the left. Stretch and imagine you're an Indian warrior. Feel like you are linking earth and heaven. Hold to a count of ten. Inhale and come up.

FIVE SENSES MEDITATION

You can practice this meditation over and over again any time you wish. It is especially helpful if you do it right at the beginning of each session in the red level, after the standing postures. Each time you journey consciously into the inner space of the Red World you will have a deeper experience if you prepare yourself with this meditation.

Speak slowly leader. The (. . .) mean to pause and give yourself plenty of time.

Get into the relaxed state of the basic meditation given on page 54 When you are centered within, then it is time to explore the five senses from inside-out. Close the eyes. Draw all your attention to the point between the eyebrows behind the forehead in the center of your brain . . . draw all your attention to that one spot . . . try to imagine what it would be like to be blind . . . to have been born blind without any memory of sight . . . what is it like to not be able to see anything and to never have seen anything . . . no colors . . . no light or dark . . . how would you know what things were like if you couldn't see them? . . . yet the seer who makes sense of what the eyes see is still awake within.

Now pretend you have never heard anything; from birth you have been blind and deaf. You have never heard voices or sounds, all is still . . . how would you tell about life without sound or sight . . . how would you know anything?

Now let's remove the sense of touch . . . there are people who are born without any sense of touch, hearing or sight . . . what does it feel like? . . . How would you know what space is or what objects in space are without touch? All you would have left would be smell and taste . . . What is it like to just be able to relate to the environment through smell and taste? . . .

Let's remove the sense of smell as well . . . you have never smelled your food or body odors or perfume or flowers . . . what is it like to be unable to smell? . . .

Now let's remove the last sense of taste, you can no longer taste anything . . . you have never tasted anything, neither your mother's milk which is the first thing babies taste nor the taste in your own mouth. What is it like to not have any senses or memories of sense experience?

There are no sense objects there to experience. There are no things, no time, no space between things. . . (long pause) . . . what is left? Just your awareness. Just the inner light of consciousness waiting to make sense of the senses when you bring them back to life. . . As you bring the senses back try to keep identifying with the inner light rather than with the senses, so that when you open your eyes you will see in a new way with the inner light of consciousness rather than with the physical eyes.

Let's bring the sense of taste back, taste the taste in your mouth . . . Now add the sense of smell, sniff the air gently . . . then touch, feel the ground, your body, move a bit . . . now add the sense of hearing . . . listen to the sounds in the distance . . . and now when you open your eyes look at the different forms of light energy crystallized into objects around you and look at them without any concepts or images of what they are . . . no thoughts . . . look afresh at them with the pure light of consciousness . . . don't say the word "book" or "wall" or "chair" in your mind, just let the form rest and be . . .

unconditioned by any previous experience or by these words . . .

See if you can stay in this pure state . . . note when you become aware that old patterns of thinking and acting are recurring . . .*

PRACTICE THIS MEDITATION AFTER THE STANDING YOGA POSTURES FOR THE RED LEVEL AND EACH TIME BEFORE YOU BEGIN A VOYAGE INTO WORLD I.

---

* "Five Senses Meditation", originated by Christopher Hills, also found in DIRECT PERCEPTION, by Christopher Hills and Deborah Rozman, published, University of the Trees Press, 1978.

Children doing the sense perception game where they feel objects while blindfolded.

SENSE PERCEPTION

Exploration

3

Red World

PREPARATION:

Blindfolds for everyone (since blindfolds are used in many of the explorations, it is a good idea to tear up an old sheet or old towels to make enough to have on hand)

Different smelling spices or flower oils, extracts, roses or other flowers, etc. at least three or four different smells

Sugar, salt, cinnamon, pepper, each in a little saucer or cup

A rough rock, smooth stone, waxy leaf, piece of cotton, fur or sponge, velvety flower petals, other living, natural things of different textures

(Be sure to prepare these items well beforehand and keep them out of sight until they are needed.)

GOAL: To become more aware of each of our five senses, deepening our sensitivity to each.

Some people wonder: exercises on smelling, tasting, touching, etc.? I do that every day, that's nothing new. Why go through all the fuss and nonsense?

To become more aware of our five senses and to deepen our sensitivity to each makes our daily living more fulfilling. We have to *practice* using the senses. When babies discover each new sense, they delight in the ecstatic thrill of the experience. As we grow older we take them totally for granted as a given, not realizing there is a vast world of unexplored territory even in this physical level that we are most familiar with. So in this game we take the time to give attention to the senses, and become like the new born baby who is feeling, seeing, tasting, smelling, hearing, and touching for the first time. It's a new experience!

This game is a series of exercises where we become like Alice in Wonderland in the world of our senses.

EXPLORATION:

1. Begin the session with yoga and the Five Senses Meditation. Keep silent until you are asked to speak. Have your journal in front of you.

    The leader reads the following one at a time.

Sound: a)   Listen in the silence to the sounds you can hear, both in your body and outside, near and far. Write down as many sounds as you possibly can. Strive to identify very subtle sounds.

With young children who cannot write, you can do this step verbally where they share what they hear and you share what you hear, both of you trying to get so very quiet that more and more sounds can be detected.

b)   Now, still without conversation, put your thumbs over your ears to block up the canal and listen for inner sounds. Get comfortable so that you can listen for several minutes as the sounds will change the deeper you go into them inwardly. You might hear a bell gonging, or the ocean roaring, or a bee buzzing, or a high-pitched ring, or body sounds. Listen to them as quietly as you can without moving and put your mind into them.

c)   Now, chant the sound OM three times. Take a deep breath first and let out a long OOOOOOOOMMMMMMMM on the outbreath. After each time listen for a while to the deeper stillness. Hear how quiet your mind and breath are, and how calm you feel. The inner listening is awakening. Don't think as you do this, just be.

Smell: Everybody put on a blindfold except for the leader. Sit in a circle, near to each other so you can pass items from one person to the next.

The leader passes around different smelling things that have been prepared ahead of time.

Take a deep whiff of whatever is coming around and note how

much more intense your sense of smell becomes when your eyesight is blocked off. Try to identify the different smells, but don't say your guess out loud or you'll give the answer away to others who are still guessing. How do the smells make you feel?

The leader can observe the expressions. Does a rose smell under everyone's nose bring many smiles? Does a strong spice smell bring a wrinkly nose?

Now that all the smells have been passed around say your guesses out loud.

Taste: *The leader passes around the plates with the different items to taste, not telling anyone what they are.*

Wet your finger with your tongue and take a bit from each plate, putting it on your tongue. Pass each plate around one at a time. Note how the sense of taste is also intensified by having no eyesight. See if you can notice which parts of your tongue react to the taste of the different items. Savor them by rolling them over your tongue to explore what taste is. Then try to guess what each is.

Touch: *Next, the leader passes around, one at a time, the different objects collected to feel for different textures.*

Feel the smooth, rough, moist or dry surfaces. Share your impressions verbally as you pass the object around, both trying to guess what it is and expressing the feeling that it gives.

Sight: Finally, take off your blindfolds, and as you do try to be aware of how dominant the sense of sight is. What is the first thing that catches your eyesight and attracts your attention? Share this with each other. We will do more with sight in the next exploration.

2. Share your experiences. What did it all feel like to you? What sense did you like the most? Which did you like the least? What sense are you most attracted to in life? Eating? Smelling? Touching? Hearing music? Seeing sights, paintings, etc.? The sense you are most attracted to controls you most and conditions your perceptions at the expense of the others. Each sense also relates to a higher brain

function. Internal vision or being able to "smell" a clue are examples.

3.   HOW WELL DO WE REALLY LISTEN?   Think of a brief episode that happened today. It could be something funny or sad, or you can go back a few days if something special happened. Write it down in no more than three or four short sentences. Now one person volunteers to begin. Whisper your story into the ear of the person next to you. Then that person whispers what you heard to the next person and so on until the last person receives the story and repeats it out loud to the entire group. The originator must say how accurate the transmission was. Repeat with the next story. After each story try to find out what goes wrong. Where did the communication break down in the circle? See if you can all listen better so that the last stories are conveyed with perfect communication. If there is time, repeat until everyone has a turn. Children often play this game at birthday parties and call it "Telephone". It is an excellent exercise in being able to really listen. With this game you can tell how gossip gets all screwed up and one of the reasons it can be so destructive. You can also tell how human communication and media are likely to get distorted.

4.   Journal writing.

SIGHT AND LIGHT

Exploration

4

Red World

From here on it is assumed you are beginning each exploration with the first two important steps, yoga relaxation and meditation.

PREPARATION:
2 White cards for each person. Draw a large green elephant on one and place a small black dot in the center of the other.

2 wads of red construction paper
1 wad of blue construction paper

Colored acetate, available from an art or stationery store. As many sheets of different rainbow colors as possible.

Scotch tape

Sheets of blue, green, red, yellow, orange, or white construction paper or felt pieces.

GOAL: An introduction to colored light and its effects on you. Color therapy is gaining recognition as a successful method of healing by exposure to certain colors. We want to become more sensitive to color in this game so that we can know how colors affect us and how we can use them creatively in our lives. Thus we become an artist of life. Introverts usually seek neutral or cool colors of blue, green, or grey, while extroverts often prefer bright reds, oranges and yellows. Of course if you are an introvert trying to become an extrovert or vice versa you may be hungrily seeking the opposite shades.

Just as some people are color blind, others are color sensitive. Often we don't know how aware we are of colors. This exercise is to bring us to a closer working relationship with color so we can learn to actually feel the psychological effects of each color on us.

EXPLORATION:

1. Take your two white cards with the elephant and dot on them. Look at the green elephant for thirty seconds, then immediately stare at the dot on the other card. Presto, the elephant then reappears— but in pink! This effect is called the after-image. If you stare at a yellow object and then look at a white wall you will see a violet after-image. Why does the after-image always appear in a complementary or opposite color?* It is important to understand after-images. Many people dismiss the aura around a person's body as merely an after-image of his clothes or hair. We do have to be careful because we may be seeing an after-image! But when we learn what the after-image looks like we can then see that the true aura is different. This is a beginning step in training to see auras. You will find more on auras in Level 6.

* For more on color read *Nuclear Evolution.*

2. *Everyone gathers at one end of the room. The leader places two red wads of paper at the other end of the room at exactly the same distance from the group and about a foot apart. In a moment he discreetly moves one an inch forward or back, hiding his action. He steps aside and asks how many can see any change and what the change is. Note how many people detected the change correctly.*

   Next the leader takes the blue wad of paper and puts it in the place of one of the red ones. Again in a moment he alters the distance discreetly and asks if anyone notices a change. He notes the correct answers.

   More people should be able to judge the juxtaposition of objects of the same color, but a color that is brighter, more luminous, like the red one, usually seems larger and therefore closer, even though the blue object is in front.

3. Sheets of colored construction paper or felt cloth are placed in separate positions on a table or on the floor and numbered. Each participant is carefully blindfolded. Each person places one hand palm down over the colors and attempts to "feel" their emanations. The leader records their guesses for each number. If you have more than five or six people, work in pairs and cut up the sheets of paper so each pair has one. One person will be blindfolded and the other will practice rearranging the colors, two colors up at a time, putting a strong one and a weak one next to each other so the blindfolded person has a better chance of feeling the contrast. For example, cool blue next to warm red, or cool green next to cooler white, or warm orange. Compare notes as to which is easiest to "feel".

4. *The leader places the colored acetate over a light bulb located in a small room such as a bathroom or closet. Tape the acetate so that it rests securely without actually touching the bulb. Do not use colored eye coverings as the entire face, neck and hands need to be exposed to the colored light. Make as many as possible of the following colors: red, orange, yellow, green, blue and violet. You can put several acetate sheets over each other to create a color if you do not have enough colored sheets.*

This next exercise is an introduction to what color therapy is like. Each participant stands alone in silence under the light for thirty to sixty seconds, noting and analyzing the effect of the colored light on his emotions. Is it stimulating or depressing? Does it give you a spiritual feeling? A sensual sensation? Make notes in your journals. The leader puts up a new color and the procedure is repeated for each color. When this is completed, describe the effect the colors had on you to the other people. Compare your results with those of the "Color and You" game on page 64 and discuss your experiences then and now. Note the correlations between how you felt under the light and the color psychology you see in yourself from the earlier game.

5. Journal writing.

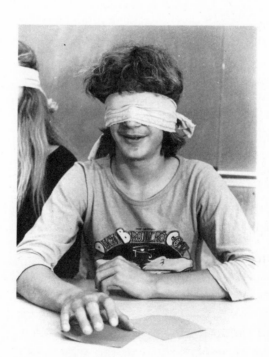

High school student learning to see colors through the fingertips.

87

MAKING CONTACT

Exploration

5

Red World

GOAL: To release tension through touch.

Guilt about sex has prevented people from making even nonsexual physical contact, which is a natural expression of affection. Most of nature plays, touches and tumbles. If you watch animals interact they play with each other. Children love physical roughhousing and contact. So in this game we release our physical tensions and some social tension and achieve an elevation of spirit that comes from acting with a new dimension of freedom. Stimulation of circulation and psyche comes from this red level action, bringing another opening of the doorway into heightened awareness and perception.

PREPARATIONS:
It's funny how the most simple and natural game that every child plays is considered the most risky to a group of "big kids". Do you dare be yourself?

Choose a spontaneous red-level leader.

whistle
blindfolds

EXPLORATION:

1. Everyone stand in the center of the room as you do for yoga. Begin with a dance. *The leader reads:*

    Everybody slaps their whole body rhythmically, rapidly, moving to the rhythm. Arm, chest, leg, foot, back, arm, thigh, buttocks, chest, hand, all over in a beat. Do this for several minutes until you really loosen up. Help those who need encouragement to let go and be free. *The leader waits until he feels everyone is really into it –into their physical being-before stopping.*

2. When the dance is stopped everyone gently feels their own body. Start with the head, neck, arms, all the way down to the feet. Now do the same, feeling with care, the person in front of you. Feel the energy, the alivened tone of the body like a child, "ready to go". Turn to another person and physically touch him or her in the same way.

88

3.   **TRUST WALK (INDOORS)** Clear the room of chairs and obstacles so you can move all over in a large space. Do this exercise with a partner. One person is blindfolded, the other is the navigator who leads the blind person around the room. Try to understand the personality of the person who is pushing, pulling, twisting you around the room. When the leader blows the whistle the seeing partner hands the blindfolded person over to another partner. As you get passed from partner to partner (the leader blows the whistle every few minutes), try to feel which partner you have and feel the personality differences. No talking allowed.

When the leader blows the whistle twice your partner lets you go but keeps watch on you. Everyone touches, grapples, bumps in and brushes against each other like Dodge'em cars. The partner keeps watch for your safety and remembers who touched you. Feel hands and try to tell who's touching or brushing you. This enlarges perception.

4.   *At some point the leader interrupts by calling out:*
     "Anyone feel like a tickle party?"
     "Go ahead."

5.   As the tickling stops we sit up with whomever we are with. Turn to your partner and touch hands, face, hair. Give each other a head massage, a back rub, or foot rub, or read palms, but share one-to-one physically, giving and receiving in turn.

6.   **THE AMOEBA ROLL** This should be done only if the floor is clean and carpeted. Everyone lies down on the floor and pretends they were the original amoeba. The leader tells the following story as all roll over and over, on top of each other, brushing sides, etc.

> You were at the very dawn of creation, the original one-celled organism, the amoeba waking up. You are wriggling as one body. Everyone rolls over each other and around in one writhing mass. . . *pause*

Now at the sound of OM you feel an evolutionary spark to divide into two and the cell reproduces by everyone standing, slowly coming to their feet as the OM is sounded and splitting into two, continuing to move in and around each other only in two groups. . . *pause*

Now at the sound of OM again you feel an evolutionary urge and split again into four . . . and now a series of short Oms spaced a bit apart while you glide to and fro in the primal energy and split again and again and again until all are individual one-celled amoebas. . . *pause.*

Now the leader asks everyone to join in a continuous OM as the individuals exploring on their own slowly come together to unite again as a whole, hands clasped in a circle, all toning the One Sound, OM.

(This movement can be done to music for a beautiful effect. Vivaldi's "Four Seasons" is a wonderful accompaniment.)

7. Discuss the experience you have had together. What barriers did you let down? What inhibitions came into your thoughts or movements? Could you let go and be yourself?

8. Journal writing.

NONSENSE
FOOLING THE SENSES

Exploration

6

Red World

GOAL: Can we believe our senses? Can our eyes, ears, touch, etc., give wrong information to our brains and thus to our minds? How can we double-check ourselves? The senses interpret only a small number of vibrations amidst the huge amount of vibrations that penetrate through the cosmos. Distortion often occurs, just as it does when we turn on the radio to intercept a radio wave. We have to have fine tuning or we won't be right on frequency and there will be distortion.

Our goal is to become more trusting, both to learn to trust ourselves and each other. Since the senses distort we have to learn to trust an inner sense to guide us. We become master of the senses then, not a slave.

The red level of our senses and nervous system is the Tree of Knowledge. In order to refine our sensory perception so that it is more accurate, we learn to bring in the intuitive, indigo world that awakens our Tree of Life which is non-sensory, and gets its messages by nonsense.

EXPLORATION:

1. a) Everybody should be sitting in a circle close to each other. Shake hands with the person on either side of you. After this takes place everyone shake hands again but this time with the left hand, and notice how it feels to shake hands with the left hand rather than the right. Does one hand feel more passive, one more aggressive? Discuss.

91

b) Now everyone shake hands again using the right hand and this time hold the grip for as long as necessary to attain the same degree of feeling as you experienced with the left hand. Note whether you need to hold longer with some partners than with others to attain the feeling. Can you feel which partner is receiving energy and which is sending? Are both of you actively sending? Are both passively receiving? Try to be aware of all of these possibilities as you shake hands.

2. Arrange the chairs or pillows so that the group is divided into two rows and is facing each other on opposite sides of the room. *The leader goes into another room for the juice can and coffee can and returns.* The leader asks two people, one at the end of each row, to stand up and face the group. Each is asked to hold palms up, waist high. The leader places the cans on the hands of the first person and asks which is heavier. Then he gets an opinion from the second person. Then he blindfolds them both.

3. The leader goes out of the room and brings in the two plates and places them on the hands of one of the blindfolded persons, then asks if there is any weight difference. The two cans are placed on the plates. He switches the cans to opposite hands and asks again, "How about now?" Then the second blindfolded person does the same thing. Usually the two blindfolded weighers will declare the coffee can heavier on the first go around with no blindfold, even though it is lighter. And when blindfolded they usually detect no weight difference, showing how sight can fool you.

4. The group all experiments with the cans and the weights without blindfolds and discusses the experience as the leader goes out of the room for the three buckets. Six people are to be blindfolded before he comes out. *He fills one with lukewarm water, one with ice water (removing all unmelted ice) and one with hot water from the tap (not so hot it will burn).*

5. Nobody is to talk while this experiment is taking place. *The leader comes out with the cold bucket and places it in front of the first blindfolded person and then places the hot bucket in front of the*

blindfolded person opposite him. He places the lukewarm bucket in the center between them. Each blindfolded person places his right hand in his bucket and holds it there without saying anything for thirty seconds. Then the leader guides the hands of both to the center bucket and asks each to put the same hand in that bucket in turn for just a second or two. Then the two discuss the temperature of the center bucket with each other and come to some conclusion, still blindfolded.

6. Without comment from the audience, the procedure is repeated with the other two blindfolded pairs. They also discuss what they felt. Blindfolds are removed. The non-blindfolded group members can try their hand in the buckets too before the whole group discusses the obvious reasons for the different feelings of the water. Talk about opposites, relativity and how our senses tend to compare things for a relative picture of life. Can we list other examples of relativity?

7. BODY CONTROL   Our senses also fool us when we try to control the body, as the following experiments will show. Pair off, clear a wall so there is space and one person from each pair line up along the wall, back to the wall.

    a) Each partner pretends to thrust his hands (clasped in prayer fashion) in the face of each standee, but his hands part, right at the critical moment, and slap against the wall. What you want to find out is how many times must this be done before the standee can control his blinking. Practice until the standee can trust that the hands won't come crashing into him so he doesn't have to blink.

    b) Next, the standees stand with their right side to the wall and their right wrist pressing onto the wall with the right arm straight. They exert strong pressure for sixty seconds. Then the partner says, "Face me and stand at attention." Was the standee aware that the right arm had a tendency to float upwards and was this corrected quickly?

    c) Each partner, about one foot away, faces the standee, who stands still. Then the partner leans left, right, backwards, maintaining a stiff body. Does the standee waver or stay calm and still?

d) Each partner asks the standee to stand on one foot for as long as possible without losing balance. After a few moments the stand-ee is asked to do the same thing only with eyes tightly closed. Did this make a big difference? Now the standee is asked to concentrate the eyes on a spot on the opposite wall and not take the eyes or mind off the spot of focus as the knee is raised while standing on one foot. Does concentration with the eyebeam make a difference? Switch roles and do steps a) through d) again. How firmly can we stand, feet on the ground, without faltering? Here we discover our balance and how grounded we are.

8. TRUST WALK (OUTDOORS) If we can't always trust our senses can we trust others?

Do this exercise outdoors on a nice, warm, sunny day. Pair off with someone near your size. One of the pair is blindfolded. The other person is the guide and holds the blindfolded person's arm. You are responsible for your blindfolded person. If it's safe go barefoot. Lead the blindfolded person outdoors into shade and sun. You are going on a trust walk together for ten minutes. Lead the person to feel different textures in nature: plant leaves, flower petals, grass, rock, mud. If barefoot, let the person squish his toes in the nice mud and smooth grass. Watch out for the feet, so the person doesn't trip or step on sharp things. Note how well you can trust each other. Then switch roles. Do you get more relaxed and trusting as you go along? Does your trustee goof and make you afraid? If so make sure you try again if the trustee is sincere, so that you don't leave with mistrust. Or else trade partners to be with someone you can trust more easily, who may be closer to your size or temperament.

If you are doing this trust walk with young children, you may want to go in threes with one adult always accompanying one child for safety.

9. Discuss your experience in trusting.

10. Journal writing.

The Trust Walk is a voyage of discovery.

HAVING NO SENSE

GOAL: In the Five Senses Meditation we go beyond the senses while in a passive state. In this game we go beyond the five senses as much as possible while interacting and being active with others. We try to see what it would really be like to go around with no sense. Then we are in a state of Supersense.

PREPARATION:
Moistened tissue paper to serve as ear plugs and nose plugs for everyone.
2 towels or gloves for each person
toilet tissue
blindfolds
cookies
salt
teaspoons for everyone

EXPLORATION:

1. We begin with an exercise similar to the Five Senses Meditation, only with the eyes open. The group sits in silence, looking at one another.

    The leader signals:

    "Hearing"—Imagine this sense is being eliminated. . . (long pause) . . .
    "Taste"—Imagine your sense of taste is being eliminated as well. . . (long pause) . . .
    "Smell"—Eliminate your smell sense. . . (long pause) . . .
    "Touch"—You no longer have the ability to feel with your skin . . . (long pause) . . .
    "Sight"—Try to eliminate your sense of sight without closing your eyes. See but do not see anything. Can you do this?

    Who is communicating in the silence? The True Self within. If we know our Self, then we know the true Self in others.

    After a minute with all five senses imagined to be gone again, the leader brings everybody back and continues on.

96

2.   **LOCKING UP THE SENSES**

Ears   Everyone puts in ear plugs. Then participants begin to circulate with each other and "communicate"—verbally or non-verbally. Lip-read, touch, look into the eyes for the meaning. Do this for one or two minutes.

Smell   Now the nose plugs go on and everyone communicates again, but now with two senses closed down. Note how much of your interaction is affected by smell and sound. Communication should be personal, heart to heart about feelings, not intellectual ideas.

Touch   Now each person wraps the towels or gloves around both hands to shut off their use. If you want more of the skin sensitivity deadened, wrap the toilet tissue around other exposed body parts. More circulating and communicating, noting how it feels to have another sense closed.

Taste   The leader brings out a plate of salt and a teaspoon for everyone. Salt is poured into each teaspoon and everyone holds their teaspoon in their mouth for as long as possible before rejecting it. This deadens the taste sense. Cookies are then passed around to be eaten. They won't have much taste. Note the effect.

Sight   Finally blindfolds are put on everybody. Several people may have to remove the towels to be able to help put them on. Then put towels back on the hands. There are a few final minutes of non-sensory interaction.

Finally everyone sits down and gets comfortable again for a deep relaxation. This time the senses are blocked for real, not just imagination. The leader will have to speak through your ear plugs:

> Relax the body as you have learned to do in the meditation. . .
> Do this on your own. When you are relaxed concentrate on the
> stream of consciousness flowing through your mind. Visualize a
> brilliant white light as filling the room on the other side of your
> blindfold. This white brilliance is the same thing as love. It

grows brighter and as it does love wells up in you more and more—love for yourself, for the group, for the universe. The light and love are you.

3. When the meditation ends everyone comes back to normal sense and shares their feelings of the experience. After sharing with each other everyone writes down their impressions in their journal. If this exercise ends before the group wishes to break up, the leader could have another game ready to do if everyone wants to.

4. Journal writing.

Smelling and touching are both enhanced when sight is removed.

SUPERSENSITIVE TOUCH

GOAL: Our goal is to research a new level of sensory awareness.

PREPARATION:
blindfolds
2 colored garments (such as a dress or shirt with or without design) provided by the leader and kept hidden until all are blindfolded.

We are often so afraid to touch things, lest they break, or to touch each other lest someone get the wrong idea. In this exercise we want to purify our feelings of touch so we can experience a new level of this important sense. Babies need to be touched or they die or become retarded. Adults too need the love that is exchanged in physical contact. To touch is to share, to explore, to make contact.

EXPLORATION:
1. Stand up in a circle. Remove jackets, sweaters, and as much clothing that will leave you feeling comfortable. Turn to a partner, preferably one of the same sex. *The leader will take the group through the following, allowing about one half minute per item.*

    a) Place both hands over your face, closing your eyes and feeling the skin of your face. Sense the looseness of the folds, any lines, the tightness of the nose and cheekbones. Get a feel for what your face is like from the outside-in.

    b) Place your hands over the face of your partner. First the left hand then the right hand, then both. Feel the face, the contours, the personality in the face. Feel his hands. Feel the *feel* of the hands.

    c) Place both your own hands on your own neck. Feel the contours of your neck.

d) Slap your own left forearm a number of times with your right hand. Slap your right forearm with your left hand. Feel the hardness or softness of the forearm. Feel the tingle caused by the slapping. Do the same with your left thigh and then your right thigh.

e) Turn to your partner and gently slap the back of his neck, the shoulders several times, then the back, working down to the buttocks and the backs of the legs. Then turn and let yourself be slapped this way.

f) Now both face each other and "frisk" each other as if you are looking for hidden objects.

g) Now choose another partner, preferably of the opposite sex and repeat the same exercise a) to f), trying to get to know the being, feeling the person, not the sex. Try to sense the spiritual awareness through the sense of touch. It is difficult because it's doing things backwards. It shows us how dependent we are on touch and what we have to escape from to find the indwelling seer who programs and edits the sensations presented to our ego. Light affects sensation. A low soft light increases our sensitivity. Daylight or artificial light hinders sensation. Blue light would help you tune into spiritual sensations.

h) Now hug your partner of the opposite sex and feel his or her sexual vibration. Is it strong? weak? passive? active? Does it feel pure or impure? Note your reactions and thoughts. Repeat with someone of the same sex as you are.

i) Choose a new partner. Use your hands as stethoscopes and feel each other breathing in turn. Breathe deeply and slowly. Feel the rib cage expand; feel the stomach movement; feel the back.

Discuss the experience of physical touching in this superaware way.

2. ETHERIC TOUCHING   In the following exercises we learn how to touch with our inner supersense not with our skin.

a) In this exercise everyone is to go outside and feel five different things. Three different things are to be felt with one's hands and two things in some other way. Discuss any impressions when you come in.

How hard was the hardest material?

What was the most nonmaterial feeling of touch experienced? The wind? The night?

b) Everybody is blindfolded. The leader brings out the two garments and passes them to each person to feel and try to sense what they are. Try to sense the material they are made out of, sense the colors and whether they are solid colors or a particular design. Everyone describes what their experiences are. Finally blindfolds are removed to see how accurate everyone was.

c) Everyone stands and lines up in a row. One person goes to the wall and faces it and waits there until the approach of two hands can be felt as someone quietly walks towards him. As soon as the energy from the hands is felt he says "NOW". The person approaching stops. The blindfolded one tries to determine how far away the fingers are and whose fingers they are. Everyone takes a turn. If the group is large you can divide into two groups.

d) Everyone pairs off and one partner holds both hands palms up while the other holds both hands palms down over the partner's palms but not touching. The person whose palms are on top visualizes energy flowing through them and into the palms of the partner. Both have their eyes closed. As soon as the partner feels a tingle, or a warm or cool sensation which signals the energy is coming in, he relaxes to receive more of it. When enough has been received switch positions and the other person becomes the one to channel energy into the other partner's hands.

e) Everyone lines up and holds their hands out palms up. The leader walks along the line and holds the hands about two inches over each pair of hands, palms down, spending only a minute with each person. Then he moves to the third person while the first person he sent energy to does the same thing, following the leader down the line. Each person follows in turn until all have experienced the sensations which emanate from different hands.

Note, are some stronger than others? Some lighter vibrations? Some heavier?

3. Discuss together the difference between the feel of physical touching and etheric touching or touching through vibration alone.

4. Journal writing.

Etheric energies can be touched several feet from the body.

LETTING GO

PREPARATION:
Each person will need one big pillow.

GOAL: To get in touch with the body by releasing tension and opening feelings. Through sound we can do wonders to let go of constricting inhibitions. Toning works on tension and enables us to enjoy the power of our own voice. The "silly feeling" will vanish as you get into it. Let society and culture go, to be yourself. Many wonderful healings have occurred when groups or individuals have used toning primal sounds and chanting.

EXPLORATION:

1. Everyone stand in the center of the room facing the leader. Space out just as you do during the yoga postures. Everyone let go by flopping. Bend at the hips and fling your arms downward towards your legs. Bounce up and down all floppy like Raggedy Ann. After bouncing several times add a loud grunt or groan and visualize yourself relieved of all worldly burdens.

    The leader encourages all weak grunters to loosen up more and let it out. Be very watchful to help and encourage any shy ones by doing the flop and groans with them. With every bounce and groan, a tension, an old pain, and the day's labors are let go. . . Make a sound that describes you. What sound do you feel like? It may be an animal sound, or anything that comes to you.

2. After several minutes of sounds, rise up and then sit in the circle. How many feel a sense of relief from tension already? Share.

3. Now go to your pillows. Place the pillow on the floor and kneel by it. Pound the pillow and at the same time imagine you are letting go of the most painful thing you can remember has happened to you. Or visualize some anger you have hidden, either at a family

member, or a friend who has hurt you, maybe an old lover. As you pound express your feelings by letting sound come up from your gut with each punch. Let it well into shouts or screams.

The leader encourages the ones who find it hard to let it out by bringing his pillow near and doing it with them. Then he circulates and shouts "Harder, Harder," "Come on, Louder, Louder," "Really get into it," "We're going to let it out for good!" But remember, no one should be pushed if they continue to feel they don't want to do it.

The group should be very supportive of anyone who begins to cry at the feelings that are released. If anyone does feel like crying, someone can comfort him and then the group together can give that person a gentle massage as he lies down on his stomach.

4. Everyone come back to the center of the room and become Raggedy Ann again. This time as everyone is bent forward the leader begins by quietly toning a very low note. OMMMMMMMM. As he rises gradually the tone is raised higher and higher until the body is erect, hands reaching for the sky and the voice singing as high and as loud as it can. All follow and repeat the exercise several times.

5. *The leader reads the following:*

> Toning is a way to release locked up forces of love, power, and energy residing inside. Tensions are blocked energy, and through sound this energy can be converted into a powerful force to free you and help others. In Colorado a group of women have brought healings by using and teaching toning as therapy. At the University of the Trees in Boulder Creek, California, chanting is used to open up different states of consciousness. Now we are going to have a discussion on the effects we felt from toning. However, the discussion is going to be toned or sung, not spoken. Let it evolve spontaneously. You let it wax operatic if that is your mood, or just speak musically. Let rhythm, volume, pitch reveal what you are feeling. *Leader begins.*

6. Now that everyone has had a chance to "vent", it will be easier to tune into the primal sound of the universe. Mystics in all the world's

religions intone a sound of OOOMMM or AAAAAOOOUUUMMM Everything vibrates to this primal sound, and OM is the human way of expressing the sound that comes from the universal music of the spheres, the movement of the galaxies and planets. One person with a strong voice begins with an OOOOOOOMMMMMMM. Everyone listens very carefully to follow suit and be on the same note, to stay in tune. Keep it up for one minute. Then the person with the strong voice chants the sound again three times as everyone holds their palms out in front of them, palms facing away as if in a blessing. Try to feel the sound in the palm. You can actually learn to hear with the palms of your hands by sensitizing them to vibrations.

7. Now everyone chants the OOOOOOMMMMM sound again, all on the same note, staying in tune by listening carefully, this time with the eyes closed. Keep it up for three or four minutes. Then come to a stillness. Everyone will notice how still the mind becomes, how centered and quiet everything is. Meditate on stillness for a few minutes. Feel the peace.

8. Share feelings if you want to or go directly into journal writing.

MUSICAL INSPIRATION

Exploration
10
Red World

PREPARATION:
The leader for this session should be someone who is into music, and who would like to provide a phonograph and the needed records, or who will put all the excerpts on tape ahead of time and provide a recorder.

A large room, furniture pushed back. Excerpts of 2-4 minutes of different music like: symphonic, soul, jazz, opera, country and western, folk, band, romantic, waltz, other. About 40 minutes in all.

Art materials—paints, paper, watercolors, crayons or charcoal or magic markers, whatever media you have.

GOAL: The goal is to react in movement and expression to the music. We do this by getting inside the sound and letting the mood move us. A childlike freedom to express, both in movement and in drawing or painting what the soul of the music is about, is what we want to experience. Feel your body. Feel your being expressing through this instrument of your body.

Be as free as a bird by moving to get in touch with your body and let your being out. You have to not care what anyone else thinks of how you look. Just be whatever you want to be.

EXPLORATION:

1. *The leader discusses the goal with everyone and then prepares the room for the experience with everyone joining in.*

   The first selection is introduced by name, orchestra, and composer, as is each subsequent selection. Anyone may get up at any time and move, dance, walk, lie down, do yoga, T'ai Ch'i or whatever form of movement comes naturally. At this point there should be no talking or singing, no partnership or teamwork, just tuning into one's own feelings and the music.

   The first selection begins. The leader encourages people to over-

come their natural reticence and begin to move. After fifteen to twenty minutes the music is temporarily halted.

2. The more active people now pair up with the more passive people and move together to the music again for 10 to 15 more minutes.

3. *The music is stopped again.* The people who so choose may now paint or sketch what they hear the music saying to them. Use lines, color, shadings and form to show how the music moves you inside-out. Others can continue to move to the music. People can move back and forth, painting or dancing as they feel. Play the music over again as long as the group is letting go and is into it, perhaps for another twenty minutes or so. Some groups get very spontaneous. The enthusiasm can become contagious and spread to everyone for quite a long period.

    The leader should keep watch, keep encouraging and keep pace with what people want.

4. After the action slows down take a break. Get some fresh air, some refreshments perhaps, and share and discuss the artwork and the experience.

5. Journal writing.

MAKE UP

PREPARATION:
Greasepaint makeup, lipstick,
rouge, face powder, eye shadow, etc.,
(whatever is available)
coldcream, soap for cleansing
one mirror per person

A book on physiognomy (face-reading)
(optional)

GOAL: Our goal is to change our physical features to whatever caricature we want to be, or as others fantasize us. Here we blend the physical and the social a bit by making ourselves and each other up as we would like to appear, or as we would like them to appear. This exercise is a kind of therapy that releases inhibitions and brings out personal mannerisms.

EXPLORATION:

1. The first part of the exercise will be to let yourself surrender to whatever grotesque results might occur when your partner is through improvising on you. Pair off. The make-up artist should create an exaggerated yet still real and valid impression of the personality of the receiver. You may have a secret image of her, or a flash on a possible "past-life" fantasy, or just an idea of how to make her more glamorous. Whatever the motive try to create a caricature of some part of the person. Everyone can work all at once or a few pairs can work at one time while the others enjoy watching.

2. When finished, the group gives both the artist and the receiver feedback on the general impressions. The make-up artist explains why he exaggerated eyes or lips and others question and comment.

3. Roles are reversed, and the process is repeated until everyone has a chance to be made up and to make-up someone else. Discuss the personality expressions, how you feel about your new face, whether the caricature is meaningful to you, or not too real.

4. Faces can be washed and those who feel moved make themselves up

according to their own mood, self-image, or fantasy. Feedback is given.

5.   Discuss facial features, and what they reveal about each other's personality. If you know any physiognomy (face reading) you can look for personality traits in the shapes and sizes of the features. Can we read each other's personality through body language? Try a hand and see what results you get. This is also a way of giving feedback. Don't hesitate to say if you feel someone is on or off, but see if what they say is a valid impression.

6.   Journal writing.

BODY TALK

GOAL: Here we study the ABC's of what attracts us physically about others, and what repels us. What do swinging hips, flirtatious smiles, winks, ticks, twinges, etc. mean? We ask many questions to become aware of how a smile affects us, what do we see in the eyes— shifting, steadiness, power tripping? We are going to sensitize our sight to pick up subtle meanings in the vibrations and "talk" of others' non-verbal expressions.

PREPARATION:
Sharpen your eyeglasses!

If you do not have all the combinations in your group as are called for in the game, then improvise and do what you can with the people you have.

sheets for one-half of the group

EXPLORATION:

1. Two volunteers, preferably husband and wife, if not then two people who are good friends, go into one corner of the room. The rest of the group huddles in the opposite corner. The pair carry on a conversation for two minutes on some matter which involves them—an argument, a problem, a plan, a sharing, whatever is real to them. They do this in a whisper so they can hear each other but no one else can hear them. When they are done the rest of the group guesses the topic of conversation and the positions of the two who participated. Everyone takes a chance guessing. After everyone has shared, the partners reveal what took place. Were there non-verbal signs that showed these two were familiar with each other?

2. This is repeated by two men, then two women. Look for the differences in how people non-verbally relate. Do the men have a different stance with each other than the women? Are there roles that crop up immediately?

110

3. The exercise is repeated once more by a mixed couple who do not know each other very well.

4. CHARADES
    a) The group is divided into teams of two or three or four. Each team goes into a corner or a separate room to plan a fictional situation with more emphasis on words than actions. (Example: four people playing tennis argue about whether a ball was in or out—it would not do to include too much of the action of the game as this would be too obvious, or a few people discuss what movie they should go to among several choices.) It is the facial and body expressions we are looking for, not the acting out. Each team has its turn while others try to guess what they are saying. Are they frustrated, happy, confused, elated, etc.? It's not so important as to who guesses first, but how well the team as a whole communicates.

    b) After this is done a traditional game of charades can be played with action. Again, look for the communication that comes from body language.

5. Each person spends a few minutes observing every member of the group. Then, in turn, each member goes out of the room and returns, having altered slightly something in his appearance—taken off something, put on something, done his or her hair differently, changed shoes, jewelry, etc. This should be a very slight change so as to provide a real test at observation. Each person writes down what he thinks has changed. After all have had a turn each person announces what the change was.

6. The group is divided into two halves. One half goes out of the room and they cover themselves with sheets. They emerge, one at a time, walking so the sheet covers the ankles and shoes so no identity is given away. Remember the order that they enter in. The other half writes down who they think is under each sheet by the sway, the vibration, the body position, etc. The person in the sheet makes no sound nor tries to give away his identity in any way, nor does he try to mask his identity by walking unnaturally. When all have walked

across the room they walk back out again, take off their sheets and return in a different order. Each of the other group says who was who and the errors are totaled. The group switches roles and the others guess who was who.

Discuss the effects of not having facial expressions to identify someone. Some Halloween masks have very dead expressions painted on them. Have they ever given you funny feelings about the people wearing them?

7. Non-verbal communication in pairs. Pair off and sit knee to knee for about five minutes. Look into each other's eyes until you tire, then touch, dance, gesticulate, whatever, but make no verbal sound. Try to communicate your feelings though; have purpose to what you share non-verbally. *The leader calls for the pairs to break up and for a general group non-verbal communicating, for another five minutes.* This can be uncomfortable for some, so relax and let your vibration speak.

8. At the end discuss verbally your experiences. Discuss each other's non-verbal sharing. Then entertain the following questions about each person, going around the circle.

  ● Is each person's smile friendly, phony, disarming, a cover-up for another feeling? Is it an expression of pleasure or a self-conscious showing of teeth?
  ● Is eye contact deep or self-conscious? A person who cannot look you in the eyes usually has a feeling of inferiority, or is influenced by strong social custom. Are the eyes shifting?
  ● What about each person's head? Do they look down, look away or look around while you are talking? Do they hold their nose in the air, or look down on you?
  ● What is there about a person's manner that gives a feeling of warmth or coldness or maybe hostility?

See if you can be open and honest with everybody and try to explore why people have the body talk they have. Don't leave anyone out of your feedback, so that everyone leaves feeling they have had some insight into the way they come across.

9. Journal writing.

EXPLORING HABITS

Exploration
13
Red World

PREPARATION:
coffee
blindfolds
ashtrays
matches
wide-mouth, tapered, delicately
shaped tea cup

beer mug
paints, or crayons or magic markers
drawing paper
clay for modeling
cardboard to rest clay on

GOAL: We want to become more aware of how habits dull our senses. Whenever we do something positive to break daily habits we release energy that has gone into the habits. This brings us a spurt of new awareness. Some part of us feels more alert and alive. Whether that habit is some drug—aspirin, alcohol, nicotine, caffeine, etc.—overindulgence in food or sex, reading the newspaper, a habit of twiddling your hair or smoothing your moustache, it is a binding of energy into that one action. Eat something different. Put on a new hat. Reach out to a new friend, drive to work by another route, etc. to break the routine. Each new experience that is different from the usual habits is quickening to the awareness. When you shake hands with the left hand you *feel* the other person. Your consciousness is turned on and awakened by new sensations and it is put to sleep by sensory habits. Here we are not trying to change your habits, but to give you a different experience of them.

EXPLORATION:

If there are no smokers or coffee drinkers skip to Step 4.

1. **FOR CIGARETTE SMOKERS** All smoking members of the group go to the center of the room and are blindfolded. Each is asked to take one of his or her own cigarettes and light up and to place the pack on the floor in front of them. The leader asks: "Are you sure you are smoking your own brand of cigarettes?" When this is confirmed the leader and non-smokers take the lighted cigarettes

away and begin switching them around. Each time a switch is made the leader notes whether it is the same brand as the pack in front of the smoker or a different brand. With each switch the leader asks the smoker whether he has his own brand and records his response. Sometimes a smoker gets his own brand but a different cigarette. Often smokers cannot guess their own correctly in this exercise. Smoking dulls the taste buds, but the eyes being blindfolded also affects taste sensations. Dampening one sense sometimes dampens and sometimes enhances the other senses.

2.　Air the room and discuss the experience.

3.　FOR COFFEE DRINKERS　*The leader secretly, in a different room, prepares coffee and pours some into a big beer mug and some into a tapering, wide-mouthed delicately shaped tea cup.* The leader brings two cups into the room the group is in and asks each coffee drinker to sip black coffee from both cups to decide which is the stronger coffee. *The leader tries to convey the impression that they are two different brands. Some people get the mug first, others get the tea cup first. But the leader should keep a record of who gets which container first, and also write down who feels which is the strongest.* Usually the results are as follows:

> The wide-mouthed cup sipped first has the most votes for the strongest
> The wide-mouthed cup sipped second—tie for second
> The mug first—tie for second
> The mug last—least votes.

Explanation: The first taste is always the best. The antennae are really poised for the first taste impact; the second never makes as much of a taste impression. Also, the sense of smell adds to the sense of taste and the mug shape inhibits vaporization on which smell depends, while the tapering cup enhances it and makes it smell better. Discuss the experience.

4.　Some of the best musicians have been deaf like Beethoven, and some great painters have even gone blind. What is it like to work with media normally requiring one sense without having that sense?

Everyone is blindfolded so the habit of sight is not at work, and given
a) paper and paints or other drawing instruments
b) clay and a cardboard piece to rest it on.

Try to express an inner vision in the artwork without your visual sight to enhance it and learn to see through your sense of touch.

5. Discuss the experiment.

6. Discuss the habits that you have and how you feel about them. Are they comforting? Compensations for something? Something you would like to stop? Everyone has habits. See if there is some common denominator that motivates all your sensory habits.

7. Journal writing. Write to yourself about your own habits.

SUPERSIGHT

GOAL: The physical eye picks up sense signals of certain vibrations, but it is the mind that makes sense of the senses and interprets them. Our mental eye is an inner sixth sense which we will explore deeply in the intuitive, Indigo World Six. Here we want to explore the difference between the physical sense of sight and the intuitive to gain understanding of our seeing capacities.

PREPARATION:
2 platters or trays each fitted with
15 different household objects, such as:
salt shaker, spool of thread, scissors, spoon,
bar of soap, screwdriver, paper clip,
envelope, etc. Be imaginative and different
in your selections.

Cover each platter with a towel so nothing
can be seen.

a watch or clock with second hand
4 small sheets of paper per person

EXPLORATION:

Immediately after the yoga and meditation read the goal and without discussion go to Step 1.

1. Half the group lines up face to face with the other half so that each looks into the other's eyes for a few seconds. Keep switching partners by one of the lines moving to the right until everyone has looked into every other members eyes.

2. Discuss the differences you see in each other's eyes.

3. Now pair off and sit knee to knee. Look into each other's eyes for three minutes. *The leader announces when to end.*

What new things do you see in this deeper looking? Do you notice more details? Size of the pupil? Does it get larger or smaller? Or do the eyes water? Does your mental eye get a chance to see more deeply and pick up a feeling from the eyes, perhaps hostile, loving, fearful, hypnotic, dreamy, clinging, innocent, etc.? How does it affect you?

4.   Did anyone get scared? embarrassed? Discuss why.

5.   Everyone takes four small sheets of paper and numbers them 1, 2, 3, 4, then writes their name at the top of each.

6.   The leader brings out one of the covered trays and lays it before the group. Then he reads the following story:

> This is a true story that has become a classic in New England. Several children were lost. When they did not return by evening a posse was sent to search the nearby woods for them. They searched all night without success. They still had found no trace of them the following noon, when someone noticed that a blind and deaf child, of the same parents as one of the lost children, had been "looking" off in a certain direction while gesturing and pointing and making small cries. A man in the searching party decided to consider this clue. He headed in that direction and within an hour found the huddled group of frightened youngsters.

7.   Everyone now tries to perceive with his mind's eye what is on the tray and list any common household objects that come to him on paper #1. "Common household objects" is the only clue given. The leader then collects all the #1 papers.

8.   The towel is then removed by the leader and he announces it will remain removed for sixty seconds. In that time all the group should look at the objects and memorize them. After sixty seconds he replaces the towel. Everyone writes down what they remember they saw on paper #2. Leader collects the #2 papers.

9.   Now the second tray is brought in. But before we tune in with our inner sight to this tray we will do a special meditation to activate our inner eye. We want to relax so that the inner eye can take charge. This meditation will also improve the teamwork of the physical eye and the memory. Stronger powers of awareness can appear when mind and body senses are relaxed.

10. Place your writing materials (paper #3) close to you. Sit comfortably. *The leader reads:*

Sit erect and close your eyes. We are very comfortable. . . we sit limply. . . we concentrate on our feet. . . We wiggle our toes to make sure the muscles are all relaxed. . . We let our feet rest heavily on the floor. . . The limpness makes our legs and thighs heavy and relaxed. . . It creeps up the hips into our back. . . We sit heavily and limply. . . Our whole body feels loose, limp and heavy. . . It is a pleasant feeling. . . Our face loosens. Our eyes droop and the eyelids feel heavy. We relax our mind, permitting it to concentrate on the instructions and not go to sleep or wander to other thoughts. . . Now even my voice will stop and your mind will go to the objects on the covered tray I have just brought in. . . Permit pictures of what lies on that tray to enter your mind. . . When pictures come, open your eyes, reach for your pen and paper, write what comes to mind and then close your eyes again until more pictures come, then write them again. . . . Trust yourself. . . . . Begin. . . (pause for one minute) . . . You have one minute to go. . . (pause for another minute) . . . Okay time is up. At the count of three open your eyes feeling refreshed and full of energy. One, two, three! The leader collects papers #3.

11.   The towel is now removed by the leader and as before everyone has sixty seconds to memorize what is on the tray. After sixty seconds the towel is put back on. Everyone writes down what they remember they saw on paper #4. The leader doesn't collect them.

12.   All papers are now passed back to their owners. The leader calls off the objects on each tray as each member checks his right answers on the lists. Scores are shared. Was there improvement after the meditation? How much?

13.   Discuss the experience.

14.   Journal writing.

FOOD AWARENESS

PREPARATION:
Everyone bring a dish for a pot luck meal.
Be sure to include an unsliced loaf of bread
and juice or wine, as well as a pastry dessert.

GOAL: Our goal is awakening sensitivity to taste and discovering a new experience in eating. Most people eat without fully tasting what they chew and its various flavors. Many don't even remember what they had for their last meal. Having a meal together can be a form of communion, so the purpose is two-fold: to deepen friendships and to grow in self-discovery through having a meal you will always remember by eating in a very special way.

EXPLORATION:

1. After meditation everyone joins hands in an unbroken chain for a minute of relaxed union.

2. Breaking bread is a ritual that many ancient cultures use. Each person passes the loaf to the person next to him who holds it while he splits apart a chunk. This whole bread passing should be done in silence and in slow motion. It's as important to watch the bread being passed gingerly, watch it being cracked and torn, as it is to watch it being eaten. When each person has a piece then everyone can begin to eat slowly, aware of each other eating. Then the drink is served and this is taken slowly with attention as well.

3. Silence — When the main course is served, everyone eats in silence concentrating on the color, smell, taste, subtle flavors of the food. Be aware of every bit and eat *slowly*. Don't eat too much. Save room for dessert. You will need less food when you eat this way.

4. When the leader serves the dessert he announces that each member is to feed another and in turn be fed. Pair off and feed each other,

becoming aware of the right time to feed and the right time to receive. This too is done in silence.

5. When the leader announces that everyone has finished dessert, talking can begin. Discuss the non-verbal sensory sharing experience you just had together. Did you notice a new sensory delight? What did you learn about your usual food habits? Was it difficult to eat more slowly than usual?

6. This is the last journey into the Red Level—World I. Discuss as a group your experience of the Red Energy Level. Do you notice more examples of Red Level Energy in yourself and in others you know in your daily lives? What is the Red Energy Level like in the world as a whole? How does it affect humanity?

7. Journal writing.

ORANGE WORLD
THE SOCIAL LEVEL

The Mirroring exercise brings deeper social contact.

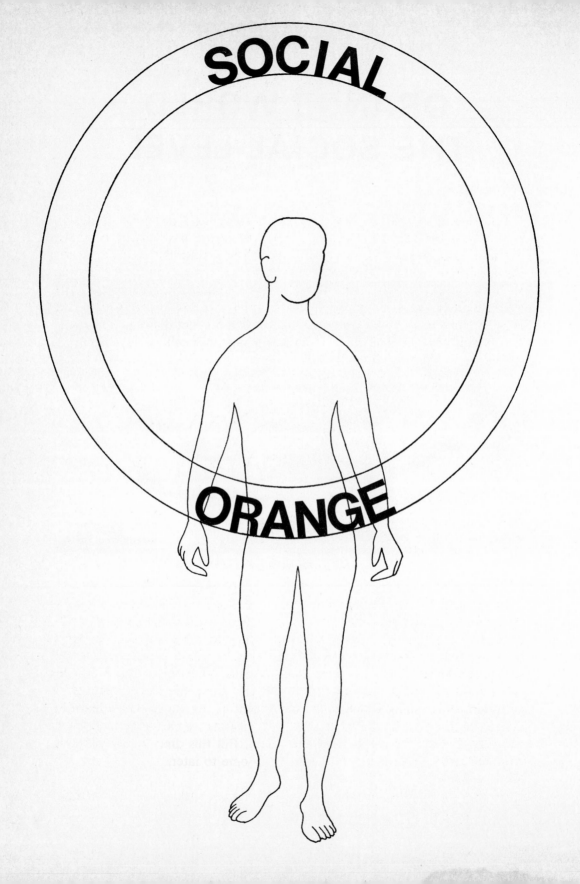

ORANGE
II

The Orange world of other people, society and our relationship to humanity is the next level of unfoldment. Once we have experienced the red level of our senses and sensory objects we must then encounter the world of other beings. While the senses still are a large part of our relating to life, regardless of which level we are functioning from, they are unconsciously taken with us into the other worlds. Each world that evolves includes the earlier worlds and yet is a distinct dimension in itself. The worlds are really spheres within spheres within spheres.

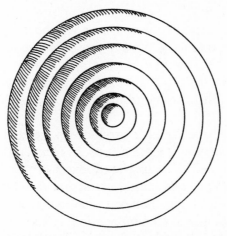

In the social sphere we become aware of others as distinct individuals. As a child we are first aware of Mommy, Daddy and then family as made of distinct persons. We expand from the family to friends, to cultural ways of doing things and to the social standards expected of us. The social scene teaches us what we may and may not do. Although this provides for some sense of order, custom and law in the group life, it also acts as a cultural brainwashing which limits our potential. As we grow, we learn to discriminate which traditions and learned customs we can scrap and which we need to keep for the good of the whole. But this discrimination needs another level of awareness which we will come to later.

In the social level we respond and explore within the given limits society places on us. We all need some limits within which to explore, just as children like to know exactly what their limits are as defined by the adults around them. They of course will test these bounds and instinctively try to expand beyond restrictions, but the sense of well-being and freedom is dependent on knowing just what is permissible and what is not. Freedom only exists as the other side of restraint. Without limits there is no freedom, the word becomes meaningless.

The way we respond to this social world in ourselves and in our experiences determines whether we will be socially ambitious or a loner, involved in social service or seeking to grow for ourself alone, a good citizen or a social outcast—a criminal or deviant in some way, concerned with prestige or not caring what others think of us.

Since this book is primarily a group book (most of the exercises are done with people) it is a challenge to our social awareness all the time. The social level of group consciousness will be developed in all the levels because a group dynamic is always present. In exploring this entire book you will be intensifying your deeper social awareness strongly. In this orange level world we want to explore going beyond otherness, to see others as ourself. This is real group consciousness.

The group will learn the basic groundwork needed for more real relating with people. To deepen relationships it is necessary to listen to each other's beings, beyond the superficial levels of communicating. Empathy, sympathy, compassion and caring are social responses that are awakened when we learn to be open, honest, centered and integral in our relating. Most important to good communication is our learning to give understanding which is a skill we will develop. When we go beyond "otherness" in our social relating to see all as part of our greater being, we will awaken a desire to serve the whole.

YOGA POSTURES II

The forward bending postures of yoga are the ones that are related to the chakra or center in the spine which governs the orange, social level of awareness. By practicing these yoga postures we learn to tune in and get in touch with that part of our nervous system to feel how it affects our relationships with people. The social center is located about four inches above the tailbone. Its energy relates to the pancreas, spleen, intestines and digestion. By practicing forward bending postures we stimulate the hormone secretions and organ functions into better balance and working harmony with the rest of our system.

FORWARD BEND

Stand straight in what is called THE MOUNTAIN posture. Head up, chin straight and parallel to the ground, chest out, shoulders back, stomach in, feet and toes together, legs straight. Inhale and then exhale. As you exhale bend forward and down keeping the back as straight as possible. Fall forwards so your head is near your lower legs. Each time you exhale stretch a little further. Stretch only on the exhalations. Hold as relaxed as you can, and remember to KEEP THE LEGS STRAIGHT throughout the bending. If

you can only bend a little ways without bending your knees, that's okay, as it is more important to keep the legs straight and do the posture correctly. Eventually you will be able to go farther as you practice this posture correctly. When you are holding in the down position put your mind inside the lower spine about four inches above your tailbone. Relax into and feel the whirling chakra there, distributing energies to the organs around it. Come up slowly as you inhale and raise your head first, then raise your shoulders, then the back. This way of rising up lets you keep the back straight at all times. Come up slowly.

HEAD TO TOE (3 variations)

1.   Lie down on your back on a carpeted floor or on a mat. Your arms are down at the side, relaxed. Inhale and sit up. Bend the right knee and put the right foot on top of the left thigh close to the stomach. Put both your palms flat on the ground and lift your buttocks in the air (off the ground) and push your pelvis back as far as possible, then sit down again. This will help you sit up straight and maintain a correct posture with your back as straight as possible. Inhale and stretch both arms and chest forward, exhale and stretch the rest of the body forward so that you can touch your ankle or left foot with your hands. Don't strain if you can't reach that far. Only go as far as you can, rest, then inhale again and wait until the exhalation to stretch again. Stretch only on exhalations. Don't worry if you can't reach because as you practice (especially if you practice every day) you will soon be able to not only touch your toes but rest your chest on your knee as well with no discomfort. Each time you inhale bring the head up, then thrust the chest forward, exhale and stretch again, moving closer to the toes. This is the way you should try to lengthen your stretch. It will also put you in touch with the inner energies along the spine. When you do this posture correctly you can feel the etheric body inside your physical body. As you hold feel the energy in the second chakra area. When you are ready inhale, slowly raise just the head, then the shoulders, then the chest and sit up. Exhale.

2.   Repeat #1 above only this time bend the left knee and rest the left foot on the right thigh close to the stomach. You will be stretching towards the right foot.

3.   The third variation is the complete Head to Toe posture. This time you keep both legs straight out and you bend forward to touch both feet, keeping the chest as close to the legs as possible. Eventually you will be able to lie down on your legs. This posture is said to be a posture of humility, and those whose backs are supple enough to be able to relax into it are said to have humble natures. Is this true in your group?

MEDITATION FOR RELEASING CULTURAL BRAINWASHING

Like the other meditations given at the beginning of each level, this meditation is to be practiced over and over again at any time, and especially before each session in the orange level after having done the forward bend yoga postures. This meditation prepares the way for the exploration into the inner space of world two.

The leader reads the following meditation, speaking slowly and pausing at the three dots (. . .) to give everyone plenty of time to let the essence sink in.

We begin with the centering meditation on pages 54-55 using the heart as the point of focus . . .

When everybody is calmly centered and feels connected in love with everyone else become aware of the society that is living inside your body right now. Meditate on the zillions of atoms everywhere, inside you, outside, moving in and out of your skin, in and out of walls, the air, the space around; meditate on how atoms can pass right through the boundaries that our flesh cannot pass through . . . Each atom is an organized society too. Some have lots of protons all huddled together inside the center with just as many electrons whirring around like satellites orbiting around the nucleus where the protons are huddled, just like planets moving around the sun. Oops, there went an electron, knocked off its orbit by a powerful force and now there are more protons than electrons, the atom is not balanced anymore and becomes very excited, hopping around and radiating energy in its excitement. Some atoms have such a big distance between their nucleus and their first electron orbit that to them it is equal to the size of a football field. Meditate on how the atom moves and interchanges particles according to a definite law and order . . . Now several atoms have decided to live together and are interlocking to form a molecule. A molecule of water in your body is made up of one oxygen atom and two hydrogen atoms married together . . . Your body is 90% water. Other atoms have joined together too, to make different kinds of molecules . . . Now in a feeling of love the molecules want to bond together and they form the first cell. But to stay alive the cell has to have fresh molecules come in as old ones die and food to give them energy to keep going. So the cells learn to work together so they can have enough food to keep going. Some cells decide they will be the carriers and they become blood cells, some cells keep on the lookout for what's happening in the environment and they become skin cells, some cells decide they had better put full time in keeping the organization of the whole going and they become brain cells. You see, the cells are specializing and banding together to do a better job than they can alone, just like society. The cells become organs as they bond together. The organs soon learn they have to work together too for the good of the whole or they might not get what they need to stay alive, and pretty soon we have an entire body all working together harmoniously as one whole! The lungs cooperate with the heart, the brain with the nerves and heart, and the digestive organs respond to all the other organs, and there is one grand symphony playing away to the the tune of ---. Of what? Of some invisible, intelligent conductor who has some unfolding purpose to it all . . .

Our minds affect our bodies and if we feel disturbed or separate, it makes our cells feel bad too. Some people get disease or even cancer when a cell rebels. Human society is the same, everyone playing different specialized roles to keep the governing process going smoothly. But is it? What happens when there is not good communication between brain and liver, or between the nucleus of the cells and the molecules that carry the messages from one part of the cell to the other? There is a breakdown! When some parts of society make money and exploit the whole at the expense of others, or satisfy their own private needs at the expense of other people, then there is a breakdown in social life. When people disregard the suffering and needs of others they do not always realize they are disregarding their own needs, and that the good of their own life is not separated from the good of others . . . Why, if the lungs were to grab more oxygen just for their own gratification, the heart would beat so fast it would freak out and the brain would hyperventilate and black out until consciousness in the whole body would break down and there would be no life left at all, not even for the greedy offender in the beginning – the lungs . . . So let's meditate on our relationship to the whole . . .

Now tune into the family and explore the different roles we all play and the harmonious functioning of them. Are everyone's needs fulfilled, and if not what might be the cosmic plan evolving to fulfill everyone? What is our part in it? . . .

Cultural codes, morals, all the things we are told we should do and be, these may or may not be of service to the real good of the whole. Government may be corrupt, and rules may be outdated. Let us let go of all the social rules, the media, the pollution of our minds and environment by the mass mind of humankind. Let's let go for now of all government or beliefs, or some authority who told us so, and of the herd instinct which wants to follow the crowd or do what others do. Become the purity of your own true being that is in tune with the will of the cosmic conductor that directs evolution and knows what and how to fulfill all beings in its great society. To experience the Inner Self is to experience that Self in all others. Then whatever you do causes no harm to anyone and you are free – free to be in tune with the whole and to do what is needed to keep the great show unfolding and expanding its way of Love. . . Focussing on the heart center feel the One in the many, this One Love flowing into the group, in and through the hearts of all, bonding us all together as One Being. . . *(Silent meditation)*

When you are ready come back to your body, continuing to feel you are part of a greater whole. Take a deep breath, blow the air out and open your eyes. Look around. See the others as your self.

PRACTICE THIS MEDITATION AFTER THE FORWARD BEND POSTURES FOR THE ORANGE LEVEL AND EACH TIME BEFORE YOU BEGIN A VOYAGE INTO WORLD II.

SOCIAL CONTACT

GOAL: For most people the most severe form of punishment isn't physical torture, which still takes place in inhumane households of child abuse and wife-beating and in many prisons. Rather, the worst punishment is often a long enforced period of solitary confinement where no contact with another is possible.

When all human relationships are gone, the personality of man begins to break down. On the other hand, an abundance of rich human relationships can be the greatest blessing. With a continuing flow of meaningful experiences with other people, a person's growth in life is assured, his or her mental stability becomes more unshakeable and more and more full potential on all levels is realized.

The answer appears to say, be a good mixer. But this is not necessarily inviting *rich* human experiences. As we meet right now, there are social meetings and millions of other get-togethers happening throughout the world. Yet, when goodbyes are said, people go home with very little more than what they brought with them. The purpose of this journey is to understand that the average social get-together can be empty compared to a growth in awareness get-together, and we need to experience the difference.

EXPLORATION:

1. Social time. Everyone socializes for around one-half hour. *The leader does not read the above goal until step 1 is completed. The first part of this session will be a social get-together. The leader does not say how long, but encourages everyone to start socializing and monitors the talks, encouraging people to mix and meet with everyone during the time. This is so that the usual rather superficial discussions will take place between the small groups that cluster together in social sessions. The leader keeps this in mind but says nothing to the group until after this first period which will be around one-half hour.*

2. *The leader ends the social time and reads the goal. Without discussion the group is led into the second exercise of the journey.*

    Each person greets every other person with a traditional continental hug, cheek to cheek, first on one side, then on the other. The leader can begin the hugging by greeting the person on his left and continuing around the circle; everyone hugs everyone else until all are contacted.

    Then when everyone is finished, pair off and sit on the floor or on chairs in two rows, knee to knee facing each other. For five minutes you examine your partner's face, eyes, and communicate non-verbally. Look into each other's eyes and soul, see if you can go deep into each other's being by just being aware and looking. At the end of five minutes the leader asks everyone to change. Pick another partner and do the same thing for another five minutes, feeling the change in vibration, the difference in this new person's being from the one before. Change again after five minutes if there are enough people and until you have had a chance to share non-verbally for fifteen minutes with three different people during that time. If the group wants to continue you can do more combinations, but the leader should be sensitive to whether people are really into it or have had enough.

3. Everyone sits in a circle again, comfortably, and meditates quietly for a few moments on the three events that have taken place, the socializing, the embracing and the non-verbal sharing. After three minutes the leader announces that there will be a discussion on the methods of social contact liked best. One person will be chosen to give a three minute talk, and everyone needs to prepare. The group is given time to prepare the talk for a few minutes more. The leader picks the person to give the talk after everyone has had a chance to prepare their piece. When the person completes the brief talk, discussion is opened to everybody. By everyone preparing, the effect is a charging up so that each person is bursting to say what he feels. Then the discussion will be lively when everyone joins in. The leader makes sure that everyone has expressed themselves. Every group comes alive and finds this sharing a rewarding experience.

4. Now the leader asks, "What do we want from our social relationships?" Together the group explores what each member feels his weakness is and what his strength is in social relationships. Try to give each other feedback in a kind way, drawing upon your experience of that person so he will know how he comes across socially. Make certain everyone is the center of attention for awhile and has his turn.

5. In light of the meditation at the beginning, what is the difference between being free to consider the good of the whole and being culturally brainwashed? Discuss.

6. Journal writing.

RIGHT ACTIONS

PREPARATION:
A willingness to trust.

GOAL: To explore our social lives to see how we shape our behavior. To discuss right and wrong in terms of our daily lives, enables us to see how we live in this second world of awareness in relation to our fellow man. It is a getting to know you exercise for level two where we nurture the feelings of unity and confidence to build trust and openness. We want to make this group experience both enlightening and gratifying to our social level.

EXPLORATION:

1. Everyone sit comfortably in a circle. We want to create a relaxed atmosphere to discuss the following social level questions, one at a time. First deal with all of a) then b) then c). Stick to the point and be watchful not to wander off into many stories. *The leader should be aware if answers are getting too long and help everyone to stay one-pointed.* In addition to discovering each other's social experience, we will also practice the first step of "getting inside the world of another person," to be able to feel with them. This important first step is commonly called "Active Listening". Listening is the key, because only by being receptive can we really experience the being of another. As everyone answers the questions, we listen to their being and expression. If we wish they would say more, or do not understand their expression in some way, we "Active Listen", instead of passively listen, by responding to them, repeating what they have said to acknowledge it and to assure them we have heard. This opens the door for them to feel accepted and to go deeper. For example, Ruth replies to Question #1 by saying, "Oh I can't stand a dirty home. I vacuum and dust daily, and am always picking up."

The "Active Listener" says, "You really like to have a neat home and not have a mess." This playback confirms the reality of Ruth and makes her feel accepted. It opens the door for her to share more deeply what she really feels. Practice the "Active Listening" response as much as you can during these questions and answers, especially when someone needs to be drawn out.

a) How clean do we like our homes to be?

How often do we vacuum, dust? straighten? Do we feel tied to housekeeping? When in others' houses can we remember times when we tracked in dirt when we entered without remembering to wipe our feet? Is this a habit? Have we dropped ashes on others' clothes, floor or upholstery? Do we have any social habits that have been annoying to others?

b) How do we feel towards personal cleanliness?

How often do we feel the need to bathe? Do we prefer showers or baths? Have we had people tell us we need to bathe, use deodorant or mouthwash? Has it been embarrassing? Do we resist? Could we tell anyone they need to clean?

c) How about our cleanliness of mind?

Do we like political games, or get some satisfaction out of them? Do we like to make others think or behave the way we do through social pressures? gossip? preaching? nagging? Do we have close relations who use any of the above methods to influence us? How often do we have negative or grumbling thoughts about others and what they should or shouldn't do going on in our heads? Discuss openly.

2. Are you content in society?

a) Are you content with yourself in your contribution to society? What more would you like to do? Can you do something about it, a step in that direction this week?

b) Do you live entirely in your own little world, selfishly from the social point of view? Ask yourself honestly. Do you care about others?

c) Do you limit your generosity to your own flesh and blood or just to your own immediate circle of friends?

d) How would you expand your social awareness? How can you see other members in the group expanding their social awareness in a truly useful way?

Now is the time to probe more deeply into our natures, not to criticize or hurt anyone's feelings, but to question our mental habits and each other's ways of living to find out what can bring us more fulfillment.

3. How strong are we in standing up for what we are convinced is right and true? Write your answers to the following in your journals.

a) Do you believe what you see and hear or read in the news?

b) Are you too conditioned by society and its authorities for your own satisfaction?

c) How able are you to go against mass opinion or community feeling to express your own sense of what is right? Would you have been different in Hitler's Germany? Would you speak out for human rights?

d) How do you feel about the present news of human rights violations in countries all over the world, both dictatorships and communist? What sense of social responsibility do you feel, if any? Are you speaking out now?

Share your answers and discuss. Again, we are not interested in judging each other, but in drawing each other out to understand one another. This is not to say we shouldn't express our feelings, but they need to be expressed in terms of our own experience, not by telling others what to do. Watch for the impulse to preach.

Continue writing your answers in your journals.

4. In what way are you interested in the study of yourself and society? Do you separate yourself and society?

5. In your choices and actions do you follow only your personal will or do you consider a universal will?

    a) Do you try to get what you can out of the world?

    b) Do you try to tune into some kind of self-surrender to universal laws?

    c.) Do you invite a cosmic plan to work through you?

    Share your answers and discuss.

    Throughout this session the leader will have to be very watchful to keep the conversation moving so the group doesn't get bogged down in any question or get off on tangents. This can be one of the most dynamic and fruitful sessions when it stays on track, yet goes deep by allowing everyone to share. Try to keep your antennae out for fine-tuning as to where people are "at". Ask them to explain themselves if you don't understand.

6. At the end of the discussion on these five areas everyone meditates together in silence for a few minutes to tune into what the cosmic plan wants for them in relation to their fellow man. Why were you brought together here?

7. Share your insights.

8. Journal writing.

MANNERS AND QUIRKS

GOAL: How much are we afraid of being socially rejected for making some kind of "faux pas"? Manners can be a sign of grace and thoughtfulness; they can reflect something of our level of consciousness. They can also be a sign of self-consciousness where we are constantly trying to appear "proper". The goal in this game is to discover our own unique manners of expression so that we may be aware of them and, if we choose, change them. Where do good manners stop and where does fresh, natural behavior begin? What is truly impolite behavior? We will search for our own codes of propriety.

PREPARATION:

If the group chooses a party atmosphere, provide whistles, gongs or bells

If the group chooses a quiet atmosphere, a yardstick or baseball bat or a gavel will do

A dining table set with chairs, coffee or tea and a snack. Serve the snack with silverware. Use cups, saucers, plates and napkins setting the scene as formally as you can.

EXPLORATION:

1. It is often hard to see our own quirks, and usually we don't like them in others. But our quirks are seen easily by others too. People may react to us or judge us without our knowing why. One company executive used to say the word "alright" at every comma and period in his conversation. He never realized that he was doing this until a drunken colleague mimicked him at a party. In a few weeks he was out of the habit. Many of us have the habit of saying "um" or "you know" or of running on sentences with lots of "and, and, and," as we talk. Other non-verbal habits are also common. In this game we will make a noise with our noisemakers (if we choose the party vibe) or we will hold up the "rod of power"—the bat or stick—(if the quiet vibe is chosen) whenever we notice a social quirk during the discussion. The quirk may not be verbal, but may be someone pulling his beard, wiping his nose, constantly playing with or patting

his hair, rubbing his toes, or any repetitive mannerism. Other mannerisms to note may include burping, interrupting and any action traditionally considered "bad manners".

Whenever a "quirk" or a "manner" is brought to light it is briefly pointed out to make the person aware of it. Then the discussion is resumed. The discussion will be on the social level and will focus on the following statement. The group decides which vibe they want— party or quiet.

The leader reads the following on the social level:

GROUP CONSCIOUSNESS–TOGETHERNESS

There is something about group action, group awareness, which nourishes togetherness. At the root of this nourishment is the ability in each of us to see the best in others, and the ability to use the worst as an opportunity *to look into ourselves*—to see if we have the same defects and to grow thereby. . . (pause) . . .

At first, the goal of the group is to prosper in being together, to study and to grow both as individuals and as a group. We invoke this spirit of unity so that we won't argue as individuals over one another's defects. In all close relationships people know each other's problems and weaknesses.

It is important not to play on each other's faults, because faults always exist in all of us. Instead we should aim at reaching that high potential of overlooking defects. The body we live in is itself a defect since the best teacher, the only perfect one, is the master within us—the pure light of consciousness. A great being is one who contacts this master and who becomes aware of *the facts about* others, not the faults of others. In this way we attain peace. Facts do not disturb, faults do. A sure sign of insecurity and immaturity is a person who is always finding fault with others for the purpose of putting everyone down and himself up. This kind of person may be sweet on the outside and critical inside, or may elbow his way around. When he does speak, it often creates arguments and a battle of words.

To reveal faults as facts for the purpose of growth, with the motive of love, is an act of service when done in a creative, positive way. When we feel secure and trusting of each other's care and respect, it is easy to share the negatives in a light-hearted way. The negative person negates others, the virtuous person devotes the fruits of his education to serving others. In the lives of the saints of history, it is obvious that all their physical energies were devoted to serving others. How much do we serve others and how much do we find fault with others?

The next step in Group Consciousness for humanity is to see others as ourself. This is only possible in the spirit of service. The physical body is much more than just a lump of protoplasm. It is a marvelous network of nervous systems, cardiovascular blood pumping systems—all kinds of systems working together, making a greater whole governed by an indwelling intelligence. We need to understand how this intelligence manifests itself through all our physical organs. Understanding this will lead to the development of potential brain awareness not yet used by many—such as refined organs of perception and sensitivity. We'll be helping nature to develop instruments of increased sensitivity in ourself which are already programmed into our brains, waiting to be awakened.

Nature has been doing this evolving since the time of the first amoeba, the single cell which developed sensitivity to respond to its environment. So we, as a complex group of organs in a body, and as a complex group of unique people, have still to develop an awareness that there is greater potential in coming together. When humans can work together as one group body, like many brains working together to become one greater organism serving a vaster purpose, as the atoms, molecules, cells, and organs came together in evolutionary advances before us, then we will be taking another great leap in evolution of the whole. This is the purpose of Nuclear Evolution,* to reveal the evolu-

---

* More details of Nuclear Evolution are available in the 1,000 page book of that name published by University of the Trees Press. For this present book all we need to know is that evolution proceeds from level to level in steps.

140

tionary future in the Cosmic Intelligence for mankind, through every person seeing it for himself, proving it and testing it in his own experience.

We begin our exploration of what "Group Consciousness" really means by discovering the life force and intelligence behind the personalities of others. In training to see how consciousness works through each other we develop awareness of our unity and our individuality.

2. *The leader begins a discussion on what was just read, asking specific questions if necessary to get things rolling.* Manners and speech defects are pointed out as indicated in step 1. How do you see what was read occuring in your lives? Have you ever thought about the potential of group consciousness? What do you think it is? Discuss.

3. When the discussion comes to a natural close, after about twenty to thirty minutes, the table is prepared for a snack. Half the group eats as they normally would while the other half sits on the other side of the table and silently observes. Those who eat will discuss the value of social etiquette. *The leader takes the observing half aside and goes over the following list secretly with them. They will be writing down what they notice about each person's eating habits, looking for any social violations. This should be done with as little knowledge on the part of the eaters as possible.* After about ten minutes the groups switch roles. Only this time the people eating their snacks will mimic the manners of the first group of eaters.

Check for the following:

Elbows pointing at neighbors' ribs	Burping
Using a fork as a shovel	Eating with your fingers
Slurping	Licking your fingers
Holding the fork like an ice pick	Reaching across the table
Chewing with mouth open	Wiping your hands on your
Stuffing the mouth full	clothes
Talking while chewing	Speaking loudly

4. The new observing half notes down all the violations they see, the manners and quirks, and at the end the group finds out which were intentional and which were not! Share your feelings about the exercise. Were you more on guard about your manners than usual? Did you learn anything about yourself? Go around the circle and ask. If you do not see something new about yourself, discuss habits or bad manners from the past. People can even bring up some they know they have now but keep well-guarded. Don't let anyone leave the session without some sharing on habits and some feedback from observant group members.

For families this game is fun to play over a meal, pointing out to each other habits but without judgements. We're not trying to change each other in this game, just pointing out and becoming aware of what we do. This requires acceptance. Change may come later.

5. Journal writing.

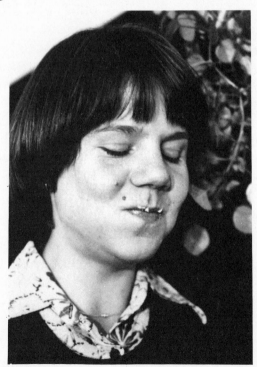

How do you tell someone not to talk with the mouth full?

YOU DON'T UNDERSTAND ME

PREPARATION:
an attitude of openness

GOAL: To discover the roles we play. Are we who we think we are? How can we become who we would like to be? In this game we take a role from life in order to see ourselves in action. We discover:

1) How do others receive us? How do they receive our roles?

2) What do we expect of other people?

One important goal in this exercise is to understand our ability to "understand". If our major expectation from others is for them to understand us (as it is with most people) then how understanding are we of others? Understanding is the foundation for love. To the extent we can understand and communicate so that we are understood, we will feel love.

EXPLORATION:

1. Everyone writes down in their journal a description of the kind of person they would like to become. To make it clear, you can take a character from history or drama who best describes the kind of person you'd like to be, or maybe you can describe someone you know and admire.

2. Ask yourself these questions. Are the qualities there in me to become this person? What needs strengthening? What is missing? Write these down. Allow at least five to ten minutes for writing. Share what you have written when all are through writing.

3. Others now give feedback as to what qualities they see need strengthening in each other for becoming the person each wants to be. Or do they feel it is unrealistic? (For example, someone wanting

to become a pop star singer who cannot sing on tune.) What other roles or potentialities do you see in the person that you feel he should unfold? You must be honest and direct to make your real feelings understood. Since you will be giving positive suggestions you can be positive and compassionate about what you feel that person's real potentialities are. We are practicing understanding.

We need to watch for feelings of "I'm better than you are," which is a tempting thought to play in our minds. If such thoughts come just let them go, not giving them any fuel. Similarly, thoughts of I'm worse than you are, poor me, are also untrue. In this game we all have true potentialities to uncover. Each person should be the subject of discussion for at least *five minutes.*

4. After everyone has had a chance to express and receive feedback discuss the following questions one at a time. These are deep questions, and cannot all be fully answered at once. They will be food for thought for you after this exploration and before the next session with the group. You can jot your thoughts and feelings down in your journals during that time. What we want to do now is share the more obvious answers that will come to mind if we are open. An example from our own life will come into our inner T.V. screen or on our inner radio wave if we are receptive to it. Go around the circle for each of the five questions, questioning each other or discussing along the way when you feel a need to understand more.

    1) What do you openly or even subtly expect of other people?
    2) Do you feel misunderstood often? By those closest to you?
    3) How much can you understand others' experiences?
    4) How does your ability to understand (or your inability) affect your relationships? husband/wife? girl friend/boy friend? friends of the same sex? children/parents? What do you see in your own life?

5. How well do you understand yourself?

6. Journal writing.

MIRROR, MIRROR ON THE WALL . . .

Exploration

20

Orange World

PREPARATION:
self-honesty

A small hand mirror for each person. Everyone is to look at themselves intently in the eyes, gazing into the mirror for five minutes, before beginning the session and while waiting for the entire group to arrive. No one is to talk while this preparation is taking place. While looking into the mirror each person is to ask the question:

"Am I always truthful with myself?"

GOAL: In this game we begin to understand how wanting to look good in other's estimation plays an important part in our social relationships. This is an area where we tend to be very ego-sensitive, where we get easily embarrassed, and we need to trust and love to be willing to see truth.

Most of us enjoy compliments and flattery. So it becomes a way of life to flatter others too to be socially "in". How much does flattery keep our relating superficial? Many friendships break up or cool down when one friend stops flattering another or when one friend challenges another's self-image. For example, if John's self-image is that he's a good communicator and you give him the accurate feedback that he's not so good so that he may correct himself and become better, he may take it as a put down and a criticism. Have you ever really liked certain people and praised them for their good qualities and either it's gone to their heads or else your own vanity is not fed in return? You might feel disappointed that such people aren't on your side. What are we seeking from our friends? Affection? Esteem? Social position? Respect? Power?

Until we can understand how vanity colors and often destroys friendships we will not be able to have closer and more lasting relationships or a refreshing, loving honesty in friendships.

EXPLORATION:

1. For the first ten minutes everyone circulates and purposely socializes and flatters each other. Try to be as flattering as you can be, perhaps as you have seen done at cocktail parties. Don't let up until the leader tells you to. Feel what it's like to give flattery and how it feels to receive it. Can you tell what is phony and what is real? Note whether you like it anyway. Can you feel how flattery is different from true loving positive feedback?

2. Next, sit in a circle and discuss flattery versus positive, honest feedback. What is the difference? How many times in life do you remember flattering someone to cover up a criticism you really felt? What was the depth of your conversation in step 1? What is your social depth of conversing usually? What does it take to be genuine and integral in friendships? Make sure everyone has a turn to answer these questions, sharing themselves.

3. Everyone write in your journal the answers to the following questions about yourself, being as integral, as truthful with yourself as you can be. The leader will read the questions aloud one at a time, allowing enough time for you to answer yes or no and describe why you see yourself that way.

    1) Am I honest with myself? with others?
    2) Am I overly materialistic?
    3) Am I overly sensual?
    4) Do I get pulled away from loftier humanitarian purposes? By what?
    5) Am I vain?
    6) Am I pushy? or wishy-washy?
    7) Am I inconsiderate?
    8) Am I greedy?
    9) Do I seek power? or social position?
    10) Do I crave affection and attention?
    11) What is my greatest strength socially?
    12) What is my greatest weakness socially?

4. After each person has finished writing, break up into two groups if there are more than eight people present.

One person at a time reads his or her answer to each question, and asks the group members, after each answer, to comment on how they see him or her. Have they noticed any examples of vanity or deceit or pushiness or other behavior as something for that person to work on? This feedback is given in a gentle, caring way, and if anyone disagrees with anyone else's perceptions they should feel free to express themselves. For example, Mary feels Bob is vain because he's always combing his hair to make sure it's just so, but Don says, "Hey, Mary, you're always patting your hair in place too." In another example, Bob tells Mary she's a bit pushy to get her turn and Sarah shares with Bob that she hasn't experienced Mary that way. If there are many disagreements in the group we can ask for an overall group perception. We don't view each other always the same, and often our own weak points may irritate us in others. Bob is too aggressive so he may feel Sarah is wishy-washy. Here we can use the entire group integrity to give a more complete mirror than any one person can give another. Everyone is entitled to their perceptions, we don't deny each other's reality, but by seeing with several mirrors we try to get a better look at the whole reality. The success of this game depends on you sharing your feelings and not holding back out of social embarrassment or fear of saying the wrong thing. Remember: Caring plus Honesty equals Sharing.

Discuss any confusions or uncertainties you may have as specifically as you can. *What are each person's social strengths and social weaknesses is the question you should give the most time to if you cannot do them all and are limited for time. If you are limited for time this session can be continued. It is usually a deep, meaningful experience for everyone.*

5. How many people feel they know each other better and feel a deeper love? Are there any hurt feelings? What is the cause if there are any?

6. Journal writing.

A MASQUERADE

GOAL: To have a party where we can *unmask*. Masquerade parties are so much fun because we get to be someone else, and put our usual self away for awhile. Actually, we are more likely to be our real selves at a masquerade party and less inhibited, which is the real reason we can have more fun. The "mask" we usually wear in our day to day personal life is set aside. We are protected by the party costume and can be ourselves rather than being what we want others to think we are. Here we penetrate into a deeper level of our social selves, a hidden social being that we may not know very well.

In sensing people and understanding their behavior in everyday life, we are constantly coping with having to distinguish between the games people play and their real intentions. Our goal is to see beyond the personality by temporarily changing it.

PREPARATION:
Everyone is to arrive in their outfit with the requirement that each person wear a mask so no one can be recognized.

party snacks

Everyone should have street clothes they can switch into later.

EXPLORATION:

1. Choose a costume of someone your secret self-image would like to be in your fantasies. For the first half-hour socialize and enjoy each other's costumes. (If you want to make this a full-fledged party you can spend longer.)

2. Remove the masks and everyone sit in a circle. Over snacks, each person comment on the outfit of the others. Were you fooled when the person arrived? Is there any relationship between the person and the costume he chose (a deep personality need or the exact oppo-

site?) What made you finally recognize who it was?

3. Two or more people get together to put on a spontaneous play or skit. They confer for a few minutes to decide on roles in keeping with their costumes. In the middle they stop, leave the room and put their regular clothes on. Then they continue the same skit. When it's over, the others comment on the differences in acting or behavior between the costumed performance and the non-costumed part. Another group of two or more can do the same thing, act out a skit, only with a different theme, to go with their costumes. Repeat the skits until everyone has the opportunity to play a part.

4. Discuss.

5. Journal writing, or, IT'S A PARTY!

FULL-LENGTH MIRROR

PREPARATION:
Your love

*(optional) If the leader has
access to a full-length mirror,
each person can spend a moment
looking at his or her image in the
mirror and finding the most positive
thing they can see in themselves.
This should be done prior to the
yoga postures or meditation.*

GOAL: In this game the group will enjoy an exhilarating experience that derives its strength from the need to be loved and appreciated. Life's competitive environment provides a constant downward push to us as others try to better themselves at our expense. Even husbands and wives compete, and the result is usually ego-depression and downgrading. Love can have dramatic positive results when expressed in affectionate and non-sentimental caring terms.

Without love, understanding and some appreciation, we wilt. We turn inward. Awareness is dulled. We even insulate ourselves from the outside world to prevent awareness of it. Some people want to sleep all the time. All of us react in some way. Just to what extent is hard to say. Some people lose their appetites and waste away when the one who loves them most turns away. Others compensate by overeating when the love they want is not there.

Full-length mirror is an exercise in appreciation.

EXPLORATION:

1. Everyone stands along the wall of the room. Each person is mirrored in turn by each other who reflects what he or she sees in the person before them that is good. Each statement must be constructive and positive. No criticism is permitted. You might

comment on a person's looks, radiance, personality, character, or some special quality you see in them. It does not matter whether the person is seen for the first time or is your mate. Speak about the qualities you sense. Look into each other's eyes and souls until you tune into the unique beauty of each being. If you react to something you don't like in someone, let it go as it is probably related to something in yourself. Let go and look deeper into the beauty of the soul and you can also feel the beauty of your own soul. Each statement should take about a minute or two, but no time limit is imposed. Say what you like about the person.

2. Line up. The leader is number one at the beginning of the line. He moves to face number two, shares his feelings, then faces number three, then number four and so on. At the end, number one takes a place at the end of the line in turn to become a receiver. Then number two does likewise, and number three, etc. until the line is restored to its original position and all have been both a mirror and a receiver to all.

There may be tears or other feelings released by a soul contact with a mirror. When someone sees into your very being it brings forth tears of joy at times. Because these are positive mirrors that see only our good, not the weaknesses, the emotional shock is one of relief, as limited or distorted self-images are restored to their proper high potential.

3. Gravitate to the people whose remarks made the most impact on you, to discuss privately some discoveries about the Self. After a warm period of close conversation in small clusters the leader requests that everyone come together again, and share their experience with the whole.

4. Close with a love circle. Everyone hold hands or lock arms and close your eyes to commune in the silence for awhile, sharing good feelings. The hearts are open. Chant the OOOOMMMMM together, and feel the love in the silence.

5. Journal writing.

Use the Full-Length Mirror anytime you want to feel good!

THE MIRRORING EXERCISE

GOAL: To learn the skill of communication. If children, adults, teachers, all people, were to learn and practice this one exercise of mirroring in their communication, 99% of all arguments would be eliminated. Arguing is usually based upon mis-understanding of the other person or of some facts. Most disagreements can be settled when there is understanding. But to understand each other we have to be able to get inside the other people's worlds and look out through their minds, eyes and hearts. Mirroring is based on being able to truly listen. So this most basic exercise begins with learning how to listen, not with the physical sense of hearing, but with the inner ear that hears the being behind the words.

Mirroring is the essential feature in "Creative Conflict" or "Creative Communication", a technique devised by Christopher Hills to solve problems which you will read more about in Part III. It is a more advanced exploration of consciousness requiring a deep commitment to truth.

This mirroring exercise is a beginning skill.

PREPARATION:
The leader should do several minutes of chanting with the group, chanting OOMMM after the yoga postures and meditation. Chanting, the use of sound, has a calming effect on the heart and mind enabling us to listen better because we become more receptive. Feel the receptivity in the silence after the toning.

EXPLORATION:

1. *The leader leads the group in several minutes of chanting (toning the OOOMMM) after the yoga postures and the meditation, to awaken receptivity.*

2. Pair off. One couple sits in the middle of the room, knee to knee, facing each other. The others gather so they can see the couple's faces. Now we close our eyes and tone the OOMMMM once more and let go into the sound so that we feel the receptive space opening up in our hearts in the silence. (This preparation cannot always be done in the heat of a crisis of course, but it is an aid in learning the skill.) As you sound the tone listen to the ear of the ear inside, the inner ear that experiences the ear hearing the sound. You can feel it inside. Be aware that it is the same one pure consciousness in everyone else listening too. Tone OOOMMMM again, long, and listen intently. Now in the silence, feel the deepening of the stillness. This tunes you beyond the mind. Open your eyes. Decide which of the pair will be first. The first person says how he feels about himself right now in just a few sentences. The other in the pair listens, with the mind empty, like a photographic plate receiving the words, feelings, and thoughts behind them. As the listener you have to be really open without playing any of your own thoughts in your mind about what is being said. Just listen to receive the real being of that person. If you think *about* what the other says, you are putting your own mind into it and are not fully listening. After you have listened you will then become a mirror and say back to the person what he has told you, not word for word necessarily like a parrot, but the essence. It's the being and the meaning you want to mirror back. When you have finished, the first person says if it feels right and if you included everything in your playback. Everyone else in the circle notes if any points were missed out. Often the projector won't remember what he's just said either. This listening process requires real concentration. Now you switch roles and you be the speaker while the other person mirrors.

3. Choose another pair until everyone has had a turn to express themselves and mirror. You will be amazed at how difficult it is to mirror perfectly. With practice you learn to do it, and when you can do it all the time, arguments will stop as you will know how to hear another person's being. Ninety-nine percent of people have more difficulty mirroring properly if they are at all upset, or if the problem

with them is deep, which is why differences between people often get worse and worse in a discussion. People often miss half of what the other says or twist the meaning in some way. Mirroring is the most important tool for real communication and it is essential in the process known as "Creative Conflict" (see Part III). Keep the exercise moving. It is quite a deep experience when we don't allow long gaps between speakers. If it's dragging at all, it means you need to get more concentrated.

4.   Keep in your pairs. Continue the mirroring, as in Step 2, only this time with the question, "How do you feel about your partner right now?" If there are a lot of people, you will want to break into smaller groups, but make sure there is at least one pair observing the pair mirroring at all times, to give objective feedback.

5.   Now, again continue the mirroring with the question, "How do you feel about your relationship with the group?" If the group is small, it is nice if this particular question can be mirrored before the entire group, so that everyone knows how everyone else feels. If time prevents this, then share the essence with the whole group afterwards.

6.   Choose someone you are having a difficult time with (either someone in the group or someone from your daily life—an employer, wife, friend, husband, child, etc.). Choose somebody in the group (*not* the person you have difficulty with) to role play that person. Prompt the role player with the details as fairly as you can. Now pretend he is that person and do the mirroring exercise you learned in Step 2. Then switch roles and the role player try to play the part and say how you feel. This role playing can be done with great success and will help you understand and iron out the difficulties without the real person even being there. Almost always the role player can tune into and hit on the real issues. See if your relationship with the person changes during the week.

7.   Use the mirroring tool whenever you don't understand someone or

whenever you want to be *sure* someone has understood what you are saying. Ask them, "Will you please mirror what I said back to me so I can feel sure you understand what I am meaning?" *Especially* use mirroring if tempers are rising or if you are having a sticky problem. A lot of hurt feelings can be mended quickly, or avoided in this way —through taking the time to understand.*

8.　Discuss your experience.

9.　Journal writing.

* In a family it is sometimes difficult to mirror, and especially for very young children if they are upset or embarrassed. At these times another member can role play the person who is unwilling or is having difficulty, not mocking them, but really trying to speak their true feelings for them. Sisters and brothers often feel for each other in such a way that they can do this role playing easily. This type of role playing often makes the person having a hard time feel very much loved, because his inner being is understood, and it brings him out to express himself eventually.

APPLIED AWARENESS
(A Return Journey)

PREPARATION:
*Because this journey takes into
account all the seven levels
(even though it deals with social
reactions) it is really best done when
you have already explored in each of
the seven worlds at least once, and are
familiar with each of the levels inside you.*

GOAL: Everybody expresses their awareness and attunement with the Cosmic Intelligence in their daily life. Aware people are calm, helpful, sympathetic, wise and diplomatic. They are aware of the thoughts they are thinking, the words they use and the motives behind their own actions. They begin to feel like a smoothly functioning instrument in a universal symphony. They challenge themselves before challenging others; but aware people, just by being aware, do not need to compete with others. They are at peace with themselves.

The aware group is a close circle of friends or families bound by much more than social niceties or blood relationships. They have experienced a deeper part of life together in many ways than have soldiers in a war or many husbands and wives. Life challenges the group to move on.

Aware groups around the world form a network of nuclei that are providing energy for man's awakening to a new level of relationships and a new step in the evolution of life on earth. Yet it all comes from the quality of inner life, from the individual and his everyday awareness. In our daily lives we constantly react to events and people. That reaction is the key to our awareness and our evolution. Is it derived from fear or confidence? Do we react from greed or a sense of service,

157

from our own pet ideas or from openness? Are our life styles self-chosen, or
reactions to the status quo? In this game
we learn to better apply our new awareness to our social situations, using all the
seven levels.

EXPLORATION:

1. Everyone writes in their journal their honest reactions to the follow-
    ing situations in fifty words or less. *The leader reads them one at a
    time.*

    a) You open your front door one night all ready to go out for the
        evening. On the doorstep is a basket containing a tiny baby.
    b) You are waiting for a train to take you away for a long weekend
        holiday. Just before it arrives you discover you have left one
        suitcase behind.
    c) You are driving two young children to school when you come
        upon the scene of a serious automobile accident.

2. Everyone reads their reactions to the first situation in order of their
    primary or favorite level of consciousness. If they haven't yet been
    able to discover what level their personality is most strongly on,
    then they go with their favorite color. By now, though, they should
    have some idea of the inner world they live in most of the time.
    Even if their written reaction is probably red level, if they know they
    are primarily yellow level, then they should stay with the yellow
    level group in this step. All the people identifying with the red level
    begin by reading their descriptions for the first situation. Then the
    oranges, the yellows, greens, blues, indigos and violets. Then do the
    same with the second situation and the third situation.

3. Can we see a noticeable similarity in the kind of action taken by a
    particular person in all three situations? Are some people's solutions

consistently practical? impractical? emotional? theoretical? imaginative? possessive? socially conscious? intuitive? See if you can define the real level of consciousness now in all of your own reactions, then discuss them with others and see if you are all in agreement as to each other's levels in what has been written.

4. Now regroup according to the levels that you have decided you actually wrote. For example, someone who thinks of herself as red level may have written very yellow or green level reactions, and vice versa. Someone who thinks he is very blue level (thinking of the past) may have written reactions that put off all decisions to the future, worrying about the future (really indigo). So join the group that you actually manifested in your writing, not what you thought you were before.

5. Now three more situations will be read by the leader. This time react to them orally, but in order of groups, so all the people in the red level group react first.
    a) You are sitting quietly in an ancient cathedral when you see a man rifling the collection box.
    b) You are at a restaurant alone, when a member of the opposite sex walks up to you and asks if you believe in love at first sight.
    c) You pass your neighbor's house, and find the man and his wife in a loud argument. As you approach he strikes her across the face.

6. Now compare your reactions as you did in step 3. Did they keep in line with the colors you were regrouped into, or do they more fit what you originally chose, or is it difficult to really tell what level it relates to? If it is difficult to tell, you may want to re-read or refer to some of the descriptions of the levels at the beginning of each of the worlds.

7. Now choose some real life incident from your own recent experience where you reacted in a way that is characteristic of your own level. Share what happened with the group. How would you like to modify your reactions? What level do you feel you need more of?

8. Journal writing.

LUSCHER COLOR TEST
(A Return Journey)

Exploration

25

Orange World

PREPARATION:

THE LUSCHER COLOR TEST, by Dr. Max Luscher, published by Pocket Books, N.Y. You will need at least one copy of this book.

Read Chapters one and two (or re-read) after the test has been taken, and refresh your memories of the Color and Personality awareness game at the beginning of EXPLORING INNER SPACE.

This journey includes all the color levels, and applies them specifically to your life situation right now. The Luscher Color Test reveals the inner dynamics affecting our social relationships, giving us new insights into the social mirror around us. Because it is such a deep probing into the seven levels of consciousness, it is best done when you have already explored each of the seven worlds at least once and have a working familiarity with each of the levels inside you.

GOAL: This color psychology developed by Dr. Max Luscher is a fantastic mirror, using color to reveal our personality and its relationships with others. Here we again see ourselves deeply. You will be amazed at how accurately your choices of colors and the order you put them in reveals your psychological situation. This test is a condensed form of a complex seventy-three color test used by Dr. Luscher and his associates in hospitals, schools and businesses throughout Europe with great success. It is new to the U. S. Author Christopher Hills and Dr. Luscher used different methods but found striking agreement in their independent color research and support each other's work. This eight color test used here may not be completely accurate because it is so abbreviated. Try choosing the colors again if it feels way off to you. The second time is likely to be "on" and if it is a similar combination to the first time, you can be more assured of its accuracy.

This color mirror is to give you feedback about your unconscious. In an awareness group where trust and caring for each other are the mainstays, opening the door to our unconscious inner beings is an opportunity for real insight and growth. This color test is not really a game, but a real tool for discovering your own psychology. You can change the patterns you don't like and you will see your feelings about colors will change as you change your psyche. This is serious work on yourself.

EXPLORATION:

1. Spread the eight colors from the packet in the book on the floor in front of everyone in clear view. Everyone writes down the color they like best, next best, and so on, ending with the color they like least. Write this in your journals. Write them clearly in a horizontal row. All eight colors must be listed. Don't think about what the colors mean, choose them quickly, however they strike you at the moment. These colors are not the proper spectrum colors, but are combinations selected for specific reasons.

2. Assign each color the number that is on the back of the card. Write this number above the word.

3. When everyone has finished writing, each person draws a circle around the first two numbers, another circle around the second two numbers, another around the third pair of numbers and a fourth circle around the last two numbers. Label the first pair +. Label the second pair X. Label the third pair =. And label the fourth pair –. Then write down your first color choice number and your last choice. Together they form another pair. Label this fifth pair + –.

4. Now is the time to review Chapters one and two and the Color and Personality game regarding color (unless everyone has done this prior to the session).

5. *The leader now looks up the tables in the back of the Luscher book.* The + group shows you your drives, your goals that are conditioning you now, whether secret or obvious. The X group shows your present existing situation. The = group shows something you may be indifferent to but need to look at, sort of subliminally there, and the – group shows what you are rejecting. Everything is relative and since you have to have two colors in the last position, you reject these in relation to the first two you preferred. Note whether you really didn't like those colors or whether they just

ended up last by default. The +- group means the actual conflict or problem going on (this is created by what is wanted combined with what is rejected).

Next the leader asks for the various + combinations, looks them up in the book one at a time and reads them out loud to the group. Then he proceeds the same way for the other combinations. Take notes of your own meanings read out loud by the leader so you have a composite picture of yourself by the end of the readings. Look and see if the picture fits with your life. Amazingly, many people have said, "I was like that twenty years ago, that was me. But I don't feel that way at all now." This may be true, yet the situation is still residual in the unconscious and is affecting your personality, your choices in life in some way.

6. Discuss honestly your feelings about what you see in yourself. If the group is large, break into small groups to discuss the one area that strikes you as the most significant. See if others can give you some help to better see yourself. You may want to spend two sessions on this Luscher Color Test mirror of your inner self and your relationships.

7. Journal writing.

YELLOW WORLD
THE INTELLECTUAL LEVEL

The Love Seat: Seeing ourselves as others see us.

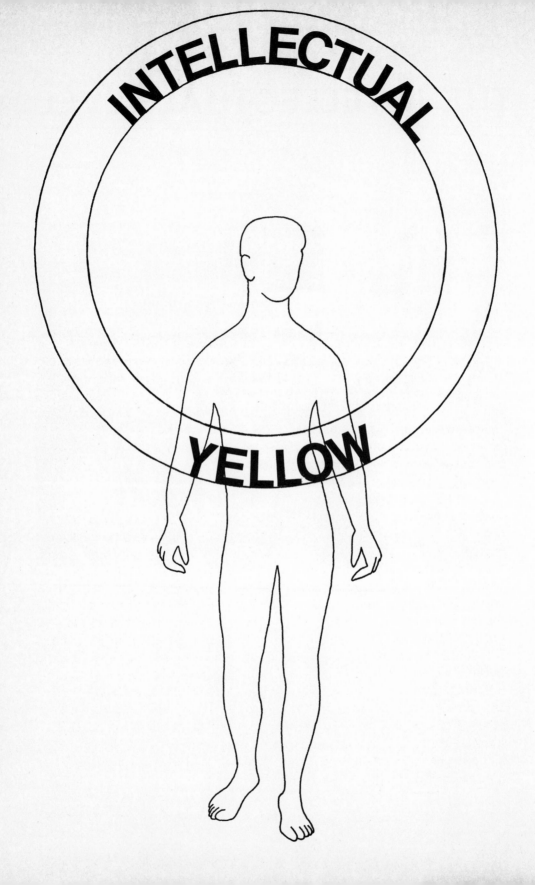

YELLOW
III

The Yellow level is the world where we feel ourself as separate from others and from anything else. Here we develop an intellect as the faculty that says "I am here in this body and you are over there in your body." "I am here thinking and the book is in front of me and space separates me from it." In this level the separated ego comes into its own and attempts to figure everything out. It analyzes, categorizes and defines the universe in order to grasp it, control it and understand it logically. All of this activity is from the intellect, born from the seed of a self-sense which is identified with living in a separate body.

In the Western world great intellect has been given high respect in society. The analytical ability applied in science and technology has never been so highly developed as it has been in the modern world. However, there is a movement emerging that recognizes the limitations of the intellect. The intellect has been sitting on the throne of truth, but science and psychology are beginning to see that there is much more to reality than the intellect can figure out. Quantum physics has shown that the observer and what is observed cannot really be separate from each other. The intellect that figures is not really separate from the thing it is figuring. If there were no object out there, the intellect wouldn't arise to see any differences, and if there were no intellect there would be no recognition of any separate object. So both "out there" and "in here" depend on each other. The intellect can only work by creating duality, and can provide no absolute truth. The intellect functions in a linear way: first x then y then z. Time in the intellectual world goes from past to the present to the future like yesterday, today and tomorrow.

A person who develops his personality mainly in this world often feels very separate from others. He is always analyzing life, trying to pin facts down, trying to figure his own emotions out without really living them. He is what is called a "head" person and misses the world of the heart because he is stuck in the ego self-sense rather than in the stream of life.

Psychology, which has been a very intellectual study of how the self works, is slowly changing its approach to include more levels of consciousness. Psychologists are beginning to realize that they must go beyond analysis, into a state where inner and outer, self and not self, subject and object, head and heart, become one. A new field of transpersonal psychology has been born which transcends psycho-analysis. The purpose of transpersonal psychology is to find ways to get out of the separated self-sense, out of the ego which thinks its body, mind and self are separate and distinct from others. This new psychology realizes that only when we transcend the separateness can we gain a greater understanding of the mind and the self. New light dawns when we escape the duality. Through transcending the ego which the yellow level represents, we transform the yellow into pure gold. Pure gold of sunlight, the radiance of enlightenment is shown in the Renaissance painters' halos. When ego separation is dissolved then *gnosis* or true knowledge comes. This is the glorification of the real Self, the one Self.

The yellow level has a love of change and novelty. New experience or new thoughts are stimulating. The urge for change can be to keep depth of feeling away so that life is superficial, or it can be a deep desire for growth and self-transformation. The strictly yellow level is computer-like and is very useful to help us organize our lives, facts and experiences. It thinks in terms of problems and solutions. When it works harmoniously with the other levels it can be a great tool and can express wisdom. Through these awareness games we want to widen the ego, our idea of self. We do this by contacting the evolutionary energy of change and transformation which is hidden in this ego-centric world to dissolve its bounds. With transcendental logic we become a conscious participator in our own evolution with the Cosmic Intelligence. By working on ourselves, exploring our seven faculties, sharing, feedback, meditation, keeping a journal of our experiences, yoga and energy awareness, we prod each level of ourself into conscious growth.

YOGA POSTURES III

The spinal twists are the yoga postures which stimulate and balance energies of the chakra or center in the spine which gives us the level of consciousness of the intellect. Our analytical ability is closely connected with our ability to discriminate, and with a sharp intellect we can avoid many pitfalls. The areas of the body that are related to the intellect are the solar plexus and the adrenal glands. By practicing spinal twists we can get into conscious touch with the energies of this physical-etheric area of our body and experience its functioning in our consciousness.

SPINAL TWISTS

There are many variations of the spinal twist postures. Three are given here, but if you know others you may do them as well. The important part is to put your consciousness inside the spine in the area of the chakra being stimulated.

1.   SITTING TWIST— Sit up with your legs extended in front of you. Inhale and put the right foot to the left side of the left thigh as in the picture. Exhale and stretch your body around to the right so the torso is twisted to the right and then put the left arm around the right knee so the left elbow and the right knee touch. Grab your right foot with your left hand. This will be difficult at first, but when you get the hang of it,it is very easy. Look around to the right and put your right arm around your back.(See picture.)Straighten your back, feel like it is a corkscrew. Put your mind in the spine as you do this, and feel the energy spiral up the spine and around to the top of the head. Slowly come out of the twist. Take a few deep breaths and repeat on the other side.

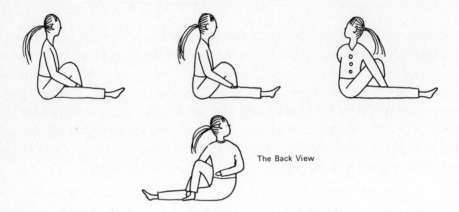

The Back View

2.   STANDING TWIST – Stand up and twist your hips from side to side. Put your mind in the spine as you do this and feel the energy around the solar plexus area that is twisting.

3. LYING TWIST — Lie down on your back with your arms down at your sides. Raise the right knee and place the right foot on top of the left knee. Bring your arms out to the sides as in a cross. Put your left hand on top of the right knee and turn your face to the right. Now exhale and bring the right knee down to the left side of the body by pushing the knee down with your left hand. Keep your face turned to the right. Try to touch the right knee to the floor and keep your shoulders on the ground as much as possible. Feel the twist in the spine. You may hear some bones "cracking"; this is loosening up tensions in the spine. Don't strain. Move only as far as you comfortably can go. Hold, while feeling the energy in the solar plexus area. Inhale and come up, arms out in the T or cross position again and bring your right leg back down so you are lying flat again. Feel how the right side of your body is stretched, your right leg may even feel longer than your left. Now repeat on the other side. Inhale, raise the left knee and place the left foot on the right knee. Put the right hand on top of the left knee, turn your face to the left. Exhale and push the left knee towards the ground on the right side of your body with the right hand. Relax the back as you stretch and feel the twisting. Keep your shoulders on the ground as much as possible to enhance the twisting effect. Feel your spine from the inside out and put your mind in the solar plexus area. Inhale slowly and come up. Stretch your legs out and lie relaxed for a moment feeling the effect of the stretching on your entire energy body and physical body.

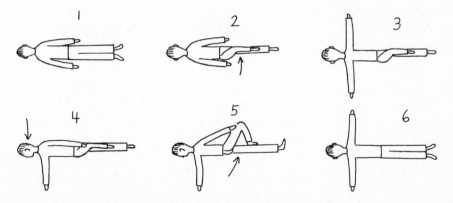

PRACTICE THESE POSTURES BEFORE THE MEDITATION AND THE AWARENESS GAMES IN THE YELLOW LEVEL.

MEDITATION FOR DISCOVERING "WHO AM I?"

Do the centering meditation on page 54, concentrating your energies in the point between the eyebrows. When the group is centered continue with the following:

The intellect lives in the world of problems, questions and answers. The most basic question we can ask is "Who Am I?" All the great sages have said "Know thyself". Let us begin to ask ourselves inside, slowly "Who Am I?" . . . Be aware of the answer as it comes to your mind. "Who is that?" Ask again . . . (pause for thirty seconds) . . . "Who Am I really?" . . . Let the feeling or thought come to you and consider, is that who you really are? . . . Go deeper . . . "Who Am I?" . . . (another pause for thirty seconds) . . ."Where did that last thought come from?" . . . "Who is this being I call myself?" . . . "If I am not just a body, not just my mind, then who am I?" . . . (long pause) . . . Now let's chant OM in a loud and clear tone, putting our whole self into the sound—OOOOOOMMMMMM. In the silence that follows let all thoughts fade away, dissolve in the stillness . . . "Who am I in this stillness?" . . . (silent meditation).

After a few moments when you begin to feel your mind returning to normal, reach for your pen and journal notebook and write down the answers that now come to you, that seem most real to you. "Who Am I?"

An alternative group meditation instead of the individual meditation above, or in addition to it, is the following. If you are alone, look into a mirror.

Before the centering meditation pick a partner (a new partner at different sessions). Decide who will be #1 and who will be #2. Sit knee to knee. (Do the centering meditation on page 54 .)

Slowly, as you come out of the meditation look into each other's eyes as you open your eyes. After a moment partner #1 asks the question "Who are you?" to partner #2. After partner #2 answers, wait a moment for the answer to settle and see if there are any more thoughts to share. Then partner #1 asks the question again, "Who are you?" Continue this questioning for five minutes. At times you may want to ask the question "Who are you really?" or "Where did that thought come from?" or "What were you before that?"

After five minutes switch roles so partner #2 becomes the questioner.

When you are through, write down your feelings in your journal or take a few minutes break to just feel the entire experience, what it has done to your being. DO NOT DIS-CUSS. (After a period of silence the leader begins to read the goal of the awareness game.)

If you are alone, look into a mirror and ask yourself the above questions.

PSYCHOANALYZE THE WORLD

Exploration

26

Yellow World

PREPARATION:
A willingness to go beyond the limits
of your little usual self.

GOAL: Just as it is very difficult to psychoanalyze oneself, so is it really just as difficult to analyze a group, a town, a state or any other entity of which any of us are part. And we are part of the world. It feels easier to analyze someone else, because we think we are separate from them. But even then, as we will see, we are often coloring the analysis with our own self.

To be so-called "objective" we have to be able to step away from our own private thoughts and get another view. We talk of a bird's eye view, a point of view that provides a broad scope and a wide perspective as when in the air above. An ant's eye view might give, however, important details that would be missed from the sky. Similarly there are different view points in levels of wealth, in different races, religions, cultures, languages, in social status.

We need to practice seeing the world from different view points so we aren't solely locked into our own limited perspective. We are part of the world and the world is our expanded self. This greater view is what we want to experience in this awareness game.

EXPLORATION:
1. *The leader reads the GOAL and then chooses a place familiar to all the members in the group. For example, in San Francisco this might be the Golden Gate bridge, in New York City it might be*

Times Square, in Philadelphia the corner of Broad and Market, etc. In every town there is a well-known park, building or intersection. Once you have decided on a place known to all, each member will describe that place from one of many viewpoints.

The leader begins by naming the place and giving one of the viewpoints from the following list to the first person in the circle. That person describes what the place looks like from that view. Then the leader reads the next perspective on the list and the next person takes that position, and so on until everyone has had a turn. If you come up with some more good examples you can continue and go around for another round, or you can add them to the list to be done at another time. If you have more people in the group than the examples listed, the leader will have to think of some more.

The leader chooses for everyone so that you will have to respond spontaneously to whatever challenge is given, and not limit yourself to your own personal preferences. *One variation of the game is for the leader to write down all the examples on little bits of paper, fold them up and put them in a hat or box. Let everyone draw their chance.*

A baby in a carriage	A worm
A bird in the sky	An invalid in a wheelchair
A truck driver	A tree
A newspaper seller	An ant
A policeman on duty	A drug peddler
A minister	A beggar
A toddler, age two	An artist
A puppy	A lawyer

2.   The object was to get into someone else's world. But would a bird really have all those emotions? Are our descriptions imaginative or realistic? Do we *project* our own human ways onto these others as if we were seeing through their eyes? What emotions does a bird or an ant feel? Discuss.

3.   The leader now directs the discussion to one major controversial

world problem going on at the time to be selected by the group. Perhaps the nuclear threat, human rights, energy, ecology, hunger, etc. . . . The leader leads a two or three minute centering meditation where everyone puts themselves into the minds and hearts of those most affected by the problems chosen to be discussed, both the victims and those in government, or those responsible for inflicting the problem or keeping it going. At the end of the meditation everyone shares their experience. We want to discuss the problem now, not from the view of politics, but to analyze the effects on the lives of people involved.

4. Now discuss, how does this problem threaten you? What solutions do you see? What is your responsibility?—are you separate from it—subject-object separation, or is it part of you?

5. What would you say, individually, is the major problem in the world today? Everyone goes around sharing whatever they think it is. The leader records all the answers. Then each person gives a two minute impromptu speech on why he or she thinks it is the major problem.

6. Did the problems everyone picked reflect their own personalities in any way? Do you see any correlations between the level of consciousness each person generally lives in and the problems they saw?

7. Journal writing.

I DO UNDERSTAND YOU

Exploration
27
Yellow World

PREPARATION:
a large lump of plasticine or clay
enough for two people, and boards
to rest the clay on

two sheets of paper and pencils for everyone

a cloth or towel

GOAL: Real communication is beyond the word level, but sometimes it is difficult to get across our thoughts and feelings without words. The yellow level is a level of self-expression where the intellect works to present our ideas and feelings. Here we go another step out from the orange level of social relating into exploring the difficulties experienced in communicating. We have to understand psychologically what is happening inside people to take this next step. Most people on this level can "hear" only that which they can relate to—what is already within their experience. If you have no experience to hang words on, you usually will have a gap in your ability to understand. If your experience is too vivid it may make you too sensitive to hear the words as the other is really experiencing them. You will color them with your own experience. This is called a "projection" in psychology. You project your own inner reality onto another.

In this journey we are going to analyze how well we understand each other's communication.

EXPLORATION:
1. *The leader reads the GOAL and then, immediately reads one or more of several passages he has chosen beforehand from several books of wisdom, e.g., The Bible, The Bhagavad Gita, The Prophet, The Sayings of Lao Tsu, Nuclear Evolution, etc.—any book that speaks in a universal way.* Someone states what that passage means

to them. . . Does it mean exactly the same to everyone else? Others describe the differences they see in it. Here are some sample passages:

1) *We choose whether or not we will give to others or radiate our love, but most of us do not fully realize that we need to give of ourselves.* —"Nuclear Evolution: Discovery of the Rainbow Body" by Christopher Hills

2) *Nuclear Evolution is most fruitful when we use it to understand ourselves and to deepen communication with other beings. . . no solution to war can be had until the tension within the individuals is lessened since it is the sum of all our tension which makes the national tensions.* —"Nuclear Evolution"

3) *Individuals who draw solely, wholly upon the Creative Forces within themselves may change their surroundings and the very vibrations within their bodies.* —Edgar Cayce

4) *Love one another, but make not a bond of love: Let it rather be a moving sea between the shores of your souls. Fill each other's cup but drink not from one cup. Give one another of your bread but eat not from the same loaf. Sing and dance together and be joyous, but let each one of you be alone, Even as the strings of a lute are alone though they quiver with the same music.* —"The Prophet" by Kahil Gibran

2. Draw with your pencil a simple sketch on your sheet of paper *in secret.* It should not be complicated. It can be a geometrical form, a symbol, a still life, a person's face or figure. The leader gives no other instructions. You have three minutes to draw your simple sketch. Do not let anyone else see your work.

3. Pair off, but still do not let each other see your drawings. Each person will need a fresh sheet of paper. The goal is to have one person draw a replica of your drawing by your detailed verbal description and instructions. No peeking. The describer will have to formulate his words and thoughts very carefully to convey exactly how and what the other is to draw. You have five minutes to do this. Then compare the results. Now switch roles and the new describer

Senior citizens engaged in the exercise on the opposite page, Step 2.

has a turn. Remember where you had difficulty understanding and see if you can communicate your directions even more clearly. Compare results. *The leader keeps track of time.*

4.   If you want to try again with a new partner go ahead, otherwise continue to step 5.

5.   The group now decides which communicator and receiver have come the closest in their original and replica. These two then decide who will be the describer and the other leaves the room. The describer takes half the lump of clay or plasticine and molds a model or a symbol or shape, as instructed by the group—following the first direction he hears, and then indicating when he is ready for the next direction. At the end of five minutes of sculpturing, the result is covered by the cloth or towel and the second person is invited back. He is given the rest of the modeling material and is instructed only by the first sculptor. At the end of seven minutes the results are compared.

6.   Discuss what happened in your minds as you tried to express in this linear step by step way, and what happened when you tried to listen and carry it out.

7.   Journal writing.

PSYCHOANALYZE YOUR SELF

Exploration
28
Yellow World

GOAL: In this level we are interested in change. Experience of a person's manners and choices may make us feel understanding or may make us judge him, depending on who we are. But to help him change requires a deeper awareness where we go into the cause of behavior.

Psychologists have several favorite methods for obtaining windows into the personality. In this exploration we will all be psychologists.

A study of a person's handwriting not only provides us clues to his personality but a tool to change it. Graphologists who see patterns in the handwriting of habitual criminals have successfully changed criminal behavior by changing handwriting patterns. Of course there has to be willingness. A man who crosses a "T" with a downward slant, indicating dejection or pessimism, can with practice learn to cross the T with an upward slant indicating hope and optimism. We want to see what our handwriting tells about us and perhaps change it.

PREPARATION:
Rorschach cards borrowed from a psychologist or make some yourself by taking white plain paper, spilling some ink on it and folding it once in half while wet. This will cause a shape to be formed. You will need two or three of these cards.

A handwriting analysis book either purchased or borrowed. You can often find them in the public library. The ones with the more recent copyrights are usually updated with the latest research. Try to discover a reputable one.

Ten words per group member. If there are seven members, you will need to create seventy words. Some may be used two or three times in a large group.

EXPLORATION:

1. Take the Rorschach cards and display them. Each person, one at a time, gets a chance to describe what he or she sees in the design— birds, guts, flowers, animals, genitals, faces are common replies. The group offers any psychological insights they may feel.

2. The psychological exercise of word association is a way into the personality. Each person is addressed in turn by the leader and

asked for instant one-word replies, one at a time, to a group of ten words. The ten words are changed for each person. Here are three sets of ten for examples for use with three people. The leader will have to make more lists of ten depending on the number of people in the group.

Night	Blanket	Sun
Sister	Food	Wave
Love	Father	Tree
Bread	Glass	Wrinkles
Car	Trip	Baby
Blood	Knife	Chair
School	Cloud	Paper
Water	Television	Kitchen
Book	Blue	Game
Rug	Breath	Fear

The group interprets the replies of each person before going on to the next. What, if any, is the significance of such associations as "night"—"fear" or "sister"—"fight" or "love"—"hate", etc.? It is doubtful whether deeply negative reactions will occur constantly, but if it happens it is a sign that the person is troubled. Look for the clues in the patterns of the one-word responses. Discuss.

3. The leader, who has reviewed the handwriting analysis book, points out some typical patterns. Every person writes down a sample of handwriting , taking a clean page out of their journals and leaving off their name. Everyone looks at each other's handwriting anonymously and analyzes it according to the characteristics basically outlined by the leader. The names of the writers are announced at the end. You write the results of your analysis in your journal and clip your paper to it. You decide what you want to change and experiment changing it. See if it changes from that point on in your journal.

4. Were these three psychological methods of analysis accurate? contradictory? enlightening?

5. How do you feel about a change? Are you willing to practice changing the personality traits you don't want in order to transform

your ego? How much do you want to work on yourself or do you want others to change instead? Choose *one thing* you want to change and share it with the group. Can we change others—mates? children? What ego battles have we felt when we've tried to change and run into a problem? Discuss.

6.   Journal writing.

Husband and wife share one thing they like about each other and one thing they feel each other needs to work on.

THE LOVE SEAT

PREPARATION:
You will need to make a chart of the
group personality. If you have less than ten
members in the group an 8½ x 11 piece
of paper will do. More people will require
a larger sheet or two. Write the first
names of everyone down the side and again
in the same order along the top. Draw lines
both vertically and horizontally forming
squares. Label the vertical lines "Reflectors"
and the horizontal lines "Senders".

GOAL: The Love Seat is a favorite awareness activity for many families and friends. It is an opportunity to share deep feelings about each other in a situation of trust, caring and openness. Both positive and negative qualities are used in this journey, and I have never failed to see a group emerge from this experience without a tremendous new awakening.

In addition to the benefits of the structured sharing for people who know each other, it is also an insightful experience for people who are seeing each other for the first time. Often our first impressions of people are deep insights into positive traits and personality flaws, which we later lose sight of because we get to know the person on other levels. Although this is a yellow-level feedback exercise, it draws from the intuition so we can see into people with penetrating insight.

Our goal is to overcome hostility and suspicion, and to demonstrate trust with each other by trusting and being open about our perceptions. Penetrating insight will come if you are willing to be honest in how you look at others and with yourself.

Still there may be those who hold back. You will not be contributing to the success of the journey by holding back. In fact, though you may feel you are preserving relationships, you may really be making them worse. Friendships are strongly cemented and people brought closer together through honesty and an atmosphere of respect for each other's views.

EXPLORATION:

1. The group forms into a circle. If there are more than thirteen people, form two circles. Each circle will need its own chart. The first Sender sits in the love seat and the rest of the group are Reflectors. One person begins and then we move around the circle until everyone has had a turn. If people are shy about volunteering for center then go around the circle in order. One person from each circle is designated as the recorder for the entire time. Choose someone who can write well and write quickly. The Sender faces one person and looks him in the eyes. That person is now the first Reflector. If you are the Reflector try to tune into the Sender and share one thing (only one thing) that you feel is positive about the Sender or one thing you like most about him, and one thing (only one thing) that the Sender needs to work on to change or grow. The reason for the term Sender is because the person in the love seat is sending his vibrations from his being.

The Reflector mirrors or reflects them back in what he says about the Sender. After the Sender has heard the first person he nods a silent thank you and *without answering* moves to face the next person in the circle and sends his being out to the Reflector. The Reflector says one positive piece of feedback and one thing that he feels the Sender needs to work on. The recorder writes down both the positive and the item to work on in the square boxes next to the name of the Sender and under the name of the appropriate Reflector.

The Sender keeps moving around the circle one by one until everyone has had a chance to express their reflection. He does not talk until he has completed with everyone even though he may be bursting to say "yes, that's right" or "no" or "that's because . . . " etc.

Before he leaves the love seat the Sender says one thing he likes best about himself and one thing he feels he needs to work on. This, too, is recorded. Then he may comment for a moment, if he wishes, on the feedback he has received from everyone. The next person takes the love seat and becomes the new Sender. When everyone has had a turn the chart will be filled.

Don't be afraid to share your feelings. The deepest thoughts, the ones you fear may not be right, are usually the ones that are most appreciated and the most right on. If you can't think of anything or your mind goes blank you can comment on simple and obvious things like dress, hair-style, make-up, warmth, coldness, introvertedness, etc. But remember it is your responsibility to make the journey work by sharing something of yourself with each person. If you won't say anything then you are in fact telling the others they are perfect in your eyes. While you may admire someone greatly, it will not help him to grow or your friendship become closer unless you can share whatever you feel *that moment* on the positive and the negative.

2. You may discuss reactions when everyone's been in the Love Seat, or go straight on to Part II.

End of Part I

PART II

You may want to do Part II the next time you come together so that you can approach it while fresh. Usually after finishing Part I the group is all energized and in a nice heartfelt vibration with each other. This next step is to analyze the chart for projections and "right ons."

1. The charts are brought into the limelight. Each person reads what he or she has said as a Reflector about each of the other people in the group. *If the handwriting is difficult to read, the leader or the recorder can do all the reading.* As the Reflector's comments are read, both positive and negative, look for the following:

    a) Has this Reflector said the same thing or very similar things to two or more people?

    b) Is what the Reflector said about this Sender more true of himself than it is of the Sender?

    c) Is what the Reflector said about this Sender right on in your eyes? Has he been very perceptive?

If the answer to a) is yes, then it is likely that the feedback to the Sender was a projection, meaning that the Reflector was seeing through his or her own personality. Sometimes the feedback may be true of both the Sender and the Reflector. This is called a "semi-projection". It is very easy to see our own good and not-so-good traits in another person because they are in ourself. If b) is true it is also a "projection." But if it is, say, 50-50, just as true in both of them then it is a "semi-projection." If c) is true and you feel "ah-ha he's really right" or if it is mostly true about the Sender and doesn't apply much or at all to the Reflector's personality then it is a "right on" or a "direct hit."

Decide as the comments are read whether they are P, S-P, or R (Projection, Semi-Projection or Right on). Call them off as the reader goes through the comments. Don't spend long times discussing, your first feelings are usually correct. It may be that one person just cannot see what others see in someone. He may be correct ("50 million people can be wrong"), but a group usually is more accurate than any one individual. That person may be "identifying" with the Sender, feeling how he would feel if he were in the Sender's shoes (which may be totally off or may be true). Identification is not clear seeing either, because it is coloring the perceptions with your own personal fears and hopes. By reading the comments we gain further insight into our personalities.

2. This entire love seat experience is an exercise in seeing how the ego works in its relationships with others. Through the group mirror we get a many-faceted picture of ourself, which is how other people do see us, and we can get a wonderful idea of what parts of our egos we need to work on to enhance our evolution. Did you have thoughts you never before experienced? Did you enjoy the opportunity to give feedback and to have your own image reflected with mature clarity? Could you feel the human similarities despite the apparent differences between people? Discuss.

3. Is the group learning how to dissolve bitter feelings or negativity with love, transcending the barrier of different inner worlds? Is the group getting beyond being offensive or defensive? Which people did you feel could have shared more? How accurate was the feedback overall? Discuss.

4. Journal writing. The group may want to xerox the chart so that everyone can keep a copy of the feedback in their journals.

GROUP THERAPY

Exploration

30

Yellow World

GOAL: Many people feel the need to open up more, to feel more, get in touch more, express more. The safe opportunities are few. Barriers are up everywhere.

These barriers can make us sick, in soul and body. It is sad that we have to go pay a psychologist usually, before we can have the opportunity for group experience where we can more easily open up and express ourselves.

Studies have found that groups of people working together on a common problem are better able to understand the differences that cause misunderstandings and harm communications. This session will not be group therapy as a professional would conduct it, but a group therapy game that stops short of the "shock treatment" of most encounter groups. It should be a fun and constructive exploration, where we can see how honest we are.

PREPARATION:
4 cards or slips of paper with the following written on them separately:

1) Pick a member of the group you relate to least and explain how it is really your own problem and how you expect to cope with it.

2) Describe your body to the group, explaining which you think are your best features and which are your worst and why.

3) Confess a failure or sin. Give details. Explain what you learned by it.

4) Name a bad habit you have and describe an embarrassing event that occurred as a result.

EXPLORATION:
1. *The leader reads the instructions:*

   This game places emphasis on honesty. A vote by participants determines if a player is "with it"—is answering true and real—or is "off"—is embarrassed or not in touch in some way. Each player picks a card and follows the instructions on it until the group votes unanimously "with it".

2. How honest are we as a whole? Do we go deep? Can we go deeper and be more real? What blocks us? Are we more real with friends or family or are we more real here in this trusting group? How can we

188

become more open and honest? Discuss what makes people in the group hold back or open up.

3.　Discuss what is needed either in the home, the school or in our group to develop a good amount of self-esteem and self-respect and dissolve the ego separations at the same time. How can we bring up children and educate them so they will build a strong ego to face the world and dissolve the ego so they can be one with the evolutionary intelligence and be fulfilled in oneness? How does the Love Seat exercise help to do this?

4.　Journal writing.

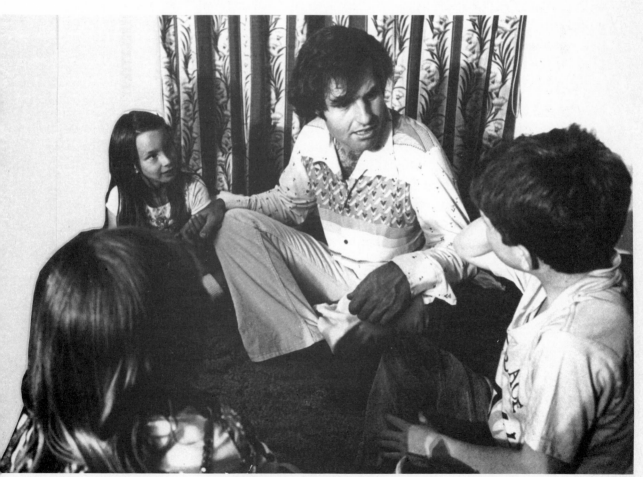

Daddy takes some feedback too!

PERSONALITY RECOGNITION

GOAL: In this journey we want to find out how well we know each other. How much have we learned about the other's goals, drives, personalities, attributes and potentialities? Our main goal is to learn how much progress we have made in getting inside others and also have some fun.

PREPARATION:
The names of each member are placed in a hat by the leader, written down on tiny pieces of paper and folded so no one knows who they are picking. Each person draws a name (if you draw your own put it back quickly and draw again). Keep the name drawn a secret.

Everyone will need paper and pencils or pens.

EXPLORATION:

1.   Everyone draws the names. Then the leader asks that a minute or two of silent meditation take place in which each person meditates on the person whose name was drawn. After meditating on the being, the vibration of that person, think of all the qualities you can in that person. Be careful not to keep looking at the member you have drawn as you may give yourself away. After a few moments the leader signals to go on.

2.   Write down a personality evaluation of the individual whose name is on the slip you have chosen. List the good and bad points, drives and goals that you see, and the chances of fulfilling them or what has to be done to fulfill them. Write at least 100 to 200 words. Do not use the words "she, he, him or her" because you will be giving a clue away. Instead use the term "this person" to keep it as secret as possible.

Short sample:
This person is very quiet and reserved. Although this person is very sensitive to others' feelings it seems to be at the expense of this person's own needs and feelings. This person has a lovely,

caring quality and, for this person's age, is very open to new ideas. This person seems to want new experiences, to grow, but holds back because of family and security. Basically this person seems quite content, but there are signs in the face that there is strain. To overcome the strain by letting go might risk the security so it puts this person in a bind. By continuing to slowly look at self and explore, a happy medium can be reached where this person can be free to be more open and still relate well to the family. In fact, there has been a real improvement since the group first began and I am looking forward to seeing what more is in store. This person would like to meditate more and tune in more, but doesn't seem to have the will power or the peace of mind to persevere, although this person seems to be getting calmer.

3. Usually the descriptions are very true to the being and the exercise brings everyone into a warm heart feeling. Each writer in the circle is given a number 1, 2, 3, 4, 5 and so on. Write this number on your paper. Read #1 aloud. When #1 is finished all in turn state who they think #1 is by writing it down on their sheets. Then the next person reads #2 and so forth until all have read their descriptions and everyone has voted on all of them. The first person who read says who #1 is and the right votes are counted. The next reveals #2 and so forth until everyone is identified.

4. Discuss which descriptions were the most accurate and which were the easiest to guess. Why? Share feelings.

5. Journal writing.

DO YOUR OWN THING

Exploration

32

Yellow World

PREPARATION:
The leader for this session must phone all the members or inform them the session before that this next journey will be an exploration in creativity and responsibility. Each person is to meditate on their idea for an awareness game that will bring about some change, something new they would like to see or experiment with in the group. This is a time for self-expression and creative thinking with every member in mind. Your game can take in any of the seven worlds and introduce some kind of change or new expression.

GOAL: Self-expression leads to growth and expanded awareness. Those who stifle themselves for fear of criticism pay in the form of dis-ease of personality and psyche. Those who express themselves unfold in health, beauty, growth and potential. They become unblocked channels through which the sunshine of creativity, intuition and inspiration can flow.

This session will be in keeping with this level of change. We will do "our own thing". We want to express the untried, the original—events designed by all the crew. As a group we know whether a game or exercise is right for us. We can tell whether or not it is aimed at our highest goals with no manipulation or disrespect for human feelings.

Change is a human need. In these games, the group responsibility for change is encouraged without the individual self-righteousness which can result from interfering with the rights of others. Society can only be really changed effectively by groups from within, where members seek valid experiences designed to melt barriers and hang-ups and blocks to communication. At the same time the group must reinforce self-esteem in each other. Confrontation with the self is *the* ultimate revolution.

These are the experiences that develop potential and that people everywhere are

192

hungry for in order to enjoy their search for truth and self-mastery. You can share this session by appointing a recorder to write a brief account of what happens and send this along with the written description of the exercise prepared by the person who originates it to the authors for further testing and possible use in future publications. People like to feel they are doing something useful. Here you will be part of a world-wide movement for change, and gain self-esteem for contributing to evolutionary development.

EXPLORATION:

1. Everyone in turn reads their description of a proposed game or event they made up and brought with them. The group asks questions to clarify the goals of any games that are not totally understood.

2. Each person votes for first, second and third choice in the games submitted. If there isn't time to do them all this time, plan for another session in order to continue. The ballots are counted by rating 3 for first, 2 for second and 1 for third. The highest scored game is played first and so on down the line for as much time as there is available.

3. Discuss.

4. Journal writing.

CLEARING THE AIR

Exploration

33

Yellow World

PREPARATION:
A tape recorder and tapes.

It is good to record this session and then play it back to hear how you sound from the viewpoint of others.

If you have access to video equipment, it is very enlightening to watch how you respond to others. The leader should video-tape the session then play it back before Journal Writing.

GOAL: Many so-called encounter groups have been described as "insult free-for-alls". Everyone trades insults and negatives and expects something positive to emerge. It is doubtful whether this works to bring creative growth. It is hard to think of people who are not worthy of some compliments. True compliments should fly back and forth just as frequently, or more so, as criticism.

Our goal in this game is to give feedback to each person for at least five minutes, clearing the air of any inner feelings and charging the group electricity. By the end everyone will feel full of united awareness. Here we want to say what we have not said, what we've held back.

EXPLORATION:

1. The key to this game is that no *idle conversation* or debate is permitted. There will be long silences when you can't think of anything to say, but these should not be considered embarrassing. People may be looking at each other hopelessly, but—behind the silence—defenses will be dropping, barriers melting, clairvoyant feelings sent and received and the group air purified. The leader begins by asking everyone to form a close circle. He sits in the center in the "hot seat" first. Any member of the circle may speak up at will with something good or bad about the leader's appearance, personality, character, effectiveness, etc. After each comment, the person in the "hot seat" is given a chance to think about what was said and to reply either "I agree" or "I disagree". Only then may another member offer the next remark. No discussion besides either

of the two statements "I agree" or "I disagree" is allowed by the person in the middle. Each person must remain in the "hot seat" for *at least five minutes,* even if no one says anything, and longer if comments are still flowing.

2. Every person in the "hot seat" selects the person they feel has been most critical to take the next turn. If you can't find anyone critical, then just pick someone to replace you in the "hot seat". Go around until everyone has had a turn.

3. Discuss the experience.

4. Journal writing.

Wendy tells Ary that she feels it's time for her to get out of her ruts.

REAL CHANGE
(A Return Journey)

Exploration

34

Yellow World

PREPARATION:
All you will need for this journey is your journal and a good pen or pencil.

Because this journey takes into account all the seven levels (even though it is about CHANGE and emphasizes the planning level) it is really a "Return Journey", one which should be done after you have already explored in each of the seven worlds at least once, and are now coming back home.

GOAL: Real change must take into account all seven inner worlds if it is to be permanent and complete. Sometimes life brings us to points of real change without our understanding what finally pushed us through. It may happen quickly or over a long period of time. Other times we try and try to change but fail. Something is blocking us. Only by going into the seven levels can we truly penetrate all the blocks to growth. Some therapies work with images, some with dreams, some with thoughts, some with analysis, some with bio-energetics, some with sexual feelings. To understand that people function on all seven chakra dimensions means any one of these forms of therapy may work sometimes for some people, but not all the time because it is limited to only one or two functions.

Through this exploration we will see very clearly on which level or levels we are blocking ourselves from changing and becoming the person we want to be.

EXPLORATION:

1. After the centering meditation and yoga postures the group comes together in a circle. Take a few minutes more to meditate on change. Come up with one thing that you would like to change in yourself. Don't pick something too drastic, like getting rich quick or some other scheme that would take an act of fate. We are going to choose our change in a special way. *The leader reads:*

   Violet   Close your eyes, and let an image flow into your

196

awareness of the one thing you would most like to change. The image of the real thing your unconscious needs to change will float before your inner eye or come to your awareness in the form of a picture or a powerful thought. When you see this image then project it into the future. See where it will go. But first spend some time getting a clear image. . . Then as soon as it comes project it into the future.

Indigo   Quickly see yourself in the future having accomplished this new change. . . What happens? Or do you get a funny feeling of unforseen upsets to the image? Is there some fear it may not happen? Some inkling of emotional upsets that interfere? You may get blocked on this level if you color your future by fear, or if your image loses power. It is necessary to keep your image very clear once you have decided, and in this intuitive level confirm your knowing that this is the right image for you to choose, the right change for you. If you have an inkling that it is not, then go back to the violet level and choose another image that your intuition feels in tune with. The image needs to be strong to keep the will flowing into it and create the future positively by seeing it free and clear-sailing to your change, knowing that any obstacles to come are temporary and can be mastered.

Blue   Now the energy of your original image is crystallizing further into mind. When it was just an image it was like steam, now as it comes through the energy levels of consciousness it gets more and more material as it becomes like water, eventually when it comes down to the physical reality it will be solid like ice. So now form a concept and build thoughts about this change in this level. Your memory comes into play and you can see how in the past you have tried to change and perhaps it didn't work or you see your own ideals and conditioning . . . all this colors the change and puts a cloak on it as it were. Let go of the mind so that you can travel through this level dynamically and free and unconditioned. Build positive ideas about yourself and this change instead. Affirm it as done. This is a level people often get hung-up on from past experience.

Green   You may already be in this next level before we even

197

mention it, since it is the heart and your security is something that pops in very quickly. It is also the level of life force and how much you really want to change. If you don't want it that much you will never get beyond this level as your heart won't be into it. The heart has to be into the image, vision, and idea in order for it to become real. If you are content for the idea to just stay in the clouds in the other levels then it will never manifest in your life. So in this level check your heart. Do you really want this change? If there is not enough will or desire energy in it, or if you really want something else more and there is a conflict of interests, go back to the violet level again and tune into a new image. Decide on something else to change that your heart is really in tune with, because it will be useless to go on from here until your heart and your head are working as one. Many people never put them together and their lives go on and on the same or in conflict. Take time to finish this level and feel good in your heart. . .

Yellow   Now when you want the change enough to do what is needed you can go to the next level of figuring out a plan of action. You need to come through this level with a clear heart where you can plan it out but are not attached to the results. If you are attached it will short circuit you as you try too hard and you'll just go around in circles. Expect success. Know that success will happen and you must create your plan of action. Now is the time to open your eyes and take up your pen. Write down in your journal step by step what you need to do to carry through the change. Remember attitudes you had to keep on the violet-indigo-blue-green levels and write these down as well so you have a nice linear progression of what has been done and where you are going to go with the change. Now in real life you jump from level to level, it doesn't always happen in order like this, but you must take in all the levels for change to happen, even if you are not aware of it. Often the image will jump right to your insecurity in the green level and get short-circuited there. Or you may intuit the future but not have enough planning to carry it out, so you'll just jump right to the red level and forget other important steps and then something will go wrong. It won't turn out like you intuited. Most psychics and intuitives see possibilities, but do not have their lives together (their levels together) and so what they intuit gets screwed-up. They often screw up other people's lives too, based on their own faulty perceptions. When they are sometimes accurate they are content with that, and don't usually go further to see how their own lives affect their inaccuracy at other times. Great psychics of course are aware of all the chakras and have them all working for them. In this level we plan as carefully as we can. Write down what you need to do, want to do and will do. *(Go on when everyone's done writing.)*

Orange We must consider this level as one of the most important in change. It is the social influence. Interference from others you live with, their needs and expectations and habits can pull you away from your plan. Others can be an excuse for laziness or you can let them sap that will-energy you need to break through. Especially if your security and emotions are involved with others, their help on taking you through or blocking your progress is important. Of course you are the one who is really responsible if you let their attitudes block you, but environment is a strong influence unless you are bound and determined to overcome it. So check out your social level. Perhaps you will find that after going through all the other levels with clear movement, it is socially impossible for you to create the change you want. The world, or your situation is just not ready for it. You will see in this level how others will affect your change.

Red This is the level where you must do it. Doing it is following through with the plan, every step of the way to make it a firm new reality in your life. If you haven't been through all the other levels (consciously or unconsciously) and cleared them, you will not have the energy to manifest on the physical level or your plans may fall short.

You want to be aware of your total being in your daily life. Keep track in your journal how you are doing this next week in putting forth your change. What happens to the energy? Note if you succeed and if you have to keep up the energy (in the case of changing a bad habit). If you fail, see on what level or levels you got blocked or failed. This will be a clue to your weak area and what chakra you need to give attention to. So begin to take action NOW.

2. Discuss which levels you felt blocked in or saw clearly in this meditation. Discuss how this journey into all seven worlds has penetrated your being. Has anything been left out? The next time the group comes together it is very important to follow up and see what changes have been made.

3. Journal writing.

GREEN WORLD
THE SECURITY LEVEL

Kids just love to stretch themselves and feel on top of the world.

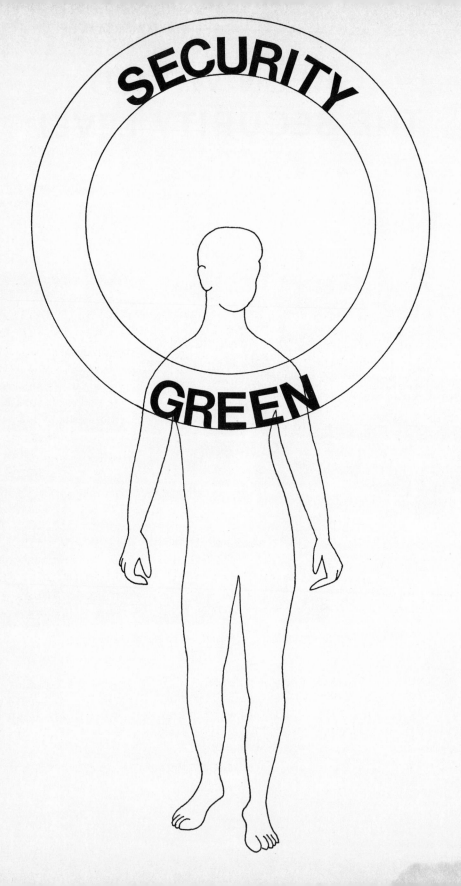

GREEN
IV

The Green world is perhaps the largest of the worlds because it affects us so deeply. Our deepest feelings of security and insecurity, longing and belonging, our desires and motives all stem from this world. Even though each of the seven worlds is a distinct vibration, they do interpenetrate each other, and in the green level we can see security or insecurity affecting our activity on all the other levels. If we are insecure about next month's rent we might travel into our imagination and fantasize how it would be to make some money, or we might escape into the past and remember the times we were rich, or we might compensate by getting drunk, or we might plan out how we're going to get more money. The motive is the need for money, but this drive colors the activity of whatever level we are operating in.

Bright leaf green is also the color of healing, which makes the body, mind or soul secure. Murky green is often a color of dis-ease, another word for insecure. We often see sickly people as green around the gills. Green is the color of life energy as revealed in nature everywhere. When positive life force is flowing, our security is assured; when negative life force is produced it is called "negative green" or "grey-green" and is the ray of death and disintegration.

The person who lives in this green world much of the time is concerned about possessions and may be a jealous person afraid to lose what he has so he holds on tightly. He likes to store up things, whether clothes, antiques, money or knowledge. This is the level where we have the urge for self-confirmation. The person on this level is in the past, present *or* future time-world depending on whether his security is threatened or safe.

If you've lost something and you were attached to it then you will be in the past, mourning your loss. If your love object is with you then you will feel snug and secure in the present. If the thing or person you love will be arriving next week then you are out in the future, feeling either uncertain until it arrives, or secure in your expectation.

As a plant reaches out towards the sun, so the green level is the level of reaching out to what we desire. Our feelings of love and security are very closely related, and this is why this feeling level of life and energy is the world of the heart.

In the awareness games of the world of the heart, we will explore what we are doing with our love, our trust and our life force, and learn ways to redirect them to feel more in tune and feel better about ourselves. After doing these exercises in our classes, people always comment on the flow of love between one another and how good it feels. No one wants to leave this space; everyone wants to hang onto it forever.

YOGA POSTURES IV

The postures that work to stimulate and open up the center near the heart are "backbending postures". They balance out our feelings in that sensitive chakra. Through one simple exercise you can change your feelings of security momentarily by contracting and expanding the area around this chakra. Take a deep breath and sit up or stand up straight, throw the chest out, straightening the back. This uplifts you in body and in spirit. Now slump forward, rounding the shoulders close together in front of you. Many people who are insecure walk around with back bent and shoulders rounded forward. Feel the constricting effect this posture has on your feelings. Now breathe deeply and sit up again with the posture of confidence. Shoulders back and chest out. By practicing opening up the chest (and heart) area through backbending postures, we open ourselves to a fresh flow of life force and a charge of positive emotions. This puts us in touch with our hearts and our oneness with life.

BACKBENDING POSTURES

In addition to the exercise given above which you can do anytime you want a pick-up, there are several back-bending postures which stimulate and balance this center. If you have heart or back problems, do these postures very gently, with no strain.

1.   STANDING STRETCH — Stand up straight with chest out, chin parallel to the ground. Inhale and clasp your hands behind your back. Pull the hands down and stretch the chest out farther bringing the shoulder blades together on the exhalation. Hold. Feel the lift up and the openness in the heart chakra. You feel good! Walk around the room in this posture. See if you can maintain the openness and confidence throughout the class.

Practice sitting and walking in this masterful posture where you are on top and in tune with life not down under. By practicing holding your hands behind your back you train your shoulders back into this position.

2.　BACKBEND— Lie down flat on the back. Put your arms up over the head and then put the palms of your hands down on the ground so the fingers point towards the toes, like the drawing. Bend your knees. Bring your feet and hands as close together as possible. Inhale and push up so the body is lifted off the ground, and stomach is high in the air. Walk your feet as close to your hands as possible. Stretch up by bringing your head down and thrusting your chest out so your back bends on the exhalation. Hold, feeling the movement of energy in your spine and in the heart area behind the breastbone. Come down slowly.

MEDITATION ON THE BREATH OF LIFE

Do the centering meditation on page 54, focusing this time on the heart center, the area where our feelings of love come most strongly, in the center of the chest, behind the breastbone. When you feel love, continue:

Now begin to watch your breath. Watch it flow up and down, up and down, like a wave on the sea of life . . .

Now inhale through your nostrils, slowly to a mental count of five – then hold to a mental count of five, then gently exhale through your nostrils for a mental count of five. Repeat this five times . . . Now that you have the rhythm of the breath, look inside your heart to your feelings. Note what they are . . . Get in touch with any insecurity, any tension, any negative feeling. Then as you exhale imagine that you are releasing the pain or negative experience . . . then as you inhale imagine that you are drawing in fresh life force, fresh love from the universe and charging yourself up with a positive, uplifting, secure feeling of oneness with life . . . Now, as you hold your breath circulate this positive feeling throughout your body, mind and nervous system, soothing and healing it as you go; then on the exhalation release the pent up energies that may still be there along with the carbon dioxide. Inhale to a count of five drawing in fresh love and light and life force, along with the oxygen. Hold to a count of five, circulating it through your bloodstream and entire being. Now exhale to a count of five, emptying the wastes of your old feelings along with the carbon dioxide and body wastes on the out breath. Repeat this imagining and breathing five times (pause). Let your feelings release and transform into something new as you discover the secret of breath. Breath is the key to life and to your cosmic clearing house of feelings and emotions. On the wave of breath you can ride to the shores of new consciousness and energy, and love. Meditate on your power to change your feelings and emotions at will (pause). . .Now let's take the new love and energy we feel and embrace the entire group in our feeling of wholeness, feeling the group love amplifying our own love into an even greater love and experience of oneness . . .(long pause).

As we come back, let us keep this flow of heart love going, circulating and sharing throughout the group and expressing in our personalities. We now open our eyes and continue to radiate the warmth we feel.

WHAT WILL MAKE ME HAPPY?

Exploration
35
Green World

PREPARATION:
Pens and your journals.

GOAL: Is the thing that we are hoping for and driving ourselves towards real? Or is it an illusion through which security and happiness will not really come? Perhaps other members of the group have goals that are more fulfilling that we might consider. In this game we are going to search ourselves to see what our own real motives are. What is it that we want?

Everybody has a goal. Some might want money or power, family harmony, travel or a new home. Some might seek marriage, children, new friends, love, sexual pleasure, etc. Everyone has an idea of what will make them happy. Even the person who wants to commit suicide has a goal—to escape from unhappiness. Many people never stop to really get in touch with deeper or unspoken goals. Now is the opportunity.

EXPLORATION:

1. Write down your goal or goals in life in order of priority.

2. After a few minutes everyone in turn reads their goals and elaborates on them. Share how you came up with the goals, whether they have been longstanding or recent, and how you feel about them. After everyone has had a chance to express themselves, discuss the goals with each other. Are these really the deepest goals within each person or are they really only superficial goals on the way to something else? Suppose we achieve these goals, then what? Whose goals feel deepest? Is it because they are more in touch with their feelings and wants? *After the discussion has reached a plateau where it is not going any deeper the leader moves on to the next step.*

THE FORCE

3.   Let us all meditate on the following statement on the Green world in nature and in ourselves, trying to see ourselves in it and its effects on our lives. *The leader reads as the others listen and meditate:*

We all possess innate drives—instinctive forces which impel us toward more complete expression of our potentials. The bank robber is responding to a drive for money as his path to fulfillment. He thinks that obtaining lots of money without working for it will make him happier. If it is at other people's expense, or if he has to knock somebody over the head in the process, this does not worry him because he is not concerned with anyone else's happiness. It is not a matter of his happiness coming first, he just does not consider anyone else.

The force that drives us toward our goals and love objects, such as money, people, or whatever we want, is so powerful that it often moves us in spite of ourselves. It can move us over other people, over the laws of society, or even over the eternal laws of the universe. Can we think of times past when that force has moved us over people, social laws or universal laws of harmony? . . . (long pause) . . .

When our goal is superficial or short-lived, we often look back and say, "Was this trip really necessary?" We feel let down. On the other hand, when the personal goal is idealistic or directed toward a long range, valid purpose, every step in its accomplishment can be a joyous, gratifying event even when it is hard work or painful. In nature there are goals. In biology there are organizers in each cell which help it to reach its ultimate structure. In the DNA there is a kind of stop-go punctuation which steers the molecular chain towards a synthesis of all of its constituent chemicals. In every organism in nature, the growth and development is regulated toward an ultimate end which can be described as part of the goal of the universe as a whole.

Human beings are not immune from this force. We, too, have a cosmic impulse that seeks growth and development, integrated with other natural forces. We may misinterpret it, misdirect it, misuse it and misunderstand it. Or we may recognize it and use our superior consciousness to aid nature in assuring our realization and fulfillment.

There is no escape from this force. We can turn on the radio as loud as our ears can stand it. We can drink ourselves blind. We can eat ourselves sick. We can bury ourselves in work or lose ourselves in pleasure. It doesn't matter. The force is still there, inherent in our organism, moving us along with all other living things in an integrated and integrating universe. It does not depend on what type of person, whether a Pygmy in Africa, a cultural revolutionary in China, an American in an affluent society, or a British traditionalist—this ultimate goal is all-pervading in nature.

Of course, people vary in intelligence. They vary in physique and outlook and philosophy, but their goals need not exceed their individual capacities. And all men have similar needs too—needs for self-respect, love and expression. Sometimes our goals do exceed our abilities. For example, a man with a diseased leg could try to win a race, a woman who doesn't have a good voice could try to get into the opera, or someone with a finely-tuned brain could try to do a job which should be given to someone with brawn. When this happens we have conflicts, failure, and stagnation. A person cannot go any further with his natural abilities without a change.   The next step must be a breakthrough to new capacities or else the goal must be re-evaluated to fit the present abilities.

Not only humans, but all living organisms will extract nutrients and vital forces from the world around them. We attract our environments according to our goals. And if these goals are limited, so will our relationships and inner wholeness be limited in this vast mass of varied processes, energies and beings around us. We extract what we need according to the goal we hold in our hearts.

Our goals can affect our immediate decisions and how well we work with others. We cannot achieve self-realization if we are out of tune or out of sympathy with the needs for self-realization in others. If every whim could be gratified when it clashed with existing needs of people and society, then we would have chaos, not harmonious integration. The understanding of our own goals comes with the understanding of the goals of others and with an intuitive feeling of the goals of the universe.

4. "What are your real goals? What lies behind the goals you have already written down?" Relax and center on your own for a few minutes to tune into the deepest part of yourself. Complete the meditation by suggesting to yourself that your deeper needs and goals will come to your imagination and mind, and you will feel in tune and relaxed, with a sense of well-being.

5. Now take up your pens again and write down your new feelings and new goals. Everyone shares their deeper goals as before, explaining what has happened to them during the meditation.

6. Discuss the overall experience. How can we be more in touch with our real drives and motives more of the time during our busy lives?

7. Journal writing.

Keeping a journal throughout these awareness activities helps you to log your inner travels and stay in touch with you inner worlds.

BREAKING THE ICE

PREPARATION:
a telephone (no party line)

an egg timer or buzzer

GOAL: This is a good getting-to-know-you game. As a beginning exercise for the green world it is especially good for teen-agers and children when supervised by an understanding adult, for it helps them let go of their insecurities in social relating. For adults it is excellent for probing the suspicious parts of our natures.

In order to let go of our insecurities we first have to get in touch with them. A person with increased awareness is one who understands people better than he once did. He is more secure in his rela-tionships with others. His biggest problem is those people who have less awareness and who are still fearful, suspicious and distrustful.

People often do not try to make contact with each other because they fear the other's motives: "What does he want from me?" Sex? Money? Does she want to take advantage of me in some way? When people have something in common, it is easier to lower the barriers. At a parade or a game or a fire, people suddenly talk to each other. They trust the other is there for the same motive and don't worry that someone wants some-thing from them.

Breaking the ice helps us to melt our own defenses and make ourselves fearless and secure.

EXPLORATION:

1. Choose two volunteers. We are going to act out a scene which goes like this:

    > Pretend you are both standing and waiting in line at a supermarket check-out counter. One person starts a conversation going. The other plays cold and resistant. The starter remains persistent until the cooler person laughs and warms up in some way. Other members of the group comment on the performance when it is over.

    How real to life was the performance? What else could either actors have said? What would you have said?

2. Choose two new volunteers for each of the following scenes and try the getting-to-know-you act again. Be sure to first pair people of the same sex and then people of the opposite sex in the following skits:

    > * One of you is sitting on a park bench as the other approaches.
    > * You are both waiting for a traffic light to change while standing on a curb.
    >   Make up more situations until everyone in the group has had a chance to play a role.

    Discuss how you experienced each actor. The actors also share how they experienced themselves.

3. In real life, do you have a problem in getting to know others? Do you always have a motive in your heart that blocks you, e.g. "I need friends", "I want you to do something for me", "I'm afraid you'll reject me"? What blocks your open sharing of yourself? Discuss.

4. Everyone offers the name of someone they know (whom others in the group do not know) who would not mind being phoned. Each in turn phones one of these people. The purpose of this exercise is to win confidence and see if you can encourage the outside person to want to continue the conversation with you. Set the timer so that you have to talk for a minimum of two or three minutes to really

warm up. When you phone, introduce yourself by name and address. Don't reveal the person in the group who knows the party, but describe yourself. You can say:

> "I live in your neighorhood" or
> "I am with a group of people some of whom you probably know" or
> "Our interest is to expand awareness and self-knowledge".

Then you can explain what it is you are doing and why this exercise for phoning them. At the end of the conversation you can reveal the name of the mutual friend (if it is okay with the friend who is in the group). When the conversation is over—don't drag it on—discuss the experience before the next call as a group. Each person takes a turn. (Children need to be supervised.)

5.   Do you feel that you have more confidence now at being able to end your fear of strangers or making contact with others? What have you seen about yourself?

6.   Journal writing.

ENERGY AWARENESS

Exploration

37

Green World

PREPARATION:
Each person brings two flowerpots
exactly the same. The leader provides
enough soil for everyone's pots and enough
seeds for every pot. Seeds should be from
the same package and of the same type, so
that the two pots each person takes home
have the same contents in them.

The leader will also need to supply a
large leafed philodendron. He might
want to borrow one from one of the
group members if he doesn't own one.

Yoghurt culture (you can get it from a
local health food store)
Three bottles (same size) of warmed, scalded
whole milk (110 degrees Fahrenheit).

GOAL: Just as sickness can be caused by negativity and insecurity, health and growth are spurred by a climate of love and harmony. This applies not only to human life, but to all life. It can be physically demonstrated with plants by some tests we will do. Plants have emotions and respond to our human actions and even to our thoughts! By tuning directly into energy we can experience it moving along our thoughts and feelings and bodies to people, plants and animals, even to things. We can see how our use of energy directly affects them.

The human body is continuously being renewed. Every part discards old cells and grows new cells. Experiments have shown that this continuous cell growth is affected by our state of mind. The new cells appear to take on the characteristics of the mental climate into which they are born. The weaker or more negative and destructive the climate, the weaker the cell. The more wholesome positive and creative the climate the more vital the cell. Like the chameleon, the cells take on the color and nature of the consciousness of the person they live in. Can we learn to control our consciousness? If healthy attitudes produce healthy cells, then how do we transform feelings of sadness or aggressiveness or irritation at events of life? By learning to be aware of these moods and feelings as energy in motion— E-motion—we can learn how to master our attitudes and feelings. Then we can

216

begin to control our cell growth with our consciousness. But first we have to become aware of how energy moves in us, and how we can move it to change our feelings.

EXPLORATION:

1. Cleve Backster of Backster Research Foundation, New York City, has uncovered much evidence that plants do have emotions. He has discovered plant reactions through use of polygraph or lie-detector equipment on plants. Sharp electro-chemical reactions were recorded on the equipment when plants were threatened. Even at the moment of the threatening thought toward the plant, such as someone planning to cut it with a scissors, sharp reactions were noted. Similar technical research has shown that plants also respond when the person who cares for them calls long distance from out of town. Luther Burbank talked to roses and cacti, and was able to cross-breed and convince some to give up their thorns through the power of love. George Washington Carver said he talked to plants who revealed their secrets to him and helped him discover scores of uses.

    We are going to communicate with plants ourselves. Everyone prepares their two flowerpots with identical soil, seeds and water. Plant the seeds at the same depth and water them with the same amount of water. Choose one plant to love as a baby, to talk to and coo to, and consider the other plant as an intruder and unwanted. Take your plants home (or leave them all at the leader's house for more scientific control) and keep them in the same amount of sunlight. Give them an equal amount of water. It is important that all physical conditions be exactly the same for the two plants. Label with a mark the flower pot of the plant that you are going to love. Do not put the plants right next to each other, but a little way apart so that each will receive the vibes intended for it. Every day, and more often if you can, send good, loving vibes to the pot that is marked, and send mean, negative thoughts—bad vibes—to the other pot or ignore it except for watering. Watch the development over the next few weeks. When you are ready to do the exploration on p. 225 bring the plants back.

2. Into each of the three bottles of warmed whole milk, place the same amount of yoghurt culture. One bottle is labeled A, the other B and the last C. A is placed in a warm place and cursed by the group. Look at it as bad culture. C is placed alongside A as a control. Don't think about it. B is placed in the center of the group circle and the group does a meditation on universal love over it. First do the centering meditation focusing on the heart. Feel love and heart energy flowing from you to the B yoghurt culture, and to everyone in the room, reinforcing their love, and then again into the yoghurt culture in the middle of the circle. Send your love to the beneficial bacteria in the yoghurt and milk to give them support in their work. Then put B next to A and C. *The leader should taste all three bottles in twenty-four hours and bring them to the group for a taste the next time they meet. He should also share with the group what the first taste of each bottle was like after the twenty-four hours.*

3. Put the philodendron into the center of the room. Now we are going to become aware of the etheric energy that moves through our bodies and acts also like a carrier for our feelings and thoughts. Everyone sits in a circle. Hold your left hand palm up and place your right hand palm down above your left with about five inches of space in between. Now imagine you are drawing energy in through the top of your head, down your right arm and through your right hand into the left palm. Keep the flow going for a minute. Can you feel something in your left palm, or some sensation of heat or heaviness between the two palms? Slowly move the two palms back and forth, closer to each other then farther away. Can you feel air pressure or a subtler sensation? Now turn your two palms upside down, so that the left palm is now above the right palm by a distance of about five inches. Give all the energy back that you took in through the left hand. Imagine the energy flowing down your arm and out of the left palm into the right palm. Can you feel the reverse flow? You may feel a tickly, hot or dry or even cool sensation as a sign of etheric energy passing. This is the same subtle stuff that flows into and through the chakras, charging your whole body with energies and different kinds of awareness.

Learning to channel The Force (Life Force).

4. Now pair off with someone. One person is the receiver and one the
    sender. The receiver holds both palms in front of the sender, turned
    up to receive the energy. The sender holds both palms over the
    palms of the receiver and imagines energy flowing in through the top
    of her head down through the arms and hands and into the upturned
    palms of her partner. Keep the flow of energy going for a minute.
    Look and see if you can see strands of light or energy going between
    the sender's and receiver's hands. Children can usually detect a
    colored light—white, yellow or blue generally. It looks at first like
    greyish or whitish threads. Now switch roles and the receiver
    becomes the sender. Where did you feel the energy most strongly, as
    sender or as receiver?

5. The next step is to form small groups of three or four. One person at
    a time gets to be the receiver in the middle. The receiver sits in the
    center of the group, palms upturned, resting on the thighs or knees
    and eyes closed. Open yourself up like a bowl to receive the energy
    and the love that is about to be channeled into your heart center.
    Everyone else in the circle is a sender. Senders, raise your right
    hand up palm facing out towards the heart center of the receiver.
    Hold the palm within eight inches of the receiver's chest. Now
    imagine energy flowing in through the top of your head down into
    your heart and down your arm and hand into the heart of the person
    in the center. As the energy flows through you, add your love to it
    and send your love piggy-back onto the energy to give to the
    receiver. This takes both concentration and feeling. The waves of
    love and energy from several people at once coming into the
    receiver in the center will bring a feeling of light or warmth, maybe
    bliss. The love energy builds in the circle and everyone is uplifted in
    a warm, cozy, joyous atmosphere. If your right arm gets tired switch
    to your left arm, but re-imagine the energy flowing in through your
    crown center on the top of the head, through your heart, infused
    with love and flowing out of your arm and hand into the receiver.
    The more you keep your concentration flowing in a relaxed way, the
    more the love energy will build up so that it is almost an over-

powering force. Take turns so everyone has a chance to be receiver of the group love, the group heart.

6. How do you feel? At this point in families, it is a wonderful time to share some feelings that you may not have been able to share before. In the vibration of heart energy and love, many problems can be ironed out. Discuss how you feel.

7. Now take this build-up of love energy and a few people at a time huddle around the philodendron in the center of the room. Move your right palm back and forth across the broad leaf about three inches away. Then move it back and forth criss-crossing your previous line of motion, and then pump the hand gently up and down towards the leaf. See if you can feel an etheric response from the leaf. It might be a tingle, or a movement of the leaf. Try to distinguish any motion caused by air from the etheric feeling of response. You will see that some leaves will respond much more dynamically to some people, even when their motions are calmer, showing that air is not the agent of motion, but some other mechanism.

8. If there is a pet in the household bring it into the center of the group. Make a close circle around the pet. Channel energy with love from your heart through your hand to the pet, just as you did with each other. Does the pet respond? Do you notice anything unusual? We will do more with channeling in the game "Exploring Nature".

9. Discuss the possibilities for channeling and being aware of this love energy. Many people have been able to stop cuts from bleeding by channeling energy to the cut with the command to stop bleeding. Does the energy feel healing?

10. Journal writing.

WHAT DOES LOVE
MEAN TO ME?

PREPARATION:
blindfold

GOAL: Why do people often find it difficult to express love? Some people have been deprived of love and cannot express it to others until it is expressed to them first. But unless we give love we do not usually receive it flowing back. So we have a cycle of non-love by non-loving. Some people do not love themselves and cannot give affection until they have a better self-image. Some people feel that expressing affection and love is a sexual come-on and will lay them open to misunderstandings, so they hold back. And some people feel it is a sign of weakness to express love and affection.

To love and be loved is the main desire for every human. Children denied parental love and affection can be stunted in growth despite a good diet of food.

What do we mean by the word love? Exploring the meaning of love is our goal in this exercise.

EXPLORATION:

1. Which of the blocks to love mentioned in the above goal do you feel you have? Are there others? How do these affect your life? Take a moment to consider and then discuss together.

2. What do we mean by love? The Greeks had separate words for three kinds of love—Eros, Phileo and Agape.

Eros is the love expressed through passion and sexual union. It is a universal love, but demonstrated by sensual means. Usually in humans it is manifested in a possessive way. The words "erotic" and "eroticism" refer to the sexual appetite as a manifestation of this love.

Phileo is a brotherly type of love. It is a deep affection for another person, such as a parent or a child or a good friend. It can also be a fondness for an animal or a love of wisdom (*phil*osophy) or love of man (*phil*anthropy).

Agape is spiritual love. It is free of personal and emotional entanglements. It flows through all life. In human relationships it is expressed in respect, esteem, understanding and mutual cooperation. It is the love we direct to the universal one and which we feel as peace and well-being. It eventually becomes pure bliss and the love that passes all understanding.

3. An engaged, married or dating couple demonstrate *Eros* by kissing and embracing . . . Note how you feel. Why should expressing love and affection before others be embarrassing?

4. The group now demonstrates *Phileo* love. All rise and mingle and embrace in the European fashion. This is a hug with heads together, first touching one cheek and then the other. Some cultures have filial hugs where people give each other bear-hugs, encircling each other in their arms and back-slapping; some cultures rub noses; and some cultures do a variation of the European hug, and kiss each cheek in turn. Try them all with each other. Tune into the meaning of *Phileo* love and affection.

5. Physical expression of affection often relaxes everyone, loosens social barriers and makes for the warm, heart vibration to encircle everyone's aura. Now is the time we can open our hearts to greater trust.

6. TRUST AND AFFECTION
    a. Repeat the falling exercise from page 62 . After being passed around from person to person in the circle, with love and care, the whole group picks up the person, holding him in a horizontal position and lifting him up in the air above their heads. Be very attentive and careful. One person should support the neck and

the head. Everybody take a different part of the body and support it as you lift it in an offering to universal love. Move the person around the room a bit or gently rock him back and forth. You can chant the tone OOOOOMMMMM with love as you rock. Then bring the person back to the floor gradually and gently. After a moment, form the circle again and continue on so each person has a turn at giving himself or herself to the group.

b) Each person takes a turn standing in the center of the circle blindfolded. Group members come up one at a time and express love in any way that they feel. This can be a kind word, a caress, a hug, a kiss, channeling, or any other demonstration of affection and esteem they feel like sharing.

7. Now everyone joins in a circle, standing and linking arms. We are going to practice *Agape*. Close your eyes for a minute or two of relaxed, meditative silence, in which you share your love by sending out a feeling of thoughtfulness and the highest feeling of bliss or spiritual love you can experience and imagine. This feeling is sent out through the heart on a wave of love and directed to the universal source. It is sent with gratitude for each other and for being alive. If it feels right, the group can chant OOOOMMMM to express the love in sound, sending it to the One in the hearts of all.

8. When the circle of love comes to its natural close, write in your journal if you feel moved to do so. Sometimes there is no desire to express this love, but a contentment just to silently experience the vibrations.

THE POWER OF LOVE

Exploration

39

Green World

PREPARATION:
Everyone brings the plant pots that were started several weeks ago and which have been given love vibes or bad vibes.

GOAL: In this exercise we explore further the power of our consciousness to change our lives through love. By creating certain attitudes in our consciousness we make room for the power of love to work through us. In this way we understand how to link the limited intelligence and capabilities of the physical world with the limitless intelligence and "miracles" of the unconscious inner worlds that lie deep within us. Doubt is the only thing that blocks building the power of these attitudes. The attitudes do come naturally to us, but we must intensify them through love, and not allow the insecure feelings to come in and create doubt. These attitudes are:

—Recognize no power of evil, only of good

—Feel oneness in the universe, not separateness

—Understand that space and intelligence are related

—Reattune yourself constantly to the universal intelligence-space through meditation

—Know that mental visualization is the fabric of things to come

—Express love continuously as "the breath of life"

—Focus this love and intelligence consciously onto a vast global network of people who are making themselves sensitive to a world-wide evolutionary plan.

We all do these things to a degree; they are not new. What is new is the awareness that life returns success to us in exactly the same degree that we can do these things. This is the Power of Love. Newton's law "Every action has an equal and opposite reaction" applies to what we do with our consciousness and what happens to us in life.

EXPLORATION:

1. After doing the meditation and yoga, the group looks at the results of the plant experiment. We have done this exercise many times with groups of children in schools and found it extremely effective in showing the children the power of love and vibrations. Discuss.

2. What are the blocks that we experience in our daily lives to manifesting the attitudes in the above Goal? How can we train consciousness to feel and be these things more? What are your blocks to really loving and accepting yourself?

3. LEARNING TO USE THE POWER OF LOVE: The heart is often a key to the awakening of the other chakras. By loving ourselves we create a relaxed vibration of acceptance and peace which opens the doors to deeper perception and the oneness of life. The next time people you know are uptight or angry, especially if you see they are angry at you for some reason, center yourself with the command to stay calm, and, whether you feel right or wrong, accept yourself. Then send a wave of love, channeling it through your heart and *mentally* sending it on a stream of light to those who are upset. The more you can keep your calm center, sending wave after wave of love, the more you will be able to understand the situation and the more people will respond to your calm vibrations. The hot air will go out of their sails as they see you unruffled and in a different state of consciousness. Practice radiating the heart vibration you have learned to feel, throughout your daily life. Discuss the results you experience the next time you meet. Children both learn

and respond well to the heart. They are like a mirror. When you're in your heart and centered, they reflect the same feeling back. When you're disturbed, they project that back. We all do this with each other, but it is most noticeable in children.

4. Decide on a group experiment to be done during the next week on exercising this power of love. Take a moment and meditate on what you can do. Share ideas, and come to a group decision about putting these ideas into practice.

5. What do you really want to put your heart into? The heart center is the center of power because it is the center of life force. Whatever you put your heart fully into will have tremendous power to manifest. Without the heart energy your work is a lifeless form. Our drive to store up power and assert ourselves comes from this center, so to discuss what we really want to put our hearts into is very important. Take a minute to get in touch and then share what you want to do with your heart. If anyone has a feeling that someone is going in an unfruitful direction, give feedback and discuss.

6. Journal writing.

SOUND AND RESONANCE

PREPARATION:
a piano, harmonium or organ—a keyboard
instrument
blindfold

GOAL: Sound has a potent effect on our etheric body. If you hear loud, shrill tones, something in you shudders or shivers. If you hear a constant rumbling your body soon feels like it is vibrating to the movement, and when the sound dies down, you feel like an incredible quiet has taken you over. If you tune your mind and heart to certain tones, it has the effect of opening your heart center and stilling your mind so that your emotions and your consciousness change.

In this session we want to explore the effect of sound on our beings.

EXPLORATION:

1. Use your harmonium, organ, or piano. Sound the notes of the scale. Each person tries to identify which note feels like his own. Hum each note, identify with it. When you feel the note that strikes your heart, makes you feel in tune, then that is your resonant note. When everybody has a note, then go on to the next step. Remember which note of the scale is yours (A-G).

2. Do a five minute meditation, everybody softly humming their own note, melting into it, feeling it, becoming one with it. Alternate the humming or toning with a moment of silence to absorb the feeling, then tone the note again. Tone it loud enough so that you can really feel it vibrating you, but not so loud that you clash with others. Channel energy from your heart into the note. After another five minutes go on to Step 3 at a signal from the leader.

3. Echo Resonance: Everyone sits in a straight line. One person volunteers to be blindfolded. The others change positions so that the

blindfolded person does not know the order. He stands about eight feet away from the line. One person stands up to face the blindfolded participant. The person blindfolded then tones his own note. Someone may have to play it again on the keyboard to help him tune it. He tries to sense an echo from the person standing facing him. Then that person sits down without a word and the next person gets up. The subject does the same toning with each person, waiting for a feeling of an echo, until he feels a resonance with some person facing him. When he is finished someone else takes the blindfold and repeats the same steps. Repeat until everyone has a chance to find an echo mate. Then the people who feel echo resonance pair off for a one-to-one discussion. Sometimes there will be more than a pair. Group as best you can according to resonance. Discuss what mutual interests you have, and whether you do feel compatible. Are your auras or levels of consciousness the same? opposite? complementary?

4. *The leader reads the following:*

> Science has found that the earth is surrounded by highly energized particles called ions and protons, created by cosmic rays from the sun and other more intense stars. When these cosmic rays collide with the nucleus of atoms in our atmosphere, a charge is released. A rain of these cosmic wave-particles on our living tissue affects the bio-electricity of all our cells. The resulting electrical force field, created by this movement of electron particles, permeates our bodies, which in themselves are bundles of vibrations. The frequency of these vibrations is affected by our consciousness and also conditions our consciousness.

> Two people with similar states of consciousness are attracted to one another because they "resonate". They feel a rapport rather than a clash. Their electro-magnetic fields have similar rates or frequencies of vibration.

Discuss as a group your experiences with people who have just "felt" like you and people whose vibrations have felt very different from your own. Whose vibrations seem most similar within the group? What do you feel they have in common?

5. Journal writing.

OPENING THE HEART THROUGH SOUND

PREPARATION:
a harmonium or organ preferred,
otherwise a piano, guitar, or other
musical instrument

GOAL: Our goal is to go deeper into sound and vibration and to see how we can direct it to open the gates of our hearts.

At the University of the Trees we have a chanting choir, where we do not sing, but chant sounds to move and send vibrations. The feeling we put into the vibrating sound, which weaves around harmonious notes, is communicated very powerfully. More can be said in toning one chant from the heart, than in any words. It is a direct expression of being, channeled along the sound. Here we will learn the first few lessons of a new style of chanting originated by the author of these games, Christopher Hills.*

EXPLORATION:

1. Chanting Step #1: Sit fairly close together so you can hear one another. In this type of chanting, listening is the most important ingredient. It is the blend of the sounds that is important, not any one person's melody. Everyone begins together on one note, called a drone. As you chant the one note, listen for the vibrations, the textures, the mood, the feeling. Put your heart and love into the chanting. Someone plays the note on the musical instrument while everyone listens carefully to stay in tune as all chant. Chant the one drone OOOOOOOOOOMMMMMMMMMMM. Keep it up for a few minutes. Most people are scared to let the sound out, but it is important that you be able to hear yourself as well as the others, to know if you are in tune. Practice chanting loud, medium, soft, then

* A series of chanting instruction tapes by Christopher Hills is available from University of the Trees Press.

gradually get louder again until you are comfortable with the sound and the ranges. Come to a gradual close, and then in the silence that follows, meditate and listen to the deep stillness. Let it come over your entire being.

2. Chanting Step #2: In this step we do the same thing as in Step #1, but we form our mouth in a certain way. We begin by chanting AAAAAAAHHHHHH sound, then as we are chanting we move just our lips into a shape of an O. We are still chanting AAAAAAAHHHHH in the back of the throat, but the lips make it into an O. AAAAHHHHHOOOOO. This makes the sound vibrate with more depth. It also helps to create high-pitched overtones and ringing sounds, called *srutis* in Sanskrit. These are unmade sounds, meaning they are not made by your voice, but by the interaction of two different sounds to form a third sound on its own. These "unmade" sounds soak up a lot of energy and you can feel them penetrate into your consciousness. The more you put your heart into the sound you chant, the more uplifting an effect it will have on you. Now try to hear and feel the *srutis* ringing as you chant again. The leader should motion when he wants the group to be louder and when he wants it to be softer.

3. Chanting Step #3: In this third step we learn to move the sound with sound and really experience the fact that sound is moving energy. Play one note. If you have a harmonium this effect is more pronounced. One person tones the same note that is being played. Now as you chant AAAAAAAHHHHHHHHOOOOOOOOO go slightly, very slightly, sharp (slightly higher)... Notice the effect on the sound. Then go back to the note, and in a bit go very slightly flat (slightly lower)... You can feel the sound move as the two vibrations interact—yours and the instrument's. In chanting if you deliberately go *slightly* flat or sharp at certain times, it creates a rich effect and many new tones that give texture to the chant. This time, everyone together chants the drone note as before. This time move around the note, going up and down, but always listen and always come back to the drone note as home base before moving around the

note some more. If you listen carefully to the others first, you will know the notes to choose and will not clash or be out of tune. Venture slowly so that you feel you are being led or moved into the notes, rather than trying to sing them. You can form chords and harmonies with each other that harmonize with the constant drone note that you will be playing all the time on the instrument. Practice this step, putting your heart and love into the sound and sending it to the entire group—each other—and to the One Life. If you have a tape recorder, tape your sounds so you can hear the results of what you do. Give each other feedback at the end of the chant and try to make improvements for the next chant. Keep the chanting session up until everyone feels relaxed, electrified and open.

4. Do not expect to be perfect chanters the first time. Feel your way into it and let it be a very moving, exciting and close group experience. It is a way to love and share on many levels. But remember you have to listen and concentrate as you chant.

5. Journal writing.

THE TRANSMUTATION OF ENERGY– LIFE ENERGY TO LIGHT ENERGY

Exploration

42

Green World

GOAL: Mankind stands in his own light and wonders why it is dark. How can we become more conscious of the intelligence that fills all space? When we sit in quiet meditation we attune ourselves to this intelligence. Every time we spend a few minutes in quiet attunement with the cosmos, we help to undo the restricting attitude of separation and permit nature to flow more easily through us. As we become more aware, we tune into the life energies and experience them as light.

PREPARATION:
a photographic darkroom

Someone who knows about photography should lead.

a leaf, or several freshly picked leaves
photographic film
photosensitive paper
a Polaroid camera and film

Psychiatrists and physicists studied Ted Serios for many years because he was able to impress Polaroid films with images from his own mind. He could project an image like a Gothic cathedral onto film with fine detail. Many people— certainly one or more in the group—can affect photosensitive materials with their life force and project an image into light. We are going to exercise our ability to do this type of channeling in this awareness game.

EXPLORATION:

1. Someone who has a good strong voice leads this step. Stand and face him with your arms stretched forward and palms out and facing away from the body. He tones the AAHHOOMMMMM in a long drawn out note until everyone can feel the tingling of the sound vibrations in the palms as the skin picks up the signals.

233

2. Now he keeps toning, but this time he adds the visualizing of life force passing through his fingers too. He holds out his palms and channels energy into the palms of the receivers as well as sound. He imagines the energy flowing in through the top of his head, down through his arms and out his hands and into the palms of the receivers. This visualization is necessary to activate the life energy. Through visualizing we make it tangible. Everyone should feel a tingling sensation or some indication that there is energy being transferred. Others may take turns sending.

3. To increase the electricity, form a circle and hold hands, linking all together like batteries. This multiplies the voltage of this life energy. Send the energy to the person who stands on your right so that everybody is channeling energy counterclockwise to the right. Close your eyes and visualize the life force coming in the top of your head down into your heart and through your right arm and hand into the left hand of the person on your right. You are pumping energy from the cosmos through your body into the person on your right. You can chant the AAHHHOOOMM as you do this to add force to your channeling. You should be able to notice a feeling of motion through you from left to right, as you receive through your left hand and send it all out through your right hand. (long pause) . . . Now the leader directs everyone to switch the flow to the left, clockwise. Can you feel the reverse flow?

4. Choose one person to go into the center of the circle. That person will turn slowly, first one way then the other, inside the circle while the others are continuing to send their energy in a clockwise motion around the circle. The person in the middle sees if he or she can feel anything. Now all extend their arms inward toward the person in the center. "Think energy" flowing from you and from the group to that person. "See" white threads passing from yourself to the person.

5. Move closer so your hands touch the arms of the person in the center. Keep visualizing and sending the life force. After a bit move the hands to a position where the person can feel the energy applied a few inches from the back of his neck. Then move to each of the

different chakras—over the top of his head, his forehead, the heart area (both in front of the chest and in back), his solar plexus, his spleen center (abdomen and lower back), and by the coccyx—the center at the base of the spine. Where is the feeling the strongest? The energy is directed over the chakras of each member of the group in turn. Everyone discovers where they feel the most intense feeling. Which of your chakras is most sensitive?

PHOTOGRAPHIC EXPERIMENT

a) For this experiment you will need a dark room and someone who knows a bit about photography. Take the leaf and photographic film and place them on a table with the photographic film on top of the leaf. One person holds his hand over the emulsion negative and maintains an attitude of complete willingness to project his own vital magnetism or energy to impregnate the film. There can be no doubts of "will this work?" You have to forget all your reservations for this to work. (If you first rotate the leaf freely on a pin and find out where it tends to stop, the leaf chooses its own position in relation to due north. This has been found to enhance the results by magnetic effect as the leaf finds its critical rotation. Then stick it down with clear tape in this position.)

When you finish your energy projection, you (the projector) must develop the film yourself by switching on a red light in a few seconds. Then take it out of the developer as soon as you see the image come up. Stop it by placing it in the fixing bath.

b) Everybody take a turn. You can use photosensitive paper as well as film or a photographic plate. We use a leaf because it is a growing thing and has its own life energy which can be activated by human life force to make a more powerful impression.

c) After everyone has had a turn, bring out the Polaroid camera and film. Someone extend a finger toward the camera lens and look intently at it while imagining life force flowing into the finger, gathering into all the fingertips and then projecting into the film behind the lens. (If this can be done in the dark room, the assistance of someone to "click" the camera when signaled can be helpful. However, do not expose the film this way under any other conditions.) Proceed with the camera's developing operation and check results. Everyone else take a turn.

6. Discuss.

7. Journal writing.

The Force (Life Force) can be felt.

THE TRANSMUTATION OF ENERGY–LIGHT ENERGY TO LIFE ENERGY

Exploration

43

Green World

PREPARATION:
waxed paper straw
needle
two corks with flat ends
wool, preferably cashmere
a piece of black cloth or a black board
a cardtable
a smooth tablecloth (preferably white)
six dice
a cardboard box or container from which to throw the dice

GOAL: Our goal is to discover more about the nature of light. How are light and love related? While physicists probe the nature of light, spiritual teachers and those committed to growth in awareness concentrate on a "single eye" to harness light's energies in a metaphysical way. What kind of light is cosmic light that we experience within ourselves? Christopher Hills' book *Nuclear Evolution* discusses the tremendous role of light in the awareness of man. Many people witness light in mystical experiences, and a 1977 survey indicated that over fifty percent of Americans admitted having had a mystical experience. "If Thine eye be single, thy whole body shall be filled with light," is a statement by Jesus who experienced light in great intensity.

Meditation and these awareness games help us to experience the great transforming power of this light. Only through direct experience do we know this light is real. When Franklin Roosevelt declared, "We have nothing to fear except fear itself", he was referring to the power of light to overcome all fear. If we dwell on darkness, we attract that; if we dwell on light, we attract the light which becomes a force of security, of good in our lives. When our eye is truly single, then there is only light.

EXPLORATION:

1. Take a waxed paper straw and pass a needle through its exact middle. Press the other end of the needle into a flat cork and set it down on a level surface. Check to make sure the straw rotates at the slightest touch. Now each person in turn places his fingers so that they are nearly touching one end of the straw. It will move right or left. The vigor of the motion is a measure of what is often called electrostatic force that builds up in the body. Yogis have found that this force can be controlled by the mind and built up by the mind at will.

2. Using another cork, place the fingertips of both hands on either side of it, nearly touching it. Wait until you feel a distinct tingling sensation in the ends of the fingers. This may eventually extend to the elbows or to the shoulders. This is a manifestation of life force. You can "will" it into the fingertips and you can eventually see it.

3. Place your fingertips a short distance apart in front of the black cloth or board. Now "will" the force to enter your fingertips. When a tingling is felt, gradually draw the fingers apart. You may see a whiteness or white "stuff" between them. This is often called the *arc of threads*. Once you have seen it, you can more easily build it up and use it.

4. Now we want to build up our use of this light to intensify our life force. In turn, each person holds the fingertips of both hands a short distance (a fraction of an inch) from the cork. Concentrate on willing the life force into your fingertips. Now, see the *arc of threads* in your imagination by visualizing the white "stuff" passing from the fingers and supporting the cork. Hold this image for a few moments before moving. Then slowly raise the fingers and see if the cork is willing to follow your fingers upward. If it does, you have succeeded in transmuting the light energy into a life force. For some people the cork feels like it wants to go the opposite way and is repelled. They feel a definite repelling sensation. If so, the energy is responding differently. It is responding but is not yet controlled.

5. Someone who has *not* had much success with the above exercises takes a seat in the center of the group. Everyone relaxes deeply. The leader holds a two-minute meditation in which everyone is to visualize a brilliant light surrounding the head and body of the one in the center. At the end of this, the person approaches the straw and tries to move it again. The results will probably be better. Others take their turn in the "light seat." Are the results at straw-moving improved? Try the "light seat" again, this time with the group holding hands in the meditation to build up the energy. Emotional involvement, concentration and a feeling of oneness with all things are the key attitudes that help make moving light successful. We all need to practice them.

6. Working with the life force and light in this way, you will eventually reach a point of saturation where you begin to feel psychically tired, that is, your attunement has peaked and is now on a downward cycle. It's best to stop at this point and recharge yourself with a few yoga or recharging exercises, a breath of fresh air, or for the most effect, turn on the tap water and hold your hands to either side of the stream. Feel your hands absorb the energy and the charge will flow up your arms until you feel refreshed. Then you can wash your hands. Be sure to let them drip dry. Do not towel dry them.

7. Take a cloth piece that you know holds a great deal of static electricity and rub your hand over it. (Each person will have to do this in turn unless there is plenty of material.) Now, using one of the hairs off your head as a crude electrical measuring device like a galvanometer, hold the hair closer and closer to the hand you have rubbed until you notice it bend towards your hand. Note the distance away when this first occurs. Now by rubbing your hand even faster for an increased number of times you will increase the charge and make the hair spring up more quickly when the charge is detected. Record the distance for say 25 rubs.

8. Now discharge your hand by putting it on the floor or on some metal ground and measure the discharged distance of the hair. Now rub your hand again 25 times on the material and place a charge on it.

Look at your hand and in your mind see it washed clean of this static charge by your psychic electricity, which you draw from the cosmos through your pores and by concentrating it in your breath and mind as you breathe. Now *will* the static charge to leave your hand. Measure the effect of your mental command with the hair. Either you must bring the hair closer for an effect or there is none at all, which proves you have removed the static electricity charge with your cosmic vital force. You can also use the same method and your *will* power to make it stay longer and get stronger and stronger.

9. WINNING STREAKS: Everyone has had beginner's luck, or a winning streak, when they just feel in tune for a bit and things go right. We are going to see if we can discover the secret of this good fortune. Someone who feels "lucky" is the first volunteer. You need to have a sense of sureness and confidence for this to work. Set up the cardtable, cover it with the smooth tablecloth, and push the table into a corner. Place the six dice in a small cardboard container. Avoid metal. The thrower of the dice now calls out a number from one to six. Visualize the number and *know* your life force is at work on the dice, transferring the light you have visualized into action. Shake the container and bounce the dice off the corner walls. One correct dice out of the six is to be expected from the law of averages. Two or more correct dice shows that you are above average if you repeat this over a period of tries. The more throws with the right answer, the higher your average is and the more likely it is that you are directing the light. If you repeat the roll four times, changing the number you call out each time, a likely average total is four, for the four rolls. If you have seven correct numbers, the odds are 100 to 1 against its happening. Sometimes this is called PK or psychokinesis, the ability to move objects with your mind. Although these games are not meant to encourage competition, sometimes by offering a prize the emotional voltage is increased and results are higher. Experiment.

10. Discuss why your heart has to be in the exercise in order to move light.

11. Journal writing.

HEALING POWER

Exploration

44

Green World

PREPARATION:
a Positive Green Pendulum (available from the publishers)
a crystal —quartz, or other (available at most jewelers, or an inexpensive one available from the publisher)
a glass of water

GOAL: The life force within us is both universal and unique. Although it has, through us, invented many instruments to measure energy, it still cannot be measured itself. It is somewhat like an eye not being able to see itself. Though invisible it is nevertheless a very real force.

Until recent years, the secrets of the life force for healing were usually hidden by medicine men, tribal chiefs, kahunas, gurus, and the church in the western world.

Spiritual healing can occur through our own awareness, but we must expand our awareness to see how we interfere with nature. The life force of positive green is nature's constant renewing, regenerating and rejuvenating energy. In this session we will discover how we misuse and how we can use this life force to heal ourselves and to prevent dis-ease.

EXPLORATION:

1. Our natural state is a healthy one. Disease enters us when we lower our resistance to bacteria—virus, germs or "bugs". We attract these to us in some way. Worry can induce gastric acids, tension can burden our vital organs and negative thoughts can undermine our emotions, body chemistry and cell growth. All of these inharmonies create vulnerability for foreign organisms to enter. The real key to spiritual healing is to change our resentments, frustrations, jealousies, envy and hatred which work havoc on our bodies. We need to substitute patience and confidence for anxiety and hold the picture of ourself in good health, brimming with vitality.

Discuss typical psychosomatic diseases and their probable causes; use examples from your own personal life and from the lives of others you know. Discuss your own health problems freely, without fear of any criticism.

2. Often people use expressions such as:"He gives me a pain in the neck," or "Oh, my aching back," "That galls me," "I haven't got the heart to," "I can't stomach her." How do these expressions relate to illness or create illness through suggestion? Discuss.

3. A game of Doctor is played. Half the group are patients and half doctors. One patient and one doctor pair off. The patient tells the doctor his troubles—health, family, business, etc. This is a serious confidential chat. The "doctor" listens but offers no remedies. This is just "active listening", allowing the patient to get his feelings off his chest. Then the doctors and patients reverse roles, but with different partners. No one gives anyone any advice, but out of the experience you should have given yourself some advice, just through the process of opening up and sharing at one time and having to be a receptive listener at the other. Share what insights you had into your own problems through opening up.

4. Although there are many stories of faith healing, laying on of hands, psychic surgery, etc., where healing power is channeled to another, in this exercise we want to learn how to direct the life force for healing power to heal ourselves. There are many techniques for psychic healing of others, but to call it healing is, at the moment, against the law. If you have a Positive Green Pendulum you can easily direct life force.

EXERCISE WITH POSITIVE GREEN PENDULUM: Everyone sits in meditation, palms upturned resting on the thighs, ready to receive life force as we did in the channeling exercises. The person with the pendulum follows instructions for tuning the pendulum that comes with it then rotates it over his left hand. Notice the direction it rotates in. Consciously rotate it to the right. When you begin to feel a tingle in your palm from the interaction of your nerves with

The positive green pendulum can also be felt by others as it swings over your hand. Water diviners can feel a sensation over water. Many animals and insects are naturally sensitive to bio-energetic radiations from objects, earthquakes, flowers, weather, etc.

the life force in resonance with the positive green energy, then mentally imagine everyone else feeling this same life force and the same feeling in the palms of their hands. Most people will be able to feel a tickling or even the circling motion in their left palms. Some will feel it more strongly in their right palms.

The person with the pendulum then walks to each person in turn holding the pendulum over the left palm. Note in which direction the pendulum spontaneously rotates. If it rotates counterclockwise over anyone, it means that there is negative energy present blocking the life force. This can often be a sign of illness. Hold in your mind the thought that the negative energy is being extracted and that it is flowing into a glass of water. The fingers of the pendulum operator's left hand should be immersed in the water (or the hand that is not holding the pendulum). At some point the negative rotation should stop. This is the time to dump the glass of water and flush it away along with all the negative vibrations dumped into it. This water has been used as a psychic dumping place so that the negative energy will not be absorbed into the operator's system as the pendulum rotates.

Then it is time to rotate the pendulum clockwise to charge the person up with positive life force. Localized points of tension in the body are also energy blocks. They will also cause negative or counterclockwise rotation in the pendulum that is held over them.

If the group wishes to devote the time, several people can practice being operators of the Positive Green Pendulum.

5. Place a lighted candle on the floor in the center of the group. The group sits in a circle. The leader reads the following for directing consciousness—light into healthy life force.

> I fix my eyes on the candle. I concentrate on the moving flame. As I watch it, my eyelids become heavier. I begin to feel that my eyes must close. I visualize them closing. Now it is almost impossible to keep them open. I let them close gently. Now I am able to relax fully. I feel the muscles relaxing in my toes, my ankles, my legs, thighs, my buttocks, my back, my stomach, my shoulders, my arms, my neck and my face. I note that I am breathing rhythmically. Every time I exhale I go deeper and deeper. I am letting go. I am now in a very deep state of blissful relaxation, yet with every breath I take I go deeper and deeper. Deeper and deeper and deeper and deeper. I now visualize myself. I see myself entirely free of health problems. There is absolutely no sign of any health problem I may have had recently. I see myself in radiant health. I now end my relaxation knowing this image to be activated into life force. I will now feel full of energy and wide awake. One, two, three! Now, continue to hold the single image of yourself as completely healthy for a full thirty seconds. You see yourself going about your usual activities in tip-top health. Know that holding this image in your mind makes it come to pass. If you have good health now, it will reinforce your good health. You feel joy and confidence.

6. Journal writing.

EXPLORING NATURE

GOAL: Attunement with nature is the greatest awareness exercise. To understand miracles we must understand nature, because nature is the greatest miracle. By being preoccupied with ourselves we are cut off from the mainstream of energy and creative flow of life from nature. We think we are important and spend most of the time thinking of our needs and our little self. But man is relatively insignificant in the pulsating life on earth and even smaller in relation to the universe. Yet the key to the universe is in each one of us and by tuning to nature we can contact the enormous undiscovered power waiting to be tapped by ingenuity and imagination.

In this exploration each person will make his own peace with nature. Each will listen and see and feel the extension of himself that envelops the trees and the ground and the sky and that includes the stars.

PREPARATION:
A potluck picnic lunch or everyone brings their own picnic, whichever the group prefers. The leader organizes the picnic aspect well ahead and chooses the day and time, planning an alternative time if the weather does not permit, and having an alternative session ready if the weather continues to prevent an outing.

a rock
a plant, freshly picked or cut
a small animal, preferably a snail, or something of similar size that won't escape.

EXPLORATION:
1. This outing includes a picnic. The yoga postures, meditation and awareness activities all take place outdoors. Find a clearing in the sun where you can exercise and meditate. The woods with a stream, pond or ocean nearby are ideal places. Try to locate a place where you will have privacy and not be disturbed by loud noises and other conversations.

2. Everyone sits quietly together, listening to the silence and to the sounds of nature. Notice the sights, the scents, touch the ground, the tree bark, the plant leaves, note the different textures.

Snails can sense our Life Force with their antennae.

The group is seated in a circle. The leader places a large rock in the center of the circle. Everyone meditates on the rock in the following way: After doing the centering meditation where all your energies are concentrated, expand them into the rock, and imagine your energy body sitting inside the rock. You become one with the rock, feeling its rockness from inside-out. What does rockness feel like? What is it like to be a rock? Hard? Old? Cool? Vibrating? The rock is part of the mineral kingdom of nature. Tune in and speak a few words spontaneously when you are ready about what you feel, calling out just the word, no long sentences or discussion. Remember you are in the meditative state, but with your eyes open.

3. When everyone has had a turn and the group vibration has a definite feeling of rockness, the leader removes the rock from the center of the circle and places a plant or flower inside instead. The plant should be green and recently picked so the leaves are fresh. Everyone centers and projects their energies into the plant to become one with it, feeling plantness. What is it like to be a member of the plant kingdom? As before, meditate on the plant, and when ready call out in the silence your feelings as a plant.

4. When the group feeling is plantness, then the leader removes the plant and puts the snail or other living creature in the center of the circle. This meditation is now on the animal kingdom. Center and then meditate on becoming one with the animal in the center. What do you feel like? Again call out the feelings you have from identifying with the creature in the center. Often small creatures will respond to the energies flowing in to them. Snails will suddenly come out of their shells and put out their antennae trying to detect the source of the stimulating energy. Now hold out your right hand and channel energy to the animal. Remember to stay concentrated. Imagine and send the light energy through your body and out your arm and hand into the creature. Notice if there is any response.

5. Contemplate for a few minutes, in the silence, the different natures of beingness of these different kingdoms in nature.

6. Discuss only if you feel moved to do so.

7. Pair off and each pair walk in a different direction. Agree to return in twenty minutes. Walk in *silence*, communicating nonverbally to each other when a desire to share is felt. Do not give in to the temptation to talk. Touch leaves and trees, stop to feel running water, look for patterns in stones and reflected light, examine a flower to know it inwardly. In all these explorations, try to feel the differences in beingness in what you touch or examine. As in the meditations on the kingdoms, try to feel yourself as whatever you touch or see, feeling yourself from the inside-out in the forms of nature. Experience the joy of attunement with it all.

8. When everyone returns share your experiences verbally, describing as best you can what you have seen and felt. If you feel words are inadequate you might be moved to write or draw in your journals. Others who can share in words should feel free to express themselves.

9. When everyone has finished expressing themselves in some way, all the group gathers together in the circle, standing and linking arms. The leader conducts a final three minute silent meditation in which the entire group combines its consciousness to dwell on all of man and womankind as a part of nature. Visualize the group as a symbol of man's search for a way toward his own natural evolution. In the end send out a feeling of love for the universe and chant the AAAAHHHHOOOOOMMMMM three times as you send out this love. Feel your AAAAAHHHHHOOOOOMMMMM sound as the universal note that lives in all the universal creation. The note of nature. Feel love and acceptance for everyone and everything, including yourself.

10. Everyone enjoys their picnic out in the woods or in the natural setting. Try to keep the conversation focused on nature and the activity around you as you eat.

BLUE WORLD
THE MENTAL/MEMORY LEVEL

Child meditating to go beyond thoughts.

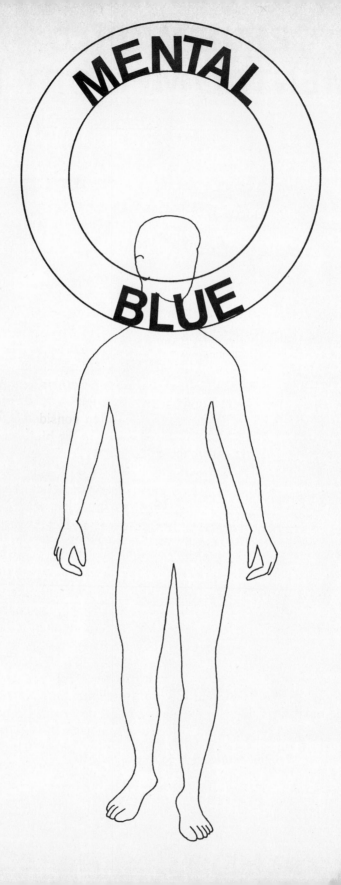

BLUE
V

The Blue level is the mental world. It is where we store all our memories of everything we have experienced on any of the other levels. Like a fantastic computer, the blue level works for us to process impressions into thoughts, ideas, concepts, and ways of perceiving. Most of our feelings are triggered by thoughts we hold about others and about life in general. Change our thoughts (our perspective) and the feelings automatically change with them. So this world is often considered the world of emotions, but in a different way than the heart. In the blue, all feelings are attached to some idea that's in the mind, while in the green, feelings of insecurity can be based on instinctual reactions and impressions coming from many other levels besides just our ideas about how life should be. The shoulds, oughts, ideals or authorities we hold dear all are built in this blue world. People with strongly blue auras usually take a long time to process incoming information since they have to think it through and consider how it fits with their presently held beliefs. In contrast, people on the yellow, orange and red levels, react or think more quickly because they are orientated to change and motion. The blue level person changes slowly, and likes to hold on to traditions and beliefs for mental stability. Many people who are strongly blue level are conservative in their actions and philosophies.

Love of authority, of peace, of family and of ideas, are strong traits of this world. The highest devotion to God, to religion, or to a philosophy, as well as the most rigid dogma, are qualities—positive and negative—of this level of consciousness. Both abhorrence of war with the urge for peace at any price, and the fanatic fighting for a cause which may mean great conflict (such as the crusades) are blue-level attitudes.

In the awareness explorations of this level of consciousness we are going to explore the memory as a great storehouse, and learn how to widen our capacity to remember what is stored. We also will explore how ideas form and how our attitudes get crystallized and condition our thinking, feeling and action. These mental grooves often become ruts which prevent our mind from expanding. Only by reexamining cherished beliefs can we tell whether they are based on truth or on mental bias.

Another way of understanding our mental level is to say that mind cannot understand mind, just like water cannot grasp water. To really transcend the mind and to go beyond its tricks we need to get beyond this blue level of concepts, in which most of us are trapped, into the sixth world of intuition or direct perception. From there, we can see the workings of the mind and the universe. We see how we build different perceptions into concepts which then become our version of reality. But is this pure reality? Or is it just the synthesis of our various experiences which may be a different combination and therefore a different program from our neighbor's? And whose truth is more true? It's like looking at the old Arab-Israeli dispute and asking whose truth is greater? When we look at the long history of tradition on both sides and the emotional beliefs that have been built over those years, we get an insight into the magnitude of the problem of mind conditioning and de-conditioning.

The mind is largely subconscious or unconscious, so to know it better we have to find a way to tap into the subconscious parts of ourselves and bring them to conscious awareness. Methods for widening our conscious mind, and then reprogramming what feels self-limiting, are what we will be exploring on this next journey.

YOGA POSTURES V

The Blue level of consciousness draws in its energy from the chakra or center near the throat. The thyroid gland is also influenced by this center, and the postures that we do to get in touch with the Blue level are neck related. The back of the neck and the base of the brain are very sensitive areas in the body. This primitive brain area is called the medulla oblongata and is the first or original brain growth in evolution. It has been called "the mouth of God" because it is a very sensitive opening for cosmic energies which put our consciousness in touch with what is called the akasha. From this center we draw mind power and this power, coupled with our focussed will, can transform, electrify, and reprogram our physical body. In the medulla are the unconscious controls to the autonomic nervous system. When we can regulate the heartbeat, breath and blood flow at will, as well as other body processes, we can demonstrate mastery of mind over body. That is the potential of this center of consciousness.

NECK POSTURES

1.   NECK ROLL— Begin by letting your head hang forward limply. Roll your chin slowly on your neck to the right and all the way around in a circle. Repeat five times. Then do the same thing only moving the chin to the left and proceeding back around the circle five times. As you do this relax your neck, and put your consciousness on the energies within the neck area, not on the moving muscles.

2. NECK DROP — With the first three fingers of both hands, rub the medulla area at the back of the neck, placing your fingers on either side of the thick spinal cord. You can feel the spinal cord if you drop your chin to your chest. When the fingers are in position, massage the areas by circling your right hand fingers in a right circle, and your left hand fingers around in a left circle. Relax and feel the soothing, peaceful easing of tensions that build up in that area. Many headaches actually begin at the back of the neck and can be relieved by massaging in this way. The forehead energies are directly connected to the medulla area. Do the rotating massage five times, then reverse directions so that your left fingers circle clockwise and your right fingers circle counterclockwise for five times. Then inhale and tense the neck as you stretch it back so your head is leaning against your back, keep the neck tensed. Count to three then exhale and let the chin fall loosely forward onto the neck with a drop. Repeat five times. Put consciousness into the neck and back of neck area.

3.   SHOULDERSTAND*– Lie down in the corpse pose, arms down at the sides, legs straight. Keep centered. Inhale and raise your feet and legs 90° in the air. Put your hands on the buttocks and boost them up in the air as you exhale. Walk hands up the spine so that only your neck and as little as possible of the shoulders are on the ground. Straighten your back and legs. Bring your elbows close together. Feel pressure on the neck. Put your mind in the back of the neck and relax. Hold for one minute to start, then increase the length you can hold still comfortably. Come down slowly. Relax for a moment lying down.

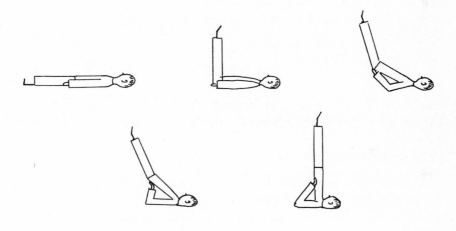

PRACTICE THESE POSTURES BEFORE THE MEDITATION AND THE AWARENESS GAMES IN THE BLUE LEVEL

*People with health problems, especially weaknesses in the back or neck, and pregnant women or women in their menstrual period should not attempt this or any other inverted posture.

MEDITATION FOR ENTERING THE COSMIC MEMORY BANK

The Cosmic Memory Bank is the Akashic Record (which we have access to for memories any time we plug into it.) You have probably heard the saying that everything we have ever done—every thought, action, feeling—is recorded in some Cosmic record book. Actually the record book is consciousness. All thoughts, feelings and actions are psychic imprints and they are printed in consciousness. The Cosmic Blue level is where we gain access to all the past, including past incarnations. Many people believe they have to go to someone who is psychic to read the *akasha*, but so often so-called psychics give them erroneous information, or tell several people they were the same person in a past life. Whether or not you believe in past lives, you can contact the storehouse of your present life and the lives of people who have lived and died before you. If you are open and continue to practice this meditation you will discover for yourself the truth about whether there are past lives or not.

The leader reads:

Relax yourself totally by sitting or lying down on your back in a comfortable position. Tense and relax each of your body parts one at a time from the toes to the top of the head. Do this slowly. Relax each body part completely by putting your mind into it fully, into the bones, blood, nerves, tissues, and imagining them all dissolving and disappearing into light energy so you can no longer feel them. . . (long pause) . . . When your body is relaxed, focus your attention on the point between the eyebrows inside the head, behind the forehead. . . Center your will there, but don't strain the eyes. Relax the emotions and relax the mind. . . Let your mind wander now over the past years of your life, going backwards from now to the time you were a very young child. Let the highlights and the lowlights flow through as you count the years backwards one by one. . . Stay alert. . . (long pause, several minutes) . . . Now see yourself as a very young child, let the impressions flow through your open mind. Don't think! Just let the thoughts, feelings and

256

images flow. Keep traveling backwards until you find yourself again in the womb, and feel how it is to be in the womb . . . go back farther and farther, before the womb . . . let your mind roam and note any impressions, flashes, images, thoughts you experience . . . (long pause) . . . stay in this akashic reverie for awhile . . . the flashes that come mean something to you now, in this life. Whatever past image or past life memory has come to you, you have attracted that particular memory to you now based on your present state of mind. Whatever you have ever been (positive or negative it does not matter) is all synthesized together to make *you* NOW! . . . (long pause) . . . When you are ready to come out, slowly bring your awareness back into your body, tense your body, then let it go . . .Open your eyes and find your journal and a pen to immediately jot down all the impressions you can remember, however fleeting or unrelated they seem to be. Do not edit them. Just write. When you are through writing then consider what your entire experience has been. Share with each other.[*]

[*] "Akashic Record Meditation" by Christopher Hills, taken from *Direct Perception* to be published by University of the Trees Press.

DISCOVERING HOW
YOUR MIND WORKS

Exploration
46
Blue World

PREPARATION:
a steaming cup of coffee
a dictionary
a Bible

GOAL: Mind is where you store your experiences and impressions and then sort them out into meaningful ideas. Since all objects and people are experienced in your mind, you need to discover how mind does this. By identifying yourself with an object or a person more completely you get out of yourself and into the other thing or other body. This helps you to let go of your usual mind tracks so that you can see them. You can't see your mind patterns while you're in them. It's like looking into a mirror–wherever you move, the mirror person moves with you, you can't get away from it. So in this exercise we work together to discover how mind works. We also strengthen the mind's abilities to penetrate the worlds of others and encompass more of reality.

EXPLORATION:

1. A cup of steaming black coffee is placed on a small table or on the floor in the center of the group circle. Each person in turn tells how he feels about that cup of coffee, expressing *one* idea only. That idea might be different for each person. There are all sorts of possible reactions to a simple cup of coffee.

2. It can be very enlightening to find out how the internal consciousness of other people identifies with such a simple object. When everyone has expressed their thoughts, look for what similarities there are among personalities of those who expressed similar thoughts. If someone's thought was unique, did it provide any insight into the personality or internal consciousness of that particular person?

258

3. What do people really mean when they say, "Would you like to have a cup of coffee? Discuss. What do you mean when you say that to someone (or tea, or other beverage, depending on your preference)? Discuss.

4. Remove the coffee cup and place a dictionary in the center of the group circle. How does each person identify with that dictionary? What kind of ideas, reactions or feelings does it evoke? Go around the room and express you minds in turn, speaking whatever thoughts come.

5. When everyone has spoken, discuss the responses. For some the dictionary is holy, enshrining the thoughts of people throughout history who have coined words in order to describe some human experience. For some it is an authority to be respected as the last word in a game of Scrabble, or in any argument on the meanings of words. For some it is a storehouse of knowledge and ideas. See if you can relate people's responses to their personalities or even to their dominant level of consciousness. Discuss.

6. Discuss the merits of books in general. What are your attitudes toward books? Do they take up where conversation ends? In Ecclesiastes it is stated that knowledge which can be put in books is vanity. Some people, though, live their lives by the book. Jesus never wrote a book, yet millions have been influenced by books written about him. Can you relate your feelings about books to your level of consciousness?

7. The dictionary is removed and a Bible is placed in the center of the group. Each person reacts and expresses his or her thoughts on the object.

8. How did the reactions to this object compare with those to the coffee? Were they more heated? Did people penetrate more deeply into this object? Did you gain greater insight into the worlds of the participants talking about the Bible than with the coffee or dictionary? Discuss.

9. Now one person volunteers to become the center of attention. He or

she sits in the middle of the room on the floor or in a chair. Remember how the three previous objects in the center gave you different feelings, each a whole different computer program for your mind. Now, put yourself inside the being of the person before you. See if you can identify so completely with him or her that you feel your feelings, thoughts and body merging. The volunteer needs to relax and receive all the vibrations of the different minds around with eyes closed. Watch to see if anyone is defensive (maybe the arms are folded or legs crossed protectively). Help each other to trust and relax in the love that is present.

For those who may be having difficulty forgetting the mind and identifying with the person in the center, do the centering meditation again for a moment . . . After centering, the mind can expand and dissolve its bounds to become one with what it expands into in a positive way. Allow the person's being and mind to merge into your receptive awareness. Share your experiences afterwards.

10. Repeat the exercise with several volunteers. Feel the different, unique vibrations of each one. If you still have trouble receiving them and becoming one, you may want to do the channeling exercise of the green, heart world, to open the flow of love. The greater the love and trust and self-forgetting, the greater your ability to open your mind to include the worlds of others, remaining in your peaceful center. Sometimes people identify with others' feelings in sympathy and get dragged down by their emotions and problems. This is negative identification and means you are not centered in your real being. Egoless people are saintly because they can feel the cares, woes and joys of others without losing their inner contact with truth, with their own spiritual Self. By practicing this identification exercise we expand the mind beyond its usual judgements and reactions, to include others and still feel centered in the oneness, our Self!

11. Discuss your ability to empathize and be one with others, versus getting pulled off center by sympathizing too much on one hand or else shutting yourself off from others in self-protection on the other hand.

12. Journal writing.

MIND GROOVES I

PREPARATION:
paper and pens for everyone

a print or reproduction of high quality
by a famous artist

GOAL: Very few of us realize that we only receive and understand a limited portion of what is communicated to us from others or from the environment. Because our minds learn to work in grooves, they shut out many of the vibrations coming in, or they misinterpret them. Most of us are unaware of this occurring because we are locked into our mind grooves. Until we open up the higher centers (which are governed by the frontal lobes of the brain) we can only hear, understand and playback that which is already in ourselves—what is stored in our minds. This human situation is behind the Biblical words: "He that hath ears to hear, let him hear what the spirit says..."

In this awareness game, we have several exercises to bring out the extent of our own understanding and our tendencies to color things positive or negative. We want to take a look at some of our basic grooves.

EXPLORATION:

1. One person in the group recounts some incident that happened during the day, or a vivid incident that happened recently and is still fresh in the mind. The others draw the incident as it is being told, and continue for a moment to finish it up when the story is over. Then the drawings are all displayed in the center of the room and reviewed by the entire group.

2. Note the positions of the persons in the drawing who are carrying

out the action described by the storyteller. The drawing reveals whether the receiver took the story as negative, positive, muddled it or missed the point of the story altogether and drew something off the point. Whatever is there in the drawing reveals the mindstuff of the receiver. Discuss without judging. You may want to repeat the exercise with someone else telling another real incident and the group drawing it in detail as before.

3. Someone in the group tells of an incident from the past that has had deep personal importance. If no one can think of anything right off hand, meditate until an idea floats into someone's memory. Then as that person tells the story, others doodle. Repeat with several stories and several doodles before stopping to look at them.

4. Now, as before, spread all the work out in the center of the room and discuss what mind patterns can be seen in the doodles. Remember when you doodled as a kid in school, or even now when listening to a talk, or on the phone? What patterns do you usually doodle in? Some people always doodle with curves, some in flowers, some with squares or straight lines. Some people doodle curves when they feel good and straight lines when they feel frustrated. Share.

5. The leader brings out a reproduction or a print of a well-known artist's painting—something of very good quality. Everyone meditates on what they see in the painting as it lies in the center of the circle, or is placed on a wall where the details are easily seen by all. Write down on your own papers what you see, what impresses you the most, and what you feel about the painting and why. Then share your descriptions.

6. When everyone has shared, discuss the different "mind views" of the painting. What mental patterns do you see in the individuals that have come out in their descriptions? When looking for mental patterns (or mind grooves) we are not evaluating good or bad, but rather patterns in the ways a person looks at life, or at others, or at things. Can you link any of what has been said to that person's level of consciousness? Can you link what you have said to your own dominant level of consciousness, or to the mood and level you are in

now? Write down the answers to these questions, then share the answers.

7.   Close your eyes and reflect on any usual patterns of mind—grooves—in which you often find yourself.

The leader reads:

> It could be a typical thought of worry or fear, or a wish or a fantasy that keeps recurring to your mind. Some people have fantasies into which they escape that are ongoing serials like the ones on TV. Some people have a repeating pattern of anxiety when afternoon comes because they feel another day has gone and nothing has gotten done, or a dissatisfied feeling every time they go out socially that causes them to think over and over, "I wish I were at home." We all have some repeating patterns of thought that happen in our minds daily. Can we get in touch with any one of them? . . .

> Habits of body are often effects of habits of mind. The desire to light up a cigarette, or overeat or to do anything compulsively often comes when one of our mind grooves starts operating. In kids, the refrains "I'm bored" or "I can't" or "No" to whatever is asked become habits of mind. These mind grooves set in while we're very young, but we don't often notice them until we are much older when they get deeper and deeper, or until we begin to look for them as in this exercise.

After meditating for awhile on your mind grooves write down in your journals what you perceive, then discuss with each other what you've seen.

8.   It may take some follow-up watching of your thoughts during the day or week to really get in touch with your patterns. The mind tape recorder keeps replaying its old tunes and tapes in everybody's heads but we aren't always aware of them. Try to discover what yours are. One way to do this is to carry around a tape recorder or a small notebook for a day. Every fifteen minutes talk into the tape recorder or write down the last thoughts that have been running through your mind. If you can't manage every fifteen minutes then

try every half-hour. This exercise will bring you closer to your subconscious mental patterns throughout the day, and you'll be able to watch your thoughts at work. Then, at the end of the day, replay the tape or review the notes in your notebook and you will see certain moods or patterns that recur. Bring your results to the next group meeting and share your discoveries.

9. Journal writing.

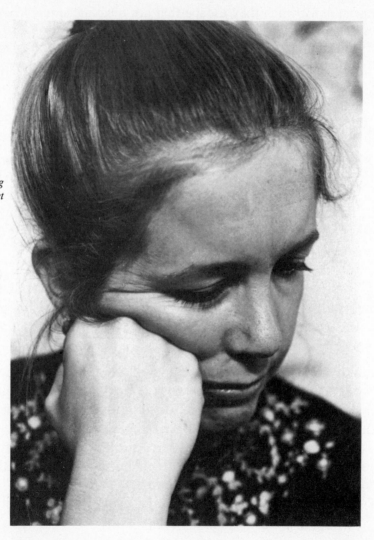

The mind is always working or reflecting until we can let it go.

MIND GROOVES II

PREPARATION:
*You need to choose some topic of the day
about which the group members hold
differing or opposing beliefs.
The more volatile the topic the better.
You may have to try a few out before you
find one that has emotional impact
for at least several of the group members.*

GOAL: As we experience feelings in life, and as we are taught different ideas to believe in, we etch our mind grooves based upon these experiences. The mind *identifies* with its experience, and believes that it is reality. Even though others may experience an event totally differently from you, because their security is *not* threatened by it and yours is, you will identify that event in terms of your fear and that will condition or color how you view life now and in the future. Mind grooves, then, are our detours and shadings from reality. How do we get rid of the grooves to re-experience the pristine pure reality? Is it ever possible? Some people refer to the learning and unlearning of mind patterns as the "game of life", why we're here. Because mind grooves are such strong influences on our behavior, it is important to devote more time exploring them specifically.

Often people create differences between themselves by identifying themselves with their different ideas (which come from different experiences). Such differences can lead to hate, blows, even nuclear attack if we are not aware of the cause. The awareness comes only by understanding how mind creates differences by what it identifies with from past experiences. Only with such an understanding of mind, can we root out the cause of dis-ease, in ourself and in the world.

265

EXPLORATION:

1. After the Goal is read, an issue of the day is discussed. The topic should be one of great controversy, something to do with economics, or politics, or pollution, ecology, industry, abortion, religious beliefs, etc. Take a minute to choose something that will polarize the group into different views, and that has a highly emotional charge in the community. Everyone states where they stand on the issue, and the two sides take opposing positions in the room. As you stand there, on two sides, looking at each other, what do you feel? Do you wish you weren't doing this exercise, because it means you have to get into your differences with others rather than dwell on the good feelings you have in common? Does it make you feel angry that others differ strongly from you? Do you feel you would like to convince the other team to agree with your views? Do you feel love and care in the heart despite the differences in the head? Get in touch with how you feel.

2. Now for the next fifteen minutes the two sides engage in an unstructured "free for all" debate on the issue, with anyone speaking his mind who is moved to do so. Note your feelings and reactions.

3. Discussion can now revolve around several questions to get things moving: Did you feel defensive? aggressive? hurt? afraid? Discuss how you felt. Did you waver in your position?

4. Now the teams change seats. The "pros" are now the "cons" and vice versa. Each side now attempts to see and express the good in the others' point of view. You must put yourself inside their "mind sets" and see from their experiences and feelings as much as possible to present their case as your own. Here, we take a vacation from our own ideas and mental position for awhile. After fifteen minutes of this switching everyone joins in a circle together.

5. Note how you felt during the switchover. Did you have a hard time really feeling the other position? Did you feel resentful? Did identifying with the other view make you doubt your own? Was this doubt threatening and if so why? Discuss your feelings.

6. How much do you want to hang on to your mind grooves and how much are you willing to let them go? The above exercise shows us how attached to them (green level working through blue level) we all really are. By your reactions you will know how unbounded you are. The more you are able to enter into the inner world of others and feel, see and speak from their viewpoint, the more you will be able to be both understanding and free of mind ruts. Your own position will be modified or strengthened based on a greater truth. Feeling all views from center enables you to get closer to Reality. Discuss why this is so.

7. Write down your description of what occurred during steps 1 to 6 in one column on a piece of paper, as far as you can remember. Then in another column write down what was important to you and whether it was positive or negative. When everyone has written their columns, the leader collects all the papers and reads them aloud. Discuss people's differences and how you feel about them. At some point the leader asks that everyone close their eyes and take a moment to dive into memory and see what created their mental positions in the above exercise. See what images float into your memory. Even seemingly unrelated thoughts may have a great bearing on the cause of why you believe what you do and how you are influenced. Share what you recall.

8. Journal writing.

HIDDEN WISDOM

PREPARATION:
a recently refreshed knowledge of a few fairy tales

paper and pens
tape recorder if you have one, with a blank tape

GOAL: Much of the wisdom recorded by humanity throughout history has been hidden in fables and stories that have been passed down through many cultures by word of mouth or written down. It is amazing that the essence message, the wisdom, has remained intact in spite of all the minds the story or legend has had to pass through. Perhaps it has remained because so often the wisdom has been hidden in images in the stories. True wisdom speaks to many levels of consciousness, like the crystal reflects many colors of light. One person may feel strongly that his is the right interpretation. Another person can feel just as strongly that her interpretation is correct. Sages who see through all the levels constructed their stories in layers so that all of humanity could identify with them. For those who can delve deeper, there is always another layer of meaning. People stop only when the "shoe fits", when their level is reached and they can see themselves reflected.

Fairy tales, like Cinderella, the Princess and the Pea, Rumpelstiltskin and others, have themes that also occur in fairy tales from other cultures, some from far away lands. Some myths and legends traced back to their origins by linguists and specialists appear to have been based on true stories from real periods in the history of man, such as King Arthur and the Round Table in England. To discover the truths and wisdom in the collective memory of humanity we need to look into the historical writings for the human patterns. The only secrets that are hidden in the universe are hidden under our own skulls, in dormant powers of perception—in consciousness itself.

EXPLORATION:

1. After the Goal is read, everyone discusses one or two common fairy tales, such as Sleeping Beauty or the Emperor's New Clothes. Share the meanings you feel are being expressed in the story. See how many different levels of meaning you can pool together and from which levels of consciousness they come.

2. Each person writes a short fairy tale or story with a hero. The hero should be a well-known person, either someone in the group or someone in politics or some famous fictional character, but his name should not be revealed in the story. Each story should contain some message cloaked in symbolic terms. Take about fifteen to twenty minutes.

   Each writer reads what he or she has written, and the other members attempt to identify the main character and the message hidden in the story. The messages hidden in the mind of the writer are what we are really trying to read.

3. Mental activity is sometimes blocked by tension that has built up from one of the other levels—physical, social, security, etc.—so take a break and do some movement or groaning, whatever helped you to relax from one of the earlier sessions. Take a visit to one of the other worlds to release tension in any way that "comes naturally". The important thing is to forget the other person's mind and "let yourself go".

4. One person starts a story or fairy tale *about the group* in the spirit of "Once upon a time . . ." then the next person takes over to continue the tale and so on, until the story is finished. Do not finish the story until everyone has had a chance to contribute. Tape record

it if you can. Is there meaning to it with reference to the goals of the group? What does it reveal about the group personality, progress, future? This group fairy tale is discussed to see if there is any "group consciousness" emerging among the participants.

5.   Journal writing.

FREE ASSOCIATION

50

Blue World

PREPARATION:
sensitive attuning on the part of the
group members

a tape recorder and several blank tapes
paper and pens

GOAL: When we truly relax, the conscious mind is laid aside and the inner subconscious mind drifts through to the surface, as in daydreaming or in the twilight place between waking and sleeping. It is a time when we become aware of our thoughts, though we do not control them. Usually the thoughts and images that float up are related to something that is a need, wish or deeper anxiety. By speaking the flow of thoughts that come in, a pattern will emerge. It is often difficult for us to see the pattern, but if we have a tape recorder nearby recording the images and feelings expressed we will be able to catch the pattern when we listen to the tape. The group members may have an insight into a pattern as we speak and they can ask us to go more deeply into some feeling or image. They can also jot down their flashes of thought on a piece of paper to be shared later. If nothing deep comes, that's okay, just go on to whatever does surface. Often something deeper will come if a question is asked to help it along.

At the end of such a session we feel rested and relieved. There is a healing power in being able to contact our inner mind and express it in words. When we talk about our troubles we get them off our chest more than if we were to keep circling them in and out of our conscious minds. This awareness exploration is to take us on a journey into the recesses of our inner subconscious mind.

271

EXPLORATION:

1. In order to loosen up and get relaxed enough so that we can get into the subconscious, we will do a nonsense exercise. Everyone stand comfortably in the center of the room. The leader sets the mood by beginning. This game is called "Glossalalia" or talking in tongues. There are many references to this in the Bible and in the history of other cultures. Many churches have had unusual experiences with it. By beginning to babble meaningless words, real meanings come forth—either foreign languages or an ancient version of English or some dialect. This babbling opens the gateway for free associating. The leader starts to talk loudly in nonsense words such as "Yubbidy Yoo Da" "Yickilty spigledum" etc. He may find himself talking pidgin English, or a Shakespearean inflection or whatever. But if he just lets it come he will be as surprised as anyone. Let the laughs fall where they may, and enjoy the release of words.

2. All join in. Voices rise and fall, first a few sounds, then a torrent. Keep it up for several minutes. Try to have a conversation in this new language with the person next to you.

3. Everyone sit down when finished and share your personal reactions and experiences.

4. Now take your pens and write in glossalalia for one paragraph. You can write a poem or whatever you are moved to do. Don't worry about making sense of what comes through you. When you have finished go back and translate the glossalalia into English. Everyone read their paragraphs—both languages. What do you notice?

5. Take a minute of centering to quiet down and relax. One person who feels moved can volunteer to begin the free association. That person lies down on the carpet or on a couch and says what he is thinking about now. Then the volunteer returns to the thoughts and feelings (speaking them aloud) which occurred during the meditation, during the "glossalalia", before arriving at the group meeting, and so on back to some incident or thought which stands out as important. If nothing moves him, a member of the group who feels some hidden meaning in the words spoken can encourage the

volunteer to go deeper into that area. Leading questions are asked spontaneously whenever the group feels they will help the expression. But let the person lying down do the talking as much as possible, describing what the inner mind sees, feels, wishes or thinks. Let moments of silence occur, but if they go on too long, the leader should gently ask, "What thought is there right now?" This will encourage the person to speak anew and not analyze, because that would be getting into the conscious mind again. With this kind of free association blocks are removed by just asking, "What are you thinking now?" and whatever it is, even a new train of thought, will keep the experience flowing. When we go deeply into the inner mind, it can become an emotional release, or we can encounter hidden fears. If we just let the person express and go through the cycle of the feeling, a cathartic release will come. Anything any group member says should be loving and caring, and anything that *is* said will immediately bring in new images and thoughts to the person. This is how the mind works—by association and identification.

6.   Repeat with new volunteers and share your insights as you go. Continue with the free association for as long as the group wants to. You may want to continue the exercise until everyone has had a chance to be in the center, either now or another time.

7.   Write in your journals what you have learned about the conscious mind, the inner mind and free association. Did you identify with anything another member of the group said? Write your own feelings and insights.

THE MANY PATHS OF YOGA

Exploration

51

Blue World

PREPARATION:
a Bible–King James version
candle
matches
candle holder

GOAL: Many people think of yoga as only the physical yoga postures, similar to the ones we practice at the beginning of each awareness journey. That form of yoga is called *hatha yoga* and is only one branch of the tree of yoga. The word yoga means yoke, or union, and yoga is a process of becoming united, becoming one with the greater Self. With yoga the different parts of us–physical, emotional, mental and spiritual–which we are accustomed to have pulling us in different directions, begin to work together in harmony. Every level of consciousness becomes heightened. Practiced in all its forms, yoga brings about a molecular change in the body for greater health, awareness and happiness. Tastes and habits change, life-force becomes enhanced, the whole person is evolved.

There are eight major paths of yoga that have been practiced for thousands of years that we will delve into in this journey. These yogas were well-established 2000 years before Christ, and it is thought by many scholars that Jesus practiced these many yogas as did Krishna and Buddha of India. The goal of exploring these eight yogas is to get closer to the oneness that yoga brings, both with each other and with the universe.

EXPLORATION:

1. The leader reads the following descriptions of the eight yogas and at

the same time another group member reads the Biblical references that have been marked ahead of time by the leader. These references show the link between the thinking of Eastern sages and Western wisdom.

1) **Karma Yoga:** The way of right action; finding some enlightening work which recognizes the needed action to bring peace and harmony to people and the world, defends the world against division, and awakens people to discover righteousness. Also, karma yoga is selfless action that does whatever work is needed with quality service and effort, keeping one's mind on the One—God—the Whole as one works, to help fulfill the purpose of the Cosmic Will.

(Mark 12:30, Mark 10:43-45, John 13:12)

2) **Sanyasa Yoga:** The way of renunciation or removing binding social forms and duties. Liberation is achieved by letting go of action in the world. When obligatory duties are abandoned out of ignorance or fear of pain and trouble, then this is not true sanyasa. Sanyasa is not just dropping out of society. Surrender is done with the trust and helplessness of a son approaching a father for his blessing. It is difficult to attain without karma yoga and dhyana yoga.

(Matt. 8:20-22, Matt. 19:29-30, Matt. 16:24-26)

3) **Jnana Yoga:** The way of knowledge. To know by philosophical reflection or wisdom. Spiritual knowledge of the highest selfhood through study of the scriptures, prophets and sages. Probing the power of the cosmic intelligence as the source of all thoughts and ideas. Probing the heart with the intellect.

(Job 28:12, Job 37:5, Prov. 1,2,14:33, Matt. 7:1-5)

4) **Mantra Yoga:** Repetition of a hallowed name, such as Hum, Amin, Om, or Amen, or chanting mentally or outloud a structured sound. A deep sigh or tone, like the OOOMMM sound, acts as a carrier wave for thoughts. *Man* means "thought", *tra* means "transfers protection" when translated from Sanskrit. Through this yoga a positive transformation of psychic electricity into cosmic vibration is manifested. Mantra tunes the life force to the greater life and intelligence as it purifies the mind of thoughts

and actions , through one-pointed concentration.
(1 Sam. 16:23, Mark 7:34, John 11:43, John 1:1-5)

5) **Bhakti Yoga:** The way of love. The aspirant selects a self-chosen and ideal manifestation of God or the universal mind which goes to the heart of the aspirant so he sees it in everything. In the West one might choose Moses or Christ. In the East, Krishna or a guru.
(Deut. 6:5, Mark 12:29-30)

6) **Dhyana Yoga:** The way of prayer/meditation and concentration of the imaging faculty. Trance states which achieve serenity and contact with the power to dispel darkness within and transmit the power of *medha* which is Sanskrit for "truth" or "wisdom" and forms the basis of the word "meditation".
(1 Chr. 28:9, James 4:8, Mark 11:22-26)

7) **Guna Yoga:** The controlling of the creative energy in yourself and the world around you and the absorption of vital forces and light.
(Mark 5:30, Mark 9:2-3)

8) **Raja Yoga:** Penetrating the seven levels of consciousness and the eighth domain of being in pure awareness.* Awareness of the material and spiritual universe with its cosmic, psychic and healing energies. Contacting the life force and cosmic intelligence and having the understanding of eternal time and karma. The "royal" yoga, encompassing many others.
(Matt. 6:1-34, John 14:2-4)

2. Having read the relation between the Eastern yogas and Western Judao-Christian teaching, can you discover which of the yogas relate to which of the levels of consciousness? In Matt. 6:1-34 (and other places in the Bible) can you see the seven levels?

3. Everyone discusses what they are doing in life, or expect to do, if anything, which may be considered within the scope of the different yogas. Consider each yoga one at a time and ask yourself the following questions:

* These levels are discussed in Part I, The Take-off.

a) **Karma Yoga:** The yoga of service. What kind of service do you do that is selfless or self-forgetting in your daily life?

b) **Sanyasa Yoga:** What does renunciation mean to you in practical everyday life? What can you let go of, in the way of activity or pleasure, as at least a one-time demonstration of sanyasa yoga?

c) **Jnana Yoga:** What books have you read which might be said to put you in tune with this path? What other books come to mind that might be as valuable as having a guru (wise teacher) teaching you in person? Of all the books mentioned, can the group agree on one or two that would be the most valuable? Why?

d) **Mantra Yoga:** Spend five minutes as a group chanting the OOOMMM sound with the AAAAHHHHHOOOOOMMMM positioning of the mouth learned in World Four, endeavoring to merge your mind and heart into the sound and into the universe. Mantra purifies if you concentrate on the vibration with full attention.

e) **Bhakti Yoga:** Now send the sound and your love out to the members of the group, embracing them in your care and love and lift the group heart into the love of your own ideal (idea of God, guru, philosophy, the highest concept you can hold), and then into the love of the whole. Discuss mantra and bhakti yoga when you finish this loving.

f) **Dhyana Yoga:** Now light a candle and place it in the center of the room. Do the centering meditation as you concentrate on the candle flame, merging yourself inside it. Let your images and thoughts melt in the fire of the flame. . . (long pause) . . . As you focus, note the changes in the background colors and environment around you. The energies will become more apparent to you as the room around you dissolves or moves in the flame. If your eyes get tired, relax and close them, continuing to concentrate on the afterimage of the candle flame inside your closed eyes. Now begin to expand the mind once you have it still and focussed. Do not expand the mind while it is full of problems, otherwise the problems will expand too.

g) **Guna Yoga:** Imagine this creative force that you have contacted is reprogramming your cells and atoms with greater consciousness and light. Project your life energy into your image. Make it powerful. Feel a sense of conviction come over you, the more your image is projected. . . When you are ready discuss the effects of dhyana and guna yoga.

h) Discuss your experience of *Exploring Inner Space* exercises on the different levels of consciousness in relation to these other yogas. They are purifiers of the various levels of awareness. Which of a) through g) do you feel most drawn to?

4.   Journal writing.

The first step in Dhyana yoga is concentration to a single point. When the point is still and the thoughts have stopped, the awareness is then expanded throughout the whole of space.

SELF-HYPNOSIS

PREPARATION:
your journals

GOAL: Most people have heard of hypnosis, and many have learned to use it for relaxing, changing habits, and killing pain. In medicine, hypnosis is very common for easing tension and creating anaesthesia. The power of the mind to control the body is best illustrated in the use of hypnosis. Self-hypnosis is taking the responsibility yourself for programming your mind. Although it may be more successful for a professional hypnotist to do it to you, it is much better for your self-mastery to retain control over your own will, learn the skill and gain the reward of changing yourself.

We call this awareness game self-hypnosis, because we acquire most of our bad habits of body and of mind through self-suggestion, hypnotizing ourselves unconsciously into believing something is real or necessary. We hypnotize our bodies into wanting a cigarette, or into feeling we need the comfort of overeating, and we hypnotize our minds into believing we are separate from each other and the world around us. By learning self-hypnosis we can then learn how to de-hypnotize ourself to be more in tune with the Cosmic Intelligence, and to leave the unreal for the Real.

Self-hypnosis should be used in conjunction with other safe practices for gaining better health physically, emotionally, mentally and spiritually.

EXPLORATION:

1. The most important factor in successful self-hypnosis is a sense of conviction or sincerity. A sincere belief in what you are doing is necessary, otherwise the doubting mind will counteract its own new program. For the mind to change the mind it has to feel and act "as if" the new affirmation or new program is true. It is true in principle, so the mind has to believe it, and then via the reprogramming methods it will be passed on to the subconscious mind which acts automatically like a computer playing out what's put into it. You have to have faith in *yourself*.

    > A woman no longer has a phobia about closed rooms.
    >
    > A woman with a spasm in her left shoulder has moved it to a less obvious location in a finger of her left hand.
    >
    > A boy stops stuttering.
    >
    > An overweight girl who has been eating a quart of ice cream a day now detests it.

    These are just a few examples of marvelous results from self-hypnosis.

2. *The leader will assist in the relaxation monologue and self-suggestion. The leader needs to be confident, at ease, and speak in a soothing, caring voice.* Everybody stands and faces the leader who leads all through a susceptibility test. *The leader reads slowly in a monotone voice:*

    > Everyone place your arms out horizontally in front of you, palms down, and close your eyes. Now I want you to visualize me hanging a shopping bag full of groceries over your left wrist. I am doing it now. It is very heavy. You can hardly hold up your left arm. It seems to grow heavier and heavier. It is pulling your arm down. Lower and lower. Now open your eyes.

    The measure of susceptibility to suggestion is the degree to which the left arm was lowered. One to two inches means you will probably do well. Anything over that indicates an excellent subject. Children are usually very suggestible. If your arm did not move at all it is a sign that you need to let go more. However, don't be discouraged, many people improve tremendously by visualizing (seeing in pictures) what they hear and by carefully practicing the "as if" principle mentioned in Step 1.

3.   The leader reads the following slowly while everyone sits comfortably relaxed in their chairs. It is important to visualize the ideas mentioned. You become your own self-hypnotizer by using the power of visualization as this is read:

> We are very comfortable. . . We sit limply. . . We concentrate on our feet. . . We wiggle our toes to make sure the muscles are all relaxed. . . We let our feet rest heavily on the floor. . . The limpness makes our legs and thighs heavy. . . It creeps up our hips into our back. . . We sit heavily and limply. . . Our whole body feels loose, limp and heavy. It is a pleasant feeling. . . Now our face loosens. The lips part. Our eyes droop. . . It is an effort to keep our eyes open. . . It feels like something is resting on our eyelids, closing them. . . Now they close gently. . . We relax our mind, permitting it to concentrate on the sound of my voice, keeping out other thoughts. . . Now even my voice will soon fade as we get so relaxed. . . (pause) . . .

When all are relaxed after a moment the leader continues:

> I now concentrate on my left hand. I see it in my mind's eye with my eyes closed. As I sit fully relaxed and breathing deeply, visualizing my left hand, I feel it move imperceptibly. With each breath I take, my left hand seems to get lighter. I visualize it rising off my lap. I say to myself, "With every breath I take, my hand gets lighter and lighter. It rises slowly from my lap toward my face. I know that when it touches my face I will be in a deep state of relaxation. Now my left hand touches my left cheek."

Regardless of how many are successful in touching their cheeks the leader continues:

> I know I can reach this deep state even more quickly next time, and go deeper and farther. I want to be able to learn to relax myself deeply at will and get in touch with my inner mind at will. Whenever I snap my fingers and tell myself to relax, that

will be my signal to my conscious mind to let go and go within. This signal will work when I snap my fingers myself. I now click my fingers and relax deeper. . . I can now reprogram any habit that I wish to change, or talk to my subconscious and program a new idea for greater fulfillment in my life. . . (long pause) . . . I have no doubts, I feel in tune with cosmic powers. . . I am now about to end this session. At the count of three my hand will drop to my lap. I will feel wide awake, revitalized and refreshed. One, two, three!

4. Anyone who is still sleepy-eyed should give themselves another command to feel wide awake, counting "one, two, three!" If they still have trouble, then the leader should say "You will feel wide awake at the count of three—one, two, three!" The reason for this is that some people may have let the leader take over instead of keeping the power of self-control. By practicing on their own they will gain the ability to tell their own minds what to do. People who master self-hypnosis cannot be brainwashed by anybody.

5. The group discusses practicing this conditioning on their own before the next meeting.

6. Either the group can continue on to the next exploration now, or end the meeting here.

7. Journal writing.

DE-HYPNOSIS

Exploration

53

Blue World

PREPARATION:
your journals

GOAL: It is natural and normal for us to experience the feelings of fear as a sign of danger. We have fear to thank for our survival. However, in humanity's early days fear was released by fleeing to safety. Today, fear has become phobia and often is based upon feelings we are not sure about, or upon hallucinations and illusions which are solely creations of our minds. Breathing increases, we perspire and other biological "memories" take over when fear arises. Often our intellect tells us, "Silly fool, there's nothing to be scared of, forget it," but for many the fear remains.

Fear wells up from the subconscious. Fear of speaking in public, of heights, of water, of animals and of the dark are common examples of conditionings often from childhood which have remained unconquered in many people. By learning how to contact the inner mind, the subconscious, we can actually reprogram it to dispel fears and phobias, guilt over past errors and other problems. Cleansing the subconscious of unwanted patterns is the goal of this awareness exploration. It is de-hypnosis.

You may practice meditation and attune yourself to the infinite through the superconscious. You may expand and improve your conscious mind to a point where your life is greatly improved. Yet, unless your subconscious mind is brought

into complete harmony with the superconscious, there will be problems and you
cannot be enlightened. We need to learn
to bring the subconscious and superconscious together to let the light in. Through
de-hypnotizing ourselves from false and
self-limiting suggestions we approach
Reality.

EXPLORATION:

1. Everyone sits comfortably. Make sure the shades are drawn and the
    lights turned off so that the room is as dark as possible. Each person
    in turn has a fantasy about what he or she feared most as a child in
    the dark. Bad men? Spiders? Black dogs? Spooks? Speak about it as
    if it were now. "Something is moving in the dark, what is it?"

2. Now light one lamp. It lights the room dimly. Sit as relaxed as you
    can, in the loving comfort of the group of people who care about you
    and about each other. You are going to practice de-hypnosis. *The
    leader reads the relaxation exercise from the last exploration on
    page 281, then adds:*

    Now everyone is enjoying a deep, blissful state of relaxation.
    Eyes are gently closed. If you'd like to go deeper, visualize
    yourself in a mine-shaft elevator going down one level deeper,
    two levels deeper, three levels deeper and so on to ten levels
    deeper. . . (long pause) . . .

    Now picture yourself in the situation you most feared as a child.
    . . . (long pause) . . . Then tune into the situation that gives you
    the most fear or guilt now. . . (long pause) . . . If the childhood
    fear was of going into deep water, see yourself going into deeper
    water which you would ordinarily have avoided. See yourself
    climbing a little higher on a ladder if fear of heights was your
    problem. Or see yourself feeling comfortable in a dark room
    enjoying the stray sounds of a quiet house.

    Switch to the situation of guilt or fear that makes you feel most
    troubled in your present life. You de-hypnotize by visualizing
    yourself in that situation, only handling it with courage and love
    the way you would like to do. Don't try too big a jump. If your

present fear concerns speaking before people, see yourself talking to a few people, not a large audience. If fear of driving is your phobia, see yourself driving well in a little traffic, not in a traffic jam at rush hour. . . (long pause). . . .

Next see yourself doing this same exercise at home in the week to follow, with the same steps progressing toward the goal of total freedom from the subconscious fear or guilt. The more relaxed and deep you go, the more transformed you will feel. You are bringing the problem to light. As much as possible, in each of your mental pictures, see yourself erect, self-confident, a picture of self-mastery. See each mental image in color and in vivid sharpness, just as if it were true. Fill the picture with light and love, sending energy from the cosmos into it. When you feel lightened and relieved, know that you will stay centered in this new light. . . (long pause) . . .

When you are ready, gradually begin to climb back up the mind shaft elevator to a count of ten levels. Always close with this suggestion: "When I count to three, I will end my de-hypnotizing session feeling wide awake, energetic, self-confident and wonderfully well. One, two, three!"

3.   Now turn all the lights on. Write your new impressions and feelings in your journal. Take some time to reflect on the new, cleansed you.

4.   If time permits you may want to repeat the trust exercise on page 62 to add some positive green energy to your new program.

MEMORY EXPANSION

GOAL: There are many courses that promise to teach us to have an amazing memory. We've all read those ads that sell a technique to enable us to be a walking telephone book. Through using the imagination to visualize, we can etch into the subconscious enormous amounts of information consciously, and then have easier access to it. However, when we combine the sixth sense of the intuition with the memory training, we have an even more powerful tool for developing memory.

Awareness can be said to be another name for the consciousness that permeates all of infinite space. It is there to be tapped by anyone whose antenna is up. The intuition provides the antenna, and in this awareness game we are going to begin to explore this faculty to enhance memory. By combining the intuition and the mind, we can begin to open new doors of perception and approach the fullest potential of the human mind.

PREPARATION:
blindfold or blindfolds depending on whether you want to do Step 3 one person at a time, several people at a time or all together

a bookshelf full of books
same number of towels as blindfolds
same number of bingo cards as blindfolds or towels

Make bingo cards using four numbers across and four down for a total of 16 squares. Put the same numbers on separate pieces of cardboard—the size of the squares on the cards. Each card needs its own set of matching numbers.

With young children you may want to adjust the time allotments in the exercises to give them more time to memorize.

EXPLORATION:

1. *The leader keeps a score card and conducts the following memory test.*

   a) First a volunteer is blindfolded. Everyone lines up facing him. The blindfold is removed for as many seconds as there are people in the line and then immediately returned. The subject then recites the names of the people in the line in order from left to right.

b) The line is reformed with everyone in new positions. Now the blindfolded subject stands two feet in front of the new first person in the line and attempts to identify who it is. He can hold out his hands to pick up the vibrations and the person in the line can hold his palms down above the upturned palms of the blindfolded subject to send his vibrations into them. No one says right or wrong to the subject's guesses until he has faced every person and said who he thinks they are. Then he removes his blindfold.

c) (optional) Now a) and b) are combined. The subject views a new line-up for the same limited number of seconds as in part a). He then recites the names he has memorized and at the same time moves down the line tapping everyone on the shoulder to feel their vibration as he goes. This familiarizes him more with the vibrations of each person. Then everyone in the line switches their places around and the subject again tries to identify them by vibration, as in part b).

Let everyone have a turn. Remembering people's vibrations helps aid the memory of names, faces, etc.

2. One person browses through the shelves of books in the room for 60 seconds, and then returns to the group to recite as many titles as he can remember. Next he turns to the shelves and sections off an area containing twice the number of books that he was able to remember. For example, if he remembered the names of five books, then he sections off ten in a row. This time he fixes his eyes on the entire group of books at once, in a relaxed state, clicking his fingers to relax himself as he has programmed on page 281. Again, in 60 seconds he returns to his seat and recites as many titles as he can. The second score should be considerably better than the first.

Each person takes a turn.

3. The skin is actually a sensory organ like the eye except that the eye is skin specialized to certain vibrations of light. Can bingo be played with the skin instead of the eye? It is possible, depending on your

degree of skin awareness. Make a bingo card using sixteen numbers —four across and four down. One person looks at the bingo card for five seconds, then it is covered with a towel and the numbers are placed on it from memory. Note the score. Now the towel is removed and the subject is blindfolded so he can't see the sixteen numbered squares now placed in his hand. He tries to feel the numbers and sense a resonance when the numbers match as he places them on the card. In matching the sixteen numbers, any score better than one is better than chance. Everyone does this in turn or, if you make enough cards, all together.

4.   Training for a photographic memory is accomplished by methods (such as the above) in which we combine intuition with relaxation and a training exercise for the mind. By practicing memorizing different things *in the relaxed state* (through the methods of self-hypnosis) we make our subconscious computer more receptive and we gain greater access to its storage cells. We can develop an auditory memory in the same way through a yogic technique called "speed tape learning" in which we run a cassette recorder with auto-shutoff while we are in the relaxed state between waking and sleeping lying in bed before sleep.* Discuss the value of memory training.

5.   Journal writing.

---

* University of the Trees has a complete Speed Tape Learning program and memory training program (see appendix) with taped instructions for those interested.

JOURNAL WRITING

PREPARATION:
First read Exploration 2 showing an outline of the different levels of consciousness.

a loose-leaf notebook with three dividers

Bring your journal which you have kept up to now so we can organize its contents into a seven-level journal from now on. If you have not been keeping a journal with these games now is your best time to start one.

GOAL: Throughout these explorations you have been keeping a journal of your feelings, reactions, ideas, creative inspiration and whatever else you felt like including. This ongoing journal is one of the most vital parts of your awareness development. You could say it is a travel log of your journey. Frequently go back over what you have written and see where you have been in your inner world and where you now are. Your journal can become a map of *your* inner space. It can tell you where you are strong, weak, or inexperienced.

Many people keep diaries. These diaries are often daily calendars rather than daily expressions of the *inner* world, which is far more honest with ourself and far more important for our growth. The "Progoff Journal Process"* is now becoming popular as a new kind of diary-keeping for spiritual growth. In this awareness exercise we are going to combine several methods with the Nuclear Evolution methods for using a journal. By keeping a daily journal of your ego reactions and your joys or fulfilling moments, you can have a daily mirror of your inner world. The diary becomes a mirror to see how your chakras are working, which levels you have been succeeding in, which you are stuck in and which need more attention.

* *At a Journal Workshop*, "Basic Text and Guide for Using the Intensive Journal", by Ira Progoff, Dialogue House, 1975.

EXPLORATION:

1.   Take the journal that you have been keeping during the course of this book. If you haven't started one yet, then obtain a notebook, preferably loose-leaf, the kind that you can take the paper in and out of. You can divide the journal into sections for a Nuclear Evolution journal. The first third of the notebook you label GENERAL LOG, the second third is SEVEN LEVELS LOG, and the last third is FEEDBACK. In the general log section you write your feelings and experiences—the raw materials by date and chronologically as they occur. In the seven levels log you list conflicts, events and experiences—also raw materials—from the class and from your daily living *when* you know which level they are on. Many times when you write your inner feelings you don't know where they are coming from until you have written them down. When you are uncertain begin in the general section. After some practice you will learn to recognize which chakra is involved in your reactions. When you know, then write in the seven levels section. You can also mentally scan each level as you prepare to write to see if any memories of recent events from that dimension come to mind. If so write them down. This gives you a record over a period of time of what is happening inside your inner world. In the feedback section you have plenty of room to delve into the meanings of what you have entered in the general log and seven levels log. For example, you may look back over your log records for a period of several weeks and see a pattern. This pattern you would write up in your feedback section. You may see that your problems with your family and in the group during those weeks were related to your insecurity. This would give you insight into what area you need to work on, and what your green level of consciousness is doing. Then you would note the time when the pressure was eased. What caused the easing? Did someone reassure you who was very important to you? Was there a change in your attitude? In class and at home, log the events in your life as much as possible. Then at least once a week reflect on what you have written in the feedback section. When you work in the feedback section, you don't analyze yourself and try to figure yourself

out, this usually blocks the insight. Rather, look for patterns, note them, then meditate upon them in the manner given in Step 4 below.

2. Look over your journal now for patterns and levels of consciousness. If you haven't kept a seven levels log, just a general log, review that log looking for the different levels. You may see repeating problems or reactions regarding any level (sexual, social, security, imaginative, mental attitudes, fantasies, etc.) or you may see "non-problem" patterns of living on any level. For example, if you spend a lot of time as a non-fiction writer, it is likely that you will be using a good deal of yellow—analyzing, sorting, etc. If you spend a great deal of time writing poetry or fiction, you are likely to use a lot of violet—images—to convey the mood of your message. If your time is spent in prayer or devotional caring for others, you may see blue level patterns. If you are very active with physical labor all day you will see red level patterns. Try to discover your everyday chakra functions. If you feel comfortable sharing your private thoughts with another, you can pair off as you do this, and help each other to see patterns that you may be blind to alone. Otherwise, share just the final results of your review with the whole group.

3. Let's now brainstorm how we can use our journals more creatively. Were there similarities in our insights?

4. Now you need to see what message the Cosmic Intelligence is writing to you through your journal. When Christ said "The Kingdom of Heaven is *within* you," he was saying that it is in *inner* space, not in some idea of heaven out there—in *outer* space. The message of the universe to you is written in your life experiences, and your liberation comes though being able to read your own history, to see the results of what you do with your consciousness. Then you gain some idea of whether your course to greater awareness is straight and direct or scattered and zig zag. And you gain clues on where it needs changing. The persons, events, dreams, memories, and feelings in your life come together. The journal can integrate them for you to show you where you are headed.

In the Progoff method mentioned earlier you identify all your experiences–with others, society, your body, your feelings, events–as experiences *within* yourself. This coincides with Nuclear Evolution which states that all is happening inside your consciousness, all is One, a projection of yourself. So with this premise, you talk with events or people or your body and feelings all as parts of yourself. Take one of the patterns you have seen and talk to it as a part of you. Get into a dialogue with it and see what it has to tell you. Write down all the feelings and thoughts that come without judging them.

5. Now close your eyes to relax deeply. Let images, feelings and thoughts float to the surface of your conscious mind. You may want to repeat the relaxation exercise on page 281. Write the images and feelings down as they come, let them flow, don't worry how they look or sound. Then close your eyes again and see what else surfaces. Dip in and then express several times, but do not evaluate what you're writing or drawing. Continue until you feel there is no more to come for now.

6. Now review what you have put on paper, and let it take you deeper into yourself, putting you in touch with new images. Even if it seems to be taking you into a different area—like an old memory, or your job—continue to write all impressions down without editing. As with free association, it will all tie together later.

7. Now read it all. Again share what insights you have gained. Each time you do this reviewing (holding up the mirror) and communicating with what is there, you become more integrated with your inner self.

8. Make an inner resolve to continue working with your journal at home, to make exploring inner space part of your daily activities, even if for only a few minutes daily.

The family can draw closer together and review its inner progress through keeping a journal of positive and negative events. When shared with children, everyone in the family can see if patterns are changing or if conflicts really are resolved. Journal Writing is a most useful tool for family development and for family communing.

THE DEPTHS OF SILENCE

PREPARATION:
watches with second hands
a large clock with a second hand if possible

books that are challenging to group members,
preferably a home library with many books
to choose from

GOAL: Concentration in the silence has been well known to every religion. The deeper the silence, the more all the energies become focussed and one-pointed to be placed on Cosmic Intelligence with heartfelt devotion. This brings a response from the universe with an uplifting feeling and often an intuitional message or other manifestation of an answer. True devotion is one-pointedness of mind on your chosen love. It's hard to maintain one-pointedness when we have conflicts or desires eating away at us.

All successful people—whether housewives, surgeons, businessmen, carpenters, salesmen, saints, etc.—find that success in any task is proportional to the amount of applied concentration. Mind power is developed through the ability to concentrate.

To scientifically open the higher centers in the brain in the frontal lobes, where our creative powers of intuition and imagination lie, we must first learn to concentrate the mind. By concentrating all the mind energies we actually go beyond mind into another world. The sixth and seventh levels are beyond mind, so we are preparing to "go out of our minds". This exploration is a series of concentration games to take us into the next dimension.

EXPLORATION:

1. There will be little discussion in this exploration as silence of mind is needed for success. Everyone must have the attitude of listener and focus their entire attention on carrying out each direction in detail, in a relaxed state, yet without great effort. First begin by closing your eyes and imagining your closest living relative in your mind's eye. Hold this image as long as possible, making the details stand out. Fit in the color of the eyes, shade of hair, face complexion and markings on the face. Work on it to make it vivid. . . (pause) . . . See more intently into this image. Can you now discover any particular details or features that you did not see before? You may. If so, make a note and the next time you are with the person, see if these impressions are correct. Spend seven to ten minutes before going on to Step 2.

2. Now take your watch off. If someone has no watch, then several people can share. Get close to the watch and sit as comfortably as you can. Follow the second hand around its complete circle, never letting your attention be diverted even for one second. Concentrate with all your powers of mind and heart effortlessly. Focus until you can no longer keep your thoughts from wandering. You will feel you cannot get them back under control and they just want to go their own way. Note the time on paper when this happens, and begin again. See how the time of control lengthens as you train your mind to concentrate. You can practice this on your own at home and build up your powers. You will notice an almost immediate positive change in your effectiveness and skillfulness in action or in work. Practice for fifteen silent minutes before going on to Step 3.

3. A few years ago KMPX-FM, a California radio station which often held ESP experiments, tried to stop the big Union 76 clock in San Francisco at 11:03 a.m. by getting enough people to concentrate the power of their thoughts toward that end. The clock is computerized and powered by an electric substation. At 11:02 a.m. that day, the clock jumped from 11:02 to 11:41, then after five seconds it went back to 11:03 and blinked off twice before going on to 11:04! Take

one of the watches, or if a large clock is available use that. Place it in the center of the group. Decide on a time a few minutes from now, and see if you can stop the clock. Everyone must put their full concentration and all their psychic forces into this one-pointed attention of mind power. For true mind power the heart has to be one-pointed as well as the mind. If your mind wants one thing and your heart something else, your devotion will be divided.

4. The next exercise is to read a page from a book in the host's library, which is not your usual style of reading. Everyone take a book and do this at the same time. Pick something difficult, or else something totally new to you. For example, if you are not a scientist, pick something technical and scientific. Read and reread the page in a concentrated state, determined with 100 percent of your being to understand what it means fully, irrespective of any technical words at which you may have to guess. Never let your attention lapse for even a second. Try to put your self into the mind of the author— what was he or she thinking when writing that? Watch your understanding grow. If you practice this at home you will also see a large expansion in your mental abilities. (Children especially can gain in mental power by playing this game frequently, using texts above their reading level, and only reading a page or two so it doesn't become too big an effort, but a challenge they can master.) Spend fifteen minutes practicing in silence before going to Step 5.

5. Visualize in your mental "TV" the face of someone who was once close to you, but who has now died. Hold this face firmly in mind; don't let it slip away. Study it until your imagination begins to fill in all the details. When you have held the image successfully for two minutes without its coming and going, place your fingertips or thumb tips on your head channeling life force to the frontal area of the brain through them. Can you capture any message from that person, either a long-since forgotten message or a new message? (Many people in our classes have been able to receive messages right away, much to their surprise. Many more who practice this "silence" exercise over and over at home have developed their abilities for

mental telepathy with those who have passed on.) Spend fifteen minutes practicing and receiving. Speak no words aloud.

6. There has been no discussion up to this time. Now discuss your desire to build concentration and mind power, and the need for regular practice at home. Do you have enough heartfelt desire? What is the the main thing you are most devoted to in heart? in mind? Are they the same? How can you increase your devotion?

7. Journal writing.

Concentrating on the second hand of your watch can be done anywhere, at any time. You can time your success and your progress. The discipline of a wandering mind is the difference between a beginner in awareness meditation and a master of oneself.

PENETRATING YOUR MIND

GOAL: In this exercise we explore the nature of karma and the highest qualities of the blue dimension. Through discovering the highest ideal we hold in our minds, we can see what we do with our love and devotion.

PREPARATION:
a rubber ball
a bell
your journals and pens

Children act out their heroes in play. Their ideal is to be like their heroes. Some people hold the ideal to be the perfect wife/husband, father/mother. Others have the spiritual ideal to expand their devotion into universal love which is not centered around a person or thing, but on Cosmic law and the unfolding Cosmic plan. The blue level holds onto its ideals as precious ideas that it holds dear. When it opens to the intuitive, then Cosmic Intelligence can expand the devotion into true wisdom. When the mind merges with violet, spontaneous openness makes the devotion universal. On what level is your devotion?

When devotion is intense and pure, one-pointed in its love of the Cosmic One, the aura turns a bright electric blue. Many saints have been artistically depicted with an electric blue cloak.

EXPLORATION:

1. *After the meditation, the leader reads the following:*

Ask yourself what you are most devoted to. Is it a person? A hobby? Your job or advancement? Facing yourself? God? Some teacher or guru or other ideal? Write it down in your journal.

Then ask yourself, what level of my awareness (red through violet) do I love most? Which do I devote most of my time or attention to? Write these answers down.

2. Keeping this in mind go on to the following. The leader reads:

You have probably heard the saying "Energy follows thought." Whatever ideas you hold in your mind, no matter how true they may or may not be, that is where your energy goes. Your love, your emotions, your desires, are all conditioned by your thoughts. The kinds of thoughts that circulate through your mind during your daily activities and at night, are what is called your *karma*. *Karma* is a Sanskrit word for the forces of action and reaction in consciousness. In grade school we learned about the law of nature Isaac Newton discovered. He proved that every action has an equal and opposite reaction. *The leader takes the ball and bounces it once.* What happens when I let go of the ball? The action of gravity pulls it down and then a reaction occurs and it bounces back. Remember, all is energy. Light and color are energy, all the levels of consciousness we are exploring are energy. So mind and thoughts are energy too, vibrating at a faster speed than the atoms of the seat you are sitting on, faster than the vibrations of anything physical. So you can't see thoughts with your eyes or sense mind with your senses. Can you see or hear or feel or touch or smell a thought passing across your mind? But you are aware of it somehow.

Thoughts work like all energy. Every thought you think has a reaction inside you. The idea that my friend might leave me, brings a reaction of fear and pain. The idea that I may not get dinner tonight may make me get hungry right now. Or the idea that you are going to be going to your favorite restaurant may set up a mental expectation in you of some enjoyment. Ideas trigger reactions on any of the levels of being, and the more energy you put into the thought, the bigger the reaction will be.

The reaction is equal to the amount of thought you put in now and over a period of time. *Karma* is the result or effect that all our thoughts and actions bring to us. It's the bouncing back of the ball. If we think of something and go and do it, then the universal law will send us back similar thoughts and actions. They may not happen right away, and we don't often see the cause and effect relationship happening in life, but that doesn't mean it's not there. The more you learn to watch your thoughts, the more you see "instant *karma*". You think a mean thought about someone and pretty soon you're bummed out and disappointed. These thoughts boomerang back to you. It's hard to believe in and learn to apply this law, because when we don't get what we want, it's human to think mean thoughts. But the more you watch your thoughts, the more you have to face the fact of how energy, your energy, works. You soon learn how to purify your mind and think positive thoughts, not because anyone tells you you should or must, but because you see for yourself the consequences and you don't want to keep making yourself unhappy.

By being aware of your thoughts you purify your blue level to reflect the clear light. You become good because you have the wisdom to know what good means and why you want to be that way. This is positive blue. Negative blue is trying to be or do good because you were told by someone you should be good in order to avoid evil, or in order to get praise, when at heart you really are selfish. So let's see if we can discover our karma by getting in touch with the thoughts we play over and over in our minds.

3. Everyone have your journals nearby. Every ten minutes during Steps 3 through 9 the leader will ring the bell and you take a few minutes to write down the thoughts in your mind, the last ones you can remember. Catch whatever thoughts you can. No one will read your journal but you, so don't leave any unwanted thoughts out. It's very important that you be as truthful and honest with yourself as you can be. Don't worry about what's happening when the bell rings, just go straight to your notebook. Ask yourself what you were just thinking or feeling, and write it down.

4. The next game which we'll be playing while the leader interrupts us every five to ten minutes is a variation of the game I SPY. Anyone can begin to talk about their thoughts, patterns and feelings. The rest

of the group listens carefully trying to hear and understand everything said and to know what is meant from inside-out. You do this by pretending you are the different people as they talk. The first person talks for several minutes then suddenly says, "A few minutes ago I said a certain key word." The rest of the group asks questions and tries to guess what the word was. Whoever guesses it has to complete a sentence or paragraph that begins with that word, only changing the subject to describe his or her own life patterns. Then after awhile he or she repeats, "A few minutes ago I said something which began with a certain key word, can you tune into what word that was?" And so on. . . Pick significant words, not prepositions or meaningless words. Everyone playing asks direct questions quickly to center in on what has been said, so the group mind is together and the various patterns are seen as part of the One mind. This technique makes us listen more intently and breaks the habit of not listening properly. Most people don't know how to listen.

5. Now review everything you've written down so far in your journal. *The leader keeps up the bell ringing.* Look back over your journals to find patterns from the past. Do you see many repeating patterns? How deep do you go with your thoughts, your mind tapes? The mind plays its thoughts like a tape recorder, or like a juke box tune over and over. We do this especially when we are listening to someone else speaking. Ask yourself: do your worries circle around and around, repeating until some circumstance or event changes the tune? Or do you resolve any of your thoughts and feelings by tracing them back to their cause and then letting them go for good? See if you can choose one pattern or conflict and trace it back to its cause, by constantly asking, what caused that thought? And then when you have an answer, ask where did that thought come from? And then where did that thought behind that thought come from? And so on.

6. Is there a block that keeps you from letting a thought or pattern go, so that it keeps going around and repeating? Contemplate what you do with your mind, and write down what comes to you. See if you can discover two or three of the most typical "tapes" you repeat in your mind. Choose the one that has given you the most trouble over

the past few months. Write it down and see if you can trace the karma, the cause and effect. How did it get so big? Is it a fantasy, an unfulfilled desire or expectation? Take some time to get in touch with it.

7. Share what you can with each other.

8. True saints are people who have discovered their karma and gained the wisdom of how to let it go. Their minds reflect the clear love and wisdom of the universal one. When the mind is pure and devoted to the universal oneness, there are no blocking patterns and karma that keep it bound or attached to anything. Purifying the mind is one of the most difficult tasks before each of us. Many people put it off and would rather keep their awareness attached, blind, dull or even drugged, so that they won't have to face their karma, their deeply rooted ideas. Then they can hold onto their dearly treasured thoughts which they believe will bring them happiness. Creative Conflict challenges each of us to look at what we are creating with our minds, and how it affects our relationships. We will deal with Creative Conflict in Part III.

9. *Mantras* are words given by many spiritual teachers as a form of meditation to clear the mind. Actually they are just the first step to quieting the mind so that it can expand into levels six or seven. *Mantras* work much like self-hypnosis, to get us out of the conscious thought processes.

    Repeating a *mantra* all day keeps us out of mental trouble—thinking thoughts that lead to feelings or actions that create more karma. The *mantra* also helps us to center the mind so that mind energy isn't wasted or distracted into scattered thinking. Choose a *mantra* for yourself of some ideal that you like: Truth, Oneness, Love, Joy, the name of someone you adore, whatever appeals to you most. Repeat it as often as you can for one whole day, as often as each breath if you can remember. It is an experiment to see what *mantra* will do for you. If you can follow through you will be in for a big surprise about yourself.

On the same day or a different day during this next week, continue this exercise of checking your thoughts and writing them down or speaking them into a tape recorder every fifteen minutes to half hour. Now that you have a feel for what penetrating the mind means, keep the energy going. Choose tomorrow if possible as your day of experiment—the sooner the better. You will have a deep insight into your karma, your real Self and its real needs. You will penetrate some deep problems or patterns you have had nagging at you for a long time. Your karma is why you are here in this school, the earth. It holds the lesson that you need in order to perfect yourself. What better devotion can you give to your real Self than to discover your karma and be free of it?

10. Discuss as a group how you will conduct your personal experiments from this exploration and make a commitment to doing them.

11. Journal writing.

A school child practicing "The Shoulderstand", a yoga posture that stimulates and balances the chakra in the area of the neck which controls the blue level of mind awareness.

INDIGO WORLD
THE INTUITIVE LEVEL

Learn to detect The Force. Teenagers detecting the biophysical energies of Life Force with the help of a pendulum that works in the same way as a water diviner's rod.

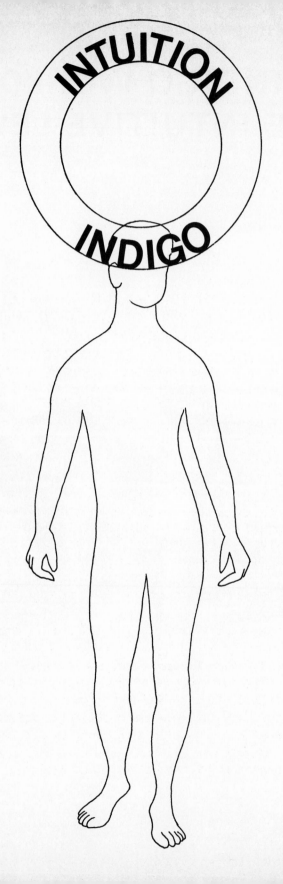

INDIGO
VI

The Indigo intuitive level of awareness is the one most commonly called psychic. Most people wish they were more psychic, hoping this would tune them better to the world, to others, and to exciting spiritual realms of extra-sensory perception. The truth is that everybody is psychic, but some people live in this world more than others. This sixth world is often called the "sixth sense", as though it were some kind of sensing device that tells us information we cannot gain with the other five "ordinary" senses. For you to know that your best friend is just about to call you on the phone, there has to be something inside you that receives the hunch. The hunch comes as your friend's vibration travels on thoughtwaves to your brain which is tuned to him or her. The mechanism is just like a radio. When the dial is set at a certain frequency you pick up signals which are broadcasting. Change the dial a bit and you are out of tune so no message or a fuzzy message comes. We pick up intuitive messages about people we love and care for most easily, because our consciousness is more sensitively tuned to them. Either we are emotionally involved and tuned in on that level, or we ride the same mental wavelength of ideas and thoughts, and so we are tuned in on that level.

This sixth sense comes from the spiritual eye, or third eye, which corresponds to the center between the eyebrows, connected with the pituitary gland. We can see the spiritual eye of in-sight in deep meditation as an orb of energy—an orange-gold circle surrounding a blue sphere, deepening to indigo or midnight blue and spiralling into a white star-like center which draws the consciousness into another energy field—a new dimension of consciousness. It can only be opened by fine tuning. By sensitively attuning ourselves to vibrations and learning to experience life in wholes (not in bits), we see with Direct Perception. We call this vision

360 degrees of awareness. When the spiritual eye is completely awakened you can see with spherical vision, seeing out of the back of your head as well as the front and seeing through matter like X-rays do.

Most people who are on the indigo level, and who consider themselves psychic, have not completely opened up their true spiritual vision. To be able to see auras, predict the future accurately, psychometrize, read tea leaves, or show other psychic abilities, does not necessarily mean you are spiritual. Certain well-known psychics have been known to be able to give readings only when drunk. Other psychics have used their powers to harm others and control their minds. Psychic ability comes when a portion of the brain, generally asleep in most people, awakens. Many primitive peoples were more psychic than people today because they exercised this part of their brain. However, this does not necessarily mean they were more spiritual or more evolved on the whole. Superstitions are also effects of this psychic level of consciousness. Visions of devils, angels, ghosts, symbols, and strange phenomena come from this abstract level of knowing.

The way most of us commonly use the indigo level in everyday living can be seen in how we relate to people through first impressions. We just feel a vibe and something about someone turns us on or off. We don't know why, we just know that's how it is. We just feel that way in our bones. This is intuitive or psychic knowing. We all have it and use it without knowing we are doing it. In fact, much of our living and our decisions come from the hunches, inklings, and non-verbal ways we feel about things. The person tuned to indigo lives in a non-verbal realm.

Indigo level people are tuned to the future, always wondering what's around the corner, and often feeling the grass is greener on the other side of the fence. They are rarely in the physical now, and so are generally late for appointments because they feel they are already there in mind and so busy themselves with something else. Indigo-level individuals may apply their sensitivity to music, to an aesthetic sense of beauty, or to entering the inner worlds of other people and knowing what they are feeling. Negatively, the indigo-auraed people may be fearful of their own sensitivity, fearful of the future, superstitious and impractical. Because they can live in a "cloud nine" dream world, they may find it very hard to plant their feet on the ground and live practically in the everyday world. And yet the dream world may be a fairy tale, far removed from Reality.

To explore the intuitive level in a healthy, creative way, we need to awaken our psychic and spiritual potential in harmony with the other levels and in tune with the good of the whole. Then our intuitive perceptions will not be delusions, but true and real tuning to higher awareness. With our group feedback we have the opportunity to test the reality of our psychic perceptions with each other.

Many psychics make predictions that are false. Anyone can do as well even without intuitive training. To open up the indigo level so that we truly unfold our potential, we need to test the validity of our perceptions constantly by being very truthful with ourselves and with each other. Then this level of consciousness becomes most powerful for human evolutionary advancement. We must always remember that just as our physical senses give varying pictures of reality to different observers and we are deceived by them, so the psychic faculty gives us impressions which are just as unreliable. Unless we train it, nourish it and get skilled in its use, then like any physical part of us it will atrophy through disuse.

This part of the book will give full instructions for anyone to practice exercises to awaken the intuition and make it work.

YOGA POSTURES VI

The Indigo level is very sensitive to the functioning of the pituitary gland. This gland of growth is little understood in terms of its effects on consciousness. Through our powers of concentration we can awaken the activity of this center, since one-pointedness focusses all the scattered energies of the human body, feelings and mind for penetration into the higher domains of direct perception. Only when we are in a receptive state without conflicting and scattered energy currents can we fine-tune to one frequency. By stimulating this chakra scientifically we gain mastery of our internal energies and greater attunement with the cosmic life. The awakening of the third eye can come with more conscious training. First we stimulate the physical vehicle with postures:

1. SHOULDERSTAND — We repeat this posture in the exercises for this center because of the close relationship between the medulla area at the back of the neck and the pituitary. Follow the instructions given on page 255. As you are holding in the inverted position, close your eyes and concentrate on the area between the brows just back of the forehead. Listen inside with the inner ear. You should be able to hear an internal sound—it may be a high-pitched ringing sound, a bell-like clanging, or a sound similar to a fog horn or the ocean. It does not matter what kind of inner sound it is but whatever you hear is a manifestation of the OM, the cosmic vibratory current throughout creation. Listen intently to it, focussing both on the sound and the spiritual eye. Feel yourself merging into the sound in one-pointedness, forgetting your body. Continue until you feel ready to come down.

2. PLOUGH — From the shoulderstand, bring your feet over your head into the posture called the "Plough". Only go as far as you can without straining. Eventually you will be able to touch your toes to the floor behind your head. Keep the legs straight and feet together as you move into the Plough. Even though your back will receive the most stretching

in this exercise, it is an extension of the shoulderstand and affects the flow of energy up the spine into the neck and into the forehead. Concentrate at the point between the brows as you practice this.

3. YOGA MUDRA — Sit crosslegged, arms behind your back, hands clasped, chest out. Inhale and stretch your arms up over the head. Exhale and lean forward and touch your forehead to the ground at the spiritual eye center. Keep your eyes closed. Relax in this position. Feel the sense of surrender and openness to the cosmic will, and concentrate on the third eye. Hold until you begin to lose concentration. Inhale and come up. Exhale and relax. Repeat several times until you get the feel of the effect on your consciousness. The intuitive level is very subtle if you are used to working from the lower levels of consciousness.

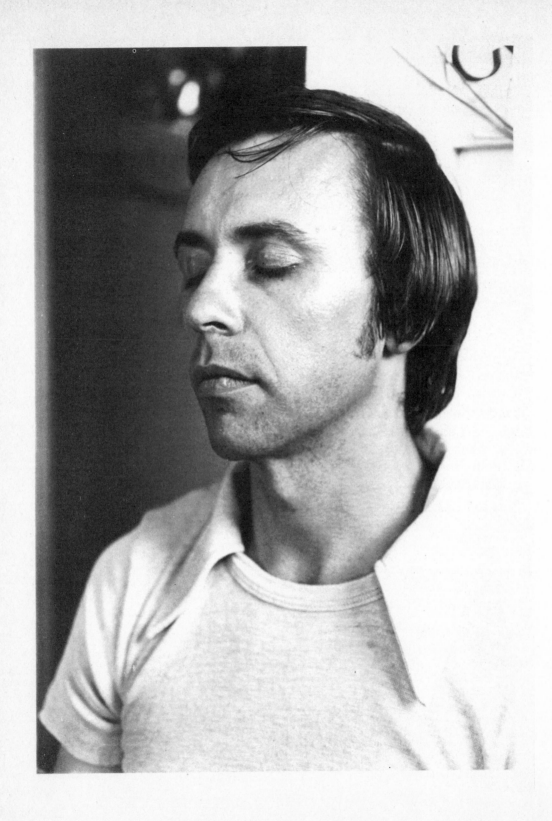

MEDITATION FOR DEVELOPING THE INTUITION

Do the centering meditation on page 54 , focussing the attention at the center between the brows, just behind the forehead. This area is the magnetic part of the mind, the inner "sensorium" that leads beyond mind into true perception. The Easterners call it Buddhi or Intelligence. We focus on the pituitary area in the front of the brain to activate that part of our consciousness. *The leader reads the following meditation when everyone is centered.*

Looking up and in, behind our closed eyes, gently, without straining, we peer into the midnight blue field, in back of our awareness. By concentrating our attention at this center, we feel its force pulling us into itself, as though we were being sucked into the center of a star, into the black hole of consciousness. To really feel this indigo center of intuition, some people imagine that the star is a magnet, attracting them into the center, or a tunnel down which they move. . . (long pause) . . . or you can imagine that there is a vacuum cleaner in the center behind the brows pulling all the energy and life force from your body, feelings and thoughts, into the one-pointedness at this center of awareness. Use the image that helps you best, and concentrate all your energies effortlessly on it. . . (long pause) . . . Now, concentrated, you have left your mind behind and are in the new energy level of intuition. . . Now project that one-pointedness into the future. . . then become receptive. . . what image or feeling or flash comes to awareness? Tune into it! Something will pop in; it may take awhile, but usually it is the first immediate flash—an insight. Don't seize it with your mind and start to work on it, because then you will be back in the mind. Just leave it and more flashes can come in, one after another. Don't worry about remembering, it will impress your memory by itself. If you *try* to hold it, you will lose the intuitive space. . .

Practice tuning into intuition and tuning yourself to people, events, things about which you want to gain more insight. Hold a picture of them in your spiritual or third eye center, project your life force into it and then wait receptively for a response. . . (long pause) . . . The more you practice this heightened, expansive, concentrated awareness, the more you will be on the intuitive level all day long. Extend your intuitive antenna. See out of the corners of your eyes in 360 degree total awareness for Direct Perception. . . (Silence. . . long pause) . . . As you come out of the meditation, open your journal and write down your impressions. Don't stop to analyze them or think about them, this will bring you down, just write them spontaneously and stay in-tu-it.

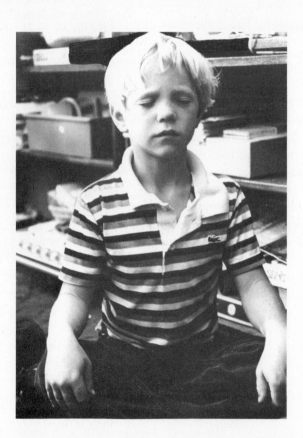

SEEING THE FUTURE

Exploration

58

Indigo World

PREPARATION:
a tape recorder with tape

Have the tape recorder ready to go
at the first step. Have your journals and
pens in front of you ready to write as well.

GOAL: One of the qualities of the intuitional level is its ability to project one into the future. Intuitive people are constantly tuned to what's happening next, where they are going, what's coming. Edgar Cayce and other famous psychics of modern times have had excellent results in predicting future events. In the blue level we explored tapping the collective unconscious for past events buried deep in memory. In this level we will expand our awareness in the direction of that universal storehouse of future possibilities which we all have the ability to tune into via intuition.

Often psychics use crystal balls, tea leaves, patterns of water (in ancient days entrails of an animal), to distract the conscious mind so that its thoughts do not block out the delicate message coming into the superconscious mind. Many tea-leaf readers are not familiar with the meanings of leaf patterns, but use them only for diverting their attention. We learned self-hypnosis in the blue level, which is also a technique for putting the conscious mind to rest, and many psychics go into a state of trance in order to see more easily into the extra-sensory realm of the future. For some people trance is not always necessary for the intuition to work.

In this session we are going to exercise our prophetic abilities, and begin to open up that area of the brain.

EXPLORATION:

1. The same free-association, dream-like space is needed to pick up the random events of the future, as it is to delve into the past. So the first step is a group discussion of "tomorrow". Each person in turn, off the top of his or her head, shares what will probably happen tomorrow from the time of waking in the morning. This exercise must move quickly and not be a process of figuring it out, an analysis or memory based on what happened yesterday or today. Rather it is a spontaneous expression of whatever comes in. First describe what you will eat for breakfast, what will happen at work or at school or at home, all the way through until bedtime. Close your eyes to tune into images that may come. These images and flashes are more likely to be the real random events of the future floating into your intuition. Tape record the descriptions.

   As you listen to each other, be aware of the mental images created by the speaker. You might find it easier and more in tune to do this whole exercise with your eyes closed. Do the images that you see include any details not mentioned by the speaker? If so, say them as you see them so they will be recorded on tape, or if you feel the timing is inappropriate, quickly jot them down so you won't forget. These images are often fleeting and if we don't write them down immediately we can lose them forever. When that person has spoken, share your glimpses, being as precise and clear as possible for the benefit of the tape recorder.

2. The next day everyone must check out whether the images, glimpses and description of the day before actually took place and record what did happen. Often there is a gap in the memory, so write down at the end of the day what did happen, then bring it to the next group meeting and compare what you have written while it was fresh, with the tape recorded predictions. Did you really meet a long lost friend? Did a dish really break? Did you really wear a red dress and someone gave you a rose?, etc.

3. Intuitive sensitivity is sharpened by practice. One person who has felt especially good with self-hypnosis volunteers to be an oracle.

He or she sits or lies down in the center of the room. Everyone together practices the relaxation and self-hypnosis learned in the blue level, suggesting to themselves: "The veils of time are lifted. We are floating into the future." The volunteer in the center announces when he or she is "ready". The members ask the oracle specific questions about problems or decisions facing them. The volunteer answers automatically, whatever thoughts come, even if they do not make any sense or are already understood and seem like common sense. Limit the questioning to ten minutes as it can be tiring. It requires one-pointed concentration to be an oracle. Don't worry about what is said, just listen and receive as the oracle speaks. No discussion should take place until the very end. Every ten minutes take turns with others who feel they would like to try being the oracle and feel "ready". One at a time, each volunteer goes into the center, or if the group is very large two oracles can tune in at the same time, answering the questions in turn. Usually the responses are amazingly perceptive and helpful. In this quiet, meditative state, pure truth can come through easily. Children are excellent at this exercise and often gain much confidence in their abilities to see and speak truth.

When everyone is through, the leader ends the session with the suggestion of renewed energy and well-being at the count of three. Take a deep breath and feel alive and refreshed, one, two, three!

4.   Discuss your experience.

5.   Journal writing.

TESTING YOUR INTUITION

Exploration

59

Indigo World

PREPARATION:
*blindfolds for everyone
an object the leader feels is very dear
or significant to him*

*four or five unusual or uncommon objects
that will be difficult to identify just by
touch alone*

*a box and some object (can be solid or
liquid, fragile or vibrating—anything)
Leader secretly places object in box.*

*ten glasses (clear) of water and a
fresh supply of water (a tap, or jug)*

GOAL: The intuitive answer comes in a flash. There is only a moment to receive it, recognize it and grab hold of it. To have this happen to us we have to learn to expect it and look for it. Aware people work with their intuition constantly, looking for the intuitive signals. They move around with their "antennae" up and ready.

Intuition involves such delicate faculties that it is just as liable to "goof" as any other aspect of human awareness, including the five senses, or human reason. When the intuitive faculty is blocked, just like any sensitive machinery it is more prone to defect and can conk out. Yet, with exercise, intuition can develop into a magnificent tool for extending our intelligence, influence and effectiveness.

While the first step is to be awake and ready for intuitive events, we must also purify our awareness of the "noise" in our environment which is made from all the passing vibrations. These vibrations create "electrical resistance". Fear, anxiety, guilt, remorse, jealousy and negative emotions also create resistance which may completely block our intuitive ability. When we let our defenses down the intuition awakens. The more we are attuned to universal energy and feel a oneness with all life, the more we are attuned to intuition. In this exercise we want to get some feedback as to where we are with our intuitive sixth sense.

EXPLORATION:

1. In this test we use a plain box. The leader places some object in it secretly. It can be anything at all. Each person in the group has to find out what is in the box. One by one everyone handles the box. Watch each other carefully and notice how each person goes about discovering what's in the box. After everyone has handled it, each person in turn guesses what's in the box.

2. It should be possible to tell a good deal about everyone by the way they handled the box, even their occupation. Are they used to working with their hands? If there was a jug of cream inside or a few eggs, did they turn it upside down or shake it roughly without taking prior care? Discuss your observations.

3. Now, working together as a team, close your eyes and meditate on the contents of the box. Do your centering quickly and one-pointedly until all your consciousness is concentrated at the intuitive center between the brows which is like a magnet. See what images flash in. Focus the concentrated magnet at the brow, then project it towards the box, imagining your energies and the energies in the box are merging into one. Wait for some thought or vision to enter. Be receptive: do not think. See your force of concentration united with the energies in everyone else for one large group-magnetized intuition, attracting an image or impression of what is in the box. *The leader brings everyone out of the meditation after a few moments.* Each person has a guess. *The leader removes the object from the box and shows it to the group.*

4. Everyone is blindfolded now, except the leader. *The leader passes unusual or uncommon objects around the group for identification.* Use your intuitive faculties to receive what the object is, remembering to concentrate, looking up at the point between the eyebrows, relax, and receive an impression, thought or image, then say whatever comes in. Don't worry if you're wrong. Practice with several things, and practice this exercise again and again at other sessions or on your own with a friend until you get the feel of the intuitive energy. It has a special feeling and soon you begin to know when you are on; you can feel you are in "synch", riding the energy of being in tune. Children, again, are very quick to recognize the feeling of the intuition, and early training will open up the center quickly and make it part of their daily lives.

5. The leader brings out the object that is significant to him and passes it around for the rest of the group to handle. Each person feels it, and tunes into it, with the same method as above, and says aloud why it is important to the leader. *The leader responds last.*

6. Everyone takes their blindfolds off for this step. *The leader places ten numbered glasses of water in a row a few inches apart on the floor or on a table.* Everyone leaves the room for a moment. The leader "magnetizes" one of the glasses by placing both hands over and around it and channeling life force, as we learned to do in the green level, into that glass. When he feels certain that he has sent energy into it and can visualize it having magnetized the water, he withdraws his hands and moves away from the glass. Everyone comes back into the room. Each person tries to sense which glass has been magnetized. Usually your first flash is correct. Your eyes may even be magnetically drawn to the charged glass.

    Everyone writes down their guess and the name of the leader. The leader then reveals which is the correct guess. Examine now this magnetized glass and open yourself to receive its vibration. Concentrate on it and on the others. Can you pick up any nuance of a feeling that makes it different? Usually it vibrates more, or has some quality that makes you feel it's different. Tune into the vibration or feeling it gives you so you can know what to look for next time. *Now the leader empties the water out and fills the glass again with fresh water.* Another person volunteers to do the magnetizing and the group leaves the room again. Repeat three or four times with a different volunteer each time. Tally the correct "hits". (The odds are even less than one correct hit for each person if you've repeated the guessing less than ten times.) Discuss your experience of the exercise. Are you beginning to recognize that intuitive feeling? Don't be discouraged if your accuracy is not high yet, even though you believe you are beginning to feel something different. Keep up with the training and testing. (Mathematical odds for the group as a whole can be computed as follows: Total number of "hits" likely equals number of participants times the number of volunteers who magnetized water divided by ten.)

7. Journal writing.

THE TAROT

PREPARATION:
A Tarot deck (traditional type) with all cards in it and instructions with interpretations or a separate book of instructions and interpretation

The leader for this session should spend some time preparing himself so he is acquainted with Tarot method and meanings.

You may want to tape record the readings.

GOAL: Another aspect of the intuition is its ability to experience truths in symbols and "know"what the symbols mean. Jung and others have explored certain symbols which seem to crop up universally in the collective consciousness of man, such as the six pointed star, the circle, the triangle, etc. The way these symbols are interpreted from culture to culture is similar. Dream symbols, too, generally have common meanings. The Tarot is a pack of cards with symbols on them. They delve deeply into philosophical truths and archetypal moods of life. Through them we can gain a mirror of our own psychological state. Gypsies of the fourteenth century are said to have created them, but it is more probable that they originated from the hieroglyphic tablets of ancient Egypt and represent the archetypal symbolism of those days. By using the Tarot cards we link or tune into the psychological states that are operating through us now.

The universal stream of consciousness, which we have been glimpsing into and probing, has no beginning and no end. While this stream is passing through us, we give it a past, a present and a future to orient ourselves and events. However, out in the cosmos, time does not take on these divisions. In the violet level we will be exploring this eternal sense. In this game, we will explore the future through the symbols we attract in the present, since whatever our consciousness is doing now creates the future. The intuition is the sensing device that picks up the future frequency in the stream of consciousness.

EXPLORATION:

1. The leader brings out the Tarot cards he has obtained and studied either briefly or for a long time. He shows the cards to everyone and explains what they include, what the symbols mean. There are fifty-two ordinary playing cards, plus one additional picture card in each suit and twenty-two numbered cards with symbols such as the Juggler, High Priestess, Empress, etc. The twenty-two cards are known as the Major Arcana. They are placed face down in a stack after being shuffled separately from the rest of the deck.

2. Each person takes a card off the top of the pack, keeping the card face down and not looking at it until his or her turn comes to read it. The leader begins by turning over his card and immediately stating the first thought which comes into his mind on seeing it. The idea is to catch the first image or impression that comes to you and to say what the card or picture means to you. Thoughts will flash in, you may not like them, but do not edit them for a second choice of thoughts. Say the first thing and then let new thoughts continue to expand on themselves as you speak. Every person in turn does the same thing with their card until all have shared their intuitive feelings about the meaning of the symbol on the card before them.

3. The leader then reads the meaning of each card as described in the instruction book. The meanings given in the book are not the only ones, and you should not discount your own in light of what the book says. For example, "The Fool" can symbolize the Divine Fool who trusts the cosmic intelligence for his every need and is greatly blessed, or it can be a small, weak, foolish person, depending on how you see yourself mirrored in it. When someone who is psychic reads the cards for you, he tunes into the feeling and images

that come to him as he experiences your vibration. These are the ones he shares. Now he may be projecting some of his own personality into the reading, but that is for you to discriminate.

4. Discuss now whether the group feels the card picked really does fit the person. One by one consider each person in turn. Generally, although it seems beyond the laws of reason, people pick the symbol (or are attracted to it) that fits them and carries a message for them as to their present situation and its outcome.

5. Now, following the instructions on how to lay out the cards in the booklet accompanying the deck, read someone's future by having them work with the whole deck. The group helps interpret the meaning of the symbols by tuning in and looking for the images and impressions that come in. Do not try to analyze or figure out the meanings based on your past knowledge of that symbol or based on the logical facts of the person's life. These will influence your intuitive interpretation anyway, but you must be open and not thinking in order to receive pure impressions.

6. Take turns until you feel tired. The energy of this level of consciousness works in cycles and until you are used to tuning to it, it can be tiring after a bit. One way to charge yourself up again is to run your hands under a tap of cold water, keeping your hands to either side of the water for a few minutes drawing in life force before wetting them. Then wash your hands up to the elbows letting them dry on their own without towelling.

7. Journal writing. It is important in all these intuitive exercises to check out whether the predictions and insights really do come true. This is the only way you can have a valid test of whether your intuition is improving. These games are for the sole purpose of exercising that psychic faculty and awakening it so you can be intuitive all the time, using it at will. Unless you cultivate it to work for you, these games will just be fun parlor games with a little mystery, and not training sessions.

THE HUMAN AURA

Exploration

61

Indigo World

PREPARATION:
room with white or light-colored walls
movie or slide projector and movie screen
chair
piece of fur or a piece of wool
(preferably fur or both)

Be able to darken the room completely,
and to vary the lighting from dim to bright.

GOAL: In this awareness game we will all learn to see auras. Whenever I have taught this exercise to a group, almost all were able to see something and gain the conviction that auras do exist and can be seen if we continue to look for them. Children see them very regularly and training them to look for them is just a confirmation of what they already feel. The aura reveals what is happening at the time in the person's inner world. It reveals the person's color level. Most people flit from one level to another rapidly, and so the aura color can be a kaleidoscopic, ever-changing pattern as we move from thinking (yellow) to reflecting on the past (blue) to insecurity (green) etc. However, we generally have one basic color to our aura, the color to which it always returns. This is called the resting color and is the frequency of our most usual state of consciousness. This frequency becomes a habit of personality which is why it is called our main level of consciousness.

A now famous story is told of a person who could always see auras. One afternoon he was waiting for an elevator after an appointment in an office building. When the door opened, the person looked inside and could see no auras around the people. The individual was too shocked to enter; the door closed, and then the elevator crashed, killing the occupants. When you are trained you can tell the state of someone's health or mood by the aura, even when there is no body language apparent. When someone is about to die the aura changes to a dark grey beforehand.

EXPLORATION:

1. The leader brings out the fur piece or wool piece. Everyone discusses its dominant color. Now take a second look. Is there a cast or sheen to the color? A blue fox is naturally dark brown, but many can also see the bluish cast. Certain animals are bred to enhance the casts in the fur. Don't focus on a single point of the garment, but allow the eye to encompass the whole by looking just a little beyond it. When eyes are slightly unfocussed more can be seen, since the focussing mechanism is not eliminating as much.

2. Practice unfocussing the eyes by holding your two forefingers horizontally with tips together in front of your eyes. Bring them close to the eyes, within an inch, so you are looking cross-eyed at them, now slowly move them away from the eyes. Keep moving them until you see a sausage-like third finger in-between the two tips. Note how your eyes feel when you see this distortion. That is the state of unfocus your eyes need to be in to allow the intuition to work through them. The mind sees aura colors, not the physical eyes, so we have to get the usual dominant physical focussing mechanism out of the way to see the aura.

3. There are several kinds of lighting that enable us to see the aura more easily.

    a) One is the bright sunlight. The person has his back to the sun and you see the sun illuminating a halo-like field around the hair and neck or coming off of the face like a sheen. Note any impressions of color you may have in this field.

    b) Another setting is a darkened room. All the lights have been turned off and shades drawn. Let your eyes grow accustomed to the darkness. Then attempt to see each other in the dark. Even if the darkness is close to total, usually something can be seen. What is it? Can you see an area where a person is? If you look at the area, it can become an aura. Again, do not focus the eyes at a particular point, but look with the slightly unfocussed gaze we learned and look slightly past the body. Those who see anything should describe it to the others.

c) Now the lights can be turned on low, so that the room is dimly lit. Look at each other, or slightly past each other to see if you can detect the aura. If the room has a light wall, white or cream-colored, have a subject sit in front of the wall, and direct the light beam onto the wall. Look at the area around the head and neck and shoulders, as well as the sheen coming off of the face. We have found this the most successful method of training inexperienced people to see auras. If you see a white halo, around one to two inches surrounding the head, this is the etheric or energy body that is like the white threads you see when you channel energy; it is not the aura of the state of consciousness.

d) One final method, which is also highly effective, is to seat people in front of a movie screen and shine the projector onto them in a very dark room. The aura can be seen reflected on the white background screen.

4. Seeing the aura is more a manifestation of an extra-sensitive person than an extra-sensitive eye. Through meditation you can develop the sensitivity automatically that enables you to suddenly discover you are seeing auras. Turn the lights on to normal brightness and look to see if you can see the same auras you saw under the special conditions, now under normal conditions.

5. Now discuss the colors you saw around each other. Is there any agreement? Does each color fit with the mood that person was in? Does it fit with their usual level of consciousness which you determined at a previous exploration? (See page 64 for a refresher of what the states and colors are.) Practice looking for auras over the next few days before the next exploration. The more you can remain in the poised, sensitive, 360 degree awareness, the easier it will be to see them.

6. Journal writing.

PSYCHOMETRY

Exploration

62

Indigo World

GOAL: Objects carry the vibrations of their story around with them. Physical things can "talk" to us if we tune into them. Many psychically able people can pick up a piece of jewelry and, by concentrating on their intuitive center, receive images and complete stories as to where it came from, what it means to its owner, and how it was obtained.

In this exploration we are going to create a climate in which we can do some psychometry games.

PREPARATION:
The leader collects together several meaningful objects, either something from his house, room, or a personal item that means a great deal to him. Four or five items will do. He also asks everyone else to bring some simple object that has a story or history to it.

a table and a tablecloth (preferably white)

EXPLORATION:

1. *After completing the meditation on the intuitive center, the leader brings out an object of his, either something in his room, or a personal item. He places it in the center of the room.* Everyone continues the intuitive meditation into a new step called "Samyama". This is a yogic exercise in which we extend our centered awareness to something or someone, and identify with it so that we become one with it. When we are in this rapport in which we feel no separation, we can feel the object's vibrations in our own being. We then can pick up impressions from its history, images of people who have been associated with it, the culture from which it comes, etc.

> To do "Samyama" we must concentrate, extend our awareness to wrap itself around the object, let go of our sense of self, and open up to receive impressions—images, feelings, thoughts.

After this exercise in oneness, the object is passed around from person to person. The first to hold it tells as many things about the object as he can describe. When he has totally exhausted all his feelings about it, he describes the facts about it, the things he

327

notices. Then he passes it on to the next person who adds to what has already been said by noting additional things about it. Perhaps the object has some scratch in the base, or some flaws in the stone or metal, or a certain thickness. Describe all the details you can about it. After all have emptied themselves of what they see and feel about the object, it is passed around the circle again. This time share your hunches about where the object comes from, and any further flashes or images you may have. After everyone has come to the conclusion that there is absolutely nothing more to be said about that object, it is handed back for a third go around. Usually there is still a great deal more to cover, and more wild guesses that are often accurate will come through. *The leader reveals the object's real history and discussion follows.*

2. Repeat with several other objects.

3. Now a person sits in the center and we do the "Samyama" exercise on the person. Everyone takes a turn saying the flashes they feel, see or intuit about that person's history. Do not worry about accuracy, share your wild guesses. Then go around again repeating the same exercise. The person should turn around and face others in the circle so everyone gets a feel from his or her whole being. Speak whatever you are feeling about the vibrations of the person in the center. When you do "Samyama" correctly you feel those vibrations superimposed upon your own, so you are reading yourself. You have become one with the object of concentration. You project yourself into the object by sending life force, then you look and see carefully what this does for your reading ability.

4. Continue with a few more people in the center.

5. Take another object and place it in the center of the circle. *The leader reads the following:*

    If you took a microscope and looked at the surface of this object you would see a lot more about it than with the naked eye. Now we want to develop a zoom lens in our mind to zoom in on something that looks simple, and blow it up so it becomes more than it appears. When we look at water through a microscope we find that there's a whole universe of living microorganisms that we never knew we were drinking. The same thing is found in all sorts of matter, such as glass. When we begin to get into the nature of materials we find that they are not even solid. Molecules and atoms vibrate at tremendous rates, the tones and harmonies of molecules are quanta of electricity, atoms with their own brand of consciousness. Molecules move with a compulsion to interact with each other through the bond which is essential to their nature. In this way we can enter into an object and find that it is made of pure electricity, like our own bodies. By doing "Samyama" and changing the way we perceive, we also, in a sense, change the nature of the object, just as a stone under a microscope is a very different entity than it is to our plain eyesight.

Now everyone does "Samyama" on this last object in terms of the above description, moving into the realms of molecules, atoms, pure electricity and light. Discuss.

6. Everyone moves to the table and places an object they have brought under the cloth in such a way that nobody can see it. It can be anything. The group takes a minute to relax and meditate in silence, and do "Samyama" on the hidden objects. Call off out loud what you feel is under the cloth.

7. Now the tablecloth is removed and each person writes down a list of the objects, then individually attempts to identify the owner by the feel or emanations of the object. People who recognize the object from knowing the owner should disqualify themselves on that particular object. When everyone has finished, the owners reclaim their objects. Any more than one or two successful choices in a group of ten to fifteen can be considered psychometry in action. Those with the greatest number of hits then continue to try to tell more about the object's history, etc., and note down the details of any direct perceptions of information which can be checked and confirmed by those present.

8. Journal writing.

DOWSING OR DIVINING

Exploration

63

Indigo World

PREPARATION:
*Each person will need a pendulum.
You can make them either from black
string or thread and wooden buttons, or
black thread and wooden spools—(wood
is the best material for accuracy, metals
can deflect energies and pick up stray
energies, and crystals or gems are
selective of different things).*

*pennies for everyone in the group
A white card or piece of paper, about
3" x 2" for each person*

GOAL: The body is a fantastic instrument of which we have relatively little knowledge, in spite of our tremendous supply of medical research. Divining is a way of sensitizing the nervous system to serve as a natural feedback unit. Many people have experimented with biofeedback machines, learning to control their thoughts and brainwaves through them. By learning how to dowse for answers to questions, for water, oil, minerals, lost objects—anything—we make use of our own built-in biofeedback system. The nervous system can be trained to communicate directly with the universal collective consciousness lying in our unconscious. Therefore we can gain a "yes" or "no" answer to any question we can imagine.

The pendulum or divining rod is merely an extension of the nervous system. We are all diviners to some degree, but some of us don't know it. When you have a funny feeling in answer to an internal question you have put to yourself, you often know that means "no –don't do it." When your heart responds with a positive feeling, you know that it's okay. Some people have their own internal codes— when they feel a flush of blood it means "no", a peaceful sensation means "yes". We usually don't use these inner messages very consciously. Yet by training with the pendulum we can train ourselves to listen

to the inner voice or inner messages all
the time. Eventually we can do away with
the aid of the pendulum entirely.

EXPLORATION:

1. *The leader passes out the string and buttons.* Everyone takes a
   wooden button and ties black string through it so that a simple
   pendulum is made about twelve inches long. The leader demonstrates
   the way the pendulum works while everyone follows along. Holding
   the string between thumb and forefinger (see picture on page 243)
   set the pendulum swinging straight forward and back, towards you and
   away, letting it swing back and forth a few times. Then, without
   influencing the swing or moving the hand, ask your unconscious the
   question, which way is "yes"? Watch and see which way the
   pendulum rotates. It should either move in a clockwise or counterclockwise rotation. For most people "yes" is clockwise. Then ask,
   which way is "no"? It will begin to swing in the opposite direction.
   Don't force it, and don't try to stop it. Many people don't experience the change because they're so afraid of influencing the swing
   they inhibit any movement at all. For best results, tune the pendulum
   in the following manner before you go on:
   To tune the pendulum to your own needs, hold the string between
   thumb and forefinger grabbing it right at the juncture where string
   and button meet. Hold the pendulum approximately two to three
   inches above your outstretched left palm if you are right-handed
   (over the right palm if left-handed). Start the pendulum swinging
   back and forth. Now slowly and gradually let the string slip between
   your forefinger and thumb until the pendulum starts to rotate (spin
   around in a circle). This is your tuning point. This point should not
   be more than three to five inches from the juncture where the string
   and button (or whatever object you use) meet.

2. Tie a knot at your tuned point. This is where you will hold the
   pendulum from now on and get best results. Again ask, which way is
   "yes"? Which way is "no"? If you are getting confusing results, give

your subconscious a command that clockwise will be "yes", counter-clockwise will be "no", or vice versa. Be definite. Your own uncertainty may be what is mixing up the message.

3. Now put down your pendulum. Hold your hand out in front of you, (use the right hand if you are right-handed and the left hand if you are left-handed.) Ask "Which finger is my 'yes' finger?" You will feel a tingle in one finger or a throb, or some distinguishing sensation. Then ask, "Which finger is my 'no' finger?" You will feel another finger respond. Children are very good at this and usually can pick up strong nerve responses in their fingers. The pendulum rotation is really triggered by a response in the nervous system communicated through the string. The pendulum just aids you in noticing it. If you feel the nerve response direct in the fingers you don't need the pendulum. Some people divine by a feeling in the heart center. See if you can develop a code with some part of your body.

4. Now everyone asks a question of their unconscious, of the universe, to which they would like to know the answer. The question should be a present-time question, not something about the future. There are too many random possibilities for the future to get an accurate answer. It should also be a question worded very clearly and answerable with a "yes" or a "no". Some questions might be: Did I do well in the test I took today? Am I making the right decision in leaving my job? Should I buy that new book? Is my lost ring in the bathroom? etc.

5. If you are having trouble, pair off with someone who can watch you and give you feedback as to how you are following the above instructions. Your attitude of mind must be open, receptive, non-programming and clear to receive a straight answer directly from the universal field. Your partner can ask questions too as you hold the pendulum. Get yourself out of the way so that the answer comes in directly.

6. *The leader passes out the pennies and the cards to everyone.* Toss the coin. Hold the pendulum over it and ask, which way is for

heads?—see if it's positive/yes or negative/no. Ask, which way is for tails? It should be the opposite. Throw the coin several times and test yourself with the pendulum to see if you get the same results. Next throw the coin, and immediately place the card on top of the coin without looking at it. Hold the pendulum over the card and see which way it rotates. An alternative is to just stay with your "yes" and "no" code and ask, Is it heads? yes or no? See what the response is. Test yourself with ten throws. The more detached, and non-caring about whether you are right or wrong, the better your results will be.*

7. You can make up some hide and seek games, treasure hunts, and other games with the pendulum. A favorite we use often at children's workshops is to put 100 pennies in a jar and hide the jar. Then give every child a penny as a witness. (Witnesses are objects, similar to the one you are looking for, which you can hold in your hand as you divine. The resonance between the witness and the object sought, amplifies the vibrations and enables you to pick up a stronger signal, getting a stronger response from your nervous system.) The rule of the game is that you have to find the hidden object with the pendulum, by asking questions like, is it in this half the room? Is it by the sofa, yes or no? No hunting allowed until you get a definite answer from the pendulum. You can hide someone's shoe and hold the other shoe as a witness. Make up a game and see how successful the group is at it. The more enthusiasm and emotional life force you put into the dowsing, the better you will be at it.**

8. Discuss everyone's experiences. The divining phenomenon is a way to train the intuition. Some people find it the easiest and most exciting of the intuition games.

9. Journal writing.

---

* If you have a compass you can see the magnetic field affect the pendulum rotation positively or negatively depending upon whether you hold the pendulum over the north or south pole. It will rotate one way over one pole, switch in the middle and rotate the other way over the other pole.

** Pendulums are available from the publishers if you wish to order them. See appendix. You can detect the colors in the aura easily with an aura pendulum.

E.S.P. AND ORDINARY GAMES

GOAL: In school and family fun we play many typical guessing games, such as chess, charades, dominoes, bridge, hangman, etc. Most of the time we use some intuition, but it is largely unconscious and untrained. In this exploration we are going to take some ordinary games that we learn as we grow up and play them, only using our newly acquired training in E.S.P. Even party games can be an opportunity for growth if played with purpose and concentration.

PREPARATION:

The leader thinks up several ordinary fun guessing games such as chess, checkers, dominoes, bridge, hangman, battleships, charades, etc.

He brings along to the evening all equipment needed to play these games.

EXPLORATION:

1. As a group, pool your ideas for some of the games you know how to play which are typical and fun. Decide whether you all want to play the same game or whether you want to break up into smaller groups and play different games. You can also use the intuition when you are playing individual games, sports, or anything that may take some guesswork! Some typical games are listed below.*

---

* (Hangman is played by two people taking turns guessing a word that the other has in mind. The person thinking of the word writes down short blank lines for each letter, showing the number of letters in the word. Someone keeps a record of each letter guessed. A rightly guessed letter is inserted by the person thinking of the word in the space where it belongs. A picture of a noose is drawn on a piece of paper or blackboard. For each wrong letter guessed, the person thinking of the word draws a part of the body: head, arm, trunk, leg, etc. If the word is a five-letter word then you have a body with five parts, an eight-letter word, you have a body with eight parts (add a foot or hair or something to make eight.) If the guesser is correct before his body is hung, he wins. On a five-letter word he'd have five guesses and so on.)

(Battleships is played on graph paper with opponents seated back to back. Each creates a game area twelve squares in each direction. The vertical rows are identified by letters across the top from left to right, A through L. The horizontal rows are identified by numbers down the left side one

2. Gather the needed equipment together and begin the game or games. Everyone tune themselves into the intuitive center, continuing to practice the meditation for this state of awareness and "Samyama", learned on page 327. To the degree that you can keep you antennae up, and your 360 degree awareness going so that you see with full vision, instead of tunnel vision, you will be activating your sixth sense during this entire session. Stay receptively focussed in the center between the brows, which means concentrated yet relaxed and open for a flash to come in.

3. Play the games with a casual, don't-care-if-I-win attitude, and yet stay attuned.

4. Discuss your results and scores. Consistent successes are signs of intuition in action.

5. Journal writing.

---

through twelve. Each player is permitted a submarine (S), a destroyer (D) and a battleship (B). He places these letters in scattered areas of his diagram. Each of these vessels can shoot into an adjoining square. That is, if an S is located in C2, it could shoot into B1, B2, B3, C1, C3, D1, D2 or D3. An S, D, or B may move either N (up), S (down), E (right) or W (left) before or after they shoot. They may shoot before moving or after moving, but they must shoot every turn. They may stand still. A submarine moves only one square at a time. A destroyer must move two squares and a battleship must move three squares. The object of the game is to hit all three of the opponent's boats before he hits yours. Once a boat is hit it is out of the game. The one who moves first says, for instance, "I shoot with my submarine into D3 and move one to the north." He may or may not hit one of his opponent's boats, but his opponent now has a fix on one of his vessels. Each party draws a line on his own chart indicating where his own vessels move to.)

TELEPATHY

Exploration

65

Indigo World

PREPARATION:
a blindfold (Make sure it is secure before-
hand so you cannot see down past the nose
or through the material.)

GOAL: In many of the earlier intuitive explorations we have been using telepathy without calling it that. Telepathy is the ability to receive or send a thought or image from one mind to another. We all use telepathy to some degree, but we need to become more aware of it to make this extra potential work for us. Tuning to other's feelings and minds can help us be better friends and expand our understanding. Like any ability, it can be used selfishly too. But especially with psychic abilities, selfish use will often rebound back and harm the person who is using the power to hurt. Selfless use has a way of returning good and blessing to the user. In this exploration we want to learn a healthful and creative use for telepathy which we can apply in our daily lives.

EXPLORATION:

1. Right after the opening meditation pair off with someone and sit knee to knee. Without talking, hold hands so that one person grasps the wrists of the other person. The person whose wrists are being held is the receiver, the other the sender. The sender visualizes one thing that means a great deal to him—his pet, or friend, or money, etc. Visualize the person or object in great detail. The receiver opens in heart and mind to receive the impression—a flash, an image, a thought—and says what he or she sees or feels. The other person shares whether it is correct. (Several variations of this exercise are: to send what was the nicest thing you did today, send a thought or picture of your mood or feeling, send a thought or picture of some object in the room.) Then switch roles so that the sender

becomes the receiver and receiver the sender. You can repeat this several times with different partners. Try to determine whether you feel you are better at sending or receiving.

2. Have you ever had the following experiences or something similar?

> You stare at the back of the neck of someone in front of you in an elevator. Soon that person turns around and you know he has "felt" your stare. Or you are the person "feeling" and turn around to see someone staring at you.

> A man looks at a girl walking in front of him in a bathing suit. Soon she reaches down to tug down her suit in the back.

3. The leader chooses two people to join him as starers. Everyone else lines up in a row with their backs turned so they can't see the starers. The three starers decide on whom they will zap with their intense energy and concentration. They all focus on the target and send energy through the center between the brows, channeling as we learned in World Four. Whoever feels a stare raises a hand. The starers have to be sure they stay concentrated and not let their energy and attention wander. Repeat with several targets. Someone who feels they can be a good, strong sender trade with one of the starers and repeat the exercise.

4. Everyone stands in a circle while one person stands in the middle blindfolded. The leader silently points to a member in the circle and everyone leans toward that person and at the same time looks and concentrates on the person in the center. The person in the center has no idea who has been chosen, but usually leans toward him or her. To be a good receiver, the person in the center should not "try", but should stand in a relaxed, receptive way. Others take a turn in the center. If the person in the center does not visibly lean, ask him or her to guess which way the group is leaning. Each person in the center repeats the exercise three times.

5. Everyone sits down and one person who will receive leaves the room. The group decides on some object in the room on which to concentrate and send to the receiver. They *do not* look at the object,

See Step 4 on the previous page for instructions to this telepathy training exercise.

but concentrate on it in their third eye only. The receiver comes back in and tunes into the minds of the senders with the "Samyama"* oneness he has learned, opening himself to pick up the thoughts and images that are being sent. He moves toward the object he intuits. If he has difficulty the group can help by saying "cold", "warm" or "hot" while still concentrating and sending the thought and image of the object. Take turns so several people have a chance to be receivers.

6. Discuss what telepathic tuning feels like. What is needed to be successful? Is it a special attitude of focussed mind and open heart? How can we practice telepathy, and what good use can we put it to so that we become more aware beings?

7. Journal writing.

Teenagers practicing the telepathy exercise on p. 336, Step 1.

*See page 327 for Samyama technique.

I HAVE A SECRET
(MORE TELEPATHY)

Exploration

66

Indigo World

PREPARATION:
several household objects that can be hidden

GOAL: In this game we want to put telepathy into action and continue to develop our ability to communicate without words or actions. Whether we are testing ESP or telepathy in a laboratory or in an awareness game, an important element is usually missing—emotional voltage. Because these games are not in real life situations, we do not give them the emotional charge and seriousness that we do to the spontaneous things that happen. Everyday ESP and telepathy take place more often than we know and most often with people who are close to us, involving real events that are meaningful to us. In this exploration we will add more feeling to our games so that our ESP becomes more intense.

EXPLORATION:

1. The group divides into two teams, A and B. The first person on Team A shares a secret with his teammates. Team B must guess what the secret is by asking questions to which Team A responds "yes" or "no". A count is kept of the total questions asked, until the secret is known, with a limit of twenty questions. Then Team B shares a secret and Team A guesses. The winning team is the one that has had to ask the fewest questions.

2. The winning team now becomes the receiving team in this next game, the other team the senders. One person on the receiving team leaves the room. An object is hidden by the sending group. The receiver is called back and told what he is looking for. One sender

340

holds the arm or shoulder of the receiver and walks with him around the room as the receiver tunes into the hidden object. The sender concentrates on the location of the object in his intuitive center, but does not look at the object or lead the receiver to it. A time limit of five minutes is placed on the receiver to find the object. When the object is found the leader makes a record of how long it took. Other senders and receivers try.

3.   This time the exercise is repeated without any physical touching, just the whole group concentrating on the hidden object while the receiver moves around to find it. The receiver can hold out his or her hand and ask "yes" or "no" questions to see if a tingle in the fingertips can aid the divining of the object. Here we put together two intuitive faculties, divining and telepathy.

4.   a) Everyone sits in a circle and meditates on the following question: If you were to be granted one wish in life, what would you want it to be? Choose something that you seriously want and select wisely. Holding the wish in your third eye is a first step to actually manifesting it in your physical life.

   b) Decide if you are a better sender or receiver. Senders now should visualize their wishes, receivers for the moment should forget theirs and open their minds so they can receive what is coming. Receivers write down all wish impressions that they pick up as well as the sender's name for each wish. In five minutes, the receivers read off their impressions. Then the senders state what their wishes were. The leader records how many correct guesses there were. Now switch roles with receivers becoming senders, and repeat the game. Do the scores show that the first sending group of people who felt they were better senders is indeed more accurate?

5.   Discuss the difference in your results when the thing you are visualizing or receiving means a lot to you (like a wish you really would like to come true).

6.   Journal writing.

THE FEELINGS OF STRANGERS

GOAL: The greatest problems that confront everyone are usually related to relationships and our communication difficulties. The generation gap, communications gap, credibility gap all have to do with our relation to people. Expanded awareness helps to close these gaps. An aware, intuitive person receives more information from what is said and vibed. Less separateness and greater oneness are felt by an aware person and from this oneness, love and understanding come. In this game you are going to test how much you have grown in awareness with new people. We have invited several guests to join us in order to gain some feedback on our sensitivity to strangers. The goal is to develop our awareness of strangers in everyday life and therefore this game can be practiced several times to develop skill.

PREPARATION:
The leader invites several guests to this session. If others in the group have friends they would especially like to have join they invite them too. However, the total number of guests should not be more than the total number of regular group members who will be present. When choosing guests, try to choose people with some basic differences in education, economic and social background. Age differences are good too. Aim for at least three guests.

blindfolds
flowers for each person
music—two selections, one each of very different moods
a phonograph or tape deck on which to play music
a large piece of newsprint or drawing paper (you can tape several sheets together) so that the group can make a group picture
scorecards and pens
magic markers, crayons or paints to draw with.

EXPLORATION:

1. After the meditation everyone sits in a circle, guests included. Go around and introduce yourselves. Tell your occupations and say whatever else you would like to say. Then ask the guests if they have any idea of what the purposes of the group are, what kinds of things the group does. Each guest comments. Note the different concepts of awareness. The group members then share some of the things that have meant the most to them.

2. The leader explains to the guests that they have been invited to give some feedback on the group's awareness and sensitivity to strangers. They are asked to be judges as to the accuracy of how the members have portrayed the group and themselves.

    Each guest is given a scorecard and a pen.

3. All the regular group members are blindfolded, except for the leader. They are all to pretend that they are blind people who can judge character only from the sound and inflections of voices. Each guest goes to a different corner or area in the room, or to a different room if one is available. The leader leads several blindfolded group members to each guest. They all sit down in a half-circle around the guest. Try to divide the group up fairly evenly among the guests. Each member in turn asks questions of the guest. No one knows with which guest they have been placed. Questions should try to draw out from the guest something of his inner world, his likes and dislikes, his life. Some questions might be: "Are you married?" "Do you like gardening?" "What are your deepest interests?" etc. The blindfolded members listen carefully to the vibrations of the replies, seeing what they can pick up from the communication. Listen to the guest as if he or she were music. What vibes do you feel? Gentleness? A yearning for contact? Sexual energy? Compassion and understanding? Defensiveness? Shyness? etc. How does the music of the voice affect you?

4. After everyone in the group has asked questions and the guest replied, then each person shares with the guest what he feels coming from him, for example: "I think you are very gentle and warmhearted," or "I feel you must be very emotional," or "You seem tense and controlled," etc. The guest keeps a scorecard and writes down a score from 1 to 5 as to how accurate he or she feels the feedback is. A 5 is for "right on", or a direct hit. A 1 is for way off; 2 and 3 and 4 are for various grades in between. Without the guest saying anything about what he feels or the scores at this time, the group members switch around and go to another guest to do the same questioning. Keep repeating until everyone has questioned all

the guests. If there are many guests you will have to move quickly spending from only five to ten minutes before switching. *The leader can keep watch and signal when it's time to switch.*

5.   Everyone remove your blindfolds and come together in a large circle. Share your scores and your feelings about the experience.

6.   The leader plays the first mood (a slow piece) music for several minutes while participants sit quietly, reflecting on the feelings the music creates. Towards the end of the piece, the leader walks around and silently gives everyone a flower to hold. When the music ends everyone comments on their feelings. Then the second piece is played for contrast. When it is over everyone talks about how it made them feel. What was the contrast? What effect did the flower have?

7.   The large sheet of newsprint or drawing paper and colors is brought out. All of the short musical pieces are played and everyone, one at a time or all together, draws pictures on the paper to the music as they feel moved. Everyone should contribute something to the group effort. Don't overwork the drawing. When two or more people feel it is complete, then consider it done. Discuss how you felt drawing to music, and how you felt about the different contributions of art.

8.   Ask the guests for feedback as to how they felt about the whole exploration. Discuss your feelings too. How attuned to the others in the ONE did you feel individually and as a group?

9.   Journal writing.

GROUP CONSCIOUSNESS
THE GROUP AS A CELL IN THE
BODY OF HUMANITY

PREPARATION:
The leader for this exploration should be someone who is musically inclined, and someone who has a strong feeling for the group sensitivity and group consciousness.

three selections of instrumental music that are inspirations from different cultures, at least one from the Eastern countries

The leader brings a musical instrument he can play.

a small mirror for each person

GOAL: The more aware we become, the more sensitive we are to the feelings and inner worlds of others. With a whole wave of people dedicated to becoming more aware, we can come together and work together for each other's evolution, thereby greatly enhancing our own and the group's awareness.

Due to easier communications through the media, groups are becoming very common, and different kinds of group activity are increasing. By becoming part of a group we change and let go of our separateness. The group consciousness of the indigo level of awareness is a different sensitivity to the group experience than the following-the-crowd consciousness of the orange level. True group consciousness is a group of people all tuned in oneness, so that together they form a greater, more aware being. This kind of group consciousness is not changing our ideas to go along with the ideas or most powerful view in the group, but to be free to see the group members as soul mirrors of the self. With the many diverging views, we can more wisely decide what feels best for us. Rather than dwell on the negatives and differences, we concentrate on our united purpose for growth and unfolding positive potential.

EXPLORATION:

1. After the meditation find a partner and sit knee to knee. Look into each other's eyes and look to see which eye is the larger or the stronger. Is one eye projecting life force more than another? Is one eye sucking you in and another sending energy? Note which is doing what. . . Now, imagine that you are looking into a mirror and those eyes are your own. Whichever eye is larger is your eye. See if you can try to balance out the eyes so they are of equal intensity by adjusting your own eyes. You may want to close one or the other for a moment, or imagine a rush of life force going through the weaker eye. . .

2. The right eye has the positive, masculine, more aggressive energy. The left eye has the negative, feminine, passive energy. The body is electrical just like a magnet. By breathing strongly through the left nostril and blocking the right nostril with the forefinger, we charge up with the feminine (called Shakti) energy. The left eye should appear larger or brighter. By sending this life force out of the left eye it will project or radiate. By drawing this life force in from the universe in a receptive way, the left eye will draw in energy. You can increase the male (Shiva) force in the same way, by blocking the left nostril with the forefinger and breathing through the right nostril. Using breath and sending or receiving, see if you can balance out the eyes in your mirror—the eyes in front of you.

3. When you have balanced as well as you can, ask yourself how you feel. Go within to see if you experience more balance, more peace and ease. When positive and negative energies are balanced within (masculine and feminine) we are poised and centered, and the energies are free to rise to a more aware state of consciousness. Pick up your small mirror and see if your eyes are balanced. If not, take a moment to breathe and send life force as before.

4. Now close your eyes and look within. Did you have fears of eye contact? Did you react to what you saw in the mirror of the other? In your own mirror? If you had fears, get in touch with what they were. . . . . Now balance your inner being again and let the reactions

346

or fears go. Can you open your eyes and look at the other person and see your real Self, without any fear? Look for the soul, the love and the being behind the personality.

5. Close your eyes again. Now ask yourself if you have a fear of dying. What if you had to die soon, could you stay in the center of love and balance? What does it feel like to be a soul at peace, rather than a personality that is always acting and reacting? Meditate on that peace.

6. Now open your eyes and come together to discuss what group consciousness means to you. What have your experiences with each other, dedicated to awareness and growth together, done for you? Share your feelings with each other.

7. If you haven't already discussed these questions, do so now. Go around the circle with each question.

    a) Does the group provide fulfilling new experiences?
    b) Does it challenge my consciousness?
    c) Does it involve everyone deeply enough?
    d) Have we melted any unwanted personality or social barriers?
    e) Does it promote love and understanding?
    f) Is it fun?
    g) What would make the group consciousness more fulfilling, more meaningful?

8. What activities do you do on your own during the periods between your group explorations to increase awareness? Discuss. What would you like to do in the future?

9. Which world has felt the most productive of growth and progress thus far? Is this the world you enjoy most? live in the most? or need to develop the most? Everyone shares their favorite world and answers these questions.

10. At this point the group can choose from previous awareness explorations to do the one that brought the members closest together, the

agreed upon favorite for group consciousness, or the group can continue on with Step 11.

11. Music and dance are group art forms that can tune a group of people in to the Source, move them with the spirit. Inspirational music is chosen for the next exploration. Dance music is played and the floor cleared. In the East there are spiritual dances of ecstasy. The dervishes in North Africa, Turkey and Afghanistan expand awareness by tuning their muscles and nerves to cosmic rhythms. In India the cobra snake symbolizes the chakras within the spinal column. Through music we can charm the energy of consciousness to rise through the spine into the higher centers in the brain. We sway to the heartbeat-like rhythm, feeling our meditation go deeper as we move in tune with the universe.

12. The leader puts on the first piece. Everyone dances alone, tuning in with Samyama* directly to the Source and to the consciousness of the composer and musician, writing and playing the inspiration.

13. The second piece of music is played and the leader calls "change" every fifteen seconds. You choose a new partner each time, moving to the person nearest to you but with whom you have not yet been paired (if possible). You dance to the cosmic rhythm together, spontaneously.

14. For the third selection, everyone forms a circle, holding hands. The circle can sway, move slowly around in one direction then another, or it can face outward and repeat these movements. It can face inward again and form a tighter circle with arms hugging each other around shoulders or waists. Move spontaneously as the music inspires you. Try to tune together as a whole to the One spirit.

15. Take a minute to relax now that the dancing is finished. Then the leader, who has brought a guitar or musical instrument, brings it out and all join in group singing and chanting. Listen to each other. We want to have clear tones and harmonies which only come when we

* See p. 327 for instruction on Samyama.

listen to the universe and each other as much as we listen to our own sound. Alternate a soft and then a powerful sound, varying the rhythm and tone.

16. Close with a two or three minute meditation.

The leader reads:

> Everyone tune into the group's strength and send light and love to each other, then to the whole room, the building, the trees and sky, earth and people in the wider community, the country, the world, the solar system, the galaxy, the universe, into the Oneness of all consciousness.

17. Share feelings.

18. Journal writing.

Part of the community at the University of the Trees who are working together on Group Consciousness.

TAPPING HIDDEN RESOURCES

Exploration

69

Indigo World

GOAL: In the awareness game to follow we are faced with a real test in real life action to see how our intuition has developed. Several situations in the world are given and we are challenged to trust the cosmic intelligence to provide and see us through.

PREPARATION:
The leader will need to supply a house with a kitchen and supplies for baking cookies, but he or she is not to prepare the utensils or food, but leave them on the shelves and in the refrigerator.

knitting needles and yarn
several small appliances that can be opened up and taken apart and put back together
a car to drive someone

To meet the challenge you will have to call on hidden resources within your soul, because you will be called on to do something outside your usual experience and knowledge. If you try intellectually to plan it all out you will block the creative flow of inspiration that makes this journey exciting and confirms your higher power. A real test of whether you are tapped into the One is your own spontaneity. You invent a way on the spur of the moment. It comes through you and out and you don't have to think about it. By feeling yourself as part of the whole, including any problem, you tune into the way through it.

EXPLORATION:

1. Each person will be going on an unusual assignment. These are serious tests of your ability to be guided by spontaneous conclusions and intuition. You may either draw lots and let the cosmos decide your task, select your own test from the list below, or you can alter the list and invent more tasks. Often we do not go beyond our fears because we don't accept challenges. We take the safe way out. Then, of course, if our fears are too strong, they will block the intuition from working for us. More than one person can be given

the same assignment, but everyone must work separately, since it is a personal test. The time limit is one hour for completing the task.

The following are divided according to tasks that men generally find more suitable and tasks that women generally find more suitable, however no distinction has to be made if you don't feel it's necessary. If you feel too afraid of the tasks given you, then openly share your feelings, and don't be afraid to share them. There's no use doing a test you don't feel in tune with or confident with—it won't work. Choose something more suitable yet still challenging.

Men

You are taken blindfolded and penniless in a car about two or three miles away to some out-of-the-way, off-the-beaten-track spot and left there to return to the group"on your own".

You are to leave and return with a book you have borrowed from someone—either a friend or stranger—not related to you, which deals with a subject on the nature of human beings or the universe.

You are to learn to knit by yourself with knitting needles and wool provided and you must knit a ring or bracelet.

You are to leave penniless and return with three kinds of fresh fruit to eat and something that is non-edible but grows.

Women

You are to prepare cookies in your hostess' kitchen without asking any questions and finding all the materials yourself.

You are to weave a small mat using whatever grasses you can find.

You are to disassemble and reassemble a small appliance like a waffle iron or clock.

2. Make up enough challenges such as the above for the entire group or double up. Make sure everyone has some challenging activity to do.

You may want to do them in shifts so that for the first hour several people in "shift one" go out and for the second hour the rest of the group in "shift two" go out. In the meantime those who remain behind can visualize and help create a successful outcome for those who've gone out. Send loving and encouraging thought waves, channeling your energy and care. Be sure you channel only one image to one person at a time. As the hour progresses see if you can tune into what is happening with each person who is on assignment. Close your eyes, tune to the person's name and vibration, visualize the face, then when you feel the being, open up to receive whatever impressions come. Take that person into yourself so that you feel one and see what thoughts arise in your consciousness.

3. At the end everyone gathers together at an agreed upon time, and discusses their successes or failures, their feelings and how their state of consciousness conditioned what happened. How did your experience draw on your spontaneity and intuition? Did you feel the energy and support coming from others in the group? Did you feel tuned into the whole and the guiding universal intelligence?

4. Everyone shares in the cookies and discusses what they need to work on to strengthen their attunement.

5. Journal writing.

VIOLET WORLD
THE IMAGINATION LEVEL

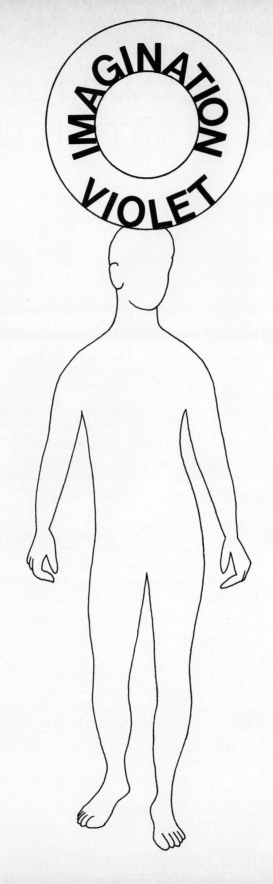

VIOLET
VII

The Violet level of imagination is not the same energy level as that of the conceptual images that flow in from the memory bank. It is, however, the creative imagination, that primal energy that becomes form and substance, that creates and projects forms in consciousness. There is often a fine line between fact and fantasy, and in the imagination level we need to distinguish between the primordial images that we all experience in consciousness, and the real hallucinatory or fantastical ones that are merely mental creations or distortions of the Real. The primordial images that form trees, clouds, humans with the same basic structure, animals, all life forms, are projections of the Cosmic Intelligence and Cosmic Imagination in which humans participate as direct experience.

By widening our own imaginative abilities we can experience the conscious co-creation of the universe in oneness with the Universal Intelligence. We transcend space and time and experience the eternal essence of things. This is the spiritual goal and challenge for mankind. In this way we can become One with Cosmic Consciousness. Then we go beyond our known universe and its seven levels into another domain of awareness.

When light is fully absorbed, the aura color is black. This darkness can be the thick darkness of ignorance—refusing to radiate any light or love—or it can be the transparent primal darkness of the black hole of pure awareness, where the Cosmic energy is absorbed before it is re-radiated into all the colors of the rainbow for pure white or the golden white aura of the master of consciousness.

The Violet level is a level in which we use images to create and recreate our reality. It is the domain of magic and invocation. Whatever we see before us, we are re-creating in our imagination from the signals passing along our nervous system to the brain. Inside the brain we project a replication or an image on our mental screen. Isn't this a magical, fantastic process? Science does not yet understand how it really works.* Very little research has been done on the creative imagination. The violet auraed person is often in a dream world, as you may imagine, seeing the world as images of light, impressions and textures of some eternal time-feeling sense.

The images first become percepts, then concepts and finally get stored in our memories and replayed in our minds. All thoughts are made of image content. The true violet level lives in the eternal now of the energy of the image which is ever-new, not in the past of memory images. A good musician hears music in his imagination; it plays him, and he merely becomes the channel to put it into writing so that others can benefit from the composition. Beethoven was deaf but he heard music in consciousness. All great artists, musicians and imaginative mathematicians function in this violet level. Time seems to stop in this world. Space extends everywhere in this eternal feeling, as form dissolves into formlessness.

Most people on the violet level have glimpses of the eternal realms, but do not live in its primordial purity. They manipulate images and fantasies to suit their ego preferences, rather than surrender to a greater Cosmic will. Although this is the highest center, a violet aura doesn't mean that person is necessarily more evolved than someone with a red aura. Many people revert to the violet as an escape from other levels which they have not mastered. A drug addict may escape into a realm of inner images which anaesthetize him from the harsh realities of practical everyday living. Someone else may use his power of imagination to create erotic fantasies, another to hallucinate images of himself as certain historical characters. The challenge to people on the violet level is to test out the reality of their images in their lives—in their job effectiveness, relationships, etc. In other words, check it out on all the other levels of consciousness. Only then can the full potential of the violet world, often called the thousand petalled lotus in the East, open up to reveal the glory of the Cosmic Intelligence.

* *Energy, Matter and Form*, by Allen, Bearne and Smith, discusses the mental replication process in depth. (See appendix)

YOGA POSTURES VII

The Violet level is the crown center or chakra on the top of the head. It is related to the pineal gland. The pineal gland has often been thought to secrete a hormone that activates the mystical experience, but very little is known about it in western medical research. In fact, in most people it atrophies gradually with misuse as the body grows older. Imagination is something we all have, but usually use unconsciously. Some people, who have studied the effects of psychedelic drugs on subjects, maintain that these drugs activate a brain chemical substance similar to the hormone secreted by the pineal gland, or even activate the pineal hormone itself, thereby quickening the imaginative-mystical experience or, alternatively, the hallucinatory experience. By stimulating this chakra scientifically we can safely probe the creative forces within us and within the universe. We can also dissolve the ego membrane that creates separation and thus experience the essential oneness of universal life.

1.   THE HARE— Kneel on the floor, sitting back on your heels. Keep your knees, inner thighs, tips of big toes together. Relax your ankles, feet and sit up straight. Now come up onto your toes so the toes bear the weight of your feet. Firmly grasp each heel with your hands. Tuck your chin on the chest, round your back as much as possible from the base of the spine to the top of your head, and roll slowly forward. Pull your stomach in toward the spine. Keep rolling forward slowly until the crown of your head touches the floor. Let your arms straighten and your hips rise off the heels. Hold, and feel the energies flow into your crown center. When you are ready, sit back on your heels and roll up slowly, one vertabrae at a time. Relax.

2.   YOGA MUDRA with Crown Center — Follow the instructions for yoga mudra on p. 311 as you did on the indigo level. Only instead of touching forehead to the floor, you place the top of the head on the floor. Keep your eyes closed and relax. Surrender to the Cosmic Intelligence and imagine your personal self dissolving in the Universal expansion of Oneness. Hold as long as it is comfortable. Inhale and come up. Exhale and relax. Repeat several times until you feel yourself surrender more and more, as much as you can. This is a posture of humility and surrender in the One.

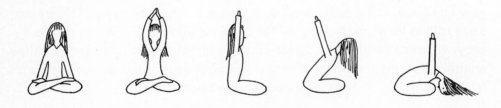

3.   THE HEADSTAND* – Sit on your knees. You may want to work in pairs so that your partner can hold you up until you gain your balance and some confidence in this posture. Alternatively, you can do this against a wall so you won't be constantly falling down and having to pick yourself up. Cup your hands and put your head in your hands. Put the hands and head on the ground, with elbows forming a stable tripod supporting the head. Inhale and raise the knees so the legs are straight and the buttocks are in the air. Make sure your elbows are on the ground. Exhale and push up. Straighten your legs in the air. When you push up and straighten your legs your partner can catch them and hold them in a vertical position. If you are doing this against a wall, try to straighten yourself as much as possible. Go slowly and concentrate carefully. Your degree of absolute concentration will do more for your success than anything. Hold for one minute, keeping your neck firm but not tense. Come down slowly, bending the knees then lowering your feet to the ground. Relax, and lift your head up slowly when the blood is redistributed through the body. Then lie down on your back and relax in the Corpse Pose.

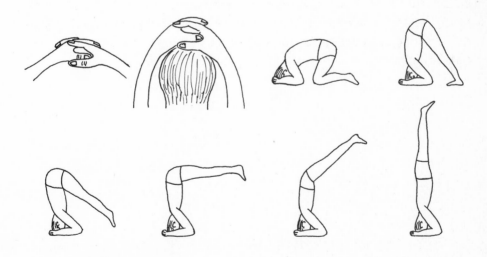

* People with health problems, especially weaknesses in the back, neck, or heart, and pregnant women or women in their menstrual period should not attempt this posture.

4.   CORPSE POSE – This posture is a good one to do after every yoga practice session on any level. It is a most difficult posture to do perfectly, since perfect relaxation is rare. Lie on your back, legs together, feet splayed out, arms down at the side. Close your eyes and go within, relaxing any tensions by imagining them dissolving and adjusting the body as needed. Tune into each of the seven chakras, from the base of the spine to the top of the head and feel your psychic being open to the universal flow. Body, feelings, mind, imagination, life force, all merged into one.

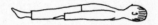

MEDITATION FOR EXPANSION INTO THE UNIVERSAL ONENESS

Begin the Centering Meditation on page 54 . When you feel centered, transfer your attention to the top of your head, the crown center. *The leader slowly continues with the following:*

Focus on the crown center as the seat of creative consciousness within you. Imagine and feel white light energy moving at the top of your head and gently flowing within you and without . . . You feel uplifted and light. The sense of lightness is both felt and seen at the same time . . . The more lightness you feel, the less you feel like a body, or a separate self. The lightness lifts you out and out and expands your feeling of "I" into the crown, into energy, into light all around you . . . Your heart feels as if it is being lifted up into your crown and then spreading out, blending with the rays of energy, flowing into the Cosmos . . . (long pause) . . . The more you can gently imagine this flow, in a relaxed way, not thinking of self, just letting be, the more you will feel bliss. Bliss replaces your sense of a self. Bliss replaces your feeling of being separate from the universe around. Your crown center becomes lighter and hotter and more intense. The energy keeps streaming out until you feel the sun glowing and spreading its rays from the center in your crown throughout the whole universe. The sun's rays are penetrating through space, shining on the earth, flowers, plants, grass, animals, clouds, sky, people, shining on all creation,*creating* the creation with its light energy . . . (long pause) . . . You go deeper into this central sun, looking for the source of bliss, and the rays of transparent light pour out more intensely, past planets, stars, into the furthest reaches of space, past galaxies, universes and all that's left is bliss . . . pure bliss consciousness . . . and you are merged in this bliss so that self and bliss are one . . . If any thought comes to bring you back to the little self let it dissolve into energy, so you keep the outpouring, the sunlight blending through all of space . . . Now even space is just an idea that dissolves. . . and there is only one . . . (long pause) . . . blissful oneness . . .

Stay in this selfless state for as long as you can. As you come out of the meditation remember **YOU ARE THE LIGHT OF THE WORLD.** Your consciousness is lighting up the world around you— your consciousness is the light by which you see this world.

The crown chakra meditation is best done in the corpse posture. But if you have a tendency to go to sleep when you lie on your back, be sure to sit upright.

CREATIVE VISUALIZATION

Exploration
70
Violet World

PREPARATION:
a large mirror, preferably full-length

GOAL: We learned in previous explorations that the power of suggestion on a receptive mind can work miracles and create amazing changes in body and mind. Through self-hypnosis we can de-hypnotize the erroneous suggestions of limitation that have been placed upon us by social thinking, and imprint true suggestions of Cosmic Oneness. In the state of receptivity in which self-hypnosis places us, our creative visualizing capacity gains great power and manifests more strongly. The choice is always yours, whether to accept a suggestion or not, and the responsibility for visualizing a change is also yours, although the combined group consciousness visualizing together with you creates a greatly enhanced, powerful effect. In this awareness game we are going to work with the group power to aid us in using our creative imagination for growth and change.

EXPLORATION:
1. The following are true examples of successful hypnosis. These are not all self-hypnosis, which is what we practice, but they still show the power of suggestion over mind and body. *The leader reads:*

> A professional golfer who was having a problem with his drive was told to visualize himself making a perfect drive and repeat the drive in his mind's eye several times. A minute of intense visualizing can equal an hour of practice. The golfer found his score improved and he now gets a full day of driving practice in eight minutes.

363

An actor who had trouble memorizing his lines and faced losing his job went to a hypnotist for help. The hypnotist taught him to suggest in hypnosis that by reading the part once it would be indelibly fixed in his memory. It worked successfully for him.

A man was told that he was being touched with a hot iron when he was actually touched with a cold coin in hypnosis. His skin blistered. And when the situation was reversed, when he was touched with a hot iron and told it was a cold coin, there was no blister.

A stage hypnotist told a woman her body was rigid. Then her head was placed on one chair and her feet on another. A man was able to stand on her midsection without her flinching or being hurt at all.

A patient hemorrhaged in surgery. All medical efforts failed, so a hypnotist was called in. He commanded the flow of blood to stop. The patient's subconscious obeyed his command.

Whether you have had success with self-hypnosis yet or not, you will improve your results if you can accept the fact that you can do it. Usually from eighty to ninety percent of all successfully hypnotized people believe that they were not really hypnotized at all. Yet their actions prove to others that they were. Even in the so-called normal state, how many of us believe we are walking around hypnotized into the dream of our self-limitations? Most people think it's real! Even watching television is a mild state of hypnosis. To improve your results visualize yourself as if you are now doing self-hypnosis, and have already done it successfully. You must really want the suggestion you give yourself to work. You must also be in a relaxed state and visualize rather than think or verbalize to yourself. A picture is more powerful than 1,000 words or thoughts in this state. You should not use your power of imaging to pick too great a change. Go one small step at a time. Neither should you use suggestion to remove nature's warnings, such as chronic pain. Don't eliminate a habit without substituting something else in it's place. Your body may have a psychological need for the habit you would like to remove—like overeating. Giving it up can produce substitute habits that might be more harmful—like smoking, etc.—so you should substitute something else until you get to the real emotional cause, which can only come by exploring your unconscious as we do in these games and soul searching. Choose something harmless, like gum chewing, to compensate instead of the unwanted habit you have. Be patient and persistent. Start with one iota of progress and let it work. Then go on. Self-hypnosis is the first step to self-change and spiritual growth. It unlocks the door to your unconscious so you can work with it creatively. Now with this added background in mind, continue on to the next step.

2. Each person stands in front of the group in turn. Everyone makes some suggestions for better posture. The person stands more erectly, making whatever changes are suggested. Look in the full length mirror and see your new image. The group also discusses other physical aspects. Now the group describes every person in the way they'd like to look, for example, an overweight person is described by everyone as looking slimmer. A boy with a bad complexion is described by the group as having clear skin. Every physical imperfection is mirrored as its opposite to form a powerful suggestion for the person who has it. After every person has had the group mirror on their improvement, everyone sits down and does the self-hypnosis, emphasizing the vivid visualization of the new physical image as that person, and the new feeling it brings. Our self-image is often made from how we think others see us. This game lets us see others seeing us in a new way.

3. Everyone continue your one-pointed visualizing for as long as you can, until your energies begin to feel slowed down, like you've had enough. Then end your own session with the one, two, three count.

4. Everyone shares some emotional attitude they would like to change or develop with the rest of the group. Describe your goals and what you wish to achieve. The group then devises a visualizaton for each person. Together you decide on the best visualization and the safest, most natural solution. When everyone has their own group-supported visualization, everyone returns to their self-hypnosis state

and begins programming and suggestion in as deeply relaxed a state as they can. The following are some helpful examples:

A person's best talents are visualized at work or at school, in perfect form over and over, seeing him a success in what he wants to do. The person can make a continuous cassette tape to be played over and over before going to sleep with the suggestion.

Someone's skill at a sport or game is visualized, in perfect form repeatedly.

Some person is at the crossroads with alcohol. If he keeps on he sees trouble ahead. If he stops now or at least makes a discipline of moderation he see happiness ahead. The entire group visualizes him choosing the way of moderation and happiness. They offer substitute drinks that he can make when the urge comes on.

A person wants to give up smoking but is having a hard time. The group suggests that he visualize every cigarette tasting like burnt rubber and each pack crawling with lice. He repeats this suggestion over and over in self-hypnosis. Then when he feels tempted he has the force of the group to help and his own self-hypnosis there to work for him and reinforce the suggestion. The group offers a substitute activity which is harmless.

Someone seeks spiritual uplifting. The group together creates an image of him radiant with joy. He visualizes himself as this image over and over. The group offers a mantram or saying to repeat in his mind and he picks the most suitable one. He repeats the mantram to protect himself against depressing thoughts.

5. Everyone discusses their experiences and makes a pact to keep practicing on their own, remembering the feeling of the group support and the group energy. Everyone also promises to take time to visualize for others in the group so an energy vortex is built up in each person.

6. Journal writing.

DREAM INTERPRETATION

Exploration
71
Violet World

PREPARATION:
Select a leader for this session who has had some interest and or experience in dream work or psychology, so he can facilitate the dream interpretations exactly as per instructions.

an easel or some board with several large sheets of paper and magic marker
or
a large blackboard with chalk and eraser
The paper is preferable.

Instruct each group member to come prepared with a dream written out for the group. If anyone cannot remember any dreams, the leader asks them to practice Step 5 for several days prior to the exploration.

GOAL: Dreams always have a meaning for our unconscious, even though we consciously cannot often understand what that meaning is. One of the most effective methods of dream interpretation is the Gestalt method. It is effective because it is based on the laws of consciousness. Although some dreams are precognitive, that is the images come into the intuitive realm of future scanning or telepathy, most dreams are projections from within us from our inner emotional, psychic memory onto the screen of the mind. The conscious mind is out of the way so the field of the imagination and memory has free play. Dreaming is the psyche's way of balancing out its inner energies, just as sleep is the body's way of resting and renewing.

People who have problems which they refuse to face in their waking hours, or which get buried in the stream of daily activities, are usually confronted by these problems through dream symbols. And the solutions to the problems are also often presented in the dreams by the unconscious. It is up to us to learn their code in order to decipher the messages. Like fairy tales and parables, dreams speak to us indirectly in a language of powerful analogy and imagery. Poetry and parable are also powerful because the image contains more content than explanatory words could ever convey. In this exploration we will delve into this inner world of dreams and learn one fail-safe method for interpreting them for ourselves.

EXPLORATION:
1. *The leader reads the following description of dream interpretation.*

The Gestalt method of understanding dreams is based upon the way consciousness works. It begins with the awareness that everything you see or experience is being created in your own consciousness. All is within you. All the objects in the room you are in are projections of the creative imagination re-creating your reality through you. Each person's reality is filtered a bit differently, although there are primordial archetypes common to all of us created by the Universal Intelligence. These universal patterns are hidden within our individual personality patterns. When we dream at night, we must own the fact that every person in our dreams, every object in the dream is a projection of us, a projection of our own energy and consciousness. It symbolizes, for a reason, some part of ourself. Whether you dream of your mother, your dog, a hairy spider, or your child, the image is a symbol for some feeling going on inside of you. This fact of how the violet level functions is more easy to see and apply to dreams than to waking reality. It is not easy to believe that this typewriter I am typing on is a projection of myself, symbolizing some quality of consciousness that mirrors my inner state right now.

In the dream work, when we apply the Gestalt process, the interpretations all seem to fall in place and we are left with an astonishing painting of our inner being. And the confirmation comes not from some outside authority (which would be a blue level mental operation) but from our own intuitive conviction. The imaginative level is one level beyond the intuition and working with imagination helps to enhance and activate the intuitive knowingness of direct perception.

Each color level is capable of seeing how the energy levels below it work (the slower frequencies) but can only glimpse one or two levels above itself because the energy is not intense enough to see farther. Similarly, by working with the imagination we will be utilizing all that we have learned about ourselves from the six other energy worlds we have explored.

In the dream work if I am dreaming I am typing at a typewriter, I might, upon waking, naturally say "Oh well, I typed all day yesterday, so I dreamed I was still typing at night." Frequently we do dream about the activities we have been involved in during the previous day, especially if they are repetitive activities like typing. But to brush them off as only that, deprives us of seeing why our unconscious chose to project that particular image to us during the night. There is choice in dreams, as fantastic as that may seem, but some awareness beyond the conscious ego is making the choice. It is our unconscious trying to communicate to the conscious mind with symbols as well as let off pressure and balance the internal energies. In the Gestalt method, if I dream I am typing at a typewriter I must become the typewriter, own it as myself and describe how I feel being a typewriter. So I may say, "Well, I'm green, I'm mechanical and rat-a-tat-tat all the time, and I am constantly going." I look at this description and I say to myself, "Yes, that's how I've been for the past few days." My very choice of description and talking about it as myself reveals something to me about my psyche, my inner state. Writing down my comments then, I describe myself as each object in the dream. I reread what I have written. Never have I failed to be amazed to see a perfectly painted portrait of my deep inner feelings and problems. In this case I might say, "My goodness, this description fits exactly how my friend told me I have been treating him this past week— insecure, talking all the time, mechanical in my movements, etc." So the objects in the dream state are a mirror of the self. And in real life, the objects at any given moment, the people in our consciousness at any given moment (which means the people around you physically as well as in your thoughts), are mirrors of yourself. In all my classes I have had people bring their dreams. We go through the Gestalt process, and everybody is amazed at how deep a reflection they get back. Often they know that it is deeper than they can understand, deeper even than they want to go, but they know, with an inner certainty, that it is true, it hits home. This astonished reaction to the portrait painted comes even with those who are initially most skeptical of the philosophy, who simply cannot accept the idea that everything is a projection of their inner world. They say, "I don't have any problems," or "that was in my dream only because it happened yesterday, it doesn't mean anything" or "that is just mumbo jumbo, silly things, I must have had indigestion." The main point we need to communicate from this imaginative level, is that nothing is meaningless, everything has cause and effect, even if it is activated by your indigestion. All is consciousness and consciousness is just what the word says—conscious—aware, intelligent. By its very definition it has meaning! So with this background let us see for ourself, and begin the group dream interpretation.

2. Everyone brings out the dreams they have logged in their journals during the past few days. Or if you have a dream from the past that has long disturbed you, or a repeating dream which is vivid in your mind, you can use one of those. The leader should select one or two dreams to begin with as examples, so the entire group can participate in the process together, and get first-hand experience of how it works. Then, when everyone feels they know the steps, each can apply them to their own dream or work in small groups and interpret each other's dreams together. If you have a large group it will be rather lengthy and tiring for the whole group to be involved in each other's dreams. It is better to work in pairs or trios to gain help of another's mirror, and not just interpret by yourself. There are many other methods of dream interpretation, from analyzing symbols, to the recently popular Jungian and Senoi dream work. For the purpose of this exploration, let us try to put aside all of our knowledge of Freudian symbols, or other ways of interpreting, until we have completed the Gestalt method from beginning to end. Then we can embellish whatever we have seen with the other ideas we may have. For the purpose of learning the Gestalt method, we must not confuse it with other methods initially.

3. Now that everyone is with the partner or group they are going to work with, choose one or two dreams from the larger group and the leader begins directing the Gestalt process.

   a) The leader goes to the blackboard or to an easel with several sheets of paper on it. He begins writing with large, distinct letters so everyone can read what he writes. He asks the person whose dream it is to share the dream from beginning to end, as much as can be remembered, including every little detail. It doesn't matter if all that is remembered is one small snatch of a dream. There is a reason that you have remembered that snatch! The leader logs the dream before the whole group and includes all images described.

b) The next step is to ask the dreamer to go through the dream again, line by line, and own each object or person in the dream as a part of him or herself. If in the first sentence there is a group of people and several objects, then take each one at a time. The dreamer describes what he or she feels like as that person or object, always speaking in the first person. (There will be a temptation to begin separating and saying he or she instead of I. Whenever this begins to happen the group should immediately help the dreamer correct it back to the first person.) As the dreamer goes through every action, object, situation and person in the dream describing it as *himself*, the leader is busy writing down this new version of the dream story on another sheet of paper. Go slowly enough so you get every flash that the dreamer speaks, every feeling, every thing. Beware of the tendency to shift from I to it, for example, "I'm a boat, I'm brown, and it's got slats and it is cut in half." This Step b is an experience of owning, and must be practiced as that, very strictly. If the dreamer starts to gloss over some descriptions, anyone in the group can ask him to go more into the feeling of being that spider, or more into the feeling of being his mother, wife, child or friend. We want to identify as much as we possibly can with the different people as ourself. At times this is threatening, and may bring resistance or tears. Be patient, give the dreamer a chance to work through the feelings. Often unconscious fears burst forth. At this time no one is to switch into analyzing or go off the track into words of comfort. It is best to keep the dreamer one-pointedly on feeling and expressing according to the instructions in the exercise.

c) After the leader has logged this new version of the dream, all in the first person, I, then most of the work is done. The Gestalt is on record. What remains is for the dreamer to then read aloud to himself what has just been logged. In this step he sees the mirror and the wholeness of the portrait his dream has painted becomes a reality to him. The story is told in all its richness, complexity, and descriptiveness. Even the most uncreative person often sits in awe at this artistic flowering of his deepest self.

d) Now, any further insights from the dreamer or from other group members about the dream or the dreamer are shared, and the feedback is completed. Usually the dreamer will continue to get insights into himself long after the session is over. The process of owning all as ourself is the key.

4. For children, this training is a tremendous aid to developing creativity, spontaneity and self-understanding. It begins to activate the pineal and crown center consciously, developing the already vibrant imaginative life. To learn as early as possible that all life is one, a projection of our real self, dissolves the little ego and expands it into universal consciousness. Now, the next step is for everyone to have the opportunity to do the Gestalt work with their own dream, so that the process, once learned, can be applied at home or anytime.

5. The leader can circulate around helping with the process and the experience. Some people do not dream much. Their unconscious life is well-integrated with their conscious experience, and doesn't need the pressure valve released in dreams. But these people are few and rare. Most people dream, but frequently do not remember their dreams because the unconscious is too removed from the conscious. If you have trouble remembering your dreams, do the self-hypnosis or the meditation for the seventh level just before you fall off to sleep. Give yourself the suggestion in this relaxed state that you will remember your dreams and that you will awaken immediately and write them down in your journal which you have at the side of the bed. If you really want to, you can remember and log your dreams in this way.

6. When everyone has finished their dream interpretation, come together as a larger group and each person share what was the most meaningful part of the experience. Discuss how you could apply this same Gestalt process to a waking scene and what it would tell you.

7. Journal writing.

EAST MEETS WEST

GOAL: In India, the art of self-hypnosis and body control has reached such skilled levels that tremendous feats are performed, considered miracles by some and "impossible" by dubious scientists. These include lying on a bed of nails, swallowing poison with no ill effects, telepathy, being buried alive, etc. The art of meditation has also achieved its greatest heights in India. Expanding the imagination to encompass the Cosmos, men and women have purified their consciousness until the hidden secrets of life and Oneness with the Creator have become known to them. In this exploration we are going to dive more deeply into meditation to direct our imagination into our cells and remind the molecules that they are connected by electrical forces to molecules in others and linked with the whole Cosmos. We are going to use the power of the seventh level to launch us beyond planetary orbits into the central spiritual sun and beyond.

PREPARATION:
Everyone will need a comfortable pillow.

a candle
the Centering symbol of Nuclear Evolution
(placed on the wall, see p. 418)
wine, juice or punch
a dimly lit room

The group sits in a semi-circle facing the clearly visible Center symbol on the wall.

The leader should be someone skilled in meditation and relaxation, with a soothing voice, capable of being sensitive to the different individuals' inner worlds in the silence. He must read dynamically, yet giving times for pause at appropriate places to assimilate the images. The success of the exploration depends on the degree of relaxation and concentration attained, so frequent reminders to stay alert and focussed may be helpful.

EXPLORATION:

1. *The leader reads the Goal then takes the group through the complete relaxation learned for self-hypnosis on page 281. When the group is relaxed and concentrated, the leader lights a candle and places it in the center of the room and continues reading.*

> Get as comfortable as you can. If your body begins to fidget, lie down with your feet facing the flame. In the world of light there are many kinds of light and many kinds of energies that all come from light. The life within us is a light that quickens our vital

functions. It is a psychic energy. The light you see before you in the candle flame is to help you visualize light and then to step up your visualization from candle flame to the sun, from the sun to the life-light within. If it moves you to visualize a religious symbol or the symbol of Nuclear Evolution in place of or in addition to the candle, use your imagination accordingly.

Look at the flame. . . Then, when your eyes begin to tire or water, close your eyes and look up inside your head to the center between the brows. Send your vision soaring upward until it is lost in the mind's eye. At first you will see the reflection of the candle flame. Steady it so that it no longer vibrates in your mind's eye. Do this effortlessly and in as relaxed a state as you can. It will disappear eventually and you will be centered in a point of light which is the central intelligence of your being. Concentrate now on this center. . .

This center is the transmitting station from which inspiration can be flashed into your intuition and mind. Now we send a message down through the nervous system from that central point to the whole brain and into the heart and then to the bottom of the feet. The message is that your whole body is tuning into its source of electrical energy. All molecules and atoms of your body are merely vibrating frequencies of electricity. As we visualize and experience this deeply, we send out a message to the whole universe. We project it on our life force through our imagination. We project that we are connected by these electrical forces to the sun and the moon and the stars. These bodies are merely masses of highly energetic oscillating electrons and atoms in space. They are whorls of energy swirling now in our own expanded field of being. . .

We are like a radio set which is enveloped in the many radio frequencies coming from the signal transmitting station. All these frequencies are passing through space continuously whether the radio set is switched on or not. We imagine now we are a radio set being switched on to consciously receive the cosmic program over the radio waves. As we do this, we become aware that our body is not limited by its physical form, and in fact its physical form is changing into vibrations of electricity and wave lengths. It can transmit to any part of the universe and receive a message back. It is like the same kind of radio transmitter that sends messages to the moon and to Mars or the sun. . .

The sun's rays are part of the sun; they are the electro-magnetic energy that has come from the central sun. Likewise, we visualize ourselves now as a burning, blazing sun, transmitting our rays of light out into the far reaches of the universe. . . As we feel this golden light enveloping us, just as the earth is bathed in the sun's light, we begin to feel its radiant warmth within. The material gross wave lengths of the body merge together and unite in the heat and effulgence. As they unite they also blend our imagination and our perception; all are fused into one. Our consciousness now controls this light. Our consciousness permits it to stream through all the sensory organs of the body, bringing our state to one of illuminated intelligence. Bask in this light, your light, the light of the universe. . . (long pause) . . .

This light is the same stuff which plays through us when we are asleep and unconscious, when the self has been put away. Then our entire nervous system and organs are regenerated with this vital force, just as they are now being revitalized. . .
Now, with our imagination, we begin to weave this light into threads, and visualize that from our head the light has flashed to the center candle flame or the center symbol or our religious symbol, whichever we chose earlier. It becomes a flashing circle from the right of our head, to the head of the figure of light, then through the center of the candle flame or symbol, completing a circle as it flashes from point to point. This radiant imagining in our mind's eye is done in a flash. We do not wander lingeringly, but move as a spark of electricity, without time for contemplation. It comes like a flash of lightning. It becomes a quickening process done over and over. It should be done quickly so that the mind does not get involved or linger over the process. It is your projective, creative imagination, flashing through time and space. Do it now. A circle of light from head to the flame and so on. Flash!

As we do this we enter into the central flame and become the light ourselves. All the separate points of consciousness merge and we become one with light and energy and vibration. It all becomes the same frequency in oneness. And then we become conscious of the pulsating movement of this light passing through us like the breath in our lungs and we begin to breathe in and out as the whole universe breathes, with pure life energy.

As we breathe in, we become conscious of gravitational forces pulling toward the center within. As we breathe out, we become conscious of outward, expanding centrifugal forces of light expanding the universe. And we continue to do this psychic breathing. We bring to our being the rhythm of eternal life energy which is actually creating our breath. . . Feel it creating your breath, the life and consciousness breathing you. . . (long pause) . . .

Then we begin to visualize breath going down into the solar plexus and down to the feet. And then the breath goes straight from the solar plexus to the infinite point of light above. We know if this exercise is repeated every day, or whenever we are worried, uncertain, off-center, angered, or feeling resentment, we will solve the problem. . .

We visually enter into this conscious breathing of the vital forces, relaxing and letting go in the universe, becoming one with the forces of light. Our own breath becomes fused with the very source of creation and we transcend the material body. We enter into its real manifestation as electrical, vibrational energy. We create a renewed body. Through the breath we integrate the atomic substance in our flesh with the whole universal process. We provide a channel for life energy to be transmitted through our inner "television station", the center of consciousness in our own life. . .

We retune ourselves and improve our receptivity to cosmic wave lengths by continuing to focus our mind with the Cosmic Intelligence. *Where* our mind is focussed is very important. For there you are, yourself, identified. Just as when you focus your mind on your desires, problems, worries, frustrations and limitations, then that focus is the cause of your unhappiness, disease and eventually the cause of your death. The focus of the Cosmic energy dynamo within is your identification with eternal life. Death may come while your body still lives, for you can be walking dead—dead to your own universal process that is going on within, because you are constantly whatever you identify with. So the daily practice of this type of exercise focusses your mind on the universal, on the energies and cosmic vital divine program. What is the Cosmic Intelligence telling you; what has it been vibrating to you along your Cosmic Connection? You have set up a hot-line to the Universal Source of Intelligence, Love, Oneness and Energy. What is it saying to you? Your thoughts, and feelings are a reflection of the message. . .Is it telling you that you need more practice and training to tune the instrument more exactly? . . . (long pause) . . .

Just as we know that all around us radio waves carry the programs of different stations, so we must learn to tune our receptivity into that wave length of the divine universal mind, and sustain our relaxation, our concentration and centering to receive its program for us. . . (long pause) . . .

2. *The leader brings the semi-circle back into waking consciousness gradually.* Now, we all suggest to ourselves that we remain centered in the oneness, the Universal Source, and continue to practice this tuning on our own.

3. There is no discussion of what anyone experienced as this leads to comparison. All verbalizings in this state take away the energy and pull you away from your attunement. And, after all, they are mere vanities, often glamorized by people needing attention, or in self-glorification of their own psychic powers. Everyone should remain in silence and ponder their experience rather than lose psychic power. Many people talk about their psychic experiences the way some people talk about their operations. It only leaks away the psychic forces and attunement; the whole purpose of this exploration is to store up these forces so that we can channel them and use them for higher spiritual experiences. Spiritual heights are typified by humility!

4. *The leader brings out a loving cup of communion wine, juice or punch. All who would like to may share in it.* It should not be offered, but rather held until those who wish to partake come forward when they are moved, in humility, to share. Some may feel embarrassed in the silence, but that embarrassment is a challenge, and they will grow by dealing with it. It is important to master the embarrassment of not speaking when there isn't anything sacred or important to say, and to let silence speak louder than words.

5. *At some point the leader may quietly break the silence and say that the object of the session has been to bring all present into a nonverbal experience of communion and fellowship in oneness, in the seventh level.* Those who wish to stay in the silence may remain and those who wish to leave may do so whenever they feel moved. A non-verbal salute of pressing the palms together in the Indian way (as in prayer) means "I salute the highest in you." It is a physical expression of the inner feeling, and may be used as a closing good-bye rather than words. The silence in this exercise is generally pregnant with energy.

6. Journal writing (optional).

REAL FANTASY

PREPARATION:
The leader brings to the session
30 or 40 magazine clippings of different
scenes and situations. They can include
nature scenes, ads, people pictures,
etc. The more artistic they are the better.
They should be interesting and colorful.

GOAL: When we hear the word "fantasy", most people have an image of something unreal, maybe an escape from what is going on in real life. A fantasy is free association of the imagination, letting images float and form into a story or a happening. It may be something we fear might happen, or it may be a fantasy of something we wish would happen. Some people have erotic fantasies, some people have fantasies of being heroes or supermen and women. We can fantasize about others or ourselves on any level of consciousness. Like dreams, daydreams and fantasies can be a way of letting off steam from inner conflicts or releasing creative energy. Whether we direct the fantasy into an art form, such as music, painting or writing, will determine how much we develop our creativity.

Children use fantasy in play, and it is a very real part of life for them. In this exploration we are going to give freedom to our fantasies and let them reveal to us some part of ourselves. We are going to go beyond the fantastical to the real inner message. We all hold a secret self-image, and through fantasy we can discover what it is.

EXPLORATION:

1. *The leader places the magazine clippings in the center of the room.* Three or four volunteers come to the center and select a number of clippings which appeal to them and each creates a collage. The time limit is five minutes. The others observe.

2. The rest of the group compares the results. Is one person's collage darker or brighter than the others? Are there people in one collage and not in another? Are there more men than women? A particular scene? What mood or emotion do you see reflected in the artwork? Why did people make those choices?

3. The artist now comments on his own collage and on the comments made by the others. What meaning or insight do they bring?

4. Repeat Steps 1 through 3 with other members of the group until everyone has had a chance to create a picture.

5. Now the clippings are all spread out on the floor. Choose one clipping each and take it to your seat. Take out your journals and have your pen in hand. Look at the clipping you have chosen and let yourself fantasize what it means to you. Write down your images and feelings in about fifty to one hundred words.

6. Now silently read what you have written and write another fifty words on why you chose that clipping, what it may relate to in your life, and what real need or feeling your fantasy relates to in your life. Write your name on the back.

7. *The leader collects the papers, with the clippings attached, and then redistributes them, making sure he does not give any back to its author.* The leader begins by reading the paper he has, but not identifying the writer. Then he exhibits the clipping and comments on any insight into a problem, personality trait or the self-image of the writer that he sees hidden in the fantasy and writing. Others comment too and offer more ideas. After this group mirror, the author reveals himself and shares what he feels about the group perceptions. The next person reads the paper he has and repeats the procedure, and so on until all papers are read and comments shared.

8. Discuss as a group how our image of our self, whether it is a low self-image or a high one, gets pictured in the fantasies we entertain in daily life. What kinds of fantasies do we live in? What levels are they mostly on?

9. Journal writing.

FANTASY POWER

Exploration

74

Violet World

GOAL: Not only can fantasy be an aid to discovering deeper parts of ourselves, but it can be a powerful tool for re-programming and transforming unwanted habits or solving problems. In this session we are going to use our fantasies to release creative energies. Sometimes the very act of fantasizing about a problem relieves it. For example, one man who had stomach pains decided to fantasize about the cause of them. In his fantasy he made himself very tiny and decided to go inside his stomach to look around. The very act of fantasizing helped him to own the problem and let it go. His pain went away for good. In fantasy it is important not to worry about whether you are on the right track or not, or whether you are right or wrong. It doesn't matter. What matters is that you just let yourself go, and be as spontaneous and as honest and real as you can. From that imaginative outpouring comes a cosmic mirror eventually. As you learned in the dream work you have to let it out freely first, before you can understand its deeper levels of meaning.

EXPLORATION:

1. Each person decides on a starting point for his or her fantasy. Choose something real. Something from the feedback you saw in the last exploration? A matter of health? A hang-up? A problem in your school or business? A personal goal? A relationship problem? A desire for improvement?

2.   Someone volunteers to be first. That person shares the problem, and shares the clipping again with the group.

3.   The person lies down on the rug in the center of the room, head resting on the pillow. Where would you like to begin your fantasy? Here are some ideas: If your clipping brought out the problem, then look at the picture and imagine yourself entering inside it and fantasize what is going on there. Or if it is a health problem, imagine yourself small like Alice in Wonderland, floating on a cell inside your body, going to visit the problem part. You can begin your fantasy by fantasizing something you wish might happen, or you can imagine you are a child in bed after the lights are out, or maybe imagine you are on a trip to the zoo and are sharing with an animal. See if any images for a fantasy flash into your mind, giving you an idea where to go, a starting point. If nothing comes, close your eyes and daydream a bit. If you still have trouble, the leader or someone close to you can help with the following intuitive method:

>   The helper imagines that he is the person lying down and begins to let his fantasy about that person range free. In what direction does it go? What images crop up? Try to get inside the inner world of the person and become him or her. Don't worry about how crazy the image that comes to you might be, speak it aloud and let the person take it up from there when it feels right.

4.   *As the person continues the fantasy, the leader tunes in intuitively and leads when necessary. The leader must listen carefully and if necessary ask such questions as:*

>   "Is anybody with you?"
>   "What do you see?"
>   "How does that make you feel?"
>   "Can you describe that more fully?"
>   "What does the fantasy say to you?"

If too many people get in the act it can be confusing. This is why one leader is usually best. However, if anyone gets a strong flash they feel would be important they should ask it in the form of a question like the above. But you have to be very careful you don't break the vibration and say something really way off base. The intuition is very important in this fantasy work. If the leader holds up his hand, that means he feels it is not the right comment at the moment. Let the leader direct.

5. If the fantasy starts to go on too long, where it is not getting any farther, the leader should gently bring the person back into the real life situation in the room, saying "Thank you for your sharing. It is now time to come back to our friends here, perhaps you can continue the fantasy again another time with us or on your own."

6. Each fantasy will probably take five to ten minutes. Some people may start to go deeper and deeper and you will want to continue longer. Repeat the exercise with everyone who wishes to try it. Leave some time in between people to discuss what happened, and to allow everyone to share how their fantasy felt.

7. How many people were really able to get a deeper view of their problem? Did you find that you got stuck in the mind or images and went in circles? If so, then you are blocking somewhere, and need to let go more into new images and freer fantasy. If you feel unresolved ask the group for more feedback before you end the session. Continue to explore with your creative fantasy at home in writing or talking to a tape recorder.

8. Journal writing.

GETTING HIGH
(WITHOUT DRUGS)

Exploration
75
Violet World

PREPARATION:
The leader for this exploration should have a calm, soothing voice and some understanding of the psychedelic experience. This does not mean he has taken drugs, since you do not need drugs to be able to "trip" imaginatively.

The leader arranges for several selections of visionary music to be brought to this session. For example: "You'll Never Walk Alone", "Aquarius/Let the Sunshine In", "Dream the Impossible Dream", Holst's "The Planets", music from "Close Encounters" or "2001", etc.

a record player to play the music on

The scene can be set with low lights, incense, maybe a black light shining on the center symbol mandala of Nuclear Evolution (see page 418) or other mandala pinned to the wall.

GOAL: Many, many people take drugs of all sorts these days. Sleeping pills, psychedelics such as marijuana and L.S.D., speed pills, downers, uppers, etc., are so common that drug traffic in them is widespread and steady. Besides physical pain relief, drugs are taken mostly to relieve psychological pain and tension. Even with the commonly smoked marijuana plant, the motive is usually to have an altered experience of consciousness, something that will bring relief and a time out from the ordinary confining demands of life.

The urge to expand consciousness is as old as life itself. It is the natural life force that has caused us to evolve beyond the level of the ape and extend ourselves into space. The drug experience, and to some extent alcohol, does alter the mind, but offers no permanent evolutionary development. This can come only from self-mastery, not enslavement to external stimuli. Marijuana can temporarily heighten sensitivity and lift us out of the usual intense identification with the body. In that "high" it brings us the realization that there is more to life and consciousness than the body. But in this awareness session we are going to use the most powerful drug of all—consciousness—to get high, and learn to recreate the high at will without drugs.

EXPLORATION:

1. There should be no discussion at all until Step 6.

2. Think back to a time when you felt high and expanded, either some memorable peak experience in nature, a drug experience that turned you on, or any moment that you cherish in your memories. Choose an experience that you would like to feel again. Write it down in your journal in as much detail as you can, trying to get into the feeling of it again as well. (The blue level memory is never quite the same as the direct experience, and all too often we build up an image of these past experiences that is more than what they were.)

3. Through self-hypnosis and the meditative state, the power of consciousness is so released that we can suggest to ourselves that the same expanded experiences we previously enjoyed will occur on command. To the degree we can open up to the creative imagination, it can re-create the experience for us completely. Under hypnosis, people have regressed to babyhood and relived traumatic experiences just as though they were happening for real now. So in this step we put ourselves into the most relaxed and meditative state that we can at this time in order to "turn on". Have your written experience before you.

Begin with the hypnosis on page 281 to be read by the leader. This preparation, combined with the meditation you have already done on the imagination will take you deeper into inner space. *The leader reads the hypnosis then continues slowly with the following:*

> You will be writing your own travel ticket for a "trip" to the recesses of lost memories, and combined with your imagination you will land in a dimension of hypersensitivity, a rainbow of vibrant colors to a wellspring of ideas, to time dislocation or to heights of spiritual ecstasy. In this deep space the power of consciousness is released to work for you and re-create the experience you most want to have again. . . . Begin to imagine yourself in a situation that will bring you this feeling you desire. . . . Let your fantasy flow and mingle with any memories that also wish to flow in. . . . Project your images and life force into

386

the flow and let them take you. If you feel yourself begin to doubt, or start to think, don't let it bring you down—just let go and continue in your fantasy and reverie realm. . . (long pause, five to ten minutes) . . .

The leader continues to read:

THE ULTIMATE DRUG: CONSCIOUSNESS

Let's trip farther into consciousness right now. Close your eyes. Pop the imaginary psychedelic into your mouth—gradually feel a funny feeling come over your skin. . . You vibrate all over. You wonder what's happening—hot and cold. You begin to gradually notice strange things happening to your consciousness. . . . Things begin to go very wavy . . . moving, something is undulating, really going on. You suddenly feel a great rush of something. . . It takes you up and up and up and you wonder if you are even going to blow off the top. . . You push your consciousness on and you experience lights flashing around in circles. There are jagged lines, triangles, all kinds of funny sounds and movements, funny words come, strange sights, new feelings, things rushing in at you, running away from you. . . (long pause) . . .

You really begin to trip now, you're in the second stage. All of a sudden things stop and you see a big black dark forest coming at you. There's nowhere to go. . . The whole universe is coming closer and closer and there's no place to go . . . it's so powerful, it might destroy you . . . so you better destroy it before it destroys you . . . so you press the button, and just at the same time it presses the button . . . and there's a huge bang . . . and the whole universe blows up inside you now . . . and you're in the middle of the explosion, blown in every direction . . . bits here and there, all over the universe you are blown. And it never stops going out and out and out, and it's like the original big bang, a huge explosion, and you begin to wonder when it is ever going to stop. Out and out, onward and onward, further and further you go. Your ego all expanded all over the universe.

Bigger and bigger and bigger you become and you can't get any bigger. And when you get the biggest you can you turn around and say to yourself, How big is big? And you continue to get bigger and bigger to see the big, big Self. A little voice says inside somewhere, "Wait 'til you see the big, big, big Self" . . . then there's another explosion, bang, and you get bigger than big, even bigger and bigger and bigger than big . . . on and on and nowhere is it going to stop . . . colors keep moving and consciousness keeps going. . . (long pause) . . . And a voice says, "Wait 'till you see what's really big!" And you go off again, past all the universe and stars more and more, and you get bigger and bigger and bigger again some more. . . Where does it all stop? The voice says, "Well, you'll find out how big I am when you can realize that I am in your heart." . . . How big can your heart blow up like a balloon? . . . How big can your heart get without breaking the heart? . . . So the heart begins to stretch . . . and get bigger and bigger . . . so much it gets painful . . . so full . . . it's going to burst . . . it gets so filled full . . . and bigger and bigger and bigger than it's ever been before . . . and you get higher and higher and higher than you've ever been before . . . so we go and penetrate into that pain of the heart . . . and feel that it's love that is hiding in there, love is going to expand inside us and make us grow. . . It's expanding, constantly stretching bigger and bigger and bigger . . . and it feels like it will be painful to grow unless we let it burst and spill our love all over. . . Who's willing to let it go? Who's willing to take the risk and let it all go? Let your love go? Let's blow it then, and let the heart go with a big bang and our love spills everywhere. We blow the heart so we have got nothing left at all to cling to, just one big empty space . . . full of love . . . and that love goes and grows until it sticks on everybody else . . . until it sticks on all the stars and all the suns . . . and all the space between the stars too. There's nothing left to experience, just love. . . (long pause) . . .

Instead of letting all this wear off like a drug experience, let's hold it so that our love is going to stay everywhere. . . (long pause, several minutes) . . .

4.   Now read the description you have written in Step 1. You have fifteen minutes to go deeply into your experience—no one is rushing

you—and the only one you have to face is yourself. Tune everything out except what is going on in your own consciousness. Let images flow, do not think.

5. *After fifteen minutes of silence the musical selections are played. If the leader wishes, he can flash the light show of colored lights projected onto the walls around the room, and create as much of a spacey-psychedelic effect as possible.* Sit up and meditate, give yourself one of the following suggestions, or just continue the experience as you are. You can rise and move around, look into each other's eyes, chant or space-out, but do not talk to anyone.

The leader softly reads the suggestions:

a) Under psychedelics the senses open to new vibrations. Colors are often heard and sounds seen as color. Kaleidoscopic images appear and blend. Impressions and ideas come in and leave like a comet or meteor falling into consciousness. When I open my eyes I will have a flow of impressions that will be meaningful and productive in reaching my goals. I picture even now the fertile areas I can tap.

b) When I open my eyes now, colors will appear in their fullest intensity, sound will be reduced to its most harmonious vibration, scents will be magnified, and I will be aware of the universe as one magnificent symphony of the senses. I see it all in my mind's eye even now before I begin.

c) When I open my eyes now, I will sit in silent communion with the very soul of the universe. We will be as one. I will feel the love and bliss that comes only with divine oneness. I begin to feel it now even before I open my eyes.

6. *After another fifteen to twenty minutes, or when the leader feels it is time to pull the group together again with words, he asks*

everyone to take three deep breaths and bring their love back to earth and back into the group.

Come together in a love circle, holding hands.

7. Everyone describe their experience, so all share in the group soul.

8. Journal writing.

TAPPING CREATIVITY

Exploration

76

Violet World

PREPARATION:
Each person brings to the exploration their
favorite method of expressing creativity,
and all supplies they may need. It could
be a musical instrument, a painting, a piece
of clay, woodwork, charcoal and paper,
writing materials, dance music, etc.

a large piece of newsprint or enough
paper taped together so the entire group
can make a group collage

magic markers, paints or crayons
to draw with

8 magnets placed in each of the top
and bottom four corners of the room
tape the magnets to the corners

GOAL: Science looks at space as a void–a vacuum of nothing filled by pieces and particles of matter and waves of vibration. The universe could not exist without space. Space had to exist before the first suns and planets were created.

Many yogis and philosophers perceive that space is a continuation of consciousness, intelligence and energy. It is the very fabric of science and all forces of gravity, levity, atomic energy and other physical phenomena are in that stuff of consciousness. Each person can absorb energy and intelligence from space and radiate energy and intelligence back into space. We are like cosmic radio transmitter and receiver sets. How we are tuned dictates both what we send out through space and what we receive from others through space.

If we consider that space is the prime source of creation itself and is consciousness—our extended awareness—then space becomes the source of all creative inspiration and originality. How can anything come out of nothing? Space becomes a very pregnant nothing when we recognize it as pure consciousness, not separated from our own. We have boxed ourselves in. We sit in bodies, corners, live in rooms and have our beings in houses. Lift up all the houses sprinkled on blocks all over cities, and you see millions of people wriggling around busy in space.

When we attune to only boxed-in space we limit our creative consciousness. In this exploration we want to become space by taking all the separating walls and boxes down. Then we expand and tap hidden creative potential.

EXPLORATION:

1. We begin with an exercise to expand our walls and then dissolve them. By expanding and stimulating the growth of our brain cells, we activate the frontal lobes—that part of our brain with expanded space awareness.

Everyone sits facing the same direction. *The leader reads the following:*

BRAIN EXPANSION EXERCISE*

Close your eyes. Imagine you are sitting in the middle of the room and the room is a big box. Imagine that each corner of this box has a magnet in it. There are eight corners, four corners on the top where the ceiling and walls meet and four on the bottom where the floor and walls meet. There you are, sitting, right in the middle. Now, imagine your mind has grown and has wrapped itself around the box so the box is inside your mind and you are sitting inside your mind too. With the eyes closed, take a deep breath and blow the breath all out and mentally send it to the front top left corner of the box. Feel the breath fasten onto the magnet. Feel the magnet pull at your brain like it is pulling the brain itself. Let the brain come back in by itself and then blow it out to the front, top, left corner of the box again. Feel that magnet tugging at your brain cells, stretching your brain. Now blow out once more to the front, top, left corner. . . This time when the breath comes in we're going to change corners and blow it out to the front, top, right corner. Feel the magnet pull at your brain cells, waking them up. Now blow out again to that front, top, right corner. Feel your brain growing. And once more to that corner. Then proceed to the back, top, right corner and blow out, feeling the back of the brain stretch in the same way. Do it three times in this corner. Be sure to feel the magnet

---

* This Brain Expansion Exercise is part of the Rumf Roomph Yoga Series called "The Science of Vibration and Transmission of Life Force" by Christopher Hills, available on tape. (See appendix.)

pulling. . . Then do this for the back, top, left corner, three times. . . Now do the bottom four corners just as you did the top four.

(The leader can continue on directing the attention three times to each of the bottom four corners, so that everyone stays together. Especially with children, this will be necessary until the exercise is learned by heart.)

Begin to feel the walls disappear. Feel like the magnets are becoming stars, centers of light energy, pulling your brain cells which are also stars—you are sitting at the center of the entire universe. Your brain cells are the 100 billion stars in the galaxy—you are the universe.

2. Now everyone goes to their favorite medium of creativity that they have brought with them and enjoys twenty to thirty minutes working with this medium in space, alone, not disturbing others. As you work, the main idea to keep in mind is the meditation experience that you are the entire universe, and that all space and time and stars and other galaxies are located inside you.

3. Now discuss how an expanded awareness affected your creativity. Could you stay expanded while you worked? Did your consciousness actually feel as if it were wrapped around the stars and that they were twinkling and burning inside your consciousness? Try to hold the expanded awareness as you work together as one consciousness in Step 4.

4. Now everyone does a group collage together for another fifteen minutes. Everyone must draw something related to the drawing of the person next to them. For example, if you draw a tree, your neighbor might draw a monkey swinging from another tree towards your tree, and your neighbor on the other side may decide to draw a meadow with people dancing on it. The object is to keep the collage linked together as a whole and a unified expression of the total group mind.

5. Now ask the group where they actually now experience the stars. How many realize that even in normal perception the stars are experienced in fact inside our heads—inside our consciousness?

6. Journal writing.

A group collage is fun sharing for young and old together. See Step 4, p. 393.

SPIRITUAL PSYCHODRAMA

Exploration

77

Violet World

PREPARATION:
The leader should feel a close kinship with psychology and with drama. As with Dream Interpretation exploration, we are aiming for a Gestalt, a wholeness in which we experience ourselves as one with each other and see the whole situation as part of ourself.

a carpeted floor where people can move, sit and act

GOAL: Psychodrama began as a form of therapy in the 1920's. It was developed by a psychiatrist named J. L. Moreno to enable people to release their feelings and to help each other see their internal blocks.* Through acting out real scenes from our lives, role playing other people's parts or replaying our own, we get a new perspective on what has happened.

In spiritual psychodrama, we use the action to help us expand our consciousness. We look at it as a form of growth, not necessarily as therapy. Healthy, normal people can benefit from this group experience as much, and often more than people with serious problems. This type of psychodrama is a spiritual tool in that it gives you training and opportunity to enter into the inner-worlds of others and experience them as they experience themselves. It also enables you to look back at yourself while looking through the eyes of others. Your angle of vision is widened from the purely personal tunnel-vision view, to a more inclusive picture from many centers. It helps develop a wholistic 360 degree view of life.

Like Gestalt dream work, spiritual psychodrama sees every situation, every disagreement, every experience and every person as a projection of your inner self. We learn to make this truth part of our understanding through the action.

*PSYCHODRAMA by Dr. Jacob L. Moreno, Beacon House, 1946.

EXPLORATION:

1. Everyone writes down in their journals a real life problem they are having, or recently have had with another person. It may be entirely an internal conflict about that person, or it may be a recent heated argument, or possibly an inability to communicate with someone. Pick a situation fairly fresh in your mind. Everyone has some difficulties in relationships with others, even if they are minor ones, otherwise their lives would be perfect. Pick out one such difficulty, and write it out. Then everyone shares their problem briefly with the group.

2. The group now decides which situation has the greatest need for group help. The decision should be unanimous. That person's problem is chosen first. That person describes the scene of the problem, the last time it occurred, and what happened between the people involved.

3. After the brief description, the group acts out the scene. Chairs are pushed out of the way so there is open space in the center of the room. The person whose problem it is will play himself. He is called the protagonist. He picks people from the group who he feels might best play the parts of the others in his scene. With just the brief facts described to go on, the others try to tune into how they might feel being in the shoes of the person they are to portray. Psychodrama is also called spontaneity theatre. No roles are memorized, you don't try to figure out beforehand how you are going to act out in some situation. Rather you put yourself in the position of the person whose role you are going to play and respond spontaneously, incorporating the few facts you know into your actions and words. It is uncanny how often your spontaneous portrayal is exactly what has happened in the real situation. The protagonist is often astonished when you say something that was exactly what the person in real life had said. As the scene is being acted out, don't worry whether it changes direction from what was described. Often in the psychodrama we go deeper into issues that are more real than what has happened in real life. The rest of the group watches, not as

observers, but as part of what is happening. When anyone has an insight or a flash, they jump up and stand behind the person who they want to speak for. They become a double or alter ego for the moment, and speak their piece, in the first person, using the word "I", just as if they are that person. They remain on stage until the others have a chance to reply, and then the double sits down and lets the scene resume, only with new light. Don't be afraid to risk hopping up and down. The more input and insight, the more angles of vision are provided. The leader will still have to direct and be astute enough to see when someone's interjection is really way off base and distracting. If this happens, the leader says how he feels and directs the scene onto the course he feels it needs to be going. Often deep emotions will come out and the action will get very intense. This action is real feeling and reaction, it is not play acting. Many people in the group will be able to recognize and identify with each other's scenes. When there is no more to say and the energy has faded, everyone goes back to their seats and the group discusses what occurred. The protagonist begins by sharing what feelings and insights came.

4.   Choose another scene and do another psychodrama if there is time. Do as many as the group has time for. It is important for people in the circle to risk getting up and jumping in to act as double or alter ego. Encourage each other to participate. Don't be afraid to make a mistake, but always have the best intentions for the protagonist's world in mind.

5.   Write any insights you have had into your journal.

Spiritual psychodrama helps us to get in touch with our real feelings and get fresh insight on them from others.

THE PLAY'S THE THING

Exploration

78

Violet World

GOAL: The goal of this exploration is to take a well-known play, such as Shakespeare's Hamlet, to act out. This acting will begin with a reading of the play, everyone taking different roles, but will end with an entirely new plot. By combining the original artist's idea with our own spontaneous fantasy as we go along, we bring new life to the play. We guide the fantasy so that it deals with real and profound human needs and feelings. Our goal is not to convert a serious play into a comedy, but to modify it according to our own real inner feelings regarding the situation or the character we are portraying.

PREPARATION:
The leader chooses a play known for its wisdom and informs everyone in the group what it is, well in advance. This timing allows the others to read the play if they possibly can beforehand. You may want to photocopy the script so each person has a copy.

No costumes are used. But if the leader has some simple props that help to identify the roles and the scene, they can be used.

EXPLORATION:

1. *The leader selects a starting point or a scene from the play.* Everyone chooses their own role or the leader can assign roles if there is disagreement. The play begins and the characters weave their parts around the author's original plot, at the same time involving their own real feelings in the plot. See how creative and artistic you can make the blend between the author's creation and the group's creation. For example, we might find we have a Hamlet who not only doesn't believe in ghosts but doesn't want to talk about them and prefers to discuss the psychology of his problems. Or we might find a Hamlet who understands beings on the other side and so he decides to hypnotize a person to become a medium and "converse" with his dead father. Remember that whatever modification you make will affect every other person in the play, so exercise your fantasy in tune with the whole.

2. The leader/director ends the play at some appropriate point. He

then states that this performance has been watched by a group of very advanced souls. They are saints and prophets of great philosophical and spiritual stature. Each person now becomes one of these great wise ones. Now in these new roles, discuss the significance of what you have just seen: a group of awareness seekers dressed as characters in a play and doing their own drama. What were the levels of perception displayed? What was revealed in these people's personalities? What words of wisdom do you have for any of these people?

3. Everyone now shares their feelings about what's been said to them or about them.

4. Journal writing.

THE I CHING

Exploration
79
Violet World

PREPARATION:
*The leader for this journey should
be the person in the group most
familiar with the "I Ching".
If no one is familiar, the leader
must spend some time before the
session getting to know the "I Ching",
throwing the coins himself, until
he gains familiarity with how it works.*

*one or more copies of the "I Ching"—
Wilhelm translation
three pennies per person*

GOAL: The *I Ching* is an ancient text. No one knows for certain how old. The two main Chinese philosophies, Confucianism and Taoism took inspiration from it. It is considered an oracle, a mathematically perceptive insight into the operations of nature and its laws. How do random events from the collective unconscious or the Cosmic Intelligence percolate through our minds and beings into actions? How do the laws of probability work to enable us to predict the future? The *I Ching* transcends time and space to take you right into the "universal now". Based upon the question asked and held in mind as you toss the three coins, the answer comes as a penetrating mirror to your internal situation.

The wisdom and advice of the *I Ching* is incredibly profound. Those who learn how to intuit the meanings of its images and symbols always find an answer to any question and a direction to take. It is written from the seventh level of consciousness and beyond. The eternal realms of harmony and universal consciousness are its very fabric. Carl Jung, noted psychiatrist, studied the *I Ching* deeply. He asks the Western reader, in his introduction to the Richard Wilhelm translation, to put aside linear reasoning that says D happens because C happened which happened because B happened as a result of A, etc. Instead he asks us to enter the level of consciousness where events are all in the same moment in the physical and psychic dimensions—the eternal now, where cause and effect are simultaneous and One. The goal of this session is to open ourselves to the Violet level through the *I Ching* and receive a cosmic message from the oracle.

EXPLORATION:

1. Everyone takes a minute to tune into the deepest question concerning them at the moment. Write this question down clearly in your journals. Confine your question to one topic only. You can always ask another question at another time. Everyone takes three pennies and holds them in their hands as they tune into their heart and open to Cosmic Intelligence. Now with full concentration on your question, not letting your mind wander, or wondering what others are doing or trying to second-guess the answer, throw the three coins as follows:

Throw all three coins and count the numbers of heads and tails. A head equals 3 and a tail equals 2. So if you throw three heads and you add up the value you get 9. If you throw 2 tails and one head you will get the value 7. Two heads and one tail is 8 and three tails is 6. You throw all three coins six different times, recording your value each time in the following manner. You list the throws from the bottom up rather than from the top down as we usually write.

				Present situation	Future prediction	
	6)	3 tails	6	——x——	——————	line change to positive
Example of	5)	3 heads	9	——o——	—— ——	line change to negative
coin throws:	4)	2 heads, 1 tail	8	—— ——	—— ——	
	3)	3 heads	9	——o——	—— ——	line change to negative
	2)	1 head, 2 tails	7	——————	——————	
	1)	3 tails	6	——x——	——————	line change to positive
				48	41	

Now one further step is necessary in order to discover which hexagram you have thrown. Each 6 translates as a broken changing line. Each 7 is a solid line. Each 8 is a broken line. Each 9 is a solid changing line. They are written as in the above example. This first hexagram is your reading for your present situation. In this example there are four unstable or changing lines. You will look up the meanings of your changing lines which are particular messages for you in the *I Ching*. These unstable lines change into their opposites and thus a new hexagram is formed. When you are finished reading the first hexagram you then read the new hexagram which is your future reading. You never read the changing lines in your future reading because there are none. The future prediction is based on the law of probability. If you heed the guidance and advice in the present situation your future will be harmonious. If you do not heed the advice or warnings, the future will bring a problem or disturbance. Sometimes the future prediction is negative. This means that the probability is that you will not follow the advice given in the first hexagram and the second hexagram is the likely outcome. When the future reading is positive, it means that you are likely to follow the path of wisdom and that you're on the right track. The *I Ching* reading is not the final word. You can change your destiny. It merely mirrors the attitude you hold in your unconscious and the place you are in at the moment of the throw. You will continue to get similar readings until your inner attitude changes. The answer puts you in touch with the Tao—cosmic intelligence.

Each hexagram you receive has many depths of meaning. Usually it is beneficial to have others help you interpret it because often it mirrors the one blindspot that keeps us down. Since this blindness is often difficult to see ourself, another might be able to spot it more readily. The more experience you have with the *I Ching,* the more you can zero right in on the meanings of the symbols, the images and judgements. However, if you keep asking the *I Ching* questions over and over again without due meditation on the answer already given, you are importuning the cosmic intelligence and you will find your answers will reflect that.

If you are sincere, the *I Ching* response will speak to a deep part of your being, mirroring for you your secret attitude, feelings and thoughts. It never fails to give a profound reply and people who get to know the text are usually in awe at how it is so deeply correct every time.

2. *After everyone has recorded their hexagrams, the leader opens up
    the "I Ching" and looks up the reading for each person, one at a time.*
    Each member reads the question asked, then the leader reads aloud
    the response of the *I Ching*. Everyone needs to be in a meditative
    space to tune into and receive the wisdom of the seventh dimension.
    At the end of the reading the person says what the answer means to
    him. Then the leader and others comment on what intuitive flashes
    they had as to the message for that person.

3. Take a break. Stand up, move around, get some fresh air for ten
    minutes or so. At the end of the break come together in a circle.
    Center again for a moment and do the Samyama exercise from page
    327, focussing the united group mind on the question: "What is the
    direction for our group?" As the group mind is focussed on this
    question, the leader throws the coins for the entire group. Read
    together the group reading and discuss what it means to everyone.

4. Now that everyone's reading has been shared, discussed and probed,
    discuss the group reading in light of the various individual readings.
    Is there any relationship? How do they affect each other?

5. Journal writing.

COME FLY WITH ME

Exploration

80

Violet World

PREPARATION:
your journals

GOAL: The very first exploration of the group is now repeated. We come full circle around to take off into a new spiral of evolution. "Man is born free, and everywhere he is in chains," is a famous comment made by the philosopher Rousseau long ago. It is still true. We spend half our lives keeping in step with everyone else—orange level conformity— and the other half convincing ourselves that it was all our own idea. Our self-image is the root of our identity. Hopefully we have expanded our self-image and developed a truer feeling of who we really are and what our potential is over all our explorations.

In this final journey we are going to see how we can make our new self-image more real, how we can bring the violet down to the red level of actual manifestation. We have learned of the tremendous power lying within the seventh level and the freedom we have in being able to re-create our future, our destiny, through what we do with our images. With this power comes also responsibility. Our responsibility to ourself is to use this new knowledge we have learned. Our responsibility to humanity and to Cosmic Intelligence is in how much we live the truths we know. Only in using what we have been given can we gain the self-mastery to open the next portal on our journey of Nuclear Evolution.

EXPLORATION:

1. Everyone goes around the group and expresses their philosophy of life. Share how it has changed or evolved since your first exploration with the group.

2. Now everyone writes in their journals their present life goal or goals. In one or two sentences state what you hope to accomplish or to become.

3. The leader reads the following as the group goes into a silent deep meditation, offering their goals to the evolutionary intelligence.

    > A child is riding in a car. A radio is playing music. The mother notices that big wet tears are rolling down the cheek of her three-year-old boy. She asks why he is crying. He replies, "The music is doing it." A few minutes later the same boy remarks, "Mother, can we take the clouds home with us? They look so lonely and they are following us."

    > The boy is certainly making his identity known. It comes through loud and clear. It is not found in his name. It is not found in his address, in his geneology or in his looks. It is found in how he interprets the universe to himself.

    > That is the mirror which we will use in our identity revelations. Contemplate yourself as this child.

4. Everyone again writes their personal life goal, and goes deeper this time, putting it into images in a short poem. It can be in rhyme or unrhymed. Attempt to express your subtlest and deepest feelings in images or inspiration that come to you. Write in silence. Tune in on any feeling you derive from the universe. You are putting together images, words, feelings and ideas that have never been put together in just that way before. It is a creative expression of beingness through you.

5. After twenty minutes or so the group comes together again and each poem is read by the author.

6. Now, discuss each of the following questions:

"What can we point to before we die and say, 'I've done this' or 'I've done that,' with the joy and fulfillment of having expressed our unique identity?" . . .

"Is it enough to be nice? A dog is nice, a pig is nice. . . How do we see our image of who we are right now? How does that condition our actions? How are we going to manifest who we want to be? What's our next step?"

7. The group forms a love circle and chants the **OOOOOMMMMM** together. Visualize launching yourself and each other onto the next stage of Nuclear Evolution.

Chanting together in small groups has a regenerating effect on your consciousness.

BLOWING YOUR MIND
INTO THE CLEAR LIGHT
by Christopher Hills

For those daring explorers who wish to go through the light barrier into yet another dimension.

(The following is a transcription of a meditation and talk given by Christopher Hills at the University of the Trees.)

Let us meditate on the nature of the impressions that we receive in our imagination. How real are the images that we see of the world around us, or the thoughts we form in our imagination from the sounds that enter the brain? When we listen to music, do we not form images? The sound of a passing car does not have the shape of the car, but the shape of sound rolling on the wet road, a swishing sound. Yet our mind and imagination transform it into a car. Or, when we hear the musical sound of the desert at night, we picture in our mind the vast expanse of the sand dunes and stillness. How does the signal come through the eyes into the brain, into the occipitals where we focus on it, and from there what interferes or enhances its reception? It is the brain which gives us our meaning, our sense of knowing something. How much noise is going on inside the brain that squelches the strength of the original signal or pattern? The original signal passes through the optic nerve into the back of the brain, and is then interpreted by the inner brain.

But what happens to the signal or the pattern if there are too many pre-formed thoughts or computers running with their own ideas, making so much noise that the original signal or stimulus is totally distorted? We can look at the human brain as a medium through which the signal passes. Depending on the clarity of that medium, the ray of light carrying the pattern or the image of the external world will be distorted. If the ray of light passes through a medium that is murky and clouded by too much going on in the mind, then the reception of the impression will also be clouded. Therefore the imagination, our faculty of seeing, depends not only on the original signal, but also on the medium through which this signal passes.

Let us meditate on this: the signal may be very weak, but the interference and the noise may be very loud. Let us meditate on the medium through which all of the impressions have to travel. If the impression is a ray of light from the sun, it travels through space, enters through the earth's magnetosphere, and hits the atmosphere which immediately distorts it, so we never see the ray of light as it really is, but only through the vapor and gases which surround the earth. What would it be like to see a ray of light without its passing through the medium? Would we know daylight as it is now? Or would we see only black around us in space? Would only the object that we are perceiving in our mind's eye be lit up by the sun's light and everywhere else in space be dark? And what of the intervening clouds which distort the signal and make the light something totally different? Is not our own mind full of such clouds, full of noises from the tape recorder which plays all of our memories and impressions back to us?

Let us chant the sound Ooommmmm deeply for the clarification and precipitation of all those unwanted images, thoughts, and judgements, so that we may hear the signals, the sounds of life, and see the pictures of the world around us as they really are. (Pause) . . . Let us feel the mind settle down in silence with all the clouds precipitated. The atmosphere inside is washed clean, transparent, so that the signals and patterns of the world around us may pass through the filter of the mind unhindered, so that we may see everything clearly, washed clean and white as snow. Let us see our imagination as a clean sheet of paper, or a perfectly white carpet of snow on which impressions will write themselves, just as rays of light impregnate a photographic emulsion, leaving their impressions behind unhindered by any human interference. Let us meditate on that clarity . . . (long pause in the silence) . . .

The first thing that you have to do to become aware of the worlds beyond your own levels of consciousness is to open yourself to them. If we limit the world around us to the limits of our own consciousness we become very closed off. We build walls around ourself which are made up of all kinds of noise-makers—the channels through which the universe has to penetrate to get to us. Those worlds have to come through a multi-channeled communication system which you have to deal with in order to be able to see into them. Many of the channels are called memories, basic assumptions, expectations, and presuppositions. All of these types of knowledge that you think you know are noise-makers which cloud the pure signals from the invisible worlds. Often the pure signals are very weak, whereas the noise that these thoughts make—the noise of our basic assumptions and the things that we think we know, the knowledge that we hang on to and all the things that we store inside our mental equipment that we believe are real—this noise is very loud inside us. It is all a blockage, a tremendous thick blanket which prevents the weaker and finer signals from the more subtle worlds from reaching us. We can only experience these worlds when we can completely dissolve the barriers and eliminate the noise-making channels by forgetting what we know and getting rid of all our thoughts which are conditioning these worlds. If we think a thing is not possible, then it is going to limit the kinds of signals which we receive from those worlds.

What we must do is to make ourselves as empty as a brand new photographic plate, every time we look at anything, or listen for anything, or listen to a person or even look at the universe. For unless we can know our ignorance, know that we are truly ignorant of the real processes that go on in life, instead of pretending that we do know and hanging on to that reality as if it were something real, we will never know those worlds. They cannot break through to us because we are clinging to the worlds we know too tightly. As if they were a security blanket, we hang onto the things we have been told by our parents, by school, by our society, by our culture and by the environment around us; we are conditioned by them. Not one of them is real; they are only impressions and pictures that we have formed about what is real. And as long as we hang onto these, as long as we think that the apparent things are real, that what appears to us is real, as long as we think and mistake those symbols, those images that we see, for the reality, then we will never see the worlds beyond our immediate consciousness.

The Sanskrit symbol for OM, the cosmic sound, is shown in the center of the Nuclear Evolution symbol.

So how do we do it? . . . by constantly correcting ourself when we are listening or looking or receiving any outside information from the outside world. Constantly question the information, is this real? Or is my own mind getting in the way? Can I put myself in a totally receptive space in which I am not thinking anything, so that I can really hear? If I am thinking, my mental wheels are turning and grinding out thoughts while someone else is speaking. How can I be listening? Or if I am even looking at the world outside, whether it is a tree or a flower or a motor car or a building or a star, or whatever, am I really thinking that I know it already? If I am, I will not be able to know it as it really is. I will only be projecting my own ignorance onto it.

So constantly we have to remind ourselves that we are not seeing what we think we see. We are not hearing what we think we hear. We are not even feeling what we think we are feeling. What we are feeling may be just some chemicals arising in our blood stream. We may be feeling all uptight or whatever, and be thinking our feeling is real when really it is only a reaction to some adrenalin in our system as it is pumped into our body. If we think the body is the only world, or that the physical world in which the body moves is the only world, then our thoughts will be so limited we will not be able to accept that there is another world. We will never believe that there really is anything else, therefore there will never be a signal for us from anywhere else. Our consciousness cannot experience anything if we do not open ourself to it.

So only when we get to that stage where we put aside everything, temporarily of course, can we experience the signal. You do not have to forget everything forever, but just to receive the signal as it is from an object, you have to de-condition yourself from what you already think about that object. And the same is true with a person. You might have lived with a person for twenty years, and you think, "I know that person very well, therefore when he is speaking I know exactly what he is saying." But do you know what that person is really feeling? Why do people get divorced after twenty-five years of marriage? Is it because they feel they know each other very well, or is it because they did not know each other very well at all, particularly when they first got married? Do they say that to themselves—"I was so blind that I could not see a half of what was in that person"? or rather are they thinking and saying it is that person's fault, "That person is the wrong person for me. I am not going to change, it is she that has to change. Not me. I am seeing clearly. I am seeing things as they really are." Isn't that what we say when dealing with another person? And yet what is the divorce rate? Practically fifty percent. People have to live so close to each other, sleep in the same bed, only to find that they are universes apart.

We can see how deluded we are in thinking that the body is capable of seeing and feeling truly. It takes us all these years to find out that a person is not suited to us, or cannot even communicate to us on certain levels. Certain worlds, inner worlds inside them are not even available to us. What about all our other faculties? We are not communicating on these other levels. Are we only married at the physical level? If we have an assumption that we know very well what our mate is speaking about, then we are going to block the message of that person's real being. We will hear it only through the filter of our own level and not from the other's level which may be quite different.

Only by completely putting aside all of our pre-conceptions about that person, even if we have known them for twenty years, can we receive a true message. Whether it is our mother or father, or whether it is the people we are working and living with, the only way that we can really hear them truly and experience them truly, from their world, is by putting aside all of our thoughts about them, putting aside all of our emotion and feelings that arise as we talk to them. It does not mean that we become like a zombie. It means that we open ourself to receive the message, and then we can come in with all of our critical faculties, and our feelings and thoughts and make a judgement, having received the true signal. Then it is a true message. But to condition the message as we are receiving it is just to distort it and we will never know that object or that person or that world. Even if we think we know it, we are not receiving it at the depth it is meant unless we put our thoughts aside.

In this very world in which we live are many other worlds interlocking in their vibrations, that we do not experience with our physical bodies and our physical senses. It is not possible to know them through those senses. But this does not mean that it is impossible to experience them. There are ways of experiencing those other worlds that are non-sensory. And if we limit them only to what we can touch, feel, see and hear, then we will never know them. We will not know them because those faculties which we have within us that can know them by other means, will never emerge. Our intuition will lie fallow, dead and unused as long as the noises from our senses are too loud. This faculty is completely squelched by physical sensation. And if we think we will ever know what our imagination is doing, which is so far beyond even the intuition (such a fine subtle sense by which we perceive the entire universe) we are deluded. For we will never experience it unless we master the senses. If we even let the intuitional impressions that float in front of our psychic world interfere, we will never know what the imagination is. Even though we use the imagination every day, even though we think with it every day and see with it every day, we will never know it. We will never know what it is without mastering the other levels. We will never know how an image gets translated into our heads from outside, just a simple image of anything, just a simple physical object.

How an image gets inside your head is profound, tremendously profound knowledge which you cannot learn at the university. No doctor can tell you the process. Doctors can tell you physical processes about neuro-transmitters and electrical stimuli, but they cannot tell you how the imagination works. To them it is just a word. They say, "Well, it's just in your imagination." And what is the imagination? What research has been done on the imagination to say exactly what it is? Nothing! Nothing in the whole of history. There is not one philosopher that can tell you. Philosophers say, "Oh, well, it all depends on the imagination." But to say what the imagination *is* is another thing. It is like saying what God is. They say, "It all depends on God." Well, what is God? You might as well say it all depends on God as to say it all depends on the imagination, because people know as much about the imagination as they know about God, if they are honest. So, to know how our imagination works and how the physical objects reproduce themselves in our consciousness means that we have to get all the images that float in, all the psychic stuff, out of our heads completely because it is all subject to interpretation by the mind.

Whatever you see going on in your psychic awareness still has to be made sense of by you, by your mind. And if your mind is screwed up, you will be screwing up your interpretation. If you are a pure channel in this cycling of images, of course you will see the images clearly, you will have clairvoyance, clear seeing. But you will still have to interpret them. And if you are a dummy, you will not make any more sense of them than anyone else who just sees physical objects and cannot see on the imagination level. Just to have perfect clairvoyance does not make you any more intelligent if you cannot understand the images you are seeing. Only when the super-clairvoyant has some intelligence and can accurately interpret the impressions when they come does that person have a gift of any use. Most of them cannot interpret accurately. They do not understand how the images get there. They say, "I do it," because they do not know how it happens. So they are no wiser about themselves. And their lives are usually much bigger messes than are the people's lives they are giving the readings for. If you look into their lives and see how they live, and the relationships they have with their loved ones and so forth, you find that they are no more enlightened than anyone else and perhaps even less. They depend on their active psychic impressions without having mastered the other levels.

And yet people run to these "psychics" for advice, to read the future and all that stuff. You can read your own future just by reading your mind, because that mind is going to take you wherever you are going, and it is going to condition everything you do and think and receive and learn. All the hang-ups you have in yourself are going to make your future. Only by getting beyond those, by being totally receptive to what the world is trying to tell you, to what life is trying to tell you, to what the universe is trying to tell you, to what other human beings, who are agents of that universe, are trying to tell you, will you understand the imagination. Only when you can take that feedback without conditioning it with your own uncertainty and with your own anger, and with your own resentments, can you have even the slightest idea of worlds that are beyond imagination. There are worlds that exist and that cannot be known even in images. If we ever knew what the imagination was we would know there are worlds still beyond imagination, beyond the conditioned scheme of things, beyond the physical realities of images. These worlds cannot be imaged but can still be experienced. Our consciousness is so wonderful that we can even experience things in it that cannot be imagined. Beyond the imagination itself, there is still consciousness that is alive and vibrating, and capable of knowing something. There is someone inside of us so pure that the consciousness of this being has no images, no thoughts, no concepts—pure consciousness, capable of experiencing its own light. Is it possible even to imagine that purity? A state of mind so pure that there is nothing in it, just the bare crude consciousness itself, without any conditioning or any thought about itself?

Only in that state does true experience (the deepest you can have) and true learning take place. All the rest is just *maya*, illusion, which we program into that pure stuff with our images and minds. We plant the seeds of all our illusions in that pure stuff and it grows them. It is helping us now to think and listen and see that consciousness is making our world in whatever way we are using our consciousness. If we are misusing our consciousness or abusing our consciousness then it will help us to do that, because our consciousness will only do whatever we do with it. If we cannot stand the thought of silence or the pure consciousness which is void of anything, because that frightens us, because we cannot let go into it, we will want to fill it up with noise, we will want to fill it up with sound, we must always have something going. We may be always chattering, always thinking, always filling up the silence because we are frightened of the emptiness which is our true self. As long as we are doing that, we are escaping. We will never know those worlds beyond, until we can make ourself totally receptive, take away all of our thoughts and just remain like a pure photographic plate, waiting and expecting something to come in, but not expecting anything in particular. If you have an expectation that is all that will manifest. But to be expectant without expectation, to have that state of mind where you do not expect anything but you expect everything, then anything can happen. Then the world becomes a spontaneous place in which to live.

Is that too far out of place for you? It is difficult isn't it? And you have got the whole of your life to worry about it. The universe is not in any big hurry. It gives you the whole of eternity in that space. Pure consciousness is eternal; it does not have anything to do with beginning life and ending life because it is beyond any concept of manifested life. It is both the manifest and the potential all rolled into one, and everything that is manifest now is the potential state for the next manifestation. So there is no difference between your potential state—what you can be—and what you are now. You see, in pure consciousness there is no difference. It sees you from the beginning to the end, as it were, in a timeless state. In pure consciousness there is no beginning and no end, because there is no one there to put a beginning or an end on it. It is a purely selfless state, where the self is not contemplating itself. It is just experiencing—experiencing self as everything else—so it is not a self-centered self looking at its own consciousness. It has become a selfless self.

It sounds paradoxical, but if you could purify your consciousness to the point where everything you saw around you in the universe was vibrating in your consciousness, not outside it, you would be that selfless self. The sun is just a burning ball of gas out in space, but you are experiencing it in your consciousness, a burning piece of gas inside your consciousness. There is no separation, it is part of you. The minute you think, "I am here and the sun is over there," your consciousness has created a division in itself—a concept, an image, and you destroy completely the purity of your consciousness. It is like pure water, absolutely transparent. If you put anything in it, you pollute it, it is no longer pure, it is something else. Your consciousness is identical to that. It is completely transparent without any thought about itself or anything else. Now when it takes itself and creates a thought with itself, then that is what it experiences.

So that is what we are experiencing now in our manifested form. Our human form is experiencing itself as human because that thought has been put into that purity. But there is no separation between *the creator of that thought and the consciousness which is experiencing that self as that thought.* The separation comes only in the consciousness that separates. This is very difficult to understand for those who are imprisoned in the flesh and sensory world, because they are clinging so strongly to their sensory phenomena as the reality that they cannot understand that the sensory phenomena and the one they call "me" are merely vibrations in consciousness. They have no reality other than that. The whole of the created universe in that sense is made of consciousness.

When I talk about consciousness I am not talking about human consciousness, but I am talking about the primal stuff of which the universe is made in its entirety, in experiencing itself, whatever it is. If it is a ball of gas like the sun, it is holding together as hydrogen, and something is holding it together as the sun. If it is a cabbage, the cabbage is not thinking it's a carrot, it's saying, "I am reproducing myself according to my own seed, according to my own image of myself, and next year I'll be a cabbage too; my seeds are not going to come up like carrots." Everything has that primordial image of itself inherent in it, in pure consciousness. So how do you penetrate that? Inside you there is that same seed nucleus—pure consciousness. Deep inside you, it is there. When you realize that nucleus you will know all of the worlds that come before your vision. You will be open to more worlds. You will discover Nuclear Evolution.

THE CENTERING SYMBOL OF NUCLEAR EVOLUTION

PART III
THE LANDING

Coming Down To Earth

Creative Conflict in action. The speaker has the rod and the reactor has the bat.

CREATIVE COMMUNICATION

Through Creative Communication we learn to grow more rapidly and find true peace of mind. Whatever work, study, hobby or action we do, we are communicating with our environment in some way. How creative that communication is depends upon our attitude toward what we are doing. Creative Communication is essential to good relationships with people, but it is also essential to successfully relating with the things we handle and sense. How aware we are when doing the dishes will determine whether one dish drops and breaks, whether they really get clean or are put in the dish drain with bits of egg left on them, and whether we get any joy out of washing them. The word communication comes from the root word *communicare,* to make common, to share in common with. If we cannot share our beings, or make our feelings common with others and our environment, we will have conflicts within and without. In essence then, the problem with communication *is* the basic world problem. All human problems arise from misunderstanding which in turn emerges out of poor communication.

The awareness explorations in Part II of this book put us in touch with the many thresholds of communication in people. They also developed our abilities to communicate effectively with people, nature, objects, different parts of ourselves and myriads of vibrations. Our practice of these instructions and our receptivity to them will determine how much we can actually bring them into use in our daily lives. In Part III, The Landing, we concentrate on specific skills to apply Creative Communication to our daily life on earth and, for those who wish to go farther, to probe the deepest blocks to communication.

Everyone has conflicts and challenges to deal with in daily life. They are the friction which spurs growth and learning. To know how to grab hold of your conflicts and use them for growth, rather than have them use you, is a rare talent. Most people allow conflicts to buffet them around. The conflicts teach them lessons in spite of themselves because they do not harness the energy of conflict. Traditionally we have been taught to face conflict by a) fighting back, b) staying cool and calm while trying to reason the difficulty out, c) turning the other cheek, or as modern parlance says "shining it on". But how much do we really gain from our conflicts? Few people realize how much dynamic energy gets bound up in a conflict. That energy can be taken hold of and released into higher creative potential when we know how. Regardless of which methods people have used to deal with conflicts we can all probably agree that most people still do not understand themselves or others very well.

At the University of the Trees consciousness research school, we have evolved some very successful communication skills that deal with the energies of conflict. We call the practice and use of these skills "Creative Conflict". In nature, creation evolves through continuous conflict-resolution. There is much violence, from the forceful collisions of microscopic atoms to giant exploding stars. On earth, positive and negative forces conflict, repel and unite in dynamic action on every level of existence, from the atomic and cellular levels to the mental and spiritual levels. Conflict is built into nature to evolve its creation, to push it along the path of nuclear evolution. Conflict is so very important because it is the major propelling evolutionary force, although it is not the evolutionary goal.

When together we can discover the keys to mastering conflict, we will be on the threshold of a new society. It is not something we can put off to the future, waiting for some government to hand it to us. We must build upon every tool we have available now, because the choice is cold and clear—mastery or suffering, even destruction. Science knows when energies build up they must be released. The negative energies in the world psyche must be understood and transmuted or they must wreak their havoc after creating too much pressure. Love is necessary, but personal devotion alone will not change the world. Self-responsibility in each of us to take hold of the forces of conflict is the only way, and everyone must do the work. No one is exempt from resolving conflict.

THE EGO AS THE ROOT OF CONFLICT

There are a number of psychological tools that have been brought forth this century which aim at resolving conflict in a variety of ways. Many have been incorporated into the explorations in Part II. Creative Conflict embraces all the useful psychological and spiritual methods of Creative Communication, and it also is a specific process which probes beyond them to the very heart of human conflict—the ego.

Dr. Thomas Gordon developed the wonderful method and communication model called "Effectiveness Training", which is gaining popularity in homes and schools. It is the best beginning process that we have seen for Creative Conflict. We only wish Effectiveness Training went farther than it does, but it stops at the door of the ego. In his book *P.E.T. In Action** (Parent Effectiveness Training), Dr. Gordon asks himself if Effectiveness Training can help all people accept what they cannot change. He responds to his own question, "I doubt it and I am at a loss to know how we could do better." The only sure way we have found to help people work with what they cannot change is through Creative Conflict with the ego to gain insights into its motivations. The ego is normally totally blind to its own rationalizations, hence Dr. Gordon's statement. A former P.E.T. teacher and educator who has introduced higher consciousness through *Meditating With Children*** into every classroom, kindergarten through sixth grade, in the suburban Los Angeles school in which she teaches, commented that she stopped teaching P.E.T. because "It just doesn't go far enough. There's more, much more." We find this true of most every psychological technique available. These techniques do teach getting inside each other's world for creative communicating, which is the essential first step for dissolving ego separation. But they do not penetrate the basic ego separations from the oneness of life. The only way to transmute conflict for good is by developing a program that includes higher consciousness and grabbing hold of the greatest human challenge of all—the separating ego.

Most people think of the ego as something they value, their individual uniqueness, and they cannot distinguish it from their real being. The idea of "getting rid of" or "working on" the ego seems foreign to them. They ask, "Is there any advantage in transcending the ego? How can it be beneficial to constantly look at my motives, the subtle undercurrents of my self-centeredness generated by my ego? What is the advantage of

---

* *P.E.T. In Action,* by Thomas Gordon, Bantam Books.
** *Meditating With Children,* by Deborah Rozman, University of the Trees Press.

being egoless? Can I really gain anything by giving up looking out for Number One? Look around, how many people really want to give up their egos? I'll be stupid if I do. I want to develop my ego, not reduce it."

But what is the ego really? It is the one sitting inside our own idea of I am. That consciousness which is in everything must express through some form or body. In getting a body it wants to be somebody special, separate and unique from other bodies and from the environment. "That's me," it says, until it realizes that by giving up its idea of separateness, it gains a much greater individuality and fulfillment and a much expanded consciousness. By giving up our separateness, we give up our selfishness, the part of us that brings our conflicts, pain and suffering. Rather than being a weak, unattractive state, egolessness is knowing who we really are. It is knowing we are one with everyone and that the whole environment belongs to us. It builds tremendous strength and courage.

Creative Conflict challenges every person to confront their ego position that separates being from being. It tackles the causes that separate human consciousness from oneness. The essentially spiritual structure of Creative Conflict has nothing to do with religion or any belief system, but just the pure relationship between energies. You can refer back to Chapters One and Two in Part I of this book for more explanation of the nature of these energies, and the link between ego, light and consciousness. Given these facts of nature, it seems a bit absurd that so few people are really willing to work on their ego, that self-centered identity which binds and limits their energy. Most people would rather cling to it or escape into some heavenly euphoria or into sense pleasures. But working directly with the ego we release the energies that block our fulfillment. We release them permanently into greater potential, greater light, and expanded understanding.

The first step in dissolving the separating ego is to get out of our little self and inside the inner worlds of others. All the good beginning communication skills available (such as Gestalt, psychosynthesis, co-counseling, P.E.T.) enable us to begin to take this step. But we then must go much farther in our own evolution and in deepening relationships by learning to watch and confront the ego's subtle motivations and reactions.

Creative Conflict methods have been used successfully with children, parents, classrooms, businesses, teenagers, spiritual groups, growth groups and labor-management relations. With some practice you will be able to apply the process on your own in all your relationships.

The most fundamental principle which Creative Conflict is based upon is the spiritual principle that since all is one, all life is a mirror of ourself. Each situation, each person, each inner reaction, is a mirror in which you can see yourself, your own real nature. Through learning to look at the mirror everywhere, you can see where it needs polishing. In a Creative Conflict group, together we can polish the mirror to see reality and reflect the glory of our own true potential unveiled. In the group we learn to see how we are creating our reality and we gain the power to put in a new program.

THE CREATIVE CONFLICT PROCESS

The best way to begin using the Creative Conflict process presented here is to embody the techniques in yourself and use them in your daily relationships. Through demonstrating your own skillfullness in communication you will affect others who will want similar skills. They will see your centeredness and ability to deal with all situations and want it for themselves. (This is as true for children as it is for adults.) A person who has insight into his or her own ego becomes specially magnetic to others who sense that he or she knows something they do not know. This is not a false sense of righteousness, which children see right through and reject. The truly wise and attractive people are those we feel drawn to because they know themselves and are therefore understanding of us. They care enough to communicate and listen. So most of the keys given here are to help you foster real listening. What is life trying to tell you? Can you hear it? What is your child or anyone trying to tell you?

The next step to implementing the Creative Conflict process on a deeper level is to form a group of people or join with a family eager to explore truth together. This group can be the next journey after you have completed the awareness explorations in Part II or you can begin immediately to use Creative Conflict along with the games. Some families have family Creative Conflict time where all members gather together regularly to practice real listening, to share in their work on themselves and to mirror and support each other, in addition to awareness exploration time.

In our village block we have neighborhood Creative Conflict to deal with the little problems that the kids create for the adults and for each other, from telling fibs to walking on the neighbor's newly planted grass after being told not to at least ten times.

There are several important attitudes we must consider before beginning Creative Conflict.

Commitment

The first attitude is commitment to each other in the heart in spite of differences in the head. Because of people's different levels of consciousness and different life experiences there are always going to be some differences in perceptions, beliefs, and preferences. These differences are welcomed in Creative Conflict as food for growth, because the underlying desire for oneness in the heart bonds us with others. Creative Conflict is a commitment to see how the ego works in each of us, dissolve its blockages, which are like negative surface tensions encrusting the positive core of love in the heart and filtering reality, and expand ourselves into greater beings. Each person must do the work, no one can do it for us.

Because people are so identified with their egos, we will all be challenged at some point on whether our commitment to getting to truth is real, whether we really do *want* to face ourselves, or whether we would rather forget it. Sometimes we will even feel like running from someone confronting a nitty-gritty part of us. The ego is very tricky at justifying its position when it feels cornered. We say, "That's me, you're criticizing me, leave me alone." Egos get hurt, protect what they want to, try to get their own way and unconsciously hurt others, not realizing that they are not seeing clearly. It is hard sometimes to see whether the person confronting you really cares or whether that person is just trying to put his or her will and opinion on you too. The Creative Conflict process sorts this out. Children especially do not like to look at their egos, until they experience what the process and the feeling of oneness can do *for* them. The delusion is that we *can* run away and forget looking or find something easier. In reality, life's lessons are harder to bear without Creative Conflict. The mirror is always with us, whether in a group or not. But it is more difficult to see into the mirror alone, even if we are working on our own growth. It is more intense, but more rapid and fulfilling to meet the challenge of life with a group of people who ask you to look at yourself, who care about you and who are committed to each other's being. This kind of group is like a greenhouse, with ideal conditions for growth. The Creative Conflict process is a modern tool for enlightenment, for breaking through the light barrier. It is a form of social yoga for everyone in the nuclear age, based on nature's laws of energy and of feedback.

To get the most from Creative Conflict, work with a group of others equally or more committed than yourself. Until the group trusts each other enough, whatever age range, it is best to use the awareness games along with Creative Conflict to carefully, gently build the understanding and caring needed for deep commitment to truth. The awareness explorations are carefully designed to guide you to deeper, higher levels of consciousness where trust is built. In Creative Conflict you have guidelines, but you must initiate the action and take full responsibility for working through the conflicts expressed. This is the commitment needed.

Many youngsters are ready for Creative Conflict before their parents, but the reverse is often true too, depending upon the ego development. The main factor for readiness is self-honesty. For teenagers, Creative Conflict is a stabilizing force when there is a committed group. It is crucial to their development of a healthy self-image and honest relationships. They learn to know when they are seeing clearly, eliminating a lot of the confusion that comes in adolescence. Several of our staff at the University of the Trees who teach Creative Conflict to children and teens have remarked that the kids do not like the ego confrontations at first. It is the first time anyone has demanded that they be real and look at themselves. But they come back for more and more just because it is real, and because they feel their inner beings accepted.

We must emphasize that the process is not that of an encounter group. We use communication techniques to clarify what we are feeling, but we do not wallow in negativity. We get into higher consciousness and from there we transform problems together. So many people have reported to us very unfulfilling encounter group experiences in which their emotions were churned up and they were left hanging, or where social one-upmanship games prevailed, or where several strong egos held sway. On the other hand they found Creative Conflict a golden opportunity to understand how they channel their energies and create their relationships. Strong egos cannot dominate because it is the ego that is being looked at! People learn how to take responsibility for directing their consciousness to the degree they are committed to the process. The training teaches identification with the One, the pure consciousness, not with the emotions and egos. Positive support is important, but massaging each other's egos only blows up the self-image and leads to problems which are just as great as self-doubt and negativity. Creative Conflict helps us build a clear and honest self-concept through identifying with the greater Self and its commitment to look at the little self. Periodically we should openly discuss our commitments and receive feedback from each other on how we are manifesting them. The Creative Conflict group is only as effective as the *commitment* of each of its members.

Motivation

Motivation is the second attitude we must consider before we begin Creative Conflict. The desire to feel at one, beyond the differences, and to improve relationships is the basic motivation for wanting to do Creative Conflict. Groups are stillborn or impotent when the underlying motives are conflicting. The depth of the motivation in each determines how effective the group force can be. Practice of the process will both test the motives and deepen the feelings for the work. So we must remain mindful of why everyone is doing this group sharing and probe our real motivations frequently.

Integrity

Integrity is the third attitude that will make a successful Creative Conflict group. Integrity means being in touch with our real feelings and expressing them. If we get turned off to the challenge to be real with others about how we feel, we will get the kind of situations and type of world we deserve through our own default. So integrity is facing ourselves and each other as honestly as we can and with a sense of responsibility. *The main reason for lack of peace in ourselves and in the world is lack of communication. The main reason for lack of deep communication is lack of integrity.* The ability to own our feelings and actions so we can take responsibility for them is developed by looking into our motivations and encouraged through the work on our ego reactions. These come out in the Creative Conflict process. Integrity makes Creative Conflict meaningful an dynamic.

The following Creative Conflict process for transcending the separating ego is the basic beginning teaching. For those who wish to go deeper into the methods there is a more in-depth pamphlet available from the publishers.*

THE CREATIVE CONFLICT PROCESS

In this process we delve deeply into specific methods to dissolve ego blocks. For most of us the ego is constantly, subtly blocking our perception. It is also usually blocking real listening, so there is very little true communication taking place, even though we may think we are high and aware beings talking to each other. We hear words, but not the layers of meaning and being behind them. We see flowers, but not the light and consciousness within them. In order to do this work on ourselves together or alone, we must balance its depth and intensity with a light heart, humor and joy. Otherwise it becomes very serious. However, if we look at it as life's garden that we are nurturing, weeding, digging, fertilizing, watering and supplying sunlight for, we can make the work light. By making work light we make *light* work. When light works for us we are in tune with nature and we can tackle anything, even making the manure of negativity into good compost to help nature grow beautiful flowers.

There are a number of keys to real listening with which we begin the Creative Conflict Process. There are also subtle blocks to real listening that we must watch for in ourselves as we use the keys.

KEYS TO REAL LISTENING – SEVEN STEPS

1. **Centering Meditation**
    Taking a moment to quiet the body, feelings, and thoughts jangling around inside to get in touch with our inner being—the center.

---

* "Creative Conflict" a pamphlet of instruction and background by Christopher Hills, University of the Trees Press (see appendix).

2. Receptivity

Putting aside all thoughts, reactions, and "tapes" playing in our heads, spinning tunes of past feelings and ideas and future expectations.

3. Active Listening

Replaying what other people are saying to you after they have spoken. This enables you to see if you have really been receptive and lets the other person feel you are in rapport. You speak back using your own words, not parroting the other's. This means you will speak back meaning, as well as words.

4. Mirroring

An extension of Active Listening. It goes deeper than Active Listening, because you are trying to mirror back what the person's being is saying to you behind the words. You mirror back the vibrations and feelings you pick up from other people as well as the words, so they feel you are at one with them and can feel their heart. You might begin mirroring by saying, for example, "Let me see if I understand you, you're really saying. . ." In Active Listening you just say back to the other what has been said which makes the other feel heard and encourages him or her to continue speaking. In Mirroring you are actually trying to experience others as they experience themselves, becoming one, and taking the communion to a deeper level of being.* The other person must then confirm or deny whether you heard rightly before going on to respond to what was said.

5. Confirmation

After mirroring you ask the other if your mirror is a correct picture. It is essential that you ask for confirmation, to know if you are tuning in properly. Then you listen for the reply, again with receptivity. If the person says, "Yes, you've got it!" then you can speak your feelings and respond. If the other says, "No, that's not what I meant," or "Those were my words but I don't really feel that way," then you ask him or her to explain again. You active listen and mirror again. You do this until you receive your confirmation from the other.

This communication process may at first glance seem laborious but it actually becomes quite fulfilling as you penetrate to deeper layers of sharing and being. It is also absolutely essential to clear understanding. The fact that 99 per cent of people cannot do this process properly

---

* A complete mirroring exercise is given in the exploration on p. 153.

without practice is proof enough that we *think* we understand but do not. The saying "Hearing, they hear not" becomes vividly illustrated.

6. Response

Only after all of the above are completed do you share your response, what you feel about what the other has said to you. Most people want to respond before the other has even finished speaking, and so miss all the important steps for real communication. It takes self-discipline to wait and respond only after confirmation is established. When you respond you use an "I-message". For example,

> I felt hurt when you gave those boxes to Ruth because it made me feel left out.

There are four aspects to an I-message which expresses a deep feeling you have:

a)   I felt (owning it is your reality)
b)   hurt (or joyful, or whatever it is you felt)
c)   when you gave those boxes to Ruth (saying what triggered the feeling)
d)   because it made me feel left out (saying specifically what it did to you)

People often forget to include the fourth part especially and this is the part that communicates the most deeply. All four aspects of the I-message must be there for your being to have fully communicated. This takes some reflection to get in touch with your feelings and it requires openness in expressing them, which you can only learn through practice.

7. Confirmation

Then you ask the other person to please mirror back what you have just said so that you can feel you have communicated. When you speak with another who is also accustomed to using these communication skills it is ideal communication and you can usually get to the place of oneness and true understanding very quickly. Most people, whether they know about these steps or not, will respect your interest and desire to have the communication clear. Just watching someone use these skills puts them in touch with a deeper part of themselves and makes them want to use them too. With a little guidance most people will also respond well to your request that they should mirror back what you have said, as it shows you really do care that they hear you.

BLOCKS TO REAL LISTENING – WAYS THE EGO WORKS TO SEPARATE ITSELF

Compliance

Compliance occurs when you adopt the opinion of someone else, or of the group mind, in order to go along with the crowd, gain a favorable reaction or omit something unfavorable in order to be liked. You may not actually believe in the opinion. You may be privately disagreeing while outwardly going along wtih the other person. This will block communication between your head and heart and with others.

In our work at the University of the Trees, Michael used often to disagree with group decisions inwardly, but go along with them compliantly so as not to make waves. He would pack books or come to group meditation as he was "supposed to", but resented being "scheduled". He went along with the group, at the same time feeling resentful because he was afraid of looking selfish and of group feedback if he did not "comply". It wasn't until he finally opened up in the Creative Conflict group and shared his problem that the group was able to help him see his ego position. Then through self-confrontation he totally changed his attitude. Now he bounces around with energy and contributes joyfully to the group work from his own self-motivated center, not from compliance. Not everyone has had Michael's problem so severely in the group, but everyone was able to help Michael see how he was creating it through separating himself from the group. It was hard for him to hear at first. The change took time, but when it came it was from the depths of his being. He changed from selfishly looking out for just his own feelings to selflessly identifying with the whole.

Negative Identification

1. One person identifies with the emotions of another and the sympathy pulls him off his own center into the center of the other person. He begins to feel the same feelings as the other and they both get stuck in the conflict.

2. One person identifies with the group mind or another person and begins to act out the other person's role as part of his own self-image. The other personality becomes a model for the individual and his opinions are held only so long as that personality has an important relationship to him. The relationship provides identity and self-esteem. It blocks real communification with others because the role image is too strong.

An example of the first type of communication:

One woman on campus, Pam, has to keep close watch on her tendency to swing into everyone else's center. She can be talking to Robert about his perception of a situation and she will sway right into his point of view. Fifteen minutes later she can be talking to Norah who has the exact opposite view on that situation, and Pam will agree with her. Pam's block is not compliance due to mixed motives, but it is wanting to be understanding and amiable. So she feels first one way then the other. Her identification blocks her from seeing truth. She has had to learn to watch her pattern of swinging and stay centered in her own feelings while listening to the other's motives behind the words.

In the second type of negative identification, Debbie tends to take on qualities and mannerisms of whomever she directs her love towards. It seems as though she absorbs their energies. When she was fifteen she took on the qualities of an admired teacher, his opinions, ideas and even handwriting, all unconsciously. Others felt she was a bit strange. When she was twenty-one she became like her boyfriend. As if by osmosis his being became part of hers, and she could feel his expressions come over her face, feel his strength and his ego as her own. In Creative Conflict she has been accused sometimes of "coming on like Christopher", but with an added flavor of superiority and not in a way expressive of her real feelings. She has to learn to watch the energies she picks up and see how she uses them and for what motive.

Basic Assumptions

Often we have a "basic assumption" about ourselves, or about life, or about the other person which may not be true. This assumption can prevent us from hearing life's real message or listening to others. It can bring pain. A basic assumption is when you feel, for example, "You didn't take me with you so you don't really love me." You are assuming this is true, but until you check it out you just don't know. Often those kinds of feelings are not true at all, even though they seem so obvious and feel so real. We even want to believe them to be true to rationalize our feelings of hurt, and yet we are relieved when we find out our assumption was wrong. People make such assumptions because they cannot see how their egos are operating. They cannot see the real possessiveness that might be at the root of such an assumption. This blocks them from being able to get inside the world of the other person to find out what the real reason is.

Projection

Another block to listening is projecting our own feelings and motives onto another. Projection is nearly always unconscious. We see life through our own filters, through our own ego position which may not be true at all. For example, "Rick is a very moody person," says Jean. She sees him that way quite clearly. But in reality Jean is moody and so Rick's moodiness looks big to her. It looks big to her, but not to others when she checks it out. Life mirrors you in how you see and judge others. What you cannot stand in another is surely in yourself. Creative Conflict brings the projections out for you to work with them.

Expectation

Expectation is expecting someone to say or do something in the way you want. Desire is at the root of expectation. For a long time in our community, Ann would bring conflicts between herself and her boyfriend Robert to the group, always expecting the group to confront Robert and prove her point. They never did! They always felt there was something fishy in Ann's position, even though they knew Robert had responsibility in their conflicts too. Ann could never understand why the group feedback would always come back to her. Her very expectation that Robert should get the feedback blocked her from seeing her own unwillingness to look at her own ego. Her tremendous desire for Robert to change, to be more the way she wanted him, created her expectation that the group would tell him to change. Her desire also prevented her from seeing the insecurity and selfishness at the root of her feelings that were fueling her desire. She was afraid to even look at the desire lest she lose Robert in the process. Through patient mirroring and her own meditation Ann was eventually able to see how her own ego was creating its pain and to release her tremendous attachment.

Internalization

Internalization is adopting a solution or an attitude because it satisfies an ego need.

Ary decided to take a vow of celibacy for a year as a reaction to being rejected by a man she liked very much. Another person in the group had recently decided to become celibate after much soul searching. Ary jumped on the "bandwagon" for a different motive and woke up a month later with nightmares and a terrible feeling of loss and aloneness. The group helped her to see that her decision to become celibate was an unconscious power play to make the man she liked respect and want her, and to make him feel bad that she was now unavailable. She had incorporated celibacy into her value system, but for the wrong motive. Nevertheless, she feels she has set forces in motion by her decision and is sticking to her vow to see if she can master herself.

Emotionalism

Emotions provide tremendous energy to help you achieve goals, overcome barriers and provide enthusiasm for group work. They can also cloud your perception when you wallow in them and use them as a defense against looking at yourself.

Whenever Wendy was confronted on almost anything, she used to start to cry. The result was people would leave her alone or try to rescue her with sympathy and her ego remained intact. One day she wondered why she was not growing and changing as she wished. The group reached a point where they saw through her defense. They confronted her on using her tears to ward off feedback and avoid looking at herself. Crying meant she did not have to change. By not buying the emotionalism and constantly confronting her with it, the group mirror presented Wendy with her real self, and not the image of the too sensitive good girl she was used to projecting. Wendy has since changed considerably as a result of getting in touch with the motive behind her tears. She has mastered a deep pattern she had for over twenty years since childhood, in spite of years of psychology and years of meditation. She is now a much stronger person. This change came, not from group therapy, but from group integrity.

Yes, but

Whenever you hear people respond "Yes, but . . . " you know they are not listening. A "yes butter" never listens to you because he is listening to his own opinions. As you are speaking he is dying to say the next thing. So whenever you hear the words "yes, but . ." coming out of your own mouth, you know you have not been receptive. If you get a "yes, but" reply from others, all you can say is that perhaps they haven't really heard, and ask them to please mirror the thought you said. That is the polite way of saying "you haven't heard me." Usually a "yes butter" cannot mirror properly. He will come on with something very different from what you have said. Even if he is trying to repeat your words exactly he will foul them up.

Playing tapes

We all have mental tapes playing unconsciously, and this block to real listening must be watched very carefully. For instance, if your friend says something to you and you hear it correctly, it goes into your memory where there are stored all kinds of existing experiences which you have had and valued, emotional experiences, truth experiences, horrible experiences, nice experiences, and if she is telling you something nice it will go into that area of your memory where you start to compare it with other things that have happened that are nice in your life and you may be thinking about them while she is speaking—so your own tape recorder is activated and you are not listening. You are listening to your own memories. Sense impressions coming in—the car on the street, the newspaper boy walking by, the wind on your shoulders—all stimuli can trigger your thoughts, preventing your listening by pre-occupying your attention. You have to learn to be very conscious if you are playing any tapes in your mind while another person is speaking.

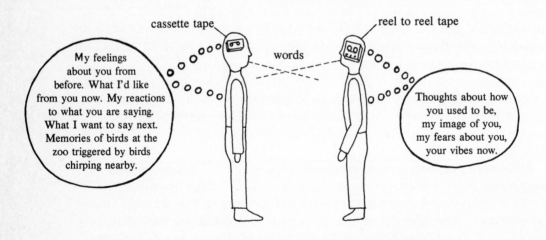

All the inner tapes filter the real communication.

Stereotyping

One of the biggest blocks in communication is labeling people. "He's a professor, he's a yogi, she's a religious fanatic, he's a scientist, she's a this

436

and that." He may have been a professor yesterday, but he could be a father today. When you fix people in your consciousness you cannot really hear them in their being. The mere fixing of an image in the mind is going to color and determine what you hear from that person. So many people react to race. He's a Negro. . . (implying all Negroes are a certain way), or She's a communist. . . (implying she must be mean and nasty because all communists want to take over the world). Stereotypes lead to many basic assumptions. Many famous movie actors and actresses have miserable lives because their public stereotype allows them no freedom to be themselves. If the image you hold of a person is not a true image of his being, then that person is not going to accept your vibration and is not going to accept what you say. You will not be speaking to him, rather you will be speaking to your private image of him. If you are afraid that people are stereotyping or judging you, your reaction might be that you will want to look good in their eyes. So you will do many things to please them. It may not be true that they feel that way about you. It may be a projection of the way you stereotype others, so you fear others will do that to you. We must always check out judgements and stereotyping of others before we try to communicate.

Self-image

The hidden image you hold of yourself, your secret self, is the greatest and deepest block to real listening and real communication with others and with the universe itself. This image colors how you see everyone else, because it is coloring your Real Self which has no color, which is pure, clear, universal, with nothing in it. So when ego penetration gets to its deepest levels, it always hits the fundamental self-image.

When Ann was afraid to look at her motives, lest she lose Robert, she was really afraid that she might come out not looking good—her self-image would be tarnished and Robert might see that and reject her. Losing Robert would not look good to others either. When we are afraid to express our real feelings for fear of rejection, it is usually a fear that we will come out looking bad. Our lily-white image of our self will be tainted. This clinging to self-image as our security operates especially strongly in love relationships, where the admiration and love of the other is important to us. We also build self-images to give ourselves a feeling of identity and worth, for example, the mother, the teacher, the good girl, the he-man, the savior. All roles we identify with are self-images. This is the deepest part

of Creative Conflict. The ego wants to preserve its idea of being somebody special and unique, and fears loss if it does not keep its image intact.
The self-image works very subtly, shifting from one identity to the other if
one is threatened until it eventually lets go and surrenders to nothing.
Then the real Self can blend with the greater Self and become truly
someone. Great sages have always said we must lose ourselves to find
our Self. Usually there are many ego battles on the way to this deeper
level before freedom is won. To get to the level of continuous penetration
through the self-images as they rise, is an advanced state of consciousness
and takes a tremendous amount of commitment to Creative Conflict.
When a group of people can help each other see where their self-images
are operating and dissolve them together, they can work in higher *group
consciousness*. Then through this clarity the group becomes a pure
channel through which the Cosmic Consciousness is able to express.

We have listed all of these illustrative examples for you to get in touch
with them in your own lives. All of the people mentioned here are healthy,
intelligent individuals who came to the University of the Trees and
embarked on the Creative Conflict process as an awareness discipline.
They are not abnormal, but have gotten more deeply in touch with their
karma, or ego blocks, than most people seeking growth. All of them
meditate, study themselves on their own and work hard, but working on
the ego by yourself is almost impossible. There are just too many nooks
and crannies in which it can hide from your real Self. To accept this as
Truth is very difficult—if you are in your ego.

THE CREATIVE CONFLICT GROUP

Once you have tested out the keys to real listening, examined the
blocks, and have decided you want to get together with a group of people
to practice Creative Conflict, it is time to form your group. Begin your
first session with a discussion of the central purpose of the group so that
all group members are in agreement and so the group mind is formed. It is
important to remind each other that everyone is responsible for cleaning
up their own ship and doing their own work. What they are embarking on
is an exciting adventure in growth which comes not through the head but
through direct perception from the heart. *Heart power* is the motto of
Creative Conflict. Ghandhi called it "soul force" and said it was the most
potent force in the world.

There is a minimum number of rules and guidelines necessary for Creative Conflict which helps to put the seven steps into practice and minimize the blocks, so that deep communication can develop. We wish there did not have to be rules at all, but we find these few rules necessary guides to the experience of loving others as ourself. The rules of Creative Conflict are the real leader of the group. The leadership is then based on truth, not on a personality.

It is possible, but *not* necessary to have a trained facilitator or leader present. But even when a leader is present, his or her role is to facilitate the use of the guidelines and keys for Creative Conflict which people do tend to forget in the beginning. Most people have ingrained habits of communication which make them forget.

It is very important not to deviate from the rules for best results, since they are based on natural models and have proved effective over and over again. Of course, you are always free to learn on your own, but the temptation to change the rules, thinking your case is exceptional, will slow your progress. Our experience has been that everytime we felt we had an exceptional situation and let the rule in question go, we wasted a lot of time and ended up going back to the rule with greater understanding of why it was instituted in the first place.

THE RULES
Implementing the keys to real listening is the first and most important rule of the Creative Conflict process.

Size
If you are beginning with a new group, it is best to limit the size to eight to ten members at first. Of course, in some classrooms and businesses, you will have to work with more people unless you can break up into smaller groups within the large group.

Setting a definite time period
It is very important that you agree upon a time period wherein everyone commits themselves to practicing the process and to attending the group sessions. We suggest ten sessions, meeting once a week for three hours. In this way we can see whether our words really match our commitment. In one group that we facilitated the commitment was made by each member

to attend each session, but when a musician came to town to give a concert on one of the dates, the priority changed for one couple. There is a need for continuity in these sessions because you are really getting nitty-gritty with people. Drifters and people who idly come in and out are not sensitive to the depths that you are trying to seek. They spoil the whole group trust and vibration. They put their own preferences first and not the souls of others. Our actions speak louder than our words, and whatever we choose to do shows where our real commitment is. By setting a definite time period we commit ourselves to looking at our integrity and working on our egos for that period. At the end of the period we can review whether or not we want to continue. This choice, at periodic intervals, allows us to have the fulfillment of completing a commitment we have set for ourselves, and gives the freedom to choose a different direction at the end of the period with integrity.

Admitting new members

We suggest that when you begin your group with a ten week commitment, that you open the group to new members at the beginning of the next ten week period. If you have an ongoing group that is committed beyond a ten week period, we have found it essential to institute a two week period of silence for admitting new members, as well as a one week probation after that to make sure all feel in tune with that person. It also gives that person a chance to become familiar with the rules and keys and be able to apply them in an experienced group. (Often it will take the new person longer.) If the group is very experienced a four-week silence period is needed. Since there are subtle energies for the newcomer to learn to tune into, this long time of learning how to listen and be receptive should be welcomed. At the end of each session the new member can share his or her feelings and the group should make every effort to draw them out. Some people are very reactive and cannot sit still for the entire period. They feel they just have to contribute their ideas and insist on speaking. Even though they may have a valid point, a test of willingness to discipline the ego is in being able to hold comments until the designated period of silence is completed. Some people are only too eager to put in their two cents worth regardless of what is happening, or to take over and dominate. They are so much in their ego they cannot believe it will take them four weeks to learn how to listen correctly. They will find out later it takes a lifetime to listen with a pure heart.

Some people want attention for themselves and some feel they are so knowledgeable about others that they do not need the humbling experience of keeping silent. Again, if a person cannot comply with this necessary rule, he is not really ready for your in-depth group.

Centering meditation

If your group has not been through the awareness explorations in Part II, it is a good idea to begin the first session with the Trust exercise on page 62 or one of the activities from the green world to loosen everyone up and get the heart energy flowing. After the exercise everyone should sit comfortably in a circle and center for a few minutes to tune the group mind to higher consciousness. You can meditate silently or do one of the guided meditations from the explorations.

Every Creative Conflict session must begin with a group centering meditation to tune all the separate energies within each individual and blend them into a united group vibration. This is the first of the keys to real listening. It helps develop the art of being centered while you interact in daily life. After you feel tuned in meditation, look into the major conflict in your life at the moment or to a conflict you feel with someone in the group or elsewhere (it may be minor). Remember, the purpose for looking into the conflict is not to give it energy, but to get to the cause of how you are creating it in your consciousness. You may feel you have no conflicts but everyone has some challenge to face. Until we are perfect, we have conflicts facing us and work to do on our egos, because that is nature's way. Try to get in touch with the part of yourself that you need to work on. The meditation helps you to release the ego-mind and identify with the oneness and the pure consciousness in which you can see clearly what you need to develop. It opens the intuition to work for you. Meditating together provides group heart power and keener insight. After a few more moments for getting in touch, one person reads aloud one of the guidelines of Creative Conflict as part of the meditation, and everyone contemplates that principle in relation to the conflict they have brought. Each session a new principle, guideline, rule, key or block is read and contemplated until all the teachings of Creative Conflict have been considered. Confine yourselves to contemplating only one teaching at a time so you can consider it in its depth. At some point someone spontaneously ends the meditation, toning the AAAAAOOOOOMMMM sound and all join in. This toning binds the group energy together and closes the meditation.

During the session, try to really apply the keys and guidelines, especially the one chosen for the meditation. If there is anyone who is confused as to its application discuss it as a group, bringing in examples from personal experience. Over the weeks the group will cumulatively study the entire Creative Conflict process. Make a list of the rules, guidelines, keys and blocks and put them up on a large piece of paper on the wall in clear view, or xerox them so everyone has a copy. Each person should read and review them all before each session, or the group can read them quickly aloud at the beginning of each session after the meditation. It is essential to memorize the entire process so that it becomes part of your way of relating. The quicker the entire group can make the process part of their being, the deeper and more effective the group experience will be.

Some people rebel at the idea of a set of rules as the authority, even though the rules are not arbitrary but have been tested and found to be necessary for many reasons. To become a craftsman at any skill, we have first to follow the directions of the teacher and be a receptive apprentice. If we feel we have failed, without having followed the guidance given, then we have no one to blame but our own egos. This entire process is very subtle, yet it works swiftly to enable you to be able to deal with conflicts on many different levels. Master it first before you modify it.

In a leaderless group, or a group in which guidelines are the leader, it is only a matter of time before natural leaders evolve. These are people who can tune into and grasp the essence of the guidelines, the spirit of truth more readily. The function of such natural leaders is to make sure that the spirit of the teachings is carried through. Everybody needs to become a leader in the Creative Conflict group and be fully responsible, if expanded consciousness is to be expressed through the group awareness. The group awareness in the Creative Conflict process is special only because it is tuned to going beyond ego to the ability to realize and express oneness and pure perception. The group must always make room for the *deus ex machina,* the spirit of truth that may come through any one of the members at any time. Through constantly listening to intuition we are always ready for it to appear. In an advanced group, the direct perception that cuts through to truth rings from one person to the next, and maintains a very high, pure energy level of wisdom throughout the group session.

The silent vote

All decisions, such as whose situation should be mirrored first, or whether we should admit a new member, should be unanimous. By taking a silent vote in meditation on the proposal or issue presented, the group can use intuition or higher consciousness in coming to any decision. The silent vote works in the following way: One person puts a proposal to the group. If there are immediate objections, the group discusses them and applies the keys to real listening to the discussion as needed, until they come up with a unanimous proposal. Then they take a silent vote on the final proposal. If anyone feels a doubt or a funny feeling concerning the proposal, they may break the silence and speak out. Then the group reconsiders in light of their input. The process is repeated until the silent vote goes through without objections. When nobody speaks during the short silence the vote has passed.

Tape recording

It is essential to tape record every group session. So much is missed in conversation. Even when we are trying our best to listen, our blind spots often prevent us from hearing. We must remember that it is not ordinary conversation we are looking for, but in-depth hearing. The group mirror may seem like too much to handle while we are present with our own ego defenses, holding onto our positions, not able to change, but it may sound very reasonable when we play the tape back in a day or two. Some people play their feedback sessions again and again and gain new insights each time. Each person can take turns supplying tapes and recording the sessions, or the person wanting to listen to the tape can purchase it from the common group stock invested in by everybody at the beginning. You can be economical by re-using old tapes over again. Most people like to save them as a record of growth and in case any dispute about who said what comes up at a later date. There is no greater authority on your ego than a tape of yourself saying something you would never dream of saying!

Sharing needs

The initial meditation, and contemplation of the guideline, rule, key or block, need not last longer than five to ten minutes. After the meditation, each person goes around the circle and shares his or her need briefly. The personal needs might also relate to some larger group need, and as the group consciousness gets stronger, many people's needs will coincide.

This is especially true in a community or a group that lives and works together. The group then decides which personal conflict or need to work with first. The decision should be unanimous. If there are differences of opinion at this point, discuss them so you can come to a unanimous agreement. Meditate a few minutes more, silently tuning into the being of the person, clearing your own filters out of the way as much as possible and focussing the group mind energy for greater perception. You do *samyama* on the person as given in the exercise on page 327 to activate oneness and intuition. When the person whose need is to be dealt with first is ready, he or she shares feelings on it as deeply as possible. Another person mirrors the problem to make sure it has been heard correctly and to bring rapport. If the conflict is with someone in the group, that person should be the mirror. When confirmation is received, the other party can share his or her feelings. The group must watch to make certain that all the communication steps in the keys to real listening are completed. When the mirroring is completed on both sides, the group mind brings deeper penetration by the different members sharing their feelings and insights.

Usually penetration, understanding and release will come in one session, but sometimes it takes a long time if the ego is stubborn or if the block is deep. The group must gently, constantly bring each other back to real listening by all giving I-messages, all saying how they actually experience the other person, mirroring their beings, and guiding them to mirror and share their own I-messages.

For beginners in Creative Conflict the temptation is to go into the most emotional needs first, but this is a trap, and not necessarily the wisest decision. To always gravitate to the most emotional issue only leads to group therapy and feeds emotionalism. The purpose of Creative Conflict is not for the group to play rescuer to a victim of a problem. Group consciousness comes from the group mind meditating upon all presented needs and tuning together to intuition for the real priority. Usually there will be a very clear feeling as to which situation is most ready for the group feedback.

During the session, bring in the guidelines, point out the blocks and apply the keys and rules wherever you can. Soon they will become part of you, and you will experience how these teachings tune you to nature. They are the lever that will help lift you and the group consciousness into full awareness for penetrating conflicts and transcending the ego. There is no other way so selfless and no faster way for transforming the ego, especially when coupled with selfless service and meditation.

Children

When working with children you will have to simplify the terms of the process with words they can understand and with examples they can relate to according to the age. Nevertheless, the keys to real listening can be taught to any age and they are the core of the Creative Conflict process.

Time limit

If you have time you can go into more than one member's need, again deciding unanimously which need is to be next. Some sessions you will be able to go around the whole group, and the other times one or two people's needs will occupy the entire group time. Decide on a time limit for your sessions or you could be there all day and night. Successful Creative Conflict creates a dynamic energy which leaves everyone feeling energized. It feels electrical, as hidden creative energies are released and direct perception is experienced. Many people come to a Creative Conflict session tired from work, and leave feeling rejuvenated and high. If the energy is flagging you must own responsibility for it and contribute the missing electricity yourself.

Review

At the end of your ten-week periods review your commitments and review what you have learned. What have you been able to carry over into your daily encounters with people? In what aspect of Creative Conflict are you still weak? These review periods are very important to help you see where you have been and where you need to go. Review what each person's role in the group has been and give feedback. You may want to do the Love Seat exercise from the exploration on page183. If after a few weeks the group energy gets stuck, use one of the games as input to get it moving again. There is usually no lack of real conflict.

Tools for effective order

Although these tools might sound a bit like arbitrary "Rules of Order", we have found them most effective for keeping the communication flowing without a lot of hassle. They also bring some humor into the group. Use them as you see fit.

A child's baton—This is the "rod of power". Whoever holds this magic wand has the floor until he or she is finished, and cannot be interrupted while speaking. When that person is through with the rod it is passed to the next person who wants to speak.

A baseball bat painted red (for reactiveness)—This is the bat of reaction which you pick up when you are itching to say something and cannot wait your turn. You feel you just have to speak next. Whoever is holding the bat is saying, without words, "I'm reacting." That person must still watch his "Yes, but" attitude, because if you are reacting it means you are playing tapes and not fully listening. As soon as the person with the rod is finished talking the bat holder has the floor next. The group must still insist on the use of the keys to real listening, and especially proper mirroring, but these tools allow for channels of expression that might otherwise result in confusion. They are especially effective in families and with children.

A CREATIVE CONFLICT EXPERIENCE

So now we are ready for a Creative Conflict session. We have a group of six or eight people who have done some of the explorations in Part II together, and who are eager to discover their blind spots. They come to the first session at one of the member's houses. As with the explorations they begin with the centering meditation. The host reads the meditation from the violet level. Everyone tunes into their deepest problem confronting them. After a few minutes the host reads the section of page 426 on commitment. Everyone contemplates the reading for another few minutes. One group member tones the AAAAHHHHHOOOOMMMMM and everyone joins in. There is a calm, peaceful, warm group feeling.

The host Bob begins by sharing his problem. He is having a hard time with his teenage son. He feels frustrated in trying to communicate with him. The boy always seems to say, "yeah, yeah," but doesn't really respond, and so Dad gets angry and then they both get into an argument. The next person in the circle, a young woman Angela, shares her conflict. The reading on commitment bothered her, because she feels that her young child may have needs that she will have to fill and so she may miss a session. She also feels that she is not sure whether she wants to share all her troubles concerning her husband since he is not in the group. She is afraid that it might rock the boat. The next person shares his conflict. He is feeling depressed lately and he doesn't know why. He cannot see any inward reason, yet something is getting him down. . . The rest of the group share their souls, and the group takes a moment to tune into which direction they should go.

One person, Ann, speaks up. "I feel Angela's need the strongest because she's not sure she should even be here." Bob pipes up and says he agrees. Other group members nod. Bob says he feels that it would be good if we all shared how we felt about our commitments. Everyone agrees. One by one every member shares their feelings. Except for Angela, everyone feels good about their commitment.(Note how the group decided to put the overall group issue of commitment first.) Now Angela's personal need speaks strongly to everyone because she is the only one in doubt about her commitment. Bob asks Angela if she would share more of her feelings about her family. He offers to be her mirror.

They go through the seven-step listening and sharing (see page 429). At one point Phil says, "You missed something in the mirroring, Bob. Angela said she really did not want to upset her husband by not going along with his decisions." The entire group is carefully listening and filling the missing links to the seven steps. After Bob has asked Angela several questions which she has answered, he has mirrored and received confirmation, he shares how he feels about her situation with her. He says, "I feel you are giving all your authority to Don (her husband) and you are afraid of the group authority. You're also afraid of following your own inner authority because you feel Don might get upset and even leave. But you want to grow and deepen your relationships, that's why you're here. You are selling yourself short. Do you really know that Don might leave, have you asked him, or is that an assumption?" Angela mirrors what Bob has just said and then answers him. Others then respond to Angela's answer and share what they are tuning into. Ann tells Scott that she feels his comment to Angela is a projection and is off the track. Phil and Bob agree. The sharing, listening, mirroring, tuning in and correcting each other, agreeing and disagreeing using the seven-step process continues and the entire group begins to feel that they are homing into the real truth, the deeper issues, in Angela's situation. Angela finally comments, "You guys are really right. I see I have to risk sharing my feelings with Don. He may not mind watching the baby. I've just been too afraid to find out. But I feel I can now. I will go and have a talk with him. This is really exciting. Thanks for all your help. I talked to my mother about this problem and a couple of friends too, but it hasn't helped. You've really been able to show me what I'm doing. I'm assuming he'll leave because I'm not happy with the relationship, so I'm projecting onto him, instead of really being open about it. It's so clear, why didn't I see that before? I'll let you know what happens."

The group energy has penetrated Angela's ego position and it has been released. Of course follow up on the issue must still be continued. The group next goes into Barbara who is also having problems with her husband. Angela, usually the quietest member, is full of energy now and is speaking out strongly. She is encouraging Barbara to have integrity and share her real feelings too. Phil points out that Barbara's situation is a bit different and she really has to make sure she hears her husband's being. It seems he's trying to tell her something and she is not listening. . . . The session goes on, with the whole group involved and everyone feeling deeply a part of everyone else. After three and a half hours, Bob says, "Incredible, it's ten-thirty already." Angela says, "This is a good time to break." Everyone looks at each other. They do not want to part and leave this beautiful feeling. They form a love circle and tone the AAAHHH-OOOMMMM. It seals the warm feeling in their hearts. Everyone leaves quietly, eyes sparkling.

Not all sessions will be as smooth as this one was, but many will be if the rules are followed. When confrontation, resistance or confusion occur, it is important to return to the seven steps. They are always your anchor. They will clear the air and bring the energy back together on a deeper level.

These guidelines and steps can be taught successfully to children with a little modification according to the age level. We hope to publish future books that will tailor Creative Conflict to every classroom.

GUIDELINES FOR WORKING ON THE EGO

GUIDELINE #1
YOU ARE WHATEVER DISTURBS YOU

If someone is disturbing you, it is *your* mind and emotions that are being disturbed, not the other's. You are identifying with your thoughts about what you see or hear and are letting those thoughts bother you. It is entirely your problem. The other might not be having a problem at all. So own the disturbance as your own. Then you can free yourself. Realize that if you hold the attitude of identifying with your pure Self and not with the ego that gets disturbed, you can gain insight into why you allow yourself to be disturbed. So when someone bothers you, point the finger first at yourself to see what part of you is reacting. What is the mirror of life, reflected from that person, trying to show *you*? This does not mean you may not have a valid perception of the other person, but if you are letting it disturb you, then you have a problem.

One major problem with conflicts and a reason why they can be so destructive is that we often refuse to own our disturbances. We lash back or say, "That's his fault. I'm all right." In Creative Conflict we cannot do that because it does not matter whose fault it is. What matters is how we are handling our reactions. Often we find that when we judge others, the next minute we are being judged. Life's mirror works very quickly at times. For example, Dave gets disturbed by Sue's authoritative manner. Sue says, "You left your milk on the table again, please clean it up", and "When are you going to take out the garbage?" Dave riles inside. Why? Does he want to be the authority? This he has to look at first. Then, instead of retorting, "Do it yourself!" and creating bad vibes between them, he can say, "You know, I have a problem with authority myself. I'd like to be aware enough to be the boss. But I do feel that you spoil your communication in the way you lay down the law and come across so strongly. I would find it much easier to accept what you say if it were expressed with a more humble, more caring vibe. Maybe others experience you the way I do."

In order to do this kind of communicating we have to be able to allow everyone the right to be whatever they are. Agree now that you are different from everybody and everybody is unique and entitled to use the *One* consciousness in any way they choose in absolute freedom.

GUIDELINE #2
I AGREE TO DISAGREE

This is the essence of Creative Conflict. In other words, you are so kind as to give others absolute freedom, when of course they already have it. We pride ourselves in giving others the freedom to be themselves, but life has given them that freedom whether we like it or not. You also have that freedom to be yourself every day. It is the only real freedom you have. So just as you demand that freedom for yourself, you give it to others. They have a divine right to say and do what disturbs you, providing they do not enforce it upon you harmfully and take away your freedom to do likewise. Pulling up the weeds of each other's hidden delusions is done first by acknowledging and accepting differences, then by confronting the motivation and truth behind each viewpoint. Only in this way can we begin the creative process. This is especially true between people or over issues in which we have a lot of emotional investment. A mother does not want to know her teenage daughter is having sex. A father does not want his son to drop out of school, as he feels it will ruin his life. One government does not like to see another government selling arms to a third country. Real peace can only come from having the self-honesty to probe the motives and causes of disagreements together, after respecting each other's right to be different.

GUIDELINE #3
I AGREE TO WORK FOR SYNTHESIS

The disagreement which does not take into account all the areas that *you do agree upon* is not creative. If the areas of *agreement* exceed the areas of *disagreement* you can have a conflict which leads to synthesis. As long as there is a fundamental unity which is stronger than the disagreements, you can work it out if you are willing. For example, you might be arguing about one particular point and getting worked up and passionately feeling your mind spinning and your emotions rushing. But there may be fifty other things you can agree on. But do you think of those fifty things at the time you are disagreeing? Creative Conflict always has this in mind, that there may be all these areas of agreement and there is just one little area of disagreement which needs to be worked out to a synthesis with the rest. Therefore at times when we feel ourselves having negative thoughts about someone, or feel poles apart on an issue, we remember this guideline and remind ourselves of some of our common areas of agreement. We reaffirm, "I agree to work for synthesis." This reestablishes the feeling of unity in the heart, the positive energy that can resolve any differences in the head.

GUIDELINE #4
I AGREE THAT EACH PERSON HAS TRUTH FROM THE POINT OF VIEW FROM WHICH IT IS SEEN

Everything is true from the level of consciousness from which it is seen. Everyone sees true from their own level of consciousness, even if it differs from another's truth. So we say to ourselves, "I agree to be the same consciousness, even when we are talking about the same object in different terms." That same consciousness is making all things seem different. In other words, the guideline "I agree to disagree" becomes agreeing to be the same in being, even though we are disagreeing mentally, because we may be talking about the same thing in different ways. One of the problems with human beings is that we never want to be the same as anybody else. The minute you share something you think others will relate to they say, "Ah, but my thing is different." They just want to be different, so they argue. Creative Conflict involves seeing that we may be egocentric in talking about picky differences, when the differences may be just a product of the ego separating itself from the experience and thoughts of others. That is why so many couples can fight one minute and make love the next. So many children can be tearing each other's hair out one minute and playing the next. People fall in love, react to praise or criticism the same, whether they are priests, hoodlums, communists or capitalists. The situation is different, but the underlying emotion is the same. So even though what is true for one person may not be true for another in the head, together we can probe our beliefs and motives and expand to a greater truth from the heart.

We can challenge another's truth, but we have to be able to see that what John says is true for him and what Mary says is true for her, even though they may be totally different truths, and from another view they may both be limiting. To get to the greater, synthesizing truth, both parties must be willing to examine themselves and be willing to change. An example of this guideline might be, "I need two women," says John. Mary replies, "I need a man who wants only me." A friend, Bill, says, "You are both identifying with your needs, but Mary's need is based on her insecurity and fear of rejection which makes her cling. John's need is based on Mary's clinging which he cannot cope with, yet he loves her and does not want to leave her." The other woman has beautiful qualities that Mary does not have, but Mary also has beautiful qualities that the other woman does not have, so John feels he needs them both and is unfulfilled with only one. In Creative Conflict, John and Mary's views are both true, but the underlying needs are the forces that are causing the views. These needs are what we must probe, share feelings about, mirror and penetrate in order to find a synthesis, a greater truth than either is seeing.

GUIDELINE #5
I WILL EXAMINE MY OWN MOTIVES FOR DISAGREEING BEFORE DOUBTING THE STATEMENTS OF ANOTHER. I WILL LOOK FOR THE BASIC ASSUMPTIONS AND THE NEEDS BEHIND WHAT IS SAID.

It is difficult to stop ourselves from reacting and ask, "What is my motive for disagreeing?" But we have to learn to get to the cause of our disturbance for conflict to be transformed. We have to continually ask ourself, "What is the basic assumption in what he or she is saying? What is my basic assumption in my position? For example, "He always thinks his way is the only right way. He assumes he's always right. What arrogance! What real feeling of inadequacy must be under all that! The need to be confirmed must be there." The underlying, unspoken assumptions form our view of truth and we base our opinions of others, and of our own egos on them. The quicker we can uncover and check out the basic assumptions in any point of view, the sooner the penetration to greater truth will take place. For example, "I'm upset, Jeff, because you didn't call me," says Laura. But Laura must examine her own motives for being upset before doubting Jeff's motives for not calling. She is upset because she is jealous and lonely. So she goes on a big trip in her mind about that, worrying for hours. Jeff finally tells her that he lost her new phone number and the operator did not have it listed. What a lot of time she has wasted worrying.

Another example, "Mary, you shouldn't handle the money anymore, " says John. Mary reacts and walks out in a huff. John is astonished. Does Mary ask what John's basic assumption is? Or check out her own? No! Perhaps John feels she mismanages money. That is Mary's fear. But John really feels that it is for his own growth that he wants the change, not for hers. He feels he needs to master handling money and Mary does it for him, so he is always feeling there is not enough because he doesn't know where it is going. We can only get to the causes of conflict when we constantly look behind the surface, behind the apparent situation, to the basic assumptions. The seven-steps, especially the mirroring step, allow us to experience directly our own and the other person's basic assumptions that we cannot normally see in conversation. We must learn to probe together and share the basic assumptions we see operating, as we are mostly blind to them.

GUIDELINE #6
RED HERRING*

One of the greatest blocks to communication is going off on a tangent, away from the center of concentration. Someone may think he has an insight and offer it, but really it is way off the point. The group mind has to be aware of this and gently but firmly say, "That is off the point, a Red Herring!" Then the group must lead the energy back to the real point. Sometimes the person being confronted will bring in a red herring. Just as you are about to share a deep feeling you haven't been able to express to that person before, the other will say, "I need a glass of water" or "Isn't it time for tea?" "Oh, I must put the baby to bed," or "The dinner's got to be made," or any number of things that short circuit the energy and deny the

---

* Origin of the term: In hunting, a red herring was dragged across the path of the quarry to distract the dogs away from the scent of the animal so they wouldn't chase after it.

communication. You usually then shut up like a clam and the conflict is pushed down inside and repressed. The group intuition must become finely tuned to one-pointedness and the energies that accompany deep soul-searching must be kept concentrated and directed. Otherwise depth will not be reached. Children are famous for bringing in red herrings to avoid facing themselves. We even go off on Red Herrings when we are alone in thought to avoid looking at ourselves. How many times have you been in a nitty-gritty situation and somebody pulls in a completely irrelevant statement which sends you off chasing that one track and you end up spinning wheels? So, then you get a wheel spinning, or what we sometimes call a "waffling" situation. The group must be able to spot this instantly and call out "Red Herring!" whenever it occurs, otherwise the session goes nowhere and is a waste of time. The Red Herring guideline is likely to be used more than any other guideline. It will train the group intuition and make the difference between a low energy session and a concentrated, electrifying and deep experience, bringing growth.

GUIDELINE #7
QUIBBLING

To define a definition of a word and then challenge the definition of the definition is to get stuck completely in the trap of quibbling. "What do you mean when you say so-and-so?" We hear this all the time. It is usually a way of diverting, of not listening to the being of the person. Some people love to get caught up in semantics and avoid the real being. When we communicate effectively we are listening to the being of a person not the words! The words are merely second-hand symbols invented by others. They are not the most important part of the communication. To use double meanings, words which are ambiguous, is another quibble. An example is, "You're too clever!" We do not mean he is clever at all. Or "You're a wise guy." Are we really thinking he is wise? A wise guy is somebody who is too clever and therefore looks stupid. This is how we speak in words that have no integrity and so we keep communication on superficial levels. To get stuck in dictionary meanings and wrong use of words is to quibble, so that all thread of the argument is lost.

Nations do the same by insisting on the legalities of actions while ignoring the actual facts. Genocide is mass murder and illegal but that does not help the victims. To stand by and say it is illegal is not telling a murderer anything new. The legality is lost on him. We do the same semantically when we quibble. It lowers the high energy-level needed for direct perception and drains the electricity which comes from being-to-being communication. The way out is for someone to say, "I feel you are quibbling." Then someone can bring in another I-feel statement to bring the communication from the semantic level to a deeper level again. We all have to be alert and take full responsibility for the direction of the group. Even one person holding back, or one person feeling bored, or dwelling on the dishes to be done at home, is deflecting the energy and is not being integral. If you are that person, ask yourself, "Why am I separating? Am I bored? Why do I not feel involved and why am I not putting in my full energies to take responsibility?" If you cannot find the cause and release it, or simply let go of yourself when you recognize it and jump in, then ask for group help at the next appropriate time, so that you can get in touch and be integral. Your *integrity* is important for group consciousness. The electricity flows in a group when all are integral.

GUIDELINE #8

I WILL SEEK OUT THE CONFLICT IN THE HEART OF EACH PERSON AND THE CONTRADICTIONS IN THEIR MINDS, BUT NOT THE CONFLICT IN THEIR WORDS AND IDEAS. I WILL NOT ENGAGE IN THEIR INTERNAL CONTROVERSY. I WILL NOT CHALLENGE WHAT I DON'T UNDERSTAND. INSTEAD I WILL SIT BACK AND LISTEN.

When you are talking, communicating, or confronting a person, you look for the contradiction in *them*, not in their words and ideas.

To challenge what you do not understand is to quibble. It is not creative to put our ignorance out onto someone else and make them explain it all in detail for us, as though we are so stupid that we do not know anything. We will need to listen better and deeper. However, it could be that the person really is expressing himself poorly, leaving half of the story out. Then we will have to ask for specific points to be clarified. What we need to watch for is the kind of attitude which believes that the whole group must be held up while "I" wait to be enlightened. It is an egocentric attitude and not creative at all. It is like the beginner saying, "I don't understand what's going on, please explain," while the rest of the group mind is just about to share an important point, vital to the conflict. You can feel the group energy start to drain or be sapped off with this kind of comment and then you must ruthlessly remind the person of this guideline. To attempt to be "nice" at this point will syphon off all the group energy. You must be firm and not be sucked into another person's confusion. Remind them to read Guideline #8.

GUIDELINE #9
MAKING A SPEECH

Under the guise of asking questions, some people will show how much knowledge they have or will display the contents of a book they have just read, ostensibly to share their insights with others. Whether those insights have been gained or books have already been read by others does not always occur to some egos. When asked to speak not from authorities or books, but from their own experience or to say what their real feelings are, they remain silent or back out of their position by saying, "I don't want to go into that now." Or they make statements about which they can offer no proof at all in their own life, only from hearsay. "Jesus said," "Marx said," "The authorities said," and they repeat all over the place for everyone's edification. But they are not prepared to test this philosophy out for themselves to prove it. They are continually coming out with suggestions which are not from their own experience. They want everyone else to test them. If they tested their own suggestions before they made them for others, then there would be value to their communication and their experience would contribute to the group energy. So before communicating we must know that our own suggestions work and that they are not just theoretical. Theoretical knowledge and comment leads only to mental masturbation. Such people should be challenged for making a speech or asked if they are contributing theoretical information or whether they are speaking on behalf of everyone present, or from direct experience. We must as a group be prepared to fight for integrity. It is not Creative Conflict unless you say, "Hey, are you speaking for yourself? I'm not at the position you're speaking from!" or "I feel you are preaching and making an assumption that we are interested in your theories and you are not really experiencing the real issues we are dealing with!" So we must remind ourselves and each other: "I (THE BIG I) CAN ONLY SPEAK FOR MYSELF FROM MY OWN EXPERIENCE. I CAN'T SPEAK FOR EVERYONE."

This guideline also should be applied when someone begins speaking for other people about their problems. Married partners and parents often fall into the trap of speaking for others. "We just want him to find a nice hobby," says the well-intentioned wife or mother. The husband or child may not feel that way at all. So in Creative Conflict we must constantly ask each person to speak for himself or herself.

These nine guidelines to making conflict creative are deep studies of how human egos normally work. By looking for these patterns throughout our daily lives we can transform ourselves into incredibly perceptive and aware human beings. If these tools and techniques were taught in every classroom, in every home and in every business where people must cooperate, from the factory to big governments, we would have a tremendous understanding of human nature and of each other. The ancient advice, "Man Know thyself!" would come true.

The following is taken from a tape transcription of a talk "Introduction to Creative Conflict" by Christopher Hills, given to newcomers at University of the Trees, Summer, 1977.

I thought I would share with you some of the basic ideas of creative conflict so that you can use them in everyday life and make them of some practical worth. Let me give you some background on how it arose.

When I retired from business in 1957 to write a book, I wrote a very idealistic book about how the world ought to be and how I would like to see it, but I realized very quickly that there was only one person at that time who was prepared to put any energy behind my own idea and that was me since I hadn't really been out in the world to find if there were other people willing to invest their time and consciousness, love and care to do somebody else's idea. I realized that not only was I in that situation but that most idealists who try to change the world first get an idea and then they get some kind of symbol or flag and they go around waving it saying, "Follow me, I've got the answers," and so either they get people who have no critical ability who follow—followers—or they attract to themselves leaders who go out on their own trip and use their ideas and so the world gets more idealists, more people who think things can be changed through ideas.

I rapidly came to realize in life, that, looking at the world with its many thousands of years of civilizations that have come and gone, it doesn't matter what ideal a society is based on; there will always be conflict in putting it over, getting it manifested or running it. As long as there are people there's going to be conflict, whether it's Christianity, Hinduism or Buddhism, Marxism or any "ism". As long as we have people we will have power seekers, we will have egos, people looking for fame and name, we will have people searching for wealth and all the other things that humans do. And in the pursuit of these many things that we want, we come up against others who are either competitive or put us down or don't like our ideas or in some way create so much conflict in the society we live in, that we cannot ever get anything done. Nothing ever seems to happen that is perfect and society often seems to be just a mess, a mess of people seeking different goals on different trips. The conflict that results from the competition between various people is destructive and divisive. It does not bring unity to people, and so as long as we have humans we are going to have conflict. As long as we have conflict we are going to have division and separation. As long as we have people around there will be strife unless we suddenly find something which can make conflict creative instead of divisive and destructive.

So I saw that I would be wasting my time to write a lot of books, or to try and put an idea over. That instead the idea must come from *within* each person. And it really did not matter how different people were in the head if they were united on one thing in the heart, if they were united in arriving at the best possible solution in spite of all the different individuals involved. That meant that we had to find a way of allowing everybody to be completely unique, not requiring them to think like we do, or to think only one philosophy—Marxist or capitalist this or that or one man's thought. We had to find a way of saying "Well we're all supposed to be different. Let's be as unique and as different and individual as we can be and still have this one resolution of conflict. Let it be our aim to create unity not by forcing people or coercing people or trying to persuade them or sell them a trip or whatever, but let the unity come as a by-product. By the interaction of all the various egos and ideas and individualities and so forth, let the result be something creative that emerges out of all this interaction." What would that result be? Growth.

If human beings are not growing, they are as good as dead. If a human being is not growing in spirit and vision and growing human awareness, they may as well just be walking automatons, robots in the flesh. So I saw that if growth came out of conflict then there would be some hope for this world because as long as people grow, as long as people become more refined human beings, whatever the pain involved, they are alive and dynamic. I saw that the pain that accompanies growth, growing pains, was not something to be afraid of, not something that needed to be pushed under the carpet, but something perhaps even to welcome in order to see why we are pained by growth when we are stretching ourselves to the limit to face somebody or someone who doesn't agree with us, doesn't even like us or think at all like us. How can we use this growth, this pain, to become a bigger person, become a finer person, who can help the world by knowing what is right action?

It is no use getting power over others or even getting monetary power if we do not know how to use it. And if you look at most politicians who get into the seat of power, whether it is President this or President that or whether it is a dictator, you always find that when in power he is subject to the same pressures that the previous person was and so he never fulfills any of the promises or very few of them. So you see that the power, unless we have the grace to know how to use it, is not much use. It is like trying to do good without first becoming good. I saw that what creative conflict could do was to make people good before they tried to do good because if they are not good and try to do good the net result will probably be that they screw up somewhere because how can they know what is good if they themselves are not good? And I saw also that good people did not need to try to do any good because they automatically do good just by being what they are. I saw that all the do-gooders in the world are wasting their time. They are trying to help the world before they have got the right insight into what the world needs.

The question arose: how can we get people together so that they get a better look at themselves in this growth process? I saw that they could get many more mirrors through creative conflict than they would get by belonging to a do-gooding group which goes out and supposedly helps others and often interferes with the lives of others without quite knowing what the others really need. I realized that there are so many people running around society who *think* they know how to help it and thousands of years go by and it does not seem to get any better. So, this is how the creative conflict method emerged.

I wrote a book, what I thought would be an ideal constitution for a group of people living together and governing themselves. They would not be governed from outside, but governed from inside themselves through free will and yet in such a way that they did not have to be coerced by an outside authority, a government. Why do we have government? Because we do not govern ourselves. We have not been self-governing creatures. We do not know how to govern our lives. We appoint others to govern us. I saw that until communities, whether the community was just like a family or whether it was like a small community like we have here, a village, or even the entire world, could come to this realization, we will have government by pressure. We pressurize those people, we lobby them, we appoint representatives, we put clout behind them if we can, if we have any. So then if we pressure enough we get some changes. So I saw that government was not really like that in nature at all. Nature achieves change and growth and things grow rather magically, they transform from one state to another, one energy system to another and all are interlinked—whether it's clouds dropping rain on the earth and evaporating from the sea—it's all cyclic. Can we learn to govern ourselves the way nature governs herself?*

In human affairs something is missing, even between two individuals. Even if you are married to a person for twenty-five years there are certain things you can't say without bringing a lot of conflict, and if you are in love with someone, it is even worse, because you do not want to lose the love of that person. So how can you say certain things about that person that you see and do not like or that you don't quite think are the way they should be? Can you go up to that person and say "Hey, look at this part of yourself?" Usually they don't want to look at that part. So creative conflict has to do with looking at those parts of ourselves that we don't really want to look at. You may say "That's crazy—attending a group of people who are looking at those parts of themselves that they don't want to look at!" Well this is the whole point. Unless the world looks at its blind spots, there will not be any New Age or any fantastic improvement in the human situation.

Where do you begin? It's no use going out there and buying advertising space or writing books. You have to begin with small communities, like a seeding process, just as in Nature.

* See *The Rise of the Phoenix, Universal Government By Nature's Laws,* by Christopher Hills, University of the Trees Press (see appendix).

The whole idea of creative conflict is to get into the kind of vibration or the kind of feeling towards others where we can tell them anything we feel and think without their getting hyper-reactive or angry, or at least if they do get angry they see the anger and are able to get a clue as to what makes them angry from the various mirrors in the group. Then we can use it to find out how to control our own minds, how to control our own selves. If we can become masters of our own emotions and the way our thoughts work then we can walk out there into the world and can be people who are centered and at peace with ourselves to such a point that nothing out there which is in conflict is going to affect us. So it's one way of creating a Master of yourself, to enter this experience as a golden opportunity, not to get only vicarious excitement by hiding behind your ego, but to say, "Okay, I'm going to *heighten* my individuality by being part of a group not lessen it. But in order to become a greater individual I will have to look at my ego, the self-sense." By ego I really mean that psychic skin which separates us inside from what we think is outside. It is really an imaginary skin because there isn't anything separating us from anything else, except our own minds. We have an idea that we sit inside this bag of skin; we say "This is inside and that is outside" and we believe that outside things affect us and make us miserable or present us with "outside" situations to which we respond, but it is not true. Most of the outside situations that affect us and that we respond to are self-created; we all have the power to go almost anywhere we want to go and to be with whom we want to be with. Strictly speaking, wherever we are at this moment is the right place, even if it is painful, even if we came "by accident" seemingly, but is it an accident? Something in us, in our mind, our soul, our being has brought us to a situation and the way we respond to it is going to determine whether we are happy or miserable.

So the whole object of creative conflict is not just to sit around and have a good time throwing dirt at each other or criticizing each other, but to see whether it is an instrument which can have a lofty vision of not only changing ourselves but of changing the situation in which we live. If we change even a little bit of the environment around us, whether it's a psychic atmosphere that we give out or whether it's a whole community we infect with our being, or whether it's the whole world, that is the only way we are going to create real change in people, instead of imposing it on them from outside and forcing them to toe the line. They themselves do it spontaneously from within. So that is the whole concept of creative conflict and that is why I wanted to talk to you about it, because we might get the idea that we are just sitting here in a group and "Hey, we had better watch what we say or we might get pounced on."

This is what does happen at the beginning when you start saying your two cents worth and the whole group seems to spring on you and say "I don't feel that's the right motive," and "What makes you say this?" and you feel attacked. You feel you are in a corner and your ego's there. It's like playing a game of chess; you are wondering what move you can make next. It's the natural reaction of someone who is trapped inside the self-sense, the ego, and we have all got an ego. The whole concept of creative conflict is not necessarily to get rid of your ego, at least not to squish it and force it down, but to bring it out so it can teach you. Your ego reactions are a way you can learn whether you are right or wrong, whether you are able to take right action and say a thing in the right way and do something in the right way.

So we don't mind the ego in creative conflict. If you have got one we had rather you had it out up front, not because we are going to tear it to shreds but because you are going to learn more about yourself if you are honest and open with your self-sense. If you think you are the greatest thing in the world, like the boxer Muhammed Ali thought, then why don't you say so? At least people will relate to you as someone who thinks he's the greatest. And they would probably say "Well, you're just an egotist." And you would say "Well, I can prove it, there are a few great things I do." And you say those things and they say "Well, we all do those things already; that's nothing." So you see, you get a picture of whether you are justified in having a self-concept that is so high without any extra-ordinary manifestation to prove it.

This is usually what happens to human beings. These people with such high opinions of themselves have very zig-zag paths through life. When you point to the track left through life, it's very crooked, it's very zig-zag. They don't really steer a straight and narrow course. The people with the highest opinion of themselves have very little to show for the opinion they hold. The most humble people, the people you would never suspect, who have achieved all kinds of things and are quiet and never talk about them much, are the people who are skillful in action. They go direct to the goal and they create very little wake behind them because they move so skillfully nobody notices.

It may be that in the creative conflict process or in the group process that you will remember these little extra ways of looking at yourself, so that when you are in the corner and your ego is out there apparently being torn to shreds, that you realize it is not something destructive that is going on, but something tremendously creative and you will be able to see how your own demon works. That is all the ego is; it's a demonic separator. It is the thing which says you are separate from everybody else, says everything is out there and I am in here. It does not create union. It is the divisive part of ourselves. It is the thing that makes us schizophrenic—the ego. It makes us separate from everyone and separate from everything outside.

So the whole process of creative conflict is to find out that separate one, to find out the tricks it plays on us, because it's a deceiver—a self-deceiver. If we're self-deluded we never can act skillfully in the world. So the whole object of creative conflict, ultimately, is to see our self-delusions, whether the delusions are grand and fed by ego-food or over-confidence, or the opposite of that. Some of us walk around with a concept that is much below our true potential and some self-concepts are far above what's real. And it often happens in the group situation that you walk out feeling ten feet taller instead of a snake on the ground.

Now most of the people residing here who have been practicing creative conflict for a number of years probably don't notice the growth in themselves because having the ego confronted many times over, you get immune to it in the end to the point where it doesn't matter any longer. But there are certain dangers in ego-confrontation, that it might even reinforce your secret ego and chase you even more behind the battlements of your own private castle so that you begin to look out of narrower slits than ever in a protective way. Now you see, that only happens if there is no willingness to change. If there is a rigidity in a human being who says "I'm not going to change; that whole group out there is all wrong and I'm right" and there's an unwillingness to look at the nitty-gritty which we have to change, then what happens reinforces the ego and that person usually leaves because he doesn't want to change, and you can't really stay in a creative conflict group unless you want to change and accept the pain of change.

Now it doesn't always mean that change is going to be painful. Sometimes it is a great joy. It depends on how resistant you are to it. If you like change and welcome it, you can absolutely be in bliss at having made a fundamental change in your self.

Another problem that comes up in creative conflict is that you can learn certain skills of how to fend off criticism, to transfer all the things that people are saying back on other people by saying for instance "That's a projection." You learn these skills and can handle yourself in the unsuspecting outside world, but in creative conflict a skillful intellect can be used to create division and protect oneself. It is sometimes very difficult to tell a person in a group that he's using the rules of creative conflict destructively and rather cleverly. It's a one-upmanship show. He says "Well, that's your projection" instead of looking back at himself as to what was said. We find such a person is one who cannot take much feedback and you will find that the feedback he takes in is proportional to his willingness to change.

You can always find one person in a group who is not willing to change. It's important for groups to always know that there is going to be at least one negative. As long as there is a positive there must be a negative. So in most groups the negative usually settles on one person. In creative conflict what happens is that the negative shifts from one person to the next. One week it's on this person and then it's on another. It is creative sometimes to be negative, to see things that are negative about ourselves and to make mistakes, get our feet wet. By opening our mouth wide we get into hot water. But if we're creative about it and we learn from it, then the next time we do it we find the negative is not us, it's someone else. In creative conflict we are learning to handle that negativity. In nature there must be a negative as long as there's a positive; the two can't exist separately—they exist within us. That's the important thing to understand that even if we're seeing all good in front of us and everybody's lovely, in the back of our head we've got to keep the negative thoughts from jumping up and coloring the vision.

We don't ask you to drop the negative or say that you must come here without negative thoughts. We are not looking for total compliance like some instructors. Good students ask awkward and difficult questions and only followers and feeble-minded people are seduced by arguments which hand Truth down from a high authority. If you join some movements they say "Oh, you can't come unless you get rid of all this questioning or unless you believe this." We say, bring all your differences because in creative conflict we agree to differ. That's the one creative thing that you begin to say from the very outset, "Well you're supposed to be different from me. You're supposed to think differently. Why are you trying to make me think the same as you?" What we do is we use all these differences. We are not afraid of them nor do we get defensive if others lay trips on us. In creative conflict we get feedback from everyone in the group. The members of the group looking at us are like TV lenses, and we look at ourselves through all those TV cameras and see a different shot of ourselves. We don't have to buy any of it. In creative conflict you don't have to say they're wrong or right. You just have to look at it. Before we point a finger out there we point it inward too, to see if we've got the same thing wrong with us that we're accusing others of. That's what makes creative conflict a growth experience. That's what gives it the dynamic for using it in everyday life like when you're talking to your husband or you're talking to a group of people or even if you're a member of a union and you're on strike with the boss. You can even have creative conflict come into union disputes or disputes between politicians like Americans and Russians. It is possible to have conflict that turns out in the end creative if everyone understands the process. Creative conflict can change the entire world, because people are involved and it's only people who will change the world. Organizations can't change the world because organizations are made of people.

All organizations, what are they formed for? What are groups of people for? Only to achieve things that individuals don't have the power to achieve. So individuals group together in some form of union or group in order to become more powerful and effective. You find that in the organization of groups, whether in companies or in the commercial world, there are also groups of people who are banded together as political parties or shareholders to achieve some economic purpose because individually you couldn't do it, but as a big company you can buy ships, railways and telephone equipment, you can do something big. The same thing applies when you're in a creative conflict group like this. You can do something much bigger than you can do as an individual.

When we examine ourselves with the help of the group we see the group is not there to put us on the hot seat, although we might find ourself on the hot seat, but the actual function of the group is to help us and that's one thing that we have to keep in the upper part of our being, because if we keep thinking that the group is all against us then there's something wrong with our ego position. It doesn't mean you have to buy everybody's opinion, but you have to look at everybody's opinion; otherwise you're not listening.

Now, one problem about creative conflict is: how do you listen to another being? This is what you are really learning. How do you listen to the being of another? It is not to listen to what they're saying, not to the intellectual garbage of the mind from the culture they live in, the family they're born into. We're all programmed beings. We've got to wash all that stuff out of our brains. There is no use for it. If there was any use to it we would all be enlightened. But if we cling so hard and so possessively to our own experience in life up to now, then we'll not be able to learn anything new. So in creative conflict what we do is temporarily take all this junk and put it on the shelf; if we love it we can always get it back again, it's easy to get back. But unless we put aside all that we know at this moment, we can't effectively listen to the being of another speaking. It is the opposite of brainwashing because we are deliberately not putting anything in, only making it more clear.

The main technique in creative conflict is the mirroring process. You have to be able to put yourself aside to be able to mirror what a person is really meaning, not just what they're saying. Often they might say with their mouths the opposite of what they mean, so you mirror back the way you received the communication. And then he or she can confirm that that is what was actually said. Once it's confirmed that's what was said, then you can answer it. But if you haven't properly received the communication how can you answer it effectively? That is the whole secret: to get rid of our own investment in our own opinion so that we go beyond opinion making altogether. In a creative conflict group we're into the nitty-gritty of our true self, not just the ideas, the things we've been told and the books we've read. That's all brainwash, which is why we have problems because we tend to think *that* is us. It isn't and what we're trying to find in creative conflict is the you, the real self, that thing, wherever it came from, that is a spark of the original creative universe—your consciousness—indestructible, immortal consciousness. It's taken many curves. It's sitting in a body right now. How many bodies has it had, how many will it ever have? You see, sitting inside each of us is the same stuff: consciousness, streaming out of our eyes lighting up everything that we see. It's the same for all of us but we're all doing different things with it. When we come into the creative conflict group, that's when we sit back and say "Hey that guy's got the same stuff as me but he's doing a different trip with it" and that is his freedom and everyone has that freedom in creative conflict to be who he or she really is.

So this is the way that creative conflict can change the world; it can re-make everyone and it can do this without any coercion, without forcing people to be docile or setting down regulations or anything. A minimum number of rules are required to create peace on earth, in fact the minimum number boils down to one rule of which the outcome is bliss. If each person were ultimately responsible for clearing up his own mess physically, psychologically, emotionally and otherwise then we wouldn't need other rules. This is a major rule "Everybody clears up their own mess."

You may have questions that you've come with, difficulties or something that you fear might happen—loss of ego, or loss of individuality or being swallowed by the group—that's the usual fear to begin with. "Are they going to take me over?"—all that stuff. If there are any questions or fears or anything that we can answer before you go into this deep experience you should voice them at the beginning. It can be a very profound and deeply threatening experience if we don't approach it in the right way. But it also can be an enlightening experience because we probe areas of our being that we never knew were there. We're all so much richer than we know. There are depths to us. And I like to use an analogy which is not too favorable to human beings, but I always like to say that we have a lot of manure deep down inside of us and that manure is very fertile soil for growing things. We shouldn't really reject it. We should thank our lucky stars that we've got some good manure down there because the most beautiful flowers grow in the richest manure.

We don't try to forget that manure; we try to use it so that it is creative and helps us to see what sort of person we are. It helps us to change more effectively because the worse you are now the more of a challenge it is for you to change, and once having changed you'll see how much better you've become. So that's why the greatest saints were always once the greatest sinners. They see how much they've transformed themselves. So they don't reject other people who are naughty; they don't do an ego trip and say "Oh look what you're doing, all that evil." They say, "Yeah, but for the grace of God there was I when I was twenty-one or thirty-one or fifty-one." They've been through those trips and so they have compassion for others who are still going through the Dark Night.

So creative conflict brings this experience to us and we're able to have compassion for others who still have got trips to go through.

Are there any questions?

Question: I have a question about creative conflict, how it can be used to help a person who isn't willing to change. Is there a skillful way of doing it without "hitting a person over the head with a hammer"?

Answer: I think the best sort of thing *is* probably to "hit him over the head", metaphorically speaking. Not even God can help a person who doesn't want to change. He's against the universe. The universe only exists because of its ability to change. Everything that doesn't change perishes. The secret of death if you want to know it is rigidity, not stability, but rigidity—mental rigidity, emotional rigidity. Now, rigidity is not the same as stability. Stability is only achieved by adaptability, by the ability to switch between the positive and the negative at the slightest fibrillation. You see, the whole universe is quivering, everything in nature is quivering and vibrating. Why? Because it is hanging between the balance point of positive and negative and when you're perfectly balanced God is sitting on his throne and everything is at peace, eternally stable. But if you have rigidity, you're dead already, you're going to be crushed because the universe is against you. There isn't anything in the universe that survives in that state of pressure.

So whether they're people who are rigid or things, they're going to be crushed by life if you don't crush their illusions yourself. So you don't need to worry about crushing a person's feelings who is unable to change. You can only hold up the vision of life and the living waters and say, "This is yours when you change. You have a perfect right not to change." And you must give him the right not to change as well as to change, otherwise it's meaningless. Freedom is meaningless unless you have the right to do wrong. Sounds funny, doesn't it?—the right to do wrong. But you have to give people the right not to change; that's their choice. You can't communicate with a person about life if he is spiritually dead. Anyone is able to change if he is willing. The will is the heart. If you have the will in your heart you can change. But don't waste time with those who are unwilling. You're wasting your time with the dilettante and half-hearted. You can take all the forces in the universe and you're plunking them down the bath hole when you're trying to change someone who doesn't want to change. No matter what you do for him, you can love him as hard as you like, he'll take your love and turn it around and hate you more. So you're wasting your time going against his real nature. Love him, certainly, but leave him be. Love him and leave him to himself because life will teach him how to change much better than you. Life is the greatest teacher.

Now if you are determined to communicate with such a rigid person you will probably find that feeling like hitting him is the end result and that's what's happening in the world, violence. It's just the lowest form of communication there is, but it *is* communicating. The stage beyond hitting is not caring at all and ignoring the person completely. That's the ultimate form of communication, ignoring a person totally, because this doesn't leave any options. Even if you had all the power of the universe and offered it to help such a person, it would be no use. There would be no receptivity. And he is getting that power anyway, don't forget; every person is subject to the same cosmic light. They're all receiving light the same way but what they do with it is all different. What they do to it determines how they are living. But everyone here is receiving the life force from the cosmos. I'm not getting any more than you. I might be using more of what I'm getting; that's a different thing.

So everyone is favored equally; no one is favored more than another. The sun shines on a rat or a blade of grass or a human being, favoring none. So it is with the cosmic life force. You cannot say to that fellow, "Hey, you must get more life force; you must change." You have to agree with him and say, "Okay, you're right from your point of view, but I'm not going to help you stick there in your smugness. I'll let life teach you."

You had a question?

Question: Yes, what if a person is consciously willing to change, but he's not changing and he can't seem to get a hold on what to do. Then what?

Answer: Well, if your unconscious mind is going in the opposite direction from your conscious mind then you have internal conflict which will definitely come out in creative conflict. That's one of the purposes—to bring out your unconscious, because what is unconscious you can't know. That's the whole problem with human beings, ninety percent of their lives is lived unconsciously, not consciously.

How do you get to the unconscious? If it's unconscious it means you don't know it's there. So most of our motivations, our emotional reactions, things we do, things we like, things we don't do are all coming from our unconscious. Creative conflict is a better way to get in touch with your unconscious than going to a psychiatrist and lying on a couch and paying him so much money. In a matter of one week or two weeks you can get in touch with far more about yourself than will ever come from association or interpretation of dreams. If you really use creative conflict you'll find out more about yourself than you can ever find out by any other method. If you're truly using it as an instrument for self-examination then the will that is in your head unites eventually with the will that is in the heart. All that creative conflict is doing is creating a union between head and heart, for if your heart and your head are going in the same direction you're in tune with the universe. Wherever your heart is, there you are. Eventually your heart is going to decide what your head is going to do, you see. And if you fall in love you know your heart always gets you into trouble. It doesn't matter what your head is saying.

If your heart is loving, it will put you through the refiner's fire with your head walking one way and your heart walking the other. You're in for trouble, but if you want to know what love is you have to walk into that trouble and face the fire. There's no other way to get to know what love is than to go through the pain, the refiner's fire. Maybe that is even the purpose of love, who knows? The true lover, even the cosmic lover, must be pained as well as joyful. He wants to share himself with everything and nothing will let him. You want to love someone and he keeps giving you a hard time and won't let you love him the way you want to love him, keeps twisting your love up and making it something different. So it's just a matter of the level that you're looking from, the head or the heart. If your heart is as big as the cosmos then your head is inside your heart, you're exploring your heart with your head.

There are certain kinds of research you can do, right? The mental kind is where you put bits together and become a scientist and look through microscopes and do analysis and you tear things apart intellectually and you have concepts and models and theories and this and that and you have just one big head. There are such people kicking around the earth—huge heads—nothing but head, no heart. So they create all kinds of monstrosities with their heads, rockets and bombs that kill people, all kinds of things. They have no heart or they couldn't do those things. They're just huge, encyclopedic brains that know everything. They can't even love properly; they're all screwed up in their emotional life. Now there is another kind of research you can do with your head by analyzing yourself, your own heart, by probing your heart with your own intellect. You can use that analytical faculty for finding out what is the structure of your heart.

What does it mean to live life from the heart and to think from the heart? That's a long trip. You can't expect to come to a few creative conflict sessions and bridge that gap overnight because the gap has been created, perhaps, through many incarnations. It means ultimate fulfillment.

Now it is possible to bridge the gap quickly, but that's what is called going through the Dark Night of the Soul—complete loss of the self-sense and ego. Not everybody's willing to let go of ego. Very few. We feel more comfortable hanging on to that which we know. That which we don't know in the unconscious is rather dark and fearsome. It's frightening. In the depth and core of the heart, which is what we mean by Nuclear Evolution, there is that black unknown self. I call it Black Night, not because it's evil or anything but because it's like the Dark Night of the Soul where you don't know what's there. It's what a scientist would call a black hole. There's no way of knowing before you get in there what it is like. You have to trust it and most people don't like to trust the annihilation of what they fear most—themselves.

Who is your worst enemy? Yourself. Yourself, the self-sense, is the worst enemy. Why did I say that? Because you really don't know your true Self, the one who sits at the seat of consciousness watching this whole thing, because everything you see is recreated in your mind and your consciousness, experienced inside, not out there.

We think it's out there. Actually it takes place inside our consciousness where we make sense of it all. That's the important part of our unknown self, to understand who is recreating the whole universe inside of us. That is the process of the Nuclear Self and the vision of its fantastic evolution. As I say, if you want to find That One, that's a big trip. You have to give up everything else in order to get there and you have to trust that this big, black, unknown self there is really worth becoming. This is frightening.

Now we don't need to go to that point in creative conflict. Creative conflict can deal with ordinary matters of living. It can be a nursery for saints but you don't

467

have to be a saint or want to be a saint to get some benefit from it. But if you want to bridge your heart and your head, to answer your question about the conscious willing of change, then you have to become a saint. That's the only way you can resolve the conflict between the world of space and time as you see it and the love which you feel—to get the two going in the one direction so that they're flowing with the cosmos instead of trying to make things happen according to how you think they should happen. When you're flowing with the cosmic energies then everything happens magically. Everything happens as it is meant to happen. Even what's wrong is right in disguise. But to get to that point is a big number. You have to take up the spiritual life and get serious about it. Even with this many splendored thing called love, there are different kinds.

The deepest love is finding your true Self. You can have a conscious will in your head but if you haven't got the will in your heart to change you're going to be miserable. That's the whole reason for pain; there isn't any other reason for suffering. And if you can understand the way your human consciousness works there is no suffering. Even suffering which you see and experience is not any big trip to enlightened minds because they see it as a teaching and so it is welcomed. Now you say, "That's a strange, weird trip to welcome pain and welcome suffering!" But a wise person learns that what is painful is not necessarily bad. It is really just the squeaky wheel that needs some oil. If there is any pain in any of our lives and we can look at it honestly and openly we will find that we are doing something inside that is not in tune with the cosmic plan. We learn to flow with the cosmic plan. That's the whole purpose of creative conflict. How can it save the world? How can it transform society? How can it have use everyday in our life? Can it change politics? How can it change the way we live and the quality of consciousness we put out in society which causes all the mess?

Human beings are a mess not because society's a mess. The mess out there is only a result of human beings not having their consciousness in tune. They are drugged by self-delusions even more powerful than dope. In fact it is these delusions that turn them onto dope and they are equal to the delusion of the dope dealer who thinks money will make him happy while he helps others ruin themselves by supplying their destructive addictions.

So the origin of all peace begins with the individual. Nations are made of individuals. If individuals don't have peace at heart, if there is uncertainty and conflict in them, then there will be no peace in the nation. So the first prerequisite is for each individual to attain peace for himself. Then he will interact with others peacefully. Then the society will be a peaceful society. It will interact with other societies and there will be international peace when individuals have peace. You can't have peace by superimposing it by military might or legislation or by trying to coerce people; it has to come from within. That's the whole object of creative conflict.

It's a lofty vision, but you don't have to go all the way, just as far as you want.

Question: You were saying that the purpose of the group is to show you that side of yourself that you don't want to see. To do that they exaggerate that side and they don't talk about the positive things, just that one thing, and make it big enough for you to see it. If you have a person who is self-doubting or not on center during the creative conflict, they can hear that in a funny way and feel very depressed and do a long trip. Are there any safeguards against that happening or anything that we could build into the creative conflict so that you can spot that happening and make something else more positive happen?

Answer: I don't see that as necessarily a bad thing in growth—to be depressed or even to have a nervous breakdown. I think if we really understand a nervous breakdown it can be a blessing if we learn from it. Most psychiatrists will tell you the same thing, that people have so many insights about themselves and situations they're in during a nervous breakdown which they would never get in their normal state of consciousness. I agree that there should be some positive feedback at the same time, not all negative. And the whole object of creative conflict is for you to get the growth feelings, that you are able to see things about yourself that help you to feel positive. Now for you to be able to live with your own negative and feel right about it is important. You don't *have* to feel so perfect, everyone else is living with a whole load of manure too, as well as you, right?

This makes it a little easier but not much good to your self-image. But your self-worth grows from your certainty about the way your ego and mind works. People are vainly striving for ego food, recognition or praise but self-worth does not work that way. Only humility works. Anything else is not worth anything, because if you get positive feedback and it just adds to your vanity and your self-concept is just mere conceit, then you'll be tripped by life even more by thinking you're somebody you're not. The emphasis of the negative in creative conflict that is placed on where you're not seeing correctly causes you to see correctly. And the only way it makes you feel depressed is if you're hanging on to your ego, proud and possessive about your opinions or your way of seeing, and refusing to see any worth in what other people are saying. Then you find it's only an attitudinal rigidity that makes you feel depressed. If your ego is very strong and you're hanging onto it and feel that you're really somebody special, it might make you depressed to find that other people don't feel you're that special. That in fact, you're rather arrogant. That can be disappointing but I see that as very positive because it's humiliating. And what does humiliating mean? It means becoming humble. I think humility is a very rare quality, and even at the cost of being humiliated, I think if you can acquire humility which is such a rare thing, it's worth it. The Bible and many religions predict this ultimate humility of humanity through violent humiliation, but I believe it can come to man another way through creative conflict.

Another way of looking at it is that if you're a really humble person you can't be humiliated by anything. You're already as close to the ground as you can get. Isn't that the way of the cosmos? It lowers the mighty and raises the humble up? So all of the things that people look on as bad I look on as good. My world is totally upside down to ordinary people's. Everything that is up for them is down for me, everything that's down for them is up for me. So it makes life very interesting. What makes other people unhappy makes me glad. What people see as foolish I see as wisdom, what they see as clever I see as foolish.

Reverse everything, turn everything in the world upside down and you'll be enlightened. Human beings live upside-down don't you know? They think they're separate from God and everything else. God's out there and they're in here. If they reversed it they'd be living in Truth. There isn't anything that's separate, that's just a mental trick we play on ourselves. How can we find this out? Only by having the mirrors come back to us with what we're really saying and thinking and feeling. It helps us to communicate with the world and with our environment and with others because it teaches us that as long as we have something going on in between our ears that we think is so important, we become self-important and as long as we're self-important we're not communicating.

So the best thing is not to go on listening to knowledge *about* creative conflict but to go out and try it for yourself. Practice it all day and every day and once a week you come to University of the Trees for a refresher class. It's something you can live by everyday. Having the courage to conflict with someone creatively, you'll find it enriches life and takes away fear. Not that you should go home and tell your husband what you think of him, because after twenty-five years he's got used to you hiding a lot. There are ways of doing things skillfully that you learn in creative conflict. You learn to say things you would normally never say to anyone, and have it received.

I also wanted to tell you what I feel is the ultimate vision that you can use creative conflict for, so that it's not just some little thing you come for once a week but something that can be totally transforming of your entire mind and soul. *It is refining your consciousness so that you will be able to be a light unto the world— where you'll actually transform the society and go out from here as leaders. Not as followers but as leaders where you will actually be masters of yourself.* If you want to take it to the ultimate, or as far as you wish to go, there are courses here at University of the Trees that can turn you into a leader. Everyone who lives here will eventually be a leader. They don't know it yet, but I only welcome strong egos because they have to be that way to stand up to mine. The problems of today's world will not be resolved by renouncing them, or by traditional religious practices of avoiding them. They will only be solved through confronting them squarely in the strength of self-mastery. The people here come with strength and that strength will eventually make them want to be their own boss and form a center and do their own trip. And they'll do it out of the freedom of their own hearts. No coercion, only for the sake of their own self-fulfillment.

The greatest thing anyone can get is to be fulfilled. Ultimately creative conflict is the method for fulfilling yourself.

APPENDIX

NOTE FOR TEACHERS

The authors are eager to link with those interested in starting alternative schools based on learning through awareness games. Our Press would also be willing to start a magazine for children if someone can offer time to edit materials and handle the subscriptions and mailing. In cooperation with local parents, we will start a school for children in 1979 with the purpose of developing their higher faculties through the methods described in this book. Anyone interested in learning the teachings behind the materials at a deeper level and becoming an authorized teacher of the methods, with the view to eventually starting their own school, is welcome to apply for training. Teachers' training fees will not be charged but the ideal of selfless service is encouraged, so those who are going to take the training are expected to participate for at least four hours a day in campus-related activities, such as audio tape production, gardening, bookpacking, mailing list, filing, typing, typesetting, editing, proof reading, algae farming, movie making, and photography, as well as working with children.

University of the Trees is a non-profit institution authorized by the State of California to grant degrees from B.A. and M.A. to Ph.d., while University of the Trees Press is a democratic industrial common ownership business belonging jointly to those who work in it on a permanent basis.

We are interested in social experiments in industry as well as education and publish research in new theories and practical teaching techniques.

All donations to the University of the Trees are tax deductible.

Dear Reader:

Many of you have come into contact with my work through the outreach of our tape learning program, books, and our courses in meditation and consciousness research, and have written asking how you can get closer to our community on campus here in Boulder Creek.

Many people come with expectations, but the criteria for living and working with us here are difficult for those not yet totally committed to being selfless, to disciplining their consciousness and to working on the ego through creative conflict. Hence many are disappointed that we cannot accept them in our very close community. But we feel that the wider feeling of "community" is also valuable and that opportunities for service abound for those who are as yet unable to give it all up, pack up, and come. I felt if I set out clearly some of the ways we can relate to you in the wider sense of community you would not need to write us so many letters asking for details and we would have more time to commune with you through the spiritual links of meditation during quiet hours, or by working directly with you from a distance, yet still feeling that you are of the family.

Here are some of the things we are doing in which you are welcome to have a part, however small.

● We are hoping to establish a peace village where our University can co-exist with new kinds of industrial organizations. These will include aquaculture farming to harness the sun's light and individual projects which express individuality and at the same time help to develop the group consciousness, e.g.

- ● Organic gardening
- ● Music
- ● Original and useful crafts
- ● Energy saving projects
- ● New architecture
- ● New social systems
- ● Awareness and yoga classes
- ● Teaching of children
- ● Any other service you can suggest that would contribute to group consciousness and awareness

● We are developing a formidable publications organization through the selfless dedication of people who are working very hard to turn the civilization around and transform it into something beautiful. Our editors and writers have voluntarily put all their royalties and profits back into the work of "conscious evolution". You can help to introduce these books and tapes to all schools, groups and bookstores, since they transcend individual cliques and bring teachings that are universally acceptable and which synthesize science and spirituality.

● We are interested in connecting with other existing communities and in founding small communities everywhere, with small groups of people who will use a spiritual code of practice for applying new techniques of *self-government* and decision-making developed from a unique constitution that avoids coercion and the present preoccupation with politics. The idea is to develop a new social organism that masters money and relationships, instead of serving mammon as an employee, in order to make our work fulfilling and joyful.

● We are interested in experiments with industrial democracy and the taking over of businesses from those who want to retire and recreate them into opportunities for spiritual service. The method is for employees to raise a loan to own the business and pay for the shares out of tax-free profits. We have a special co-ownership technique for accomplishing this economic revolution.

● You can get together like-minded friends or people interested in sponsoring seminars, lectures, TV appearances or authors' autographing visits so we can send our authors and faculty to you on tours.

● Think of anything useful you are not using or anything stored in your garage which you could send to us, such as typing paper, envelopes, Thermofax copy paper, shingles, tools, plastic bags or boxes, styrofoam packing, Jiffy bags, tapes, vans, trailers, rototillers, garden sheds, and anything you think might be useful to a community.

These are only a few suggestions that might stimulate your imagination, not to mention the basic financial requirement for any purchase of property. Most of all we are interested in you and eager to know that you are fulfilling your destiny. That is why we write the kind of books we do and why we have created a school of wisdom for a new society.

May your heart respond to the outflow of universal love from,

Christopher Hills

TEENAGERS CURRICULUM by Roger Smith and Pamela Osborn

THE ADVANTAGES OF TEACHING AWARENESS EDUCATION TO TEENAGERS

There's a real hero within every youth, ready for glory, change, dynamic action. The goal of awareness exploration with adolescents is that they may learn to get in touch with and master the energies and drives surging within themselves and in society. Every child and every person holds wisdom within them. The secret of the successful teacher is to draw it out! The effective teacher helps students get more deeply in touch with their own feelings and innate intelligence so they can learn to manifest their inner directives.

Children only respond in a real way with real feelings and enthusiasm to what is real for them; the less relevance the learning material has to their lives, the more tedious it is to learn. The closer the subject matter comes to things they can identify with and relate to personally, the more vital and impressive is the learning.

The *Teenagers Awareness Curriculum* can be used by teachers, families and teens themselves to learn keys to successful living that can be applied to new situations throughout life. It has been extremely fulfilling for us, in working with teens, to see them "come into their own" authority, shake loose of the mold of popularity that shackles them into being who they are not, and talk to each other "straight" about what they are feeling and perceiving. They leave the awareness or creative conflict session walking ten feet high with the energy that has been released from breaking out of their limited self-concept, and with the self-respect that comes from realizing their true self. Since relationships are the most important concern for most teenagers we need to provide them with skillful means of relating with each other and society so that they may have the hero's opportunity to expand into their greater self.

Teenagers Awareness Curriculum – ten weekly sessions of meditations and exercises in expansion, by Pamela Osborn and Roger Smith. Approx. 22 pgs., $3.00 photocopied pamphlet.

APPENDIX: EXCURSION MATERIALS

*MEDITATING WITH CHILDREN is, after three years, still the leading handbook that teachers and parents use to develop their children's concentration and creative imagination. Excellent results with gifted, average, retarded and hyperactive children. 160 pgs., $5.95. *D. Rozman.*

*MEDITATION FOR CHILDREN is a family guide for making conflict creative in family problems, letting others be and various meditations for children of all ages. 160 pgs., $5.95. *D. Rozman.* (Publ. by Celestial Arts)

*NUCLEAR EVOLUTION is both a book of vision and a unique book of knowledge which reveals in depth the structure of human consciousness. Hills shows how to use your powerful imagination to bring great changes in yourself. Chapter titles include: *How Humans Transmute Light; The Experience of Time; Kundalini— The Evolutionary Fire; Science and Spirituality,* and much more. 1024 pgs., $12.95. *C. Hills.*

CREATIVE CONFLICT, Part 2, is a pamphlet for those wishing to take the next step in Creative Conflict to a deeper, more unified experience of group consciousness. Approx. 30 pgs., $2.00. *C. Hills and D. Rozman.*

TEENAGERS AWARENESS CURRICULUM. A series of 10 weekly sessions of meditations and awareness exercises designed especially for teens. Photocopied pamphlet, $3.00. *R. Smith and P. Osborn.*

*INTO MEDITATION NOW is a three-year correspondence course on Direct Enlightenment in 18 sections which takes the student into a direct experience of Nuclear Evolution and the "rainbow body". Send for further details.

ENERGY MATTER AND FORM unites what is known in the psychic sciences with a spiritual vision of the nature of your consciousness. "A perfect handbook for the New Age,"—Books West. 321 pgs., $9.95. *Smith, Allen & Bearne.*

THE RISE OF THE PHOENIX is a new major work by Christopher Hills on spiritualizing politics and social yoga. It shows how we can get rid of power cliques and establish the lifestyle we desire. Offers a new constitution based on nature's models of organized self-government. To be published 1979. Write for further details.

*THE SYMBOL OF NUCLEAR EVOLUTION POSTER, sometimes called the Mahamudra or Center Symbol, is used in concentration exercises and consciousness expansion. $1.95.

*AURA PENDULUM PACKAGE includes one *Aura Pendulum* for reading auras, one *Rainbow Aura Booklet* which tells how to use the pendulum and gives the meanings of the seven colors in both positive and negative aspects, and one *Supersensonic Instruments of Knowing* book, a collection of over 25 divining instruments available and how to use them to benefit yourself. $8.95.

MEDITATING WITH CHILDREN CASSETTE is a selection of delightful meditations from Deborah Rozman's books including the favorites "Spaceship Meditation" and "White Light Meditation", read by the author herself. For all ages. 1 hr., $8.00. *D. Rozman.*

UNCLE ALF'S CIRCUS is a highly imaginative cassette tape of special children's meditations. It speaks to the heart with such guided imagery topics as "Uncle Alf's Circus" and "The Cuddly Teddy Bear" and "Animal Chanting", "Puppet Meditation". 1 hr., $8.00. *C. Hills.*

*BEGINNING MEDITATION TAPE The first step to expanded awareness if you've done little or no meditating before. Gives an understanding of the process, a direct experience of mind transcendence and instructions on how to do it yourself. 1 hr., $8.00.

RUMF ROOMPH YOGA COMMUNION is a series of 24 tapes for the advanced student or group in consciousness research. Based on the Yoga Sutras of Patanjali, these techniques and exercises bring a deep and intense experience of higher levels of consciousness. Available in sequence only. 24 sessions 1 to 2 hrs. each, total series $234.00. Write for further information. *C. Hills.*

*SPEED LEARNING INFORMATION & GUIDANCE TAPE explains how to use speed learning techniques for gaining spiritual knowledge or anything else. Side 2 is a guided meditation to put you in contact with your subconscious mind. 1 hr., $8.00. *C. Hills.*

*MEMORY TRAINING COURSE develops the various kinds of memory. It enables you to understand how your memory works and to change blocks. Write for further details. *C. Hills.*

*HILLS POSITIVE GREEN PENDULUM is tuned to life energy—what the Chinese call *chi* and in India is called *prana*. It can be used for enhancing health, checking the vitality of foods, and answering the questions of the heart center. $15.00.

* Items with an asterix indicate materials used in the Explorations.

MORE CONSCIOUSNESS BOOKS

HILLS' THEORY OF CONSCIOUSNESS is a beginners guide to the theory of *Nuclear Evolution* and lets you in on some startling ideas about life, the universe and you. It shows how many accepted concepts about time, space and who we think we are, are false. 160 pgs., $6.95, *R. Massy, Ph.D.*

YOUR ELECTRO-VIBRATORY BODY is a study of the latest worldwide research on the nature of man's *energy body* with its many energy fields. Part of the findings show that our moods, personality, health and longevity are affected by magnetic and electric fields, positive and negative ions, light and colors. 304 pgs., $9.95, *Victor Beasley, Ph.D.*

THE RAINBOW AURA BOOKLET tells very clearly what each color means and answers such questions as "What is an aura?" "Why and how does a pendulum work?" 24, pgs.,$1.00.

JOURNEY INTO LIGHT is the timely story of a woman who gives up her established place in an academic community and goes in search of her true Self. Along the way she faces many risks and tests, yet in the end love rewards her courage. 304 pgs.,$7.95, *Ann Ray, Ph.D.*

ALIVE TO THE UNIVERSE is a dowsing manual with simple exercises that will teach you step by step principles for the beginning dowser. Using such tools as pendulums and dowsing rods you'll find you can get an answer to almost any question. 288 pgs. *$9.95, Robert Massy, Ph.D.*

FOOD FROM SUNLIGHT, an answer to hunger and starvation for more than 50% of the world's population . . . Algae, how to grow it, facts and figures, the results of today's ongoing projects, as a source of energy, fertilizer and food. 384 pgs.,$14.95,*Dr. Hills and Dr. Nakamura.*

MAY YOU LIVE IN HEALTH is a book on holistic health containing many guidelines and practices for a healthful psychic and physical life. 78 pgs., $3.95, *Aaron Friedell, M.D.*

RAYS FROM THE CAPSTONE gives some refreshing answers about what's really going on inside a pyramid. It is the first to clearly set out what energies are generated and what effects these forces have on you, your food, plants, etc. 160 pgs.,$4.95, *Dr. Hills.*

POLITICS OF GOD is a thought provoking and controversial study of religion and politics by Dr. Hugh Schonfield, well-known author of *The Passover Plot.* 236 pgs., $9.95, *Dr. H. Schonfield.*

THE HANDBOOK OF NATURAL HEALING tells how to use your natural gift of healing. Basic principles of healing are included. A fun, potent little book.40 pgs., $2.95, *Dr. Michael Ash.*

INSTRUMENTS OF KNOWING describes over thirty divining tools and the hundreds of uses they have. The miracles of Christ are linked to divining. 128 pgs., $1.95, *Dr. Hills.*

THE SHINING STRANGER is an unorthodox interpretation of Jesus and his mission. Examines the miracles, economic philosophy and why and how the Gospels were written. 466 pgs. $3.95, *Preston Harold.*

All prices subject to change without notice.

FORMING AN EXPLORATION GROUP

All of the program materials can be modified for any group—adults, senior citizens, children, teens and mixed groups. The suggested program includes three steps:

1.   EXPLORING INNER SPACE—using this book of awareness activities and suggested excursion materials to explore the levels of consciousness.

2.   After a familiarity with the levels of consciousness, and a steady building of trust and commitment in the group members has been established, the next step is in-depth Creative Conflict. This includes looking at the ego and dissolving the false separation it creates.

3.   RUMF ROOMPH YOGA COMMUNION is the third and most in-depth work on states of consciousness, both group and individual. A series of twenty-four cassette tapes leads your group through six phases: *Developing Spriutal Muscles; Radicalizing the Ego Sense; Evolution of the Vehicle of Consciousness; Validation of Yogic Modes of Knowing; Mastering Self-intoxication with Self-saturation; and the Ultimate Manifestation of Being. Write the publishers for further details.*

GUIDED EXPLORATIONS INTO INNER SPACE

MEDITATIONS ON THE LEVELS OF CONSCIOUSNESS

Meditation is not intellectual knowledge but the direct experience of identification in the mind. These guided meditations trigger your consciousness so you can experience totally new worlds of being and see life anew.

C1. *Red:* The Clear Light; Becoming a Body Cell; Our Magnetic Body. 1 hr., $8.00.

C2. *Orange:* Imitation vs. Creativity; The Nature of Caring; Right Company, Right Environment. 1 hr., $8.00.

C3. *Yellow:* Precision; Abandonment of the Ego. 1 hr., $8.00

C4. *Green:* Security and Insecurity; Diving Deep into the Pool of the Heart. 1 hr., $8.00.

C5. *Blue:* Basic Assumptions; The Yoga of Wisdom. 1 hr., $8.00

C6. *Indigo:* Molding Your Future; Developing Inner Vision. (This tape is numbered MM6 elsewhere in our literature.) 1 hr., $8.00.

C7. *Violet:* The Seventh Level of Consciousness. 1 hr., $8.00.

✱ ✱ ✱ ✱ ✱ ✱ ✱ ✱ ✱ ✱ ✱

CHANTING TAPES TO INSPIRE THE SOUL

CH16. Seven Inspirational Chants. 1 hr. $8.00.

CH17. Good Chants to Start the Day. 1 hr. $8.00.

SUPERSENSONICS SEMINAR

SS1.—A series for beginning diviners given by Dr. Robert Massy, author of *Alive to the Universe*, including instructions for aura balancing.

Tape 1. A general introduction to divining. What is the pendulum?
Tape 2. The effects of color and their radiations, tuning the pendulum.
Tape 3. Divining for the life force, testing positive and negative poles.
Tape 4. Aura balancing: probing the problem, taking out negative energy, charging the chakras.

*Due to the nature of this seminar
it must be purchased as one whole. 4 hrs., $32.00.*

THE CHAKRA SERIES

This series is a dynamic look at the rainbow body of light. Each psychic center is a unique experience of time and perception and we switch from one to another. Knowledge of the centers enables self-mastery.

ADC-1. AN OUTLINE OF THE SERIES. 1 hr. 45 min. $11.00.

ADC-2. THE MULADHARA (Red center). 1 hr. 25 min. $10.00

ADC-3. THE SWADHISTHANA (Orange center). 1 hr. 30 min. $10.00.

ADC-4. THE MANIPURA (Yellow center). 1 hr. 30 min. $10.00.

ADC-5. THE ANAHATA (Green center). 1 hr. 20 min. $9.00.

ADC-6. THE VISHUDDHA (Blue center). 1 hr. 20 min. $9.00.

ADC-7. THE AJNA (Indigo center). 1 hr. 40 min. $11.00.

ADC-8. THE SAHASRARA (Violet center). 1 hr. 55 min. $12.00.

ADC-9. REVIEW TAPE, 1 hr. 40 min. $11.00.

ADC-10. NATURE OF RESPONSE TO LIGHT AND COLOR: 1 hr. $8.00.

ADC-11. QUESTIONS ON THE CHAKRAS, 1 hr. 35 min. $10.00.

ADC-12. HOW TO DISCOVER YOUR KARMA, 50 min. $8.00

ADC-13. COMMUNICATION & THE CHAKRAS, 1 hr. 50 min. $11.00.

These tapes were recorded live in a casual, at-home setting. You may hear the sounds of cars or trucks or neighbors talking while we had the windows open on a hot summmer night.

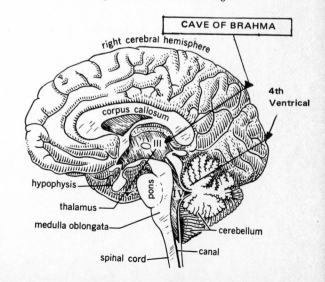

Dear Visitor,

We welcome you to the University of the Trees. Our purpose in sharing ourselves through our books and our community is to *Honor the souls of seeking people and give our hearts,* since, in essence, it's heart that we are all seeking to become.

The *University of the Trees* is located in the center of Boulder Creek, a coastal village of approximately 5000 people, nestled in a valley of redwoods about 20 miles from Santa Cruz. From there, public transportation runs hourly to the village. Visitors wishing to come and experience community life are therefore asked to come prepared for changeable weather. Summer months are often warm with scattered showers and winter is blessed with an average rainfall between 50 to 75 inches.

Accomodations on campus are few but can be made available provided that there is plenty of advance warning. We currently have a guest room available at $4.00 per night for those of you who are already associated with us and are taking the course **Into Meditation Now.** For those of you who wish a nature environment, there is Big Basin State Park, one-half hour away to the west and Henry Cowell State Park about 5 miles to the south. Finally, there are numerous motels along the main Highway #9.

Life at the University is a daily blend of meditation, Karma Yoga (running the press, divining instrument production, gardening, etc.), chanting, tea times, Creative Conflict and other weekly activities. Upon your arrival here you will be greeted by a *buddy.* Your buddy is responsible for seeing that you are informed about all that is happening and how you can join in the group rhythm.

For those wishing to come to the University on an hourly basis, we have scheduled tea times, Tuesday and Saturday at 4:00 and a group meditation open to all, usually led by Christopher Hills, Friday nights, 7:30 (summer) and 7:00 (winter). Please try to schedule your visits to these times unless you call in advance. Office hours are from 10:00 to 5:00 weekdays. For further information please write or call:

University of the Trees
P.O. Box 644
Boulder Creek, California 95006
(408) 338-3855

ORDER FORM

ORDERING INFORMATION

U.S.A.

1. Prepayment: check or money order.
2. No C.O.D.'s or stamps please.
3. We ship immediately.
4. Postage & Handling rates:

BOOKS

If your order is:
up to $4 add $1.00
$4.01-$10. add 1.75
$10.01-$15. add 2.00
$15.01-$20. add 2.50
$20.01-$40 add 3.00

For each additional
$20 add $1.50

TAPES

If your order is:
up to $8. add $1.25
$8.01-$20. add 2.00
$20.01-$40. add 3.00
$40.01-$60. add 4.00
$60.01-$240. add 5.00

FOREIGN

1. Have all checks and money orders in certified U.S. dollars
2. Expect delivery after 5 weeks.
3. Overpayments will be credited
4. Postage & handling rates:

BOOKS

1. Please include $3.50 per item. Your order will be shipped parcel post.
2. Book rate is available at $2.00 per book. We are not responsible for lost shipments under book rates.

TAPES

$0-$50 add $3.50
$51-$100 add $4.50
$101-$150. add $5.50
$151-$200 add $6.50
$201-$250 add $7.50

Description	Quantity	PRICE EACH	Total Price
	Postage & handling		
	SALES TAX		
	TOTAL ENCLOSED		

All prices subject to change
without notice.